D0791681

BEHAVIOR MODIFICATION:
What It Is
And
How To Do It

BEHAVIOR MODIFICATION:

What It Is
And
How To Do It

Garry Martin
Joseph Pear

University of Manitoba

Prentice-Hall, Inc. Englewood Cliffs, New Jersey 07632

Library of Congress Cataloging in Publication Data

MARTIN, GARRY L   DATE
Behavior modification.

   Bibliography: p.
   Includes index.
   1. Behavior modification.   I. Pear, Joseph J.,
Date   joint author.   II. Title.
BF637.B4M37   153.8′5   77-10849
ISBN   0-13-066787-0

Printed in the United States of America

10   9   8   7   6   5   4

PRENTICE-HALL INTERNATIONAL, INC., *London*
PRENTICE-HALL OF AUSTRALIA PTY. LIMITED, *Sydney*
PRENTICE-HALL OF CANADA, LTD., *Toronto*
PRENTICE-HALL OF INDIA PRIVATE LIMITED, *New Delhi*
PRENTICE-HALL OF JAPAN, INC., *Tokyo*
PRENTICE-HALL OF SOUTHEAST ASIA PTE. LTD., *Singapore*
WHITEHALL BOOKS LIMITED, *Wellington, New Zealand*

Contents

3 Decreasing A Behavior With EXTINCTION *39*
"Peter, your tantrums are driving me crazy."

4 Getting A New Behavior to Occur: an Application of SHAPING *58*
"Valerie, walk by yourself to supper"

5 Section One: Developing Behavioral Persistence Through the Use of INTERMITTENT REINFORCEMENT *73*
"Benny, you must learn to be patient"

Section Two: More About Increasing and Maintaining Behavior Through the Use of INTERMITTENT REINFORCEMENT *84*

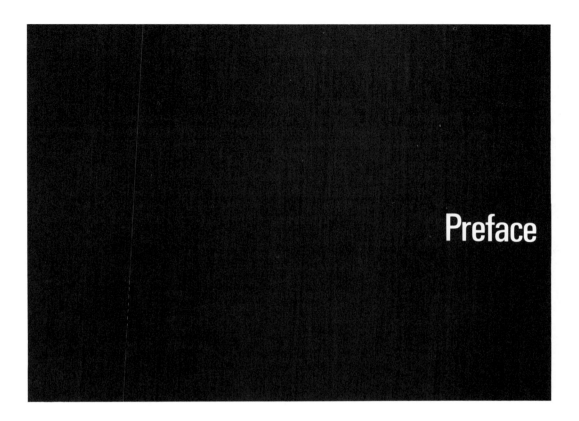

Preface

Because this book assumes no specific prior knowledge about psychology or behavior modification on the part of the reader, it should be useful to many individuals who want to know how to effectively apply behavior modification to their everyday concerns—ranging from helping their children learn life's necessary skills to solving some of their own personal behavior problems. Mainly, however, this book is addressed to the following two general audiences: (1) college and university students taking courses in behavior modification, behavior analysis, the psychology of learning, and related areas; (2) students and practitioners of various helping professions (such as education, counseling, clinical psychology, medicine, psychiatry, nursing, psychiatric nursing, social work, speech therapy, physiotherapy, and occupational therapy) that are directly concerned with enhancing various forms of behavioral development.

Our separate personal experiences over the past ten years in teaching members of both of these broad groups convinces us that there is an extreme amount of overlap in the information that they desire and require about behavior modification. Both groups seem to assimilate the principles of behavior and learn and generalize applications most effectively when those applications are explained with reference to the underlying behavior principles on which they are based. Therefore, as its title implies, this book deals equally with both the principles and the tactics (that is, the rules and guidelines for specific applications) of behavior modification.

Our goals, and the manner in which we have attempted to achieve them, can be summarized as follows:

1. To teach the elementary principles and procedures of behavior modification. Thus, we begin with the basic principles and procedures, illustrate them with numerous examples and applications, and increase the complexity of the material gradually. *Study Questions* provided at the end of each chapter promote the reader's mastery of the material as well as his or her ability to generalize to situations not described in the text. These questions can also be used for examination purposes in formal courses.

2. To teach *practical, "how-to" skills,* such as observing and recording; recognizing instances of reinforcement, extinction, and punishment and their likely long-term effects; interpreting behavioral episodes in terms of behavioral principles and procedures; and designing, implementing, and evaluating behavioral programs. To help accomplish this, we have appended two types of exercises to most chapters: (a) *Study Exercises,* which encourage the reader to analyze, interpret, and develop programs for the behavior of others, and (b) *Self-Modification Exercises,* which encourage the reader to analyze, interpret, and develop programs for his or her own behavior.

3. To provide advanced discussion and references so that readers will learn not only how to apply behavior modification, but also some of the basic empirical support and theoretical underpinnings of the field. To separate this material from the more elementary and applied material, we have presented it in the *Extended Discussion and Notes* (ED&N) sections at the end of the chapters. The ED&N sections also contain numerous references to relevant articles and books. Thus, although it is available for those with the background, interest, and time to benefit from it, it can be conveniently omitted without harm to the continuity of the text. Separate study questions on the notes are provided for those instructors who wish to include them, and as aides for students wishing to broaden their understanding of behavior modification. The ED&N sections also provide information that might be used by instructors as springboards for lecture material.

4. To present the material in such a way that it will serve as an easy-to-use handbook for practitioners concerned with overcoming behavioral deficiencies, excesses, and inappropriatenesses in a wide variety of populations and settings.

The book is divided into six parts:

Part I introduces the behavioral orientation of the book, including the rationale for that orientation.

Part II covers the basic principles and procedures of behavior modification. Each of the chapters, except for Chapter 14, begins with a case history drawn from experiences of the authors or others in the fields of retardation, autism, or early education. Such examples readily lend themselves to simplified expositions of the principles. Moreover, undergraduate behavior modification projects are often concerned with populations in these areas. Numerous examples of how each principle operates in everyday life and how it can operate to the disadvantage of those who are ignorant of it are also given. Chapter 14, which covers procedures based on respondent conditioning, may be omitted without serious harm to the continuity of the text. Most of the procedures discussed in the later parts of the text are based primarily on operant conditioning. (Chapter 26 repeats and elaborates on some of the material in Chapter 14, but can be read independently of that chapter.)

Part III covers no new principles, but rather discusses more sophisticated ways to combine and apply the basic principles and procedures discussed in Part II.

Part IV presents detailed procedures for assessing, recording, and graphing behavior. It also contains a chapter explaining how behavior modification research is typically carried out. Many instructors prefer to present much of this material quite early in their courses—sometimes even at the very beginning. Therefore, we have written these chapters so that they can be read independently of the rest of the book; they do not depend on any of the other material. We recommend that students be required to read these chapters prior to carrying out any major projects for their courses.

Part V deals with how the basic principles, procedures, and assessment and recording techniques are incorporated into effective programming strategies. In keeping with the rigorously scientific nature of behavior modification, we have placed heavy emphasis on the importance of empirically validating program effectiveness. After describing general guidelines applicable to nearly all behavior modification programs, we describe the details of developing token economies in a wide variety of settings. Then, the chapters on self-control and self-desensitization expand on the self-modification exercises of the previous chapters and discuss recent applications to important clinical problems. Finally, the chapter on cognitive behavior modification attempts to show that the same behavioral approach that is so effective with public (overt) behavior is also applicable to private (covert) behavior.

Part VI expands the reader's perspective of behavior modification. It presents an overview of the history of behavior modification and a discussion of the ethical issues in the field. Although some instructors might feel that these chapters belong near the beginning of the book, we believe that the reader is more prepared to fully appreciate this material after obtaining a clear and thorough knowledge of behavior modification. We placed ethical issues at the end of the book not because we feel that this topic is less important than the others. On the contrary, we stress ethical issues throughout the book, and, thus, the last chapter provides a reiteration and elaboration of our views on this vital subject. We hope that after reading the concluding chapter, the reader will be fully aware that the only justification for behavior modification is its usefulness in serving all humanity in general, and its recipients in particular.

The writing of this book was made possible by the help of many individuals. We gratefully acknowledge the cooperation and support of Dr. Glen H. Lowther and the staff at the Manitoba School and Sr. Bertha Baumann and the staff at the St. Amant Centre. Much of the material in this volume was generated while the authors were involved in these institutions, and without the support of the staff there this book would not likely have been written. We take special pleasure in thanking Dr. Glen Lowther for his continuing encouragement and support during the past nine years. He has been a major factor in furthering the applied work of the authors as well as in developing behavior modification in the province of Manitoba. Grateful acknowledgement is due to our many students, for their constructive feedback on earlier drafts; to Linda McDonald, who helped gather some of the material for the "guidelines" sections; to Jim Rennie, for contributing a number of study questions; and especially to Joan Lumsden, Lyle Wray and Michael LeBow for their many excellent suggestions for improvements. We also wish to thank Leila Krumm and Barb Roscoe, who cheerfully gave so much energy and their own time in typing various drafts of this text.

Finally, a special thanks to Nickie, Toby, Todd, Kelly, Scott, and Tana (from G.L.M.) and to Jonathan (from J.J.P.), who gave up so much of their time with us while this book was being written.

Completion of this book was facilitated by research grants from the Medical Research Council (Grant No. MA–5821) and the National Health Grants Program (Grant No. 606–7–255) of Canada to G. L. Martin, and grants from the Medical Research Council (Grant No. MA–5647) and the National Research Council (Grant No. A7461) of Canada to J. J. Pear.

TO THE STUDENT

This book is designed to help you learn to effectively talk about and apply behavior modification. You need no prior knowledge about behavior modification in order to read and understand this text from beginning to end. We feel, however, that very advanced students as well as beginning students will find the text informative and useful.

The text is very broad in its coverage, because behavior modification is a very broad field. The text also provides a great deal of depth, because, at its roots, behavior modification is a very complex field, with many ramifications. We realize, however, that some students will require or desire a deeper knowledge of behavior modification than others will.

Therefore, in each chapter of this book we have separated the more elementary material from the material that demands more thought and study. The former material is presented in the main body of the text. The latter material is presented at the end of each chapter under the heading "Extended Discussion and Notes." Reference numerals (like those used for footnotes) are placed above key statements in the main text to refer you to the corresponding numbered passages in the "Extended Discussion and Notes" sections. How you use the "Extended Discussion and Notes" sections is up to you and your instructor. You can ignore them altogether and still obtain a good working knowledge of the principles and tactics of behavior modification, because the main text does not depend on the material in the "Extended Discussion and Notes" sections. However, we believe that many students will find these sections very informative and that many teachers will find the sections useful in stimulating class discussion and imparting additional background information.

Another major way in which we have attempted to help you learn the material is by providing guidelines on the use of all of the behavior modification methods discussed in the text. These guidelines should prove useful as summaries of the material as well as in helping you to actually apply the methods described in the text.

Numerous study questions and study exercises (including "self-modification" exercises) are also presented in each chapter. The study questions are intended to help you check your knowledge of the material when preparing for quizzes and exams. The study exercises and self-modification exercises are intended to help you develop the practical skills you will need in order to carry out behavior modification projects effectively.

To help make your study productive and enjoyable, we progress from the simpler and more intrinsically interesting material to the more difficult and complex material. We have also deliberately tried to program an increasing complexity in the writing style. We urge you in the strongest possible terms: *Do not be misled by the seeming simplicity of the earlier chapters.* Many people unjustifiably conclude that they are skilled behavior modifiers after they have learned a few simple behavior modification principles. Unfortunately, they too often end up by once again proving the old maxim that "a little knowledge is a dangerous thing." If we personally had to pick the most important chapter in this book, in terms of the knowledge and skills that define a competent behavior modifier, it would probably be Chapter 21. We therefore suggest that you cautiously reserve judgment about your abilities as a behavior modifier until you have thoroughly mastered the material in that chapter and all of the preliminary material on which it is based.

With that word of caution, we wish you much success and enjoyment as you pursue your studies in this new, exciting, and rapidly expanding field of behavior modification.

G.L.M.
J.J.P.

BEHAVIOR MODIFICATION:

What It Is

And

How To Do It

PART I

The Behavior Modification Approach

CHAPTER 1

INTRODUCTION

If you had to think of one word common to all the people in the situations listed below, what would that word be?

When sitting on the toilet, Tommy, an otherwise normal five-year old, never urinates, instead, he does it in his pants.

Judy, a sixteen-year-old high school student, spends almost every evening watching TV or going out with friends instead of completing her homework assignments.

Larry throws violent temper tantrums whenever his parents refuse his demands.

Each morning, when medications are given to Charles, an adult epileptic retarded patient, he resists and tosses them away.

When asked, "What's your name?" an autistic child named Peter replies, "What's your name?" He never answers any questions appropriately; instead, he merely repeats them.

Fred, a "normal" adult, fixes breakfast for his kids every morning before going to work.

When driving, Pamela frequently exceeds the speed limit and sometimes runs red lights.

Richard, a delusional psychotic patient, makes absurd statements to anyone who will listen to him.

Alice is so afraid of small enclosed spaces that she will walk up ten flights of stairs rather than ride the elevator.

Have you thought of a suitable word yet? If one of the words you are thinking of is "behavior," then either you are very clever, or you are "psychic," or you cheated by looking ahead—because "behavior" is correct. Each of the above statements tells us something about the way in which a certain person behaves in a certain situation.

But what is behavior? Some commonly used synonyms would include "activity," action," "performance," "responding," "response," and "reaction." Although it is difficult to give a precise definition of behavior, we would bet that you have a good idea of what we mean by the term. Is the color of someone's eyes behavior? Is blinking behavior? Are the clothes someone is wearing behavior? Is dressing behavior? If you said no to the first and third questions and yes to the second and forth, then we are in agreement. One of the goals of this book is to encourage you to begin thinking and talking very specifically about behavior.

Now consider some examples that are a bit more difficult. Is intelligence a behavior? Is an attitude behavior? Is motivation behavior? Is creativity behavior? If not, then what are they?

What do we mean when we say that a person is intelligent? We do *not* mean that he has something inside of him called "an intelligence," for we never observe any such thing. What we *do* mean is that he tends to engage in certain kinds of behavior under certain conditions. Perhaps he readily solves problems that other people find difficult, performs well (by someone's standards) on most course examinations, reads many books, talks knowledgeably about many topics, or scores well on an intelligence test. Depending on who uses the word, "intelligence" can mean any or all of these—but whatever it means, it refers to ways of behaving.

What about an attitude? Suppose Johnny's teacher, Ms. Smith, reports that he has a bad attitude toward school. What does Ms. Smith mean by this? Perhaps she means that Johnny frequently skips school, refuses to do his classwork when he does attend, and swears at the teacher. Whatever she means when she talks about Johnny's "bad attitude," it is clearly his behavior with which she is really concerned.

Motivation and creativity also refer to the kinds of behavior a person is likely to engage in under certain circumstances. The highly motivated student spends a great deal of time studying. The creative individual frequently emits behaviors that are novel or unusual and that, at the same time, have desirable effects.

Now what about mental retardation, childhood autism, childhood schizophrenia, learning disabilities, and emotional disturbances? These also are labels for certain ways of behaving. How do specialists decide that someone is severely retarded? They make the decision primarily because they might observe that the person, after a certain age,

cannot tie shoelaces;
is not toilet-trained;
eats food only with his fingers or a spoon;
performs on psychological tests in such a way that the combined answers yield an IQ score of 35 or less.

How do specialists decide that someone has a learning disability? They make the decision on the basis of certain behaviors that they observe, such as

attending to a task for only a few seconds or minutes (typically labeled a "short attention span");
staring at an item for many minutes (typically labeled "perseveration");
moving frequently from one position, location, or task to the next (labeled "hyperactivity");
confusing spoken words, such as "thumb" for "tongue" (labeled "speech disability");
inverting words while reading, such as "saw" for "was" (labeled a "reading disability" or "dyslexia").

How do specialists decide that a child is autistic? They make this decision on the basis of certain behaviors that they observe. For example, they might observe that a child

frequently mimics particular questions rather than answering with an appropriate statement;
engages in various self-stimulatory behaviors, such as rocking back and forth, twirling objects with her fingers, or fluttering her hands in front of her eyes;
when called, does not respond, or moves away from the person doing the calling (more generally, he shows antisocial behavior);
performs much below average on a variety of self-care tasks, such as dressing, grooming, and feeding.

In all of these cases, decisions are based on observable behavior, not on invisible "mental" abnormalities. The behavior of people who are given the above labels is compared with the behavior of others of approximately the same age and perhaps with a similar amount of training and educational background, and the comparison shows that individuals labeled "retarded," "autistic," or "learning-disabled" have "behavior problems"—that is, "behavioral deficiencies" (too little behavior of a particular type), "behavioral excesses" (too much behavior of a particular type), or "behavioral inappropriatenesses" (doing the wrong thing at the right time or place, or the right thing at the wrong time or place). The same is true for individuals who are labeled "emotionally disturbed," "childhood schizophrenics," "slow learners," "neurotics," "psychotics," and so forth. The labels are applied when the person emits behaviors that are considered "abnormal." In all such cases, it is *behavior* that causes concern. Certain behaviors that parents see and hear often cause them to seek professional help for their children. Certain behaviors teachers see and hear often prompt them to have children removed from their classroom. Behaviors that can be seen or heard cause governments to set up institutions, clinics, community treatment centers, and special programs.

You may be wondering why we stress so strongly the importance of defining all of the above types of problems in terms of behavior. The reason is that there are specific procedures now available that can be used in school settings, home settings—in fact, just about anywhere there is a need to overcome behavior problems and to establish more desirable behaviors. These techniques are referred to collectively as behavior modification.* There is now a great deal of factual evidence that these techniques work extremely well in all of the above areas of concern. The main purpose of this book is to describe these techniques in an enjoyable, readable, and practical manner. We intend in this book to help the reader learn not merely about behavior modification but also *how to use it* to overcome behavioral deficiencies, excesses, and inappropriatenesses.

The behavior modification approach is different in several respects from many of the more traditional psychological and medical approaches, but it is especially different in one major respect. Many traditional psychological approaches to mental retardation, learning disabilities, and other disorders mentioned above have been strongly influenced (and still are in many areas) by what the experts call the medical model. Medicine has made great strides by looking for the underlying causes of physical illness. Things like viruses, tumors, and vitamin deficiencies, sometimes cause a variety of observable physical abnormalities and symptoms. As a result, it often seems as though a problem is caused by something inside of you that you can't see. In the past, this approach has been adopted by many psychologists and educators. The use of the label *"mental* retardation" rather than *"behavioral* retardation" is no accident. As illustrated in Figure 1-1, the traditional approach is based on the supposition that the observable behavior is a symptom of a "mental" deficiency, disturbance, or ailment of some sort.[1]

---

*The terms behavior modification, behavior therapy, conditioning therapies, operant conditioning, and learning-based therapies have at times been used interchangeably by various writers. However, the terms do not mean exactly the same things, as will become clear in Chapter 28. (Also, see Franzini and Tilker, 1972; Martin, 1974.)

Perhaps you are thinking, "Surely psychologists and educators aren't suggesting that disturbed children have little people inside their heads telling them what to do." Technically, you are right. Nevertheless, these professionals frequently assume that the disturbed behavior is primarily a symptom of some genetic, biological, or mental cause that we cannot readily observe. In that sense, they are more or less assuming that a "little person" is the cause of the inappropriate behavior. Unfortunately, the psychologists and educators have not been as successful as the medical people in accurately identifying these hidden causes (i.e., the "little people"), and therefore they haven't been able to prescribe successful treatments. Consequently, a great deal of time and energy has gone into discussions and arguments regarding the supposed causes of disorders such as mental retardation and learning disabilities, as portrayed in Figure 1-2.[2]

Behavior modifiers are different in that they assume that current behaviors are caused largely by environmental experiences. Nothing

FIGURE 1-1. *Traditional explanations of such behavior as excessive rocking back and forth, excessive crying, and clothes tearing.*

is gained by talking of the behavior as a symptom of some inner cause. Behavior modifiers agree that there are causes of the observable behavior, and that some of those causes may indeed be unobservable, complex inner "things" of some sort or another. Regardless of the cause, however, the behavior is still there and is still being influenced by the individual's immediate environment. The mother in Figure 1-2, for example, is still concerned about what to do with her retarded child and how to handle the retardation. "So," say the behavior modifiers, "let's spend a great deal of time and energy trying to teach more appropriate behavior, since we have to do something for the individual in spite of the unknown causes of the behavioral problems." Of course, if and when the causes are identified and cures involving something better than behavior modification are discovered, then behavior modifiers should be among the first to utilize them. Until that time, however, there is a great deal that can be done simply by using our existing behavior modification procedures.

FIGURE 1-2. *The experts "helping" mother with her child?*

To summarize, the behavior modification approach focuses primarily on observable behavior.[3] Individuals who are labeled mentally retarded, autistic, or whatever, are individuals who show behavioral deficiencies, excesses, and/or inappropriatenesses. Behavior modification consists of a set of procedures that can be used to change behavior so that these individuals will be considered less retarded, less autistic, or less of whatever label has been given them.

"Wait a minute," you say. "It sounds like this book is primarily for people concerned with helping severely handicapped individuals." In answer to such a query, we wish to point out that the behavior modification procedures described in this volume can be used to solve the behavior problems of any individual. Even people who are normal or average in most respects have one or two annoying habits that can be considered behavioral deficiencies, behavioral excesses, or behavioral inappropriatenesses. Such a classification may subsequently help an individual to select the most appropriate behavior modification procedure, in that some procedures increase behaviors, some decrease behaviors, and some help to change the time or place of occurrence of behaviors.

Consider the following behavioral deficiencies:

1. A normal child does not pronounce words clearly, put toys away after playing with them, or eat a reasonable amount of food at mealtimes.
2. A normal teenager does not complete homework assignments, help around the house or work in the yard, or discuss problems and difficulties with his parents.
3. A normal adult does not stop at stop signs and traffic lights while driving, express sincere thanks to others who help her in various situations, or meet her spouse or arrive home at previously agreed upon times.

Consider the following behavioral excesses:

1. A normal child frequently plays in the middle of the street, gets out of bed and throws tantrums at bedtime, plays with the dials on the television set, and throws food on the floor at mealtime.
2. A normal teenager frequently interrupts conversations between his parents and other adults, spends hours talking on the telephone in the evening, and uses abusive language with adults.
3. A normal adult watches television excessively, frequently eats candies and other sweets between meals, and bites her fingernails.

Consider the following behavioral inappropriatenesses:

1. A normal child says "da-da" when daddy is around but also when the milkman comes to the door, puts toys in the garbage can and cigarette butts in the toy box, and uses a crayon to write on walls but does not write on paper provided him.

2. A normal teenager helps a neighbor shovel gravel on a driveway but will not take out the garbage for her mother, and talks incessantly to members of the same sex but shows a great deal of embarrassment and difficulty in talking to members of the opposite sex.

3. A normal adult reads the newspaper at breakfast, when his spouse wants to talk, rather than at more reasonable times; wakes the spouse up in the middle of the night to "have sex," rather than considering his desires and timing from the partner's point of view; laughs at funny jokes, but also laughs on sad occasions.

The list of behavior problems exhibited by normal individuals could go on and on. The point at which a particular behavior is considered deficient, excessive, or inappropriate is determined primarily by the practices in the culture and by the desires, wishes, and ethical views of concerned individuals. Regardless of the reasons that a particular behavior is deficient, excessive, or inappropriate, the procedures described in this book can help to overcome the problem.[4]

In the following pages, we will describe the principles and procedures of behavior modification with examples of their application. The procedures described do *not* involve such things as psychosurgery, electro-convulsive therapy, or the use of drugs. Rather, the procedures are ways of rearranging an individual's environment and daily activities in order to help that individual function more fully in our society. We will also describe more detailed program strategies, as well as ethical considerations in the design of programs. We hope that this book will indeed give satisfactory answers to teachers, students, teenagers, adults, fathers, mothers, and others who say, "Thank you, Mr. Expert, but what can I do about it?" (the question asked by the mother in Figure 1-2). We hope also that the book will provide introductory students of behavior modification with an understanding of why the procedures are effective.

Study Questions

(for examination purposes)

1. What is behavior?
2. A behavior modifier would say that we should talk about retarded behavior, not retarded children; or autistic behavior, not autistic children. Why would the behavior modifier say this?
3. What is retarded behavior? (See pp. 5 and 6.)

the beh is not the autistic child.

4. What is behavior modification? (See pp. 9 and 10.)
5. What is a major difference between traditional approaches and the behavior modification approach to such disorders as mental retardation and autism?
6. What is a behavioral deficiency? Give two examples.
7. What is a behavioral excess? Give two examples.
8. What is a behavioral inappropriateness? Give two examples.
9. From a behavioral point of view, what is intelligence? creativity?

Study Exercises

(to be practiced by the reader)

1. Consider someone who is personally close to you (e.g., a sister, a brother, or a lover). From your point of view, identify
   a. two behavioral deficiencies to increase in that person;
   b. two behavioral excesses to decrease;
   c. two behavioral inappropriatenesses to change.
2. You and a friend observe the same child for two minutes. Working independently, each of you list all the behaviors you see. Then compare lists. Is your list identical to your friend's? (In other words, are your lists consistent?)
3. Working independently again, you and your friend observe the same child for ten minutes. This time, list only occurrences of social behavior. Are your lists identical?
4. If the lists you made in question 3 differ, can you offer any possible reasons for the difference?
5. In order to improve the reliability of their observations, behavior modifiers have learned to define very specifically the behavior they are observing. Prepare three specific and different definitions of social behavior for the child you observed.
6. Using one of your specific definitions of social behavior, redo question 3. Are your lists consistent now?

Self-Modification Exercise

(to be practiced by the reader)

Assume that you would like to make yourself a better person. The first step would be to identify areas in which you would like to change.

1. List three specific behavioral deficiencies that you would like to overcome.
2. List three specific behavioral excesses that you would like to decrease or eliminate.
3. List three specific behavioral inappropriatenesses such that you wish to keep the behavior but change the time and place at which it occurs.

EXTENDED DISCUSSION AND NOTES

1. The model in physical medicine in which germs, viruses, lesions, and other disturbances lead to the production of symptoms in the functioning of a normal human organism represented a major breakthrough in physical medicine during the nineteenth century. This view was adopted by Freud in his view of man and his attempt to describe the causes of abnormal behavior. Abnormal behavior was clearly viewed as a symptom of an underlying disturbance in a personality mechanism. The implication of this was that one must treat the underlying personality disturbance rather than the observed symptom (the abnormal behavior). A behavioral approach, on the other hand, suggests the abnormal behavior is a function of specifiable environmental causes (at least primarily). Whether or not these causes can be identified, it is possible to rearrange the environment in such a way that the behavior can be changed or improved. Although Freud also emphasized the importance of the individual's environment, that emphasis was placed on very early childhood experiences. Behavior modifiers concentrate on changing behavior by changing the individual's present environment. For a discussion of the application of the medical model to psychotherapy as developed by Freud, the reader is referred to Jones (1953). For a more detailed discussion of a comparison of the medical model with the behavioral model, the reader is referred to Ullmann and Krasner (1965, pp. 1–39). It should be pointed out that it is primarily psychologists and psychiatrists who talk about the "medical model." Physicians do indeed follow this model developed so successfully in the nineteenth century. It is also obvious, however, that physicians often treat the "symptom" directly. For example, if someone comes in with a broken arm, the broken arm is dealt with directly. It is this direct treatment of the problem that more accurately characterizes the approach of behavior modifiers.

2. For example, many writers in the area of learning disabilities have postulated or inferred that the cause of disability is some nebulous neurological entity or damage called "minimal brain dysfunction." Textbooks and articles by prominent professionals in the field simply define something called "minimal brain dysfunction" or "neurological dysfunction" as the cause of the observed behavioral deficit or disability (for example, see Myklebust, 1968; Tarnapol, 1969). There are several disadvantages to this approach.

First, as others have noted (e.g., Kahn, 1969), in the great majority of cases the diagnosis of minimal brain damage is inferred totally from observable behavior. Since such an inference is rarely, if ever, subject to some kind of direct verification, the way is open for frequent pseudo-explanations of the observed behavioral deficits. One frequently encounters situations in which the observed behavioral deficit leads to a label of learning disability and, by definition, minimal brain dysfunction. The observed behavior is then, in turn, explained by reference to either the disability or the neurological dysfunction. In many cases, this may reflect wishful thinking by those faced with the problem of improving the behavior of the underachiever. If the problem can be defined out of the realm of education and into the realm of neurology, then the educational system is not held responsible for the problem of remediation.

Second, on general scientific grounds, a suspected cause of be-

(Continued)

(Continued)

havior should be clearly delineated, independently measured, and experimentally evaluated. Variables responsible for certain behaviors or behavioral deficits should be experimentally demonstrated as causal, and not defined into existence, especially when the supposed cause of behavior (for instance, minimal brain dysfunction) has rarely, if ever, been specified.

Third, there are many individuals with measured nervous-system damage or brain injuries who do not suffer disabilities in various learning areas (for example, see Yacorzynski and Tucker, 1960). Those who appear to interpret a few positive correlations between test results and other behaviors as indications of cause-and-effect relations have many exceptions to contend with.

Fourth, there is a great deal of confusion about the particular learning disabilities whose causes individuals are searching for (for example, see the discussion by Martin and Powers, 1967, concerning attention span). It seems, in other words, that many individuals have been searching for nebulous causes of poorly specified behaviors.

3. Because behavior modifiers have been very concerned with trying to *scientifically demonstrate* the effectiveness of the various modification procedures in influencing behavior, they have emphasized the importance of *observable* behavior that can be reliably measured. Perhaps for this reason many people have mistakenly assumed that behavior modification is not concerned with private or covert behaviors. This mistaken view might also have developed because behavior modifiers initially treated primarily observable behaviors; only recently have they tackled the problem of modifying inner thoughts, feelings, and so forth (this will become clear in later chapters). Whatever the reasons, the assumption is clearly mistaken, since behavior modifiers currently deal with private activities and have recognized their importance since the early development of behavior modification (for example, see Skinner, 1953, Chapters 10, 15, 16, 17, and 18).

4. It should be emphasized that behavior modification procedures have not been limited to solving individual problems. They have extremely wide applicability in a variety of areas. For example, Skinner (1953) described how basic behavioral principles might be used to analyze the control exerted in our environment by religion, psychotherapy, education, economics, government, and law. A number of interesting applications of behavior modification have recently occurred in the community, concerning such things as litter control, urban recreation, low-income self-help programs, and group living arrangements (Martin and Osborne, in preparation). Although we will elaborate on these developments to some extent in later chapters, our primary concern is to teach behavioral principles, procedures, and programming strategies by illustrating their application to individual behavior problems.

Study Questions on Notes

1. Briefly, what is the medical model in medicine? In psychology?
2. How does the behavioral approach to abnormal behavior differ from the medical-model approach?
3. Can you think of some exceptional cases (perhaps from your in-

(Continued)

(Continued)

troductory psychology course) where even behaviorists would agree with the medical-model approach? (Hint: Remember phenylketonuria.)

4. Reexamine the behaviors of individuals considered learning-disabled that were mentioned earlier in this chapter. Describe how pseudoexplanations might be invoked incorrectly to account for these behaviors.

5. Are behavior modifiers concerned only with observable behavior?

6. Have behavior modification procedures been limited to solving individual problems?

PART II

Basic
Behavioral
Principles
and Procedures

CHAPTER 2

Getting A Behavior
to Occur
More Often With
POSITIVE REINFORCEMENT

"Charles, take your pills"

CHARLES'S CASE

Charles was a severely retarded, institutionalized adult.* He had a long history of spitting out the pills that the nurses gave him each morning and afternoon. Since he weighed about 217 pounds and was very strong and active, he was often successful in resisting most of their efforts to force him to swallow his pills. Making him take his pills was, in the words of one aide, "kind of like force-feeding a Brahman bull." Since Charles was prone to having quite severe epileptic seizures if he did not take the pills, it was clearly important that he do so. One of the psychiatric nurses, who was

*We gratefully acknowledge Dr. Lynn Caldwell, Department of Rehabilitation Medicine, University of Washington, for providing us with the details of Charles's case.

taking a course in behavior modification, thought to herself, "This is a case for positive reinforcement!"

One activity that Charles liked very much was smoking, but cigarettes were not always available to him. One morning, Ms. Peabody (the inspired nurse) sat down with him. On a nearby table, outside of Charles's reach, she placed a handful of pills. (Actually they were phony pills that looked and tasted much like the real thing.) She proceeded to hand Charles ten pills in succession, at approximately one-minute intervals, instructing him each time to swallow the pill. Charles swallowed the third pill given to him, but each of the other pills was thrown down. "So much for instructions," she said, having thus established that instructions alone would not do the trick.

For the next ten minutes, again at approximately one-minute intervals, Ms. Peabody attempted very firmly to place a pill in Charles's mouth. He spat out the first seven pills, but swallowed the eighth. The ninth and tenth pills, however, were also spat out. It seemed that force was also a "bad deal."

Note that up to this point, the only procedures that the nurse had tried were (1) instructing the patient to swallow his pill and (2) attempting to force him to take it. Her results demonstrated clearly that both procedures were ineffective with Charles.

Next, Ms. Peabody held up a cigarette and said to Charles, "If you swallow this pill when I put it in your mouth, I'll give you a puff on this cigarette." Then she placed the pill in his mouth, but once again he spat it out. During the next four minutes, Charles spat out four more pills, all the while making motions for Ms. Peabody to give him a cigarette, or at least a puff. But she remained firm. He swallowed the sixth pill that she placed in his mouth, and was immediately given a puff on the cigarette along with a great deal of praise.

During the next four one-minute intervals, Charles swallowed each of the four pills and in each case received a puff of the cigarette. Ms. Peabody terminated the session for the day. The following morning, she began another session. Again, Charles was asked to swallow the pill that was placed in his mouth and was told that he would receive a puff on a cigarette if he did so. He spat out the first two pills, but then swallowed the next eight in succession. The following three mornings, Ms. Peabody again conducted ten-minute sessions, and Charles swallowed all of the pills but one.

The results of this little experiment can be seen quite clearly in Figure 2-1.

Following the training with the fake pills, it was easy for Ms. Peabody to switch to the real pills at medication time.

POSITIVE REINFORCEMENT

The principle of positive reinforcement has two parts: (1) If in a given situation somebody does something that is followed immediately by a certain consequence, then (2) that person is more likely to

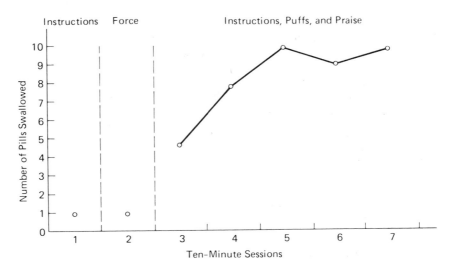

FIGURE 2-1. *Charles's pill-swallowing behavior. Each data point (o) represents the number of pills swallowed (numbered up the side) in a ten-minute session (numbered across the bottom) in which pills were presented at one-minute intervals.*

do the same thing again when he next encounters a similar situation. Such a consequence is called a positive reinforcer, a term that is roughly synonymous with the word reward.[1] Although everyone has a common-sense notion of rewards, very few people are aware of just how frequently they are influenced by positive reinforcement during every hour of every day of their lives. Some examples of instances of positive reinforcement are shown in Table 2–1. (The terms "positive reinforcement" and "reinforcement" are often used interchangeably.)

The individuals in each of the examples in Table 2–1 were not consciously using the principle of reinforcement; they were just "doing what comes naturally." In each example, it might take several repetitions before there would be any really obvious increase in the reinforced response (that is, an increase that would be really noticeable to a casual observer). Nevertheless, the effect is still there. Every time we do something, no matter what it is, there are consequences that either "turn us on" or "turn us off" or don't affect us one way or the other. Think about what you have done in the past hour, the past day, the past week, and think of the immediate consequences of some of those activities. Can you identify those consequences?

It is helpful to think about behavior in the same way that we think about other aspects of nature. What happens when you drop your shoe? It falls towards the earth. What happens to a lake when the temperature drops below zero centigrade? The water freezes.

TABLE 2-1. *Examples of Instances of Reinforcement of Desirable Behaviors*

SITUATION	RESPONSE	IMMEDIATE CONSEQUENCES	LONG-TERM EFFECTS
1. Mother is busy ironing in the kitchen. Her 3-year-old daughter is whining and attempting to get her attention.	The child gives up after five minutes and begins playing with baby sister.	Mother has just completed her ironing, and sits down to play with daughter and baby sister for a brief period.	In the future, the daughter is more likely to play with baby sister rather than annoy mother because of the attention given when she began playing with her baby sister.
2. While you are waiting in a long line of cars for the light to change at a busy intersection, a car stops in the alley on your right.	You wave to the driver in the alley to pull into the line of traffic in front of you.	The driver nods and waves thanks to you and pulls into the line of traffic.	The pleasant feedback from the driver increases the likelihood that you will engage in similar courtesies in similar situations in the future.
3. The students in a grade-three class have been given an assignment to complete.	Suzy, who is often quite disruptive, sits quietly in her desk and works on the assignment.	The teacher walks over to Suzy and says, "You're working very hard, Suzy. How would you like to help me hand out the papers during the next period?"	In the future, Suzy is more likely to work on the assignments given to her in class.
4. Father and child are shopping in a department store on a hot afternoon and both are very tired.	The child (uncharacteristically) follows father around the store quietly without complaining.	Father turns to the child and says, "You've been such a good girl. Let's go and buy an ice-cream cone and sit down for a while."	On future shopping excursions, the child is more likely to follow father quietly.
5. A woman has just tasted a batch of soup she made, and it tasted very bland.	She adds a little Worcestershire sauce.	"It tastes very tangy, just like minestrone soup," she says to herself.	There is an increased liklihood that in similar situations in the future, she will add Worcestershire sauce to her soup.
6. A husband and wife are undressing and getting ready for bed.	The husband picks up her panties and bra and places them in the laundry hamper.	His wife pats him on the bum and murmurs her thanks.	In future evenings, the husband is more likely to put her underwear in the laundry hamper.

TABLE 2-1. *(Continued)*

SITUATION	RESPONSE	IMMEDIATE CONSEQUENCES	LONG-TERM EFFECTS
7. One of the authors of this book is attempting to dictate some material into the tape recorder, but the tape recorder is not working.	The author jiggles one of the wires attached to the microphone.	The tape recorder starts working.	The likelihood of wire jiggling increases in similar situations in the future.

These are things that we all know about and that physicists have studied extensively and formulated into laws, such as the law of gravity. The principle of positive reinforcement is also rapidly approaching the status of a law. Scientific psychology[2] has been studying this principle in great detail since the 1930s, and we know that it is the single most important part of the learning process. We also know of a number of factors that determine the degree of influence the principle of reinforcement will have on behavior. These factors have been formulated into guidelines to be followed when using positive reinforcement to strengthen desirable behavior.

FACTORS INFLUENCING THE EFFECTIVENESS OF POSITIVE REINFORCEMENT

1. Selecting the behavior to be increased

The behavior selected should be a specific behavior (such as smiling) rather than a general behavior category (such as socializing). For example, Ms. Peabody chose to increase Charles's pill-swallowing behavior rather than concentrating on a vague category of behavior such as cooperativeness. By being specific in this way, you (a) help ensure the reliability of detecting instances of the behavior and changes in its frequency, which is the yardstick by which one judges reinforcer effectiveness; and (b) increase the likelihood that the reinforcement program will be applied consistently.

2. Choosing reinforcers ("different strokes for different folks")

Some stimuli are positive reinforcers for virtually everyone. Food is a positive reinforcer for almost every person who has not had anything to eat for several hours. Candy is a reinforcer for most children.

On the other hand, different individuals are frequently "turned on" by different things. In Charles's case, for example, cigarettes were very effective reinforcers. But they wouldn't have been so for someone who didn't smoke. Consider the case of Dianne, a six-year-old retarded girl who was in a project conducted by one of the authors. She was able to mimic a number of words, and we were trying to teach her to name pictures. Two reinforcers commonly used in the project were candy and bites of the child's supper, but neither of these proved very effective with Dianne. She spat them out about as often as Charles initially spat out the pills Ms. Peabody gave him. After trying many other potential reinforcers, we finally discovered that allowing her to play with a toy purse for fifteen seconds was very reinforcing. As a result, after many hours of training she is now speaking in phrases and complete sentences. For another child, listening to a music box for a few seconds turned out to be an effective reinforcer after other potential reinforcers had failed. The above-mentioned stimuli might not have been reinforcing for everyone, but that is not important. The important thing is to use a reinforcer that is effective with the individual with whom you are working.

Most positive reinforcers can be classified under five somewhat overlapping headings: consumable, activity, manipulative, possessional, and social. Classified as consumable reinforcers are such things as candy, cookies, fruit, and soft drinks. Examples of activity reinforcers are the opportunities to watch television, look at a picture book, or even stare out of a window. Manipulative reinforcers include the opportunities to play with a favorite toy, color or paint, ride a tricycle, or tinker with a tape recorder. Possessional reinforcers refer to the opportunities to sit in one's favorite chair, wear a favorite shirt or dress, have a private room, or enjoy some other item that one can possess (at least temporarily). The fifth category is that of social reinforcement. It includes affectionate pats and hugs, praise, nods, smiles, and even a simple glance or other indication of social attention. Attention from others is a very strong reinforcer for almost everyone. As anyone who has visited an institution for the retarded knows, it is particularly powerful for retarded individuals. The high frequency at which these individuals demand attention from both staff and visitors tells us something about its high reinforcing effectiveness.

In choosing effective reinforcers for an individual, it is often helpful to complete a reinforcer survey. An example of such a survey is shown in Figure 2-2.

A considerable amount of trial and error may be involved in finding an appropriate reinforcer for a particular individual. Another method is to simply observe the individual in everyday activities and note those activities engaged in most often. This method makes use of a principle first formulated by David Premack (1959), which states

FIGURE 2-2. *A questionnaire to help an individual identify reinforcers.*

This questionnaire is designed to help you find some specific individuals, objects, events, or activities that can be used as reinforcers in an improvement program. Read each question carefully, and then fill in the appropriate blanks.

A. Consumable Reinforcers: What does this person like to eat or drink?
   1. What things does this person like to eat most?
      a) regular meal-type foods _____

      b) health foods—(dried fruits, nuts, cereals, etc.) _____

      _____

      c) junk foods—popcorn, potato chips, etc. _____

      d) sweets—candies, ice cream, cookies, etc. _____
   2. What things does this person like to drink most?
      a) milk _____   c) juices _____
      b) soft drinks _____   d) other _____

B. Activity Reinforcers: What things does this person like to do?
   1. Activities in the home or residence
      a) hobbies _____
      b) crafts _____
      c) redecorating _____
      d) preparing food or drinks _____
      e) housework _____
      f) odd jobs _____
      g) other _____
   2. Activities in the yard or courtyard
      a) sports _____
      b) gardening activities _____
      c) barbecue _____
      d) yard work _____
      e) other _____
   3. Free activities in the neighborhood (window shopping, walking, jogging, cycling, driving, swinging, teeter-tottering, etc.)

      _____

   4. Free activities further away from home (hiking, snow shoeing, swimming, camping, going to the beach, etc.) _____

      _____

   5. Activities you pay to do (films, plays, sport events, night clubs, pubs, etc.) _____

      _____

   6. Passive activities (watching TV, listening to the radio, records, or tapes, sitting, talking, bathing, etc.) _____

      _____

C. Manipulative Reinforcers: What kinds of games or toys does this person like to play with?
   1. Toy cars and trucks _____
   2. Dolls _____
   3. Wind-up toys _____
   4. Balloons _____
   5. Whistle _____
   6. Jump rope _____
   7. Coloring books and crayons _____
   8. Painting kit _____
   9. Puzzles _____
   10. Other _____

D. Possessional Reinforcers: What kinds of things does this person like to possess?
   1. Brush _____
   2. Nail clippers _____
   3. Hair clips _____
   4. Comb _____
   5. Perfume _____
   6. Belt _____
   7. Gloves _____
   8. Shoelaces _____
   9. Other _____

E. Social Reinforcers: What kinds of verbal or physical stimulation does this person like to receive from others (specify who)?
   a) "Good girl (boy)" _____
   b) "Good work" _____
   c) "Good job" _____
   d) "That's fine" _____
   e) "Keep up the good work" _____
   f) other _____
   2. Physical contact
   a) hugging _____
   b) kissing _____
   c) tickling _____
   d) patty-cake _____
   e) wrestling _____
   f) bouncing on knee _____
   g) other _____

that a behavior that occurs frequently can be used to reinforce a behavior that occurs less often.* For example, one child that the authors observed ran around and screamed a lot. We therefore suggested that the staff allow the child to run and scream as a reinforcer after each correct picture-naming response. Unfortunately, although this seemed like good strategy in theory, it didn't work in practice. The problem was that once the child started screaming, the staff couldn't get her to

*The Premack Principle is elaborated on in Chapter 25.

stop. Besides, it was too noisy. However, as you can see in Figure 2-2, there are many potential activity reinforcers.[3]

It is often quite effective to allow an individual to choose among a number of available reinforcers. Variety is not only the spice of life, it is also a valuable asset to a training program. For example, a tray containing sliced fruits, peanuts, candy, and coke can be presented to a severly retarded child after each desired response, with the instruction to take one item. The advantage of this is that at least one reinforcer among the selection is likely to be strong. If the individual can read, the reinforcers can be listed in the form of a "reinforcer menu," and the preferred reinforcers can be chosen in the same way that one would order a meal at a restaurant.

One last point to emphasize is that it is always the individual's performance that tells you whether or not you have selected reinforcers wisely for that individual. When you are not sure if a particular item is reinforcing, you can always conduct an experimental test. Simply choose a behavior that the individual emits occasionally, record how often the behavior occurs without reinforcement over several trials, and then present a consequence following the behavior for a few additional trials and see what happens. If the individual begins to emit that behavior more often, then your item is indeed a reinforcer. If the performance does not increase, then you do not have an effective reinforcer. In our experience, not using an effective reinforcer is one of the most common errors of training programs. For example, a teacher may claim that a particular reinforcement program that he is trying to use is failing. Upon examination, the reinforcers used may turn out to be old, stale popcorn, hardened Christmas candy from last year, or some other item that the person doesn't like. No item should be assumed to be reinforcing without first being demonstrated to function as reinforcer for that person. In other words, *a stimulus is defined as a reinforcer only by its effect on behavior.*

3. Deprivation and satiation

Most reinforcers will not be effective unless the individual has been deprived of them for some period of time prior to their use. In general, the longer the deprivation period, the more effective the reinforcer will be. Sweets will usually not be reinforcing to a child who has just eaten a large bag of candy. A puff on a cigarette would not likely have been an effective reinforcer for Charles had he been allowed to smoke a pack just prior to the time that Ms. Peabody worked with him. Playing with a purse would not have been an effective reinforcer for Dianne had she been allowed to play with one prior to the training session. We use the term *deprivation* to indicate the time, prior to a training session, during which an individual does not experience the reinforcer. The term *satiation* refers to that condition in which the individual has experienced the reinforcer to such an extent that it is no longer reinforcing. "Enough's enough," as the saying goes.

Since an individual will be experiencing the reinforcer during the training session, satiation may occur. To prevent or delay this development, the behavior modifier should give only a small amount of the reinforcer at each reinforcement time. Ms. Peabody gave Charles only one puff on a cigarette each time he swallowed a pill. Dianne was permitted to play with the purse for only fifteen seconds after she emitted a desired speech response. In other cases, we have used only one small piece of candy, one miniature marshmallow, one piece of popcorn, one sip of juice, milk, or soft drink, or one small bite of the child's dinner per reinforcement. Another reason for using only a small amount of the reinforcer per reinforcement is to minimize the reinforcement time and thus maximize the time during the session that is available for training.

Depriving people of food and other pleasant things causes concern in many circles. Everyone agrees that it's not nice to go hungry and that deprivation, in itself, is generally bad—if for no other reason than the discomfort it causes a person. If a child is slow at learning to talk, however, depriving him of candy or a favorite toy for a few hours per day does not seem unreasonable if those items can then be used in a reinforcement program to teach him to talk. There are cases in which more excessive deprivation seems justified. For example, Wolf, Risley, and Mees (1964) had difficulty finding an effective reinforcer for getting an autistic child to wear his glasses; even candy did not work. It was crucial to establish this behavior, since the doctor had stated that if the child did not wear his glasses he would go blind within a few months. The psychologists eventually established "glasses wearing" after depriving the child of breakfast and lunch and by using ice cream as the reinforcer.[4] Once the behavior was established, it was no longer necessary to use severe deprivation to maintain it. Social reinforcers were effective.

Severe deprivation should *never* be used by the novice behavior modifier. Moreover, even highly qualified behavior modifiers should use it only when it is clearly justified on ethical and legal grounds. (See Chapter 29 for a discussion of the ethical issues involved in behavior modification.)

Often, the natural deprivation that occurs in the course of an individual's daily activities is sufficient to make a reinforcer effective. In a project devoted to teaching behaviorally retarded children to talk, we have found that bites of the evening meal during suppertime sessions generally constitute effective reinforcement. The only deprivation used is the natural deprivation that occurs between lunch and supper. If the child does not earn all of her food during the session, the remainder is given to her at the end of the session.

If the individual fails to earn lots of the reinforcer during the session, it may be because he didn't go without it for a long enough period of time and it was therefore not effective. There may be other things wrong with the procedure, but these will be discussed later. The important thing to remember at this stage of the game is that if the individual undergoes many learning trials without earning a significant amount of the reinforcer, then something should be changed. You should not conclude that there is something wrong with the individual, but rather that there is something wrong with the reinforcers or the procedures.

4. Immediacy

For maximum effectiveness, a reinforcer should be given immediately after the desired response. Recall that Ms. Peabody closely followed this rule when she was working with Charles. A positive reinforcer strengthens any response that it immediately follows. If Ms. Peabody had dallied in reinforcing Charles, then the cigarette puff might have followed some response other than pill swallowing—for instance, scratching. If this had happened, then in the future Charles would likely scratch a lot but wouldn't necessarily swallow his pills. That the failure to reinforce immediately can cause other behaviors to occur is exemplified in Figure 2-3.

Sometimes it is possible to get an individual (who can follow instructions) to work for delayed reinforcement. Telling a child that if she cleans up her room in the morning her father will bring her a toy in the evening is sometimes effective. Of course, some people do work for very long delayed goals, such as college degrees. But even for normal and above average individuals, delayed reinforcement is generally much less effective than immediate reinforcement. In fact, responding for delayed reinforcement is something that often has to be painstakingly taught to young children and severely retarded people: the behavior modifier starts with immediate reinforcement and over many trials slowly increases the time interval between the response and the reinforcement.

Some kinds of reinforcers—for instance, a movie, a picnic, or a dance—are inconvenient to deliver immediately after a desired response. We'll discuss a solution to this problem in Chapter 9.

5. Instructions

In order for reinforcement to increase an individual's behavior, it is *not* necessary that that individual be able to talk about or indicate an understanding of why he was reinforced.[5] It will probably help speed up the process if he does understand, but the principle of reinforcement works even when he does not. After all, the principle has been shown to

FIGURE 2-3. *The importance of immediate reinforcement. Regardless of mother's good intentions, reinforcement tends to influence the behavior that immediately preceded it.*

work quite effectively with animals who can't talk (at least not in a human language). Charles was able to understand simple instructions, and this perhaps accounts for the quick results obtained by Ms. Peabody. But even had he not been able to understand instructions, the same procedure would probably have worked (although it may have taken longer and required more patience). This is very fortunate, for many behaviorally handicapped individuals have no verbal skills at all. In fact, as we shall see later, positive reinforcement and other procedures can be used to establish verbal skills, even in the severely and profoundly retarded. Nevertheless, instructions should generally be used. First of all, they will speed up the process for individuals who understand them. Second, they will help to teach individuals to follow instructions. When Ms. Peabody told Charles that he would receive a puff on a cigarette if he swallowed his pill, this may or may not have speeded up the effect of the reinforcement procedure, but it probably did teach Charles something about following instructions. It probably helped him to respond appropriately the next time he was told, "If you do X, I will give you Y."

One should always behave in a manner that is consistent with the instructions she gives. If Ms. Peabody had given Charles a puff even when he did not swallow his pill, or if she had failed to give him a puff when he did swallow it, the unfortunate result would have been that Charles would have learned *not* to follow instructions. Why should he, if what the staff member says has little or no relation to what she does?

6. Weaning the student from the program and changing to natural reinforcers.

After we've strengthened a behavior through proper use of positive reinforcement, it may then be possible for reinforcers in the natural environment to take over the maintenance of that behavior.[6] For example, we have found it necessary to use reinforcers such as candy and meals to strengthen "picture naming" in behaviorally retarded children. However, when the children leave the project and go back to their wards at the institution, they often say the words that they have learned and receive a great deal of attention from the aides. Eventually, the candy and meals may no longer be needed. This, of course, is the ultimate goal of any training program. The teacher* should always try to ensure that the behavior being established in a training program will be reinforced and maintained in the natural environment. This problem is discussed in much more detail in Chapter 11.

PITFALLS OF POSITIVE REINFORCEMENT: HOW IT WORKS TO THE DISADVANTAGE OF THOSE WHO ARE IGNORANT OF IT

Those who are aware of the principle of positive reinforcement can use it to bring about desirable changes in behavior. The principle operates equally well for those who are not aware of it. Unfortunately, those who are not aware of it are apt to use it unknowingly to strengthen undesirable behavior.[7] Table 2-2 presents some examples of how positive reinforcement may work against us in the long run.

*Throughout this book, the word *teacher* is sometimes used to refer to the individual (parent, teacher, nurse, aide, or whomever) who is helping someone to overcome a behavior problem. The word *student* is frequently used to refer to the individual who has the problem. Unless prompted otherwise, please do not think just of a typical classroom situation when you read about teachers and students in this book.

TABLE 2-2. *Examples of Positive Reinforcement Following Undesirable Behavior.*

SITUATION	RESPONSE	IMMEDIATE CONSEQUENCES	LONG TERM EFFECTS
1. A three-year-old child who has been playing quietly with her coloring book gets up and looks around the living room.	The child goes over to the TV and begins fiddling with the dials.	Mother immediately comes over to her and says, "I guess you're tired of playing by yourself; let's go for a walk."	The chances of the child fiddling with the TV dials in the future increases because of the attention from mother.
2. While getting ready for work in the morning, a man cannot find his clean shirt.	He hollers loudly, "Where in the hell is my shirt?"	The wife immediately finds the husband's shirt.	In the future, the husband is more likely to holler and swear when he can't find his clothes.
3. A father is busy ironing, and his two young children are playing quietly.	One child hits his little brother over the head with a toy truck.	Father stops ironing and sits down to play with the child for a while.	The child is more likely to belt his little brother in the future in order to gain father's attention.
4. Mother and child are shopping in a department store.	Child begins to whine, "I want to go home; I want to go home."	Mother is embarrassed and leaves the store immediately with the child before making her purchase.	Child is more likely to whine in a similar situation in the future.
5. Severely retarded residents are eating their meal in the dining room at an institution.	One girl holds up her empty glass and grunts loudly, 'Mmmmm, mmmmm, mmmmm."	One of the staff members immediately comes and fills the glass with milk.	The girl is likely to hold up her glass and make similar noises in future situations when she wants milk.
6. Father is watching a Stanley Cup playoff hockey game on TV.	Two of the kids are playing in the same room and are being extremely noisy.	Father gives them each a quarter so that they will go to the store and not interfere with his TV watching.	The kids are more likely to play very noisily when father is watching TV in similar situations in the future.
7. At a party, a husband becomes sullen and shows signs of "jealousy" when his wife is dancing flirtatiously with another man.	The husband angrily leaves the party.	The wife immediately follows him, showers him with attention, and convinces him that everything is OK.	The husband is more likely to show jealousy and leave parties in similar situations in the future.

In our experience, the vast majority of undesirable activities of behaviorally deficient individuals is due to the social attention that such behavior elicits from aides, nurses, peers, teachers, parents, doctors, and others. This may be true even in cases where one would least expect it. Consider, for example, autistic and retarded children who exhibit extreme social withdrawal. One behavioral characteristic of such children is that they avoid looking at a person who is talking to them. Frequently, they move away from approaching adults. We might conclude that they don't want our attention. Actually, the withdrawn child's behavior probably gains him more social attention than he would get by looking at the adult. In a case like this, it is only natural for adults to persist in attempting to get a child to look at them when they speak to him. Unfortunately, this behavior is likely to reinforce the child's withdrawal behavior. The tendency to shower him with attention is sometimes maintained by the theory that the child needs social interaction to "bring him out of his withdrawn state." In reality, an appropriate treatment might involve withholding social attention for withdrawal behavior, and presenting it only when the child engages in some sort of social-interaction behavior—such as looking in the direction of an adult who is attempting to interact with him. The hard work of one aide or nurse using appropriate behavior techniques can be greatly hindered, or completely undone, by others who are reinforcing the wrong things. For example, an aide who attempts to reinforce eye contact in a withdrawn child is probably not going to have much of an effect if other people who interact with the child consistently reinforce looking-away behavior. Likewise, if the nurses responsible for giving Charles his pills had persisted in reinforcing him (with pleading and other types of social attention) for spitting them out, the good work initiated by Ms. Peabody would inevitably have been undone.

GUIDELINES FOR THE EFFECTIVE APPLICATION OF POSITIVE REINFORCEMENT

The following guidelines are offered for the use of parents, teachers, mental retardation workers, and other individuals who wish to utilize positive reinforcement to increase occurrences of a particular behavior.

1. *Selecting the behavior to be increased.* As we indicated earlier in this chapter, the behavior selected should be a specific behavior (such as smiling) rather than a general category of behavior (such as socializing). Also, if possible, select a behavior that will come under the control of natural reinforcers after it has been increased in frequency. Finally, as shown in

Charles's case, in order to accurately judge the effectiveness of your reinforcer it is important to keep track of how often the behavior occurs prior to your program.

2. *Selecting a reinforcer.*

   a) If possible, complete the reinforcer survey presented in Figure 2-2 and select strong reinforcers that:

      (1) are readily available;

      (2) can be presented immediately following the desired behavior;

      (3) can be used over and over again without causing rapid satiation;

      (4) do not require a great deal of time to consume (if it takes a half-hour to consume the reinforcer, this minimizes the training time).

   b) Use as many reinforcers as feasible, and, where appropriate, use a reinforcer tray or menu.

3. *Applying positive reinforcement.*

   a) Tell the individual about the plan before starting.

   b) Reinforce *immediately* following the desired behavior.

   c) Verbally describe the desired behavior to the individual while the reinforcer is being given. (For example, say, "You cleaned your room very nicely" and not, "You're a good boy.")

   d) Use lots of praise and physical contact (if appropriate and if these are reinforcing to the individual) when dispensing the reinforcers. However, in order to avoid satiation, vary the phrases you use as social reinforcers. Don't always say, "Good for you." (Some sample phrases: "Very nice"; "That's great"; "Right on"; "Tremendous.")

4. *Weaning the student from the program* (discussed more fully in Chapter 11).

   a) If, during the presentation of a dozen or so of the opportunities, a behavior has been occurring at a desirable rate, it might be possible to gradually eliminate tangible reinforcers (such as candy and toys) and maintain the behavior with social reinforcement.

   b) Look for other natural reinforcers in the environment that might also maintain the behavior once it has been increased in frequency.

   c) In order to ensure that the behavior is being reinforced occasionally, and to ensure that the desired frequency is being maintained, plan periodic assessments of the behavior after the program has terminated.

Study Questions

(for examination purposes)

1. How did Ms. Peabody know that instructions and force feeding wouldn't get Charles to swallow his pills?

2. Was Ms. Peabody recording the frequency, quality, or duration of Charles's pill-swallowing behavior?

3. What are the two parts of the principle of positive reinforcement?

4. In what way is positive reinforcement like gravity?

5. Should you tell an individual with whom you are using reinforcement about the reinforcement program before putting it into effect? Why or why not?

6. What is the *best* way to determine if something is reinforcing for someone? (See p. 25.)

7. Why did Ms. Peabody give Charles only one puff on a cigarette after each desirable response, rather than giving him the whole cigarette?

8. List the two reasons for using a small amount of the reinforcer per reinforcement.

9. Is it correct to conclude that a withdrawn child does not like attention from other people? Explain.

10. "A stimulus is defined as a reinforcer only by its effect on behavior" (p. 25). Explain what this means.

11. How might you conduct a test to determine if the social attention of a particular adult is or is not reinforcing for a withdrawn child?

12. Should severe deprivation ever be used? Explain.

13. What should you conclude if an individual does not earn much of the reinforcer during a training program? (See page 27.)

14. What do we mean by the *natural environment?* By *natural reinforcers?*

15. Briefly, what are six factors that influence the effectiveness of reinforcement?

16. Why is it necessary to be specific when selecting a behavior for a reinforcement program?

17. Ideally, what four qualities should a reinforcer have (besides the necessary quality of functioning as a reinforcer)? (See p. 32.)

18. Describe two examples of positive reinforcement that you have encountered, one involving a desirable behavior and one involving an undesirable behavior. For each example, identify the situation, behavior, immediate consequence, and probable long-term effects (as shown in Tables 2-1 and 2-2). (The examples should not be from the text.)

19. What is plotted on the vertical axis in Figure 2-1?

20. What is plotted on the horizontal axis in Figure 2-1?

21. Note that the distance between any two numbers on the vertical axis in Figure 2-1 is less than half of the distance between the same two numbers on the horizontal axis. Redraw the graph so that the scale on the horizontal axis is the same as the scale on the vertical axis. How does the appearance of your graph differ from that of Figure 2-1 on p. 19?

Study Exercises

(to be practiced by the reader)

1. For a fifteen-minute period during which you spend a good deal of time around children, carry a pencil and a small slip of paper with you. On the front of the paper, put a small mark each time you interact with (i.e., talk to, look at, or touch) a child immediately following a desirable behavior of the child. On the other side of the paper, put a small mark each time that you interact with a child immediately following an undesirable behavior

of the child. At the end of the fifteen-minute period, count up the marks on each side of the paper. We hope your instances of interaction following desirable behavior are five or six times as many as the interactions following undesirable behavior. If they are not, then we would encourage you to continue this daily exercise until this goal is reached.

2. How many times do you dispense social approval (nods, smiles, or kind words) to children during a day in which your total time with them is at least one hour. How many times do you dispense social disapproval (frowns, harsh words, etc.) during a day? Again, use a small piece of paper and a pencil and record the instances in which you dispense social approval and those in which you dispense disapproval. Ideally, your social-approval total at the end of the day will be four or five times the social-disapproval total. We would encourage you to continue this daily exercise until you have achieved this ratio.[8]

3. List ten different phrases that you might use to express your enthusiastic approval to an individual. Practice varying these phrases until they come naturally to you.

Self-Modification Exercises

(to be practiced by the reader)

1. Try to watch your own behavior for five one-minute periods while behaving naturally. At the end of each minute, describe a situation, a specific behavior, and the immediate consequences of that behavior. Choose behaviors whose consequences seemed pleasant (rather than neutral or unpleasant).

2. Complete the reinforcer questionnaire (Figure 2-2) for yourself.

3. Assume that someone (your husband, wife, friend, etc.) is going to reinforce one of your behaviors (such as making your bed daily, talking in conversation without swearing, or reading pages of this book). Select the two reinforcers from your completed questionnaire that best satisfy the above guidelines for selecting a reinforcer.

EXTENDED DISCUSSION AND NOTES

1. People have used rewards both knowingly and unknowingly, since the beginning of recorded history. It is an interesting exercise, for example, to examine descriptions of the techniques utilized by those responsible for training the Roman gladiators in order to try to identify the systems of reward that were in effect. In spite of this long history of the application of rewards in everyday life, the experimental analysis of the effects of rewards is a relatively recent undertaking. The person typically credited with experimentally identifying the importance of rewards in learning is E. L. Thorndike, who in 1898 published a description of the behavior of a hungry cat learning to pull a string to escape from a cage and acquire food. In 1911, Thorndike described the "law of ef-

(Continued)

fect," which stated in part that if a stimulus was followed by a response and then by a "satisfier," the stimulus-response connection was strengthened. It was clear from Thorndike's other writings that a "satisfier" was what we are calling a positive reinforcer. B. F. Skinner, one of the most influential psychologists of modern times, suggested later that the term positive reinforcement was preferable to terms such as satisfiers and rewards. Skinner described his reasons for introducing a new term, positive reinforcement, rather than continuing with terms such as reward, which were borrowed from the layman's everyday vocabulary (Skinner, 1938, p. 7):

> The important objection to the vernacular in the description of behavior is that many of its terms imply conceptual schemes. I do not mean that a science of behavior is to dispense with a conceptual scheme but that it must not take over without careful consideration of the schemes which underlie popular speech. The vernacular is clumsy and obese; its terms overlap each other, draw unnecessary or unreal distinctions, and are far from being the most convenient in dealing with the data. They have the disadvantage of being historical products, introduced because of everyday convenience rather than that special kind of convenience characteristic of a simple scientific system.

For additional discussion of the concept of *positive reinforcer,* see Skinner (1953, pp. 72–73).

2. What is scientific psychology? The best answer to this question might be found by examining the behavior of psychologists who consider themselves scientists. Although there is a good deal of agreement among individual scientific psychologists concerning the general characteristics of scientific psychology, there is also some disagreement. Some individuals have argued at length about what science and psychology are and are not. Other individuals, many of whom have never conducted experiments or participated in other scientific activities, have made proposals concerning the manner in which scientific psychology should proceed. (These individuals are often called philosophers of science.) For more detailed discussion of the particular brand of scientific psychology subscribed to in this book, see Skinner (1953, pp. 1–22; 1956) and Sidman (1960). This approach, generally called the "experimental analysis of behavior," emphasizes the value of studying the effects of manipulable aspects of the environment on observable behavior of individual organisms. Its immediate goals are to improve our prediction and control of the behavior of individual organisms. An additional goal is to improve our explanations of observed behavior. There are, however, different kinds of explanations. This particular approach emphasizes the importance of two types of explanation. In one sense, a behavior is thought to be explained when it is possible to demonstrate its controlling variables. In a second sense, a behavior is explained (or interpreted) when it is possible to identify demonstrated functional relationships between similar behaviors and their controlling variables. Much of Skinner's writings (e.g., 1953, 1957, 1969) consist of explanations of this second type.

3. An interesting example of the application of activity reinforcers was described by Pierce and Risley (1974). They were concerned with increasing the membership at a community recreation center in the most economically deprived area of Kansas City, Kansas. Since a number of

(Continued)

(Continued)

children were already attending the center on a voluntary basis, it was assumed that recreation activities were reinforcing for those individuals. In order to demonstrate this and at the same time solve the problem of increasing the membership, Pierce and Risley used extra recreation time as a reinforcer. An extra hour of time for recreation activity was allowed for a member each time he enrolled a new member in the center. The result was a dramatic increase in the number of new members.

4. Notice that in the experiment by Wolf et al., the autistic child initially performed best only when he was deprived of food and food was used as a reinforcer. Earlier experiments led psychologists to postulate hunger drives and thirst drives as essential components of learning when food and water were used as reinforcers. Psychologists also postulated a variety of other drives, such as a drive for approval and a drive for novelty, that were thought by many to be necessary for learning to occur. For a more detailed discussion of some of the traditional views of the relationship between drive and learning, see Kimble (1961). In general the behavioral approach adopted in this book does not resort to hypothesizing internal conditions such as drives. Rather, we identify a reinforcer by studying its effects, and then we manipulate deprivation or satiation of that reinforcer to cause it to have a greater or lesser effect. A more detailed discussion of the behavioral approach to concepts such as drives and needs can be found in Skinner (1953, pp. 141–149).

5. Although at first it may seem a little unusual to think of people learning without understanding, or to think of people being reinforced without understanding, or to think of people being reinforced for emitting a certain behavior without their awareness of it, this is much easier to understand when we consider the following observations. First of all, from experience that everyone has had as well as from basic experiments, it is obvious that animals can learn even though they are not able to verbalize an understanding or an awareness of their behavioral increases. Similarly, even the most profoundly retarded individuals who cannot speak have been shown to be affected by reinforcement (for example, see Fuller, 1949). Finally, a number of experiments have demonstrated that normal adult humans can be influenced by reinforcement to show behavioral increases even if they are unable to verbalize their behavior changes. One such experiment was conducted by Greenspoon (1951). In this experiment, university students (one at a time) sat opposite Greenspoon and were instructed to say words individually and not to use sentences, phrases, or numbers. The experimental sessions lasted for fifty minutes. One group of subjects (the control group) simply responded for fifty minutes, and Greenspoon inconspicuously counted the number of plural nouns (as opposed to singular nouns, adjectives, adverbs, and so forth) that they uttered. There were no consequences for their responses. The students in the experimental group were treated somewhat differently. During the first twenty-five minutes, each time these students uttered a plural noun, Greenspoon said "mmm-hmm." During the final twenty-five minute segment of the fifty-minute session, Greenspoon remained silent while the student said words. The result of the experiment was that the experimental group uttered more plural nouns than the control group, and most of these words were spoken during the first twenty-five minute period. When the students were asked about the experiment afterward, very few of those in the experimental group said that their behavior had been influenced in the fashion described above. Despite evidence of this sort—that learning

(Continued)

without awareness does indeed occur—it should be pointed out that this is not a settled issue in the eyes of some psychologists, who feel that the issue is not as clear-cut as we have described it above (for example, see Dulany, 1968). A discussion of awareness as behavior that develops in the same way as other behaviors can be found in Staats (1975).

6. Many behaviors in everyday life are followed by reinforcers even though no one specifically or deliberately programmed the reinforcer to increase or maintain the behavior. Reading signs is frequently reinforced by finding desired objects or directions. Eating is reinforced by the taste of food. Verbal and social behaviors are reinforced by the natural reactions of others. Typically occurring events in everyday life that function as reinforcers are referred to as *natural reinforcers*. Such events may be deliberately manipulated by psychologists, teachers, and others to modify behavior, and in such cases they would be referred to as arbitrary, contrived, or programmed reinforcers. They are called natural reinforcers when they occur as consequences of behavior in the natural environment. For a more detailed discussion of natural versus arbitrary reinforcers, see Ferster (1967) and Ferster, Culbertson, and Boren (1975).

7. Many studies in the literature have demonstrated that individuals who are unaware of the effects of reinforcement frequently and unknowingly strengthen undesirable behaviors by providing social attention as a reinforcer following those behaviors. A classic example was the early study by Zimmerman and Zimmerman (1958), in which teachers unknowingly maintained extreme tantrums in a child by attending to tantruming behavior. Another classic study, conducted by Harris, Wolf, and Baer (1966), demonstrated clearly that nursery school teachers unknowingly maintained such behaviors as excessive crawling, crying and whining, isolate play, and excessive passivity by attending to those behaviors in their children. The authors of this study taught the teachers to ignore such behaviors and to attend to desirable alternative behaviors. The results in all cases were successful in increasing alternative desirable behaviors and decreasing the undesirable behaviors. In addition, a classroom study by Hall, Lund, and Jackson (1968) indicated that attention from teachers maintained disruptive activity in children to the extent that the activity interfered with desirable study behavior. Finally, a study by Hall and Broden (1967) indicated that undesirable behaviors in brain-injured children might be maintained by attention from well-meaning but uninformed adults.

8. The appropriate ratio of reinforcers to reprimands has not been widely investigated. However, there is some support for our recommendation in study exercise 2 that a ratio of approval to disapproval should be about 4 or 5 to 1. One source of support for this recommendation comes from an investigation by Stuart (1971) concerning the dispensing of verbal approval and disapproval by parents to their juvenile-delinquent offspring. Stuart reported that juvenile deliquents and their parents tend to verbally "reinforce" each other approximately as often as they verbally disapprove of each other. Conversely, nondeliquents and their parents showed ratios of approval to disapproval towards each other of about 4 to 1. Similarly, Madsen and Madsen (1974) observed that teachers in classroom situations who disapproved of student behaviors about as often as they praised student behaviors had

(Continued)

(Continued)

higher frequencies of classroom discipline problems than teachers who dispensed praise much more often than criticism. Moreover, a training program provided by the Madsens for teachers with discipline problems led to an increase in the ratio of praise to criticism for those teachers to a 4-to-1 level or higher, and produced better-behaved classes.

Study Questions on Notes

1. Who is given credit for being the first to experimentally identify the principle of positive reinforcement?

2. State the "law of effect."

3. Why did Skinner introduce the term *positive reinforcement* rather than using the common-sense term *reward?*

4. Briefly describe a situation or experience that we might call rewarding but should not, technically, call reinforcing. Explain.

5. What two types of explanations are emphasized by the behavioral approach? Describe an example of each from this chapter (see pp. 18 and 31).

6. Why is "minimal brain dysfunction" not presently an acceptable kind of explanation for a behavior deficit? (Compare note 2 in Chapter 1 with note 2 in this chapter.)

7. What is awareness? (Hint: Recall the discussion about behavior in Chapter 1.)

8. Discuss evidence that people's behavior can be modified without their being aware of it.

9. Describe three behavior episodes in this chapter that involved *natural* reinforcers. Justify your choices.

10. What did Harris, Wolf, and Baer do?

11. How did Pierce and Risley solve the membership problem at a community center?

CHAPTER 3

Decreasing
A Behavior With
EXTINCTION

"Peter, your tantrums are driving me crazy."

PETER'S CASE

Peter, a ten-year-old boy diagnosed as autistic, was a resident at the Manitoba School.* One summer, he participated in an operant-conditioning program in which university students, under the supervision of one of the authors, attempted to teach him to talk and to engage in some basic kindergarten activities. One of the main problems encountered was that Peter frequently threw severe tantrums, during which he stamped, kicked, screamed, threw things, slapped his face, cried, and yelled "Cut,"

*This report is based on a study by Martin, England, Kaprowy, Kilgour, and Pilek (1968). The Manitoba School is a large government institution for retarded people in the province of Manitoba.

"Needle," or "Doctor" while pointing to his arm, leg, or some other part of his anatomy. These tantrums appeared to be provoked by mildly frustrating events — for instance, when he was prevented from leaving the room, or when he failed to receive a reinforcer after emitting an incorrect verbal response.

Sessions were initially conducted in a small room. Peter sat in a tablet arm-chair desk which was placed against the wall so that he was prevented from wandering around. Whenever Peter began tantrumming, Veronica, the university student working with him, simply turned away and ignored him until the tantrum had ceased for a brief period. Following the tantrum and a period of at least fifteen to twenty seconds during which the boy had been sitting quietly, Veronica would turn to him, and say, "Good boy!" and give him a poker chip which he could later exchange for food and candies. At the end of every fifteen to twenty second period in which no tantrum occurred, Peter received another chip. As a result of this procedure of ignoring tantrums and reinforcing sitting quietly for brief periods, Peter's tantrum behavior gradually decreased in the teaching situation, making it possible to begin working on developing his verbal and other basic skills. The results of the procedure are shown in Figure 3-1.

EXTINCTION

The principle of extinction, like that of positive reinforcement, has two parts: (1) If, in a given situation, somebody emits a previously reinforced response and the response is not followed by the usual reinforcing consequence, then (2) that person is less likely to do the same thing again when he next encounters a similar situation. Stated differently, if a response has been increased in frequency through positive reinforcement, then completely ceasing to reinforce the response will cause it to decrease in frequency. In a general sense, if the environment ignores a behavior, then that behavior will go away.[1]

Observation of Peter's behavior on the ward indicated that he frequently received a lot of social attention from ward staff when he threw tantrums. It is likely that this attention was a positive reinforcer in maintaining the high frequency of this undesirable behavior. In the program described above, Peter's tantrums no longer received attention and their frequency decreased to a very low level. As with positive reinforcement, very few of us are aware of just how frequently we are influenced by extinction during every hour of every day of our lives. Some examples of extinction appear in Table 3-1.

In each example in this table, the individuals are simply doing what comes naturally in their daily activities. In each example, it might take several repetitions of the behavior occurring and not being reinforced before there would be any really obvious decrease in its frequency. Nevertheless, the effect is still there. Over a number of trials, behaviors that no longer "pay off' gradually decrease. Of

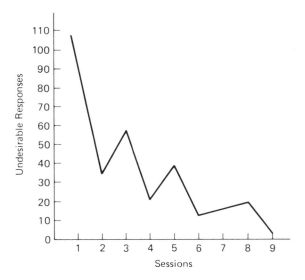

FIGURE 3-1. *Extinction of undesirable verbal responses during tantrums. Each instance of Peter's "Cut," "Needle," or "Doctor" was counted as an undesirable response. Each dot represents the number of undesirable responses in a session. A tantrum consisted of several such responses as well as crying, whining, and face slapping. The frequency of tantrums during the first nine sessions would therefore be somewhat less than the frequency of verbal responses.*

course, this is highly desirable, for if we persisted in useless behavior, we would quickly "extinguish" as a race.

Extinction, like the principle of positive reinforcement, has been studied extensively by experimental psychologists over several decades, and we are able to describe a number of factors that influence its effectiveness. These will now be discussed.

FACTORS INFLUENCING THE EFFECTIVENESS OF EXTINCTION

1. Extinction combined with positive reinforcement

Extinction is most effective when combined with positive reinforcement for some desirable alternative behavior. Thus, not only were Peter's tantrums ignored (extinction), but the behavior "sitting quietly" was positively reinforced. The combination of the two procedures probably decreased the frequency of the undesirable behavior much faster (and possibly to a lower level) than would have been the case had the extinction procedure been used alone.

It is often impractical to reinforce a child every few seconds for

TABLE 3-1. *Examples of extinction*

SITUATION	RESPONSE	IMMEDIATE CONSEQUENCES	LONG TERM EFFECTS
1. A four-year-old child is lying in bed at night while the parents are sitting in the living room talking to guests.	The child begins to make loud animal noises while lying in bed.	The parents and guests ignore the child completely and continue to talk quietly.	The child is less likely to make animal noises in future situations of that sort.
2. The next evening, the same child and parents are having dinner at the dining-room table. The child has just finished the main course.	The child holds up her empty plate and yells loudly, "Dessert, dessert, dessert."	The parents continue talking and ignore the child's loud demands. After the child sat quietly for a brief period, the mother served dessert.	The behavior of demanding dessert is less likely to occur in similar situations in the future, and the behavior of waiting quietly until dessert is served is more likely to occur in similar situations in the future.
3. A husband is standing in the kitchen and complaining to his wife about the traffic on his way home from work. The wife says, "Yes, that's too bad. Why don't you sit down and rest and you'll feel better."	The husband continues to stand in the kitchen and complain about the traffic.	The wife goes about the business of preparing supper and does not attend to any of his comments.	Continual (and probably unproductive) complaining by the husband is less likely to occur in the future.
4. A child in a grade-three classroom has just finished an assignment and raised his hand.	The child begins to snap his fingers.	The teacher ignores the child and responds to those children who raised their hand and are not snapping their fingers.	The child is less likely to snap his fingers in similar situations in the future.
5. A three-year-old child working on a plastic puzzle is attempting to put a piece in the wrong place.	The child pounds the piece to try to make it fit.	The piece still doesn't fit; it merely bounces every time it is pounded.	The likelihood of the child's aggressive pounding occurring in similar situations in the future is decreased.

engaging in some desirable behavior (such as sitting or playing quietly) in place of disruptive behavior. It is possible, however, to begin with short intervals of desirable behavior and gradually increase them to longer, more manageable intervals. For example, a child who is engaging in inappropriate crying could be ignored until he had stopped crying for a period of ten seconds. At the end of the ten-second interval, he could be reinforced with praise and perhaps a small bite of candy. On subsequent trials, the teacher could require successively longer periods of silence — fifteen seconds, then twenty-five, than a minute, and so on — before presenting reinforcement. It is important that the increase in the requirement be very gradual; otherwise, the undesirable behavior will not decrease very rapidly. Also, care must be taken not to present the reinforcer immediately after the crying ceases, as this would tend to reinforce the crying, thereby increasing rather than reducing it.

2. Controlling alternative reinforcers for the behavior that is to be decreased

Suppose a four-year-old girl, Susie, has developed a great deal of whining behavior, especially in situations in which she wants something. Her mother has decided to ignore this behavior in the hope that it will go away. On three occasions during the afternoon, mother ignored the whining behavior until it ceased, and then, following a brief period of no whining, provided Susie with the item she desired. Things seemed to be progressing nicely until early evening, when father came home. While mother was in the kitchen, Susie approached mother and in a whiny tone asked for some popcorn to eat while watching TV. Although mother completely ignored Susie, father entered the room and said, "Mother, can't you hear your child? Come here, Susie, I'll get your popcorn." We are sure that you can now predict the effect this episode will have on Susie's whining behavior in the future (not to mention mother's anger towards father).

It is extremely important during the application of extinction to ensure that alternative reinforcers (reinforcers other than those you are withholding) are not presented following the occurrence of the undesirable behavior. Failure to do this can doom your extinction program, as shown in Figure 3-2.

Reinforcers presented by other people or by the physical environment can undo your good efforts at applying extinction. Unfortunately, it is often very difficult to convince others of this if they are not familiar with the mechanics of positive reinforcement and extinction. For example, if several psychiatric nurses are ignoring a

FIGURE 3-2. *An extreme example of why attempts to apply extinction often fail. Other reinforcers must always be considered.*

child's tantruming behavior and another psychiatric nurse enters and says, "Oh, I can get this child to stop crying—here, Tommy, have a candy," then Tommy is likely to stop crying at that moment, but in the long run his crying will increase in frequency because of that reinforced trial. Since the nurse did get Tommy to stop crying, however, it would probably be difficult to convince her of the importance of extinction. In such cases, it is necessary either to control the behavior of these other individuals in some fashion, or to carry out the extinction procedure in their absence. Frequently, the latter is more feasible than the former.[2]

Extinction is sometimes criticized on the grounds that it is cruel to deprive someone of social attention during their time of need (this criticism usually assumes that an individual who is crying, whining, or showing various other behaviors that commonly evoke attention is in a time of need). In some cases, this might be a valid criticism. In general, we say, "A pox on any behavior modifier who claims that all crying should be ignored." That is simply dumb behavior modification. In many situations crying does indicate injury, emotional distress, and other forms of discomfort. We suggest that any behavior must be examined closely in terms of the desirability of decreasing it. If a decrease is desired, then extinction, along with positive reinforcement of an alternative behavior, frequently provides the right route to travel.

3. The setting in which extinction is carried out

The settings in which the extinction procedure is used can range from highly contrived situations for hard-to-eliminate behavior to everyday situations for behavior that is eliminated more easily. For an example of the latter, consider retarded children who run up to adults entering the ward of an institution and throw their arms around them or cling to their clothing. This behavior appears to be reinforced by the attention received from the adults as they attempt to free themselves from the child's grasp without "hurting his feelings." The behavior can be greatly reduced over time if the adults ignore the children who are engaging in it and give plenty of attention to the children who are politely standing a slight distance away.

The necessity of using extinction combined with reinforcement in a highly contrived situation is illustrated by the following case of a self-abusive child (Martin and Treffry, 1970). Valerie was a sixteen-year-old severely retarded girl with cerebral palsy and partial right hemiplegia (that is, she was partly paralyzed on her right side). She had been at the Manitoba School for eight years prior to the treatment to be described. She had no speech, and although she had been taught to walk with support four years earlier, she would not move unless aided by staff. When a staff member let her go, she simply dropped to the floor. Two of the undesirable behaviors she emitted were hitting her face with her strong left hand and, when placed on a chair, slouching so that she was almost parallel to the floor. Many treatments other than behavior modification had been tried during the previous eight years, but none had been effective. As a result of extensive observations over a two-month period, it became obvious that staff attention, which occasionally followed her self-abusiveness and slouching, was maintaining those behaviors at a high frequency. It was decided that a special setting was necessary before an attempt could be made to extinguish these behaviors, because the staff members were used to attending to Valerie in the natural ward setting. Therefore, the following procedure was initiated. In the morning, after Valerie was dressed, the staff would take her to the TV room and sit her on a chair that was positioned behind a sofa that had been placed across a corner of the room. Valerie was thus confined to the corner. A piece of cardboard was then placed vertically on the sofa. If Valerie sat erect on the chair, she was just visible above the cardboard. However, if she positioned herself in the undesirable fashion previously described, she could not be seen. Throughout the day, with the exception of mealtimes, the psychiatric nurses looked towards Valerie's corner approximately every fifteen minutes. If on those occasions Valerie was sitting up looking over the sofa and cardboard and not slapping herself, she was reinforced with praise, candy, or fruit. However, if she could not be seen, or if she was seen but was slapping herself, then she was completely ignored. This created a situation in which Valerie could frequently be reinforced for sitting erect without slapping, but would never be reinforced for slouching in her chair or for self-slapping behavior. The result of this combination of extinction for undesirable behavior and positive reinforcement for a desirable alternative behavior can be seen in Figure 3-3.

Over a twelve-day period, Valerie's slouching and self-slapping decreased nearly to zero and her appropriate sitting behavior increased to almost 100 percent of the observation intervals. As a consequence of this procedure, Valerie was moved from behind the sofa and placed in various ward training programs.

The case of Valerie illustrates one reason for considering the setting in which extinction is to be carried out. There is another one.

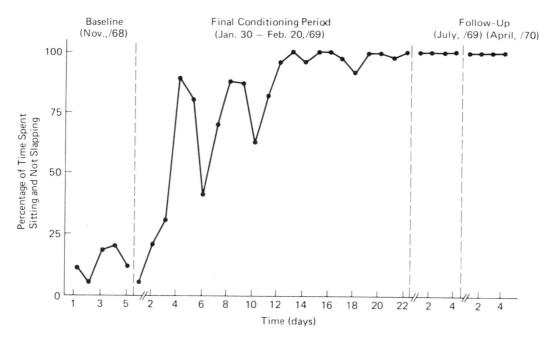

FIGURE 3-3. *Control of Valerie's self-slapping. Each entry shows the percentage of observation periods in a particular day during which the child was sitting erect and not slapping herself.*

It would probably be unwise, for example, for a mother to initiate extinction of her child's temper tantrums in a downtown department store. The child is likely to display behavior in the department store such that the nasty looks from other shoppers and store clerks would decrease the chances of mother carrying through effectively. In other words, it is important to consider the setting in which extinction will be carried out, in order to (1) minimize the influence of alternative reinforcers on the undesirable behavior to be extinguished; and (2) maximize the chances of the behavior modifier persisting with the program.

4. Instructions

Although it is not necessary that an individual be able to talk about or understand extinction, it will probably help speed up the decrease in behavior if the person is initially told something like this: "Each time you do X, then Y (the reinforcing item) will no longer occur." The points regarding instructions that were made in Chapter 2 apply equally well here.

5. Extinction is quicker after continuous reinforcement

Let's take another look at the case concerning Susie's whining behavior with mother. Before mother decided to introduce extinction, what happened when Susie was whining? Sometimes nothing would happen, because mother would be busy with other things, such as talking on the telephone. But at other times (often after five or six instances of whining), mother would attend to Susie and give her what she wanted. This is typical of many reinforcement situations in that it is clear that Susie was not reinforced following each instance of whining. Rather, she was reinforced occasionally, following several instances of whining. This type of situation is referred to as intermittent reinforcement, as opposed to continuous reinforcement, and is discussed in detail in Chapter 5. It is necessary to mention these two schedules of reinforcement here because the schedule can greatly influence the effectiveness of extinction.

The influence of the reinforcement schedule on extinction can easily be imagined if you consider a situation that you yourself have probably encountered many times. Suppose you are writing with a ball point pen and suddenly it stops writing. What do you do? Like most people, you probably shake it up and down a couple of times and try to write with it a few more times, and if it still doesn't write, you throw it away and get another pen. Now suppose that you are writing with another ball point pen in another situation. In this second situation with this second pen, the pen occasionally skips. That is, you write for a while and then the pen misses a little bit. You shake it a few times and write some more, and then it misses some more. Each time you shake it, it writes a little more. Now comes the question. In which situation are you likely to persist longer in using the pen? Obviously, the second situation, because the pen occasionally quits but it usually writes again. When the distinction is clear between a situation where a behavior has always been reinforced and a situation where that behavior is now never reinforced (such as when a pen quits suddenly), behavior extinguishes fairly quickly. When intermittent reinforcement is involved in maintaining a behavior (such as when a cheap pen occasionally skips), that behavior extinguishes more slowly.[3]

Now, let's take a look at Susie's whining. It is likely to take much longer for extinction to completely eliminate whining if whining sometimes "pays off" and sometimes does not, than if whining always paid off and then suddenly is completely ignored. In other words, extinction is much quicker after continuous reinforcement (in which each response was previously reinforced) than after intermittent reinforcement (in which responses were reinforced only occasionally). This means that if you try to extinguish a behavior that has been reinforced intermittently, you must be prepared for extinction to take longer.

PITFALLS OF EXTINCTION: HOW IT WORKS
TO THE DISADVANTAGE OF THOSE WHO ARE IGNORANT OF IT

Like the law of gravity, the principle of positive reinforcement and other natural laws, the principle of extinction operates whether we are aware of it or not. Unfortunately, those who are not aware of extinction are apt to apply it unknowingly to the desirable behavior of friends, acquaintances, family, and others. Table 3-2 presents some examples of how extinction may, in the long run, work to decrease desirable behavior.

As these examples indicate, no one can escape the effects of extinction. Even in situations where some individuals are knowledgeably applying behavior modification in an effort to help behaviorally deficient individuals, their good works may be undone by others who are not knowledgeable about extinction. Suppose, for example, that a child in an institutional program for the retarded has been reinforced by a nurse's aide for appropriate dressing. Suppose, further, that this aide had been transferred or has gone on vacation, and is

TABLE 3-2. *Examples of undesirable instances of extinction*

SITUATION	RESPONSE	IMMEDIATE CONSEQUENCE	LONG-TERM EFFECTS
1. The residents and nursing staff in an institution for the retarded are sitting in the TV room.	A particular resident has been sitting quietly for the past twenty minutes.	The nurses keep on talking, and no one responds to the child who has been sitting quietly.	The behavior of sitting quietly is less likely to occur in similar situations in the future, due to the lack of reinforcement for sitting quietly.
2. Two staff members are talking to each other in an institution for the retarded, and a resident approaches and stands nearby.	The resident stands and waits patiently beside the two staff members for several minutes. Finally, the resident interrupts.	The staff members stop talking and listen to the resident.	The response of standing beside the staff and waiting patiently is less likely to occur in the future, and the response of interrupting staff is more likely to occur in the future.
3. A man carrying several parcels is walking towards the exit door of a department store. A woman standing by the door waiting for the bus sees the man coming.	The woman opens the door for the man.	The man rushes out without saying a word.	The chances of the woman opening the door in similar situations in the future are decreased slightly.
4. A three-month-old baby is lying quietly in the crib just before feeding time.	The baby begins making cooing sounds (which, might be interpreted by eager parents as "mama" or "dada").	The mother, busily, preparing a bottle, ignores the child. When the child is picked up later she is again quiet (or, more likely, crying).	The mother has just missed an opportunity to reinforce noise making that approximates speech. Instead she reinforced lying quietly (or crying). Therefore, cooing is less likely to occur in the future.

replaced by an aide who is not familiar with the principles of positive reinforcement and extinction or with the particular program for the child. Confronted with a child who dresses himself and many children who do not, the new aide will quite likely spend a great deal of time helping the latter children but giving very little attention to the one child. It is a common human tendency to give plenty of attention to problems and to ignore situations in which things seem to be going well. It is easy to rationalize this selective attention. "After all," the aide may say, "why should I reinforce Johnny for doing something that he already knows how to do?" Despite this seemingly justifiable rationalization, we know that if the child's self-dressing behavior receives little or no reinforcement from any source, it will eventually extinguish. For any particular behavior to be maintained after it has been established, it must continue to be reinforced.[4]

A different kind of pitfall is the unexpected difficulties encountered by a behavior modifier trying to apply extinction. During extinction, behavior may increase before it begins to decrease. That is, things may get worse before they get better. Suppose a child in the classroom is constantly raising her hand and snapping her fingers in order to gain the teacher's attention. If the teacher were to keep track of the frequency of finger snapping for a while, and then introduce extinction (that is, completely ignore the finger snapping), she would probably observe an increase in finger snapping during the first hour or two of extinction before the behavior gradually began to taper off. If something is no longer "paying off," a slight increase in the behavior may be sufficient to again bring the "payoff." This phenomenon has been studied extensively in laboratory situations, and it is something that everyone who attempts to apply an extinction procedure should be aware of. If the teacher decided to introduce extinction following finger snapping, and then observed an increase in this behavior during the next hour or two, she might erroneously conclude that extinction wasn't working and give up in the middle of the program. The effect of this action would be to reinforce the behavior when it gets worse. The rule to follow here is this: If you introduce extinction, don't give up the ship in the middle of the storm. Things will get worse before they get better, but hang in there; doing so will pay off in the long run.[5]

Another unexpected difficulty of extinction is that the procedure may produce mild aggression. Again, we have all experienced this. Probably all of us have experienced the act (or at least the desire) of pounding and kicking a vending machine that took our money and did not deliver the merchandise. If we reconsider the finger-snapping example, we might see some mild aggression. If a teacher ignores a child's finger snapping, the child might start snapping her fingers louder and louder and perhaps banging on the desk and hollering "Hey." This characteristic of extinction has also been studied extensively in laboratory situations, and here again it is necessary that the teacher be prepared to "weather the storm." If an extinction procedure produces mild aggression, then giving up in the middle will not only reinforce the undesirable behavior on an intermittent schedule, it will also reinforce additional undesirable mild aggression.[6]

An additional difficulty is that a behavior that has completely decreased during an extinction session may reappear at the next opportunity for the behavior to occur. This reappearance of an extinguished behavior following a recess is called *spontaneous recovery.* Typically, the amount of behavior that spontaneously recovers is less than the amount that occurred during the previous extinction session. After several additional extinction sessions, spontaneous recovery is usually not a problem.

To oversimplify this and the preceding chapter, we suggest that if you want behavior to happen more often, reinforce it; if you want behavior to happen less often, ignore it. But beware. There is much more to positive reinforcement and extinction than first meets the eye. For maximal effectiveness in the application of positive reinforcement and extinction, one should be aware of their pitfalls as well as the guidelines for the effective application of the two principles.

GUIDELINES FOR THE EFFECTIVE APPLICATION OF EXTINCTION

The following rules are offered as a check list for individuals who wish to utilize extinction to decrease a particular undesirable behavior. As with the guidelines for positive reinforcement in Chapter 2, these rules are presented on the assumption that the person following them is a parent, teacher, or some other person who is working with individuals with behavior problems.

1. *Selecting the behavior to be decreased*
   a) In choosing the behavior, be specific. Don't plan a major character improvement to take place at one time. For example, do not try to extinguish all of Johnny's trouble-making behavior in a classroom. Rather, choose a particular behavior, such as Johnny's finger snapping in the classroom.
   b) Remember that the behavior may get worse before it gets better and that aggressive behavior is sometimes produced during the extinction process. Therefore, make sure that the circumstances are such that you can follow through with your extinction procedure on the behavior chosen. For example, be very careful if the behavior is destructive to the individual or others. Will it be harmful for you to persist in your extinction program if the behavior gets worse? You should also consider the setting in which the behavior that you have selected is likely to occur. For example, it may be impractical to extinguish temper tantrums in

a restaurant, because of obvious social pressures that you may be unable to resist. If you are concerned with decreasing a particular behavior but you cannot apply extinction because of the above considerations, do not despair. We will describe other procedures for decreasing behavior in later chapters.

    c) If possible, select a behavior for which you can control the reinforcers that are currently maintaining it.

2. *Preliminary considerations*

    a) If possible, keep track of how often the undesirable behavior occurs prior to your extinction program. During this recording phase, do not attempt to withhold the reinforcer for the undesirable behavior.

    b) Try to identify what is currently reinforcing the undesirable behavior so that you can withhold the reinforcer during treatment. The reinforcement history of the undesirable behavior might provide some idea of just how long extinction will take.

    c) Identify some desirable alternative behavior that the individual can engage in.

    d) Identify effective reinforcers that can be used for desirable alternative behavior by the individual.

    e) Try to select a setting in which the extinction can be carried out successfully.

    f) Be sure that all the relevant individuals know, before the program starts, just which behavior is being extinguished and which behavior is being reinforced. Be sure that all who will be coming in contact with the individual have been prompted to ignore the undesirable behavior and reinforce the desirable alternative behavior.

3. *Implementing the plan*

    a) Tell the individual about the plan before starting.

    b) Regarding the positive reinforcement for the desirable alternative behavior, be sure that the rules in Chapter 2 for putting the plan into effect are followed.

    c) After initiating the program, be completely consistent in withholding reinforcement after all instances of the undesirable behavior and reinforcing the desirable alternative behavior.

4. *Weaning the student from the program* (discussed in more detail in Chapter 11)

    a) After the undesirable behavior has decreased to zero, there may be occasional relapses, so be prepared.

    b) Three possible reasons for the failure of your extinction procedure are:
        (1) the attention you are withholding following the undesirable behavior is not a reinforcer for the child;
        (2) the undesirable behavior is receiving intermittent reinforcement from another source;
        (3) the desired alternative behavior has not been strengthened appropriately.

If it is taking a long time for you to complete the extinction procedure, successfully, then examine these reasons carefully.

    c) Regarding the reinforcement of the desirable alternative behavior, try to follow the rules on p. 32 for weaning the child from the program.

Study Questions

(for examination purposes)

1. What are the two parts to the principle of extinction?
2. If you tell someone to stop eating candies and the person stops, is that an example of extinction? Explain why or why not on the basis of the definition of extinction.
3. When Peter ceased tantruming, Veronica waited for fifteen to twenty seconds before reinforcing Peter for sitting quietly. Why didn't Veronica reinforce Peter immediately after the tantrum had ceased?
4. Why did mother's attempt to extinguish the child's cookie eating (as shown in Figure 3-2) fail?
5. Describe a particular behavior you would like to decrease in a child with whom you have contact. Would your extinction program require a special setting? Why or why not?
6. Why is it necessary to consider the setting as a factor influencing your extinction program?
7. If a behavior is not reinforced at least once in a while, what will happen to it?
8. Briefly describe four pitfalls of extinction.
9. Briefly explain five general factors influencing the effectiveness of extinction.
10. If you were recording some observations of an undesirable behavior prior to introducing an extinction program, what would you be looking for?
11. What are the most common reasons for the failure of an extinction program?
12. Extinction should not be applied to certain behaviors or situations. What types of behaviors and situations would these be? Give an example.
13. Describe two examples of extinction that you have encountered, one involving a desirable behavior and one involving an undesirable behavior. For each example, identify the situation, behavior, immediate consequence, and probable long-term effects, as is done in Tables 3-1 and 3-2. (Your examples should not be from the text.)
14. The graphs in Figures 3-1 and 3-3 both show the results of a successful extinction program. Yet one graph shows a decrease and the other shows an increase. Why is this so?
15. How are different experimental conditions indicated on a graph? (See Figures 2-1 and 3-3.)
16. Examine Table 3-1. Which of those examples involve positive reinforcement for an alternative response? For those that do not, indicate how positive reinforcement for an alternative response might be introduced.

Study Exercises

(to be practiced by the reader)

1. Choose a situation in which you will be able to sit and watch an adult interact with one or more children for approximately half an hour. During this half-hour period, mark down the number of times the adult attends to desirable behavior of the children and the number of times the adult ignores specific desirable behaviors of the children. This will give you some idea of how often we extinguish desirable behaviors of those around us.
2. Choose a half-hour period during which you will be interacting with one or more children. During that period, each time you interact with any of the children following their desirable behavior, make note of it. During a second half-hour period, simply sit back and observe the same children (but try to be far enough from them so that you do not have to interact with them). During this second half-hour, count the number of desirable behaviors that these children engage in that you could have reinforced if you were so inclined. Compare your two counts over the two half-hour periods in order to get some idea of how many instances of desirable behavior you yourself are ignoring, and in that sense extinguishing.

Self-Modification Exercises

(to be practiced by the reader)

1. Think of something you did today that did not pay off. Give a specific, complete description of the situation and behavior, following the examples in Table 3-1.
2. Select one of your behavioral excesses that you listed at the end of Chapter 1. Outline a complete extinction program that you (with a little help from your friends) might apply so as to decrease that behavior. Make sure that your plan follows the above guidelines for the effective application of extinction. However, do *not* try your plan at this time.

EXTENDED DISCUSSION AND NOTES

1. Extinction is but one way in which a behavior can be weakened. The reader should be careful not to confuse it with punishment or with forgetting. In punishment, a behavior is weakened by the presentation of an aversive event following the behavior. In forgetting, a behavior is weakened as a function of time following the last occurrence of the behavior. Extinction differs from both of these in that in extinction, behavior is weakened as a result of being emitted without being reinforced. (See Skinner, 1953, p. 71.)

2. One of the greatest hazards faced by an extinction program is reinforcement from a well-intentioned person who does not understand the

(Continued)

54

(Continued)

program or its rationale. This obstacle was encountered in one of the earliest reports on the application of extinction to a child's temper tantrums. Williams (1959) reported the case of a twenty-one-month-old infant who screamed and cried if his parents left the bedroom after putting him to bed at night. A program was initiated in which the parent left the room after bedtime pleasantries and did not reenter it, no matter how much the infant screamed and raged. The first time the child was put to bed under this extinction procedure, he screamed for forty-five minutes. By the tenth night, however, he no longer cried, but rather smiled, as the parent left the room. But about a week later, when the parents were enjoying a much needed evening out, he screamed and fussed after his aunt, the baby sitter, had put him to bed. The aunt reinforced the behavior by returning to the bedroom and remaining there until he went to sleep. It was then necessary to extinguish the behavior a second time, which took almost as long as the first time.

Ayllon and Michael (1959) observed the bad effect of unwanted reinforcement in extinction, which they called "bootleg reinforcement." A patient in a mental hospital engaged in such annoying psychotic talk (of the type referred to as delusional) that other patients had on several occasions beaten her in an effort to keep her quiet. To decrease her psychotic talk, doctors instructed the nurses not to attend to it but to attend only to sensible talk. As a result, the proportion of her speech that was psychotic decreased from 0.91 to 0.25. But later it increased to a high level, probably because of bootleg reinforcement from a social worker. This reinforcement came to light when the patient remarked to one of the nurses, "Well you're not listening to me. I'll have to go and see Miss — — — (the social worker) again, 'cause she told me that if she listens to my past she could help me."

3. Kazdin and Polster (1973) demonstrated the extreme persistence of intermittently reinforced behavior in an applied setting. During daily breaks in a sheltered workshop, two retarded men who engaged in few social interactions received tokens for talking to peers. At first, every interaction was reinforced, and the daily average number of interactions generally increased. Then extinction was applied, and the behavior rapidly decreased. Next, reinforcement was reinstated. One man again received tokens for every interaction, but the other man was placed on an intermittent schedule, which was thinned gradually until, after three weeks, he received reinforcement at only one of the three daily breaks. Then, extinction was again carried out for both men. The man who had been on continuous reinforcement again showed a rapid decrease in social interactions. But the man who had been on an intermittent-reinforcement schedule maintained a high rate of interaction over a five-week period.

4. Not infrequently, one meets the objection that presenting reinforcement to someone for "doing what he ought to do anyway" is "downright bribery." In a verbal exchange with a teacher, Roger Ulrich (1970, p. 337) handled this criticism quite well. First, he suggested that the teacher look up "bribery" in the dictionary. Complying, the teacher said, "Okay, the dictionary says that bribe means 'any gift or emolument, used corruptly to influence public or official action, anything that seduces or allures, an allurement. Also any valuable consideration given or promised for corrupt behavior in the performance of official or public duties.' " Ulrich then remarked, "It's quite common for people to re-

(Continued)

(Continued)

fer to reinforcement as bribing, especially when we use it for children. According to the dictionary definition, however, it doesn't seem to fit. It wouldn't seem that our efforts to get Billy to write his numbers better is really an example of trying to get him to do something illegal or something which goes against what is generally looked upon as being acceptable by our culture. Besides, Billy isn't a public official. Actually, writing numbers seems to be a good thing to be able to do and when you do good things, you often get rewarded for them."

Related to the bribery criticism is the frequently voiced criticism that extrinsic reinforcement for a behavior that a person finds (or should find) intrinsically reinforcing will undermine his motivation to engage in that behavior when the extrinsic reinforcement is no longer provided. In discussing this criticism, Kazdin (1975, pp. 50–52) concluded that "reinforcing individuals for particular behaviors in a given situation rarely leads to a deterioration of those behaviors in other situations" (p. 52). Feingold and Mahoney (1975) provided additional evidence countering the criticism. Five normal second-grade children were given two play activities, one of which was a follow-the-dots book. The number of dots each child connected was recorded over several daily fifteen-minute sessions. The number of dots was large for each child, even though no extrinsic reinforcement was given for this behavior. Then, reinforcement in the form of points exchangeable for candies, toys, and small books was given for connecting the dots. As a result, all the children showed substantial increases in their dot-connecting behavior. Next, extrinsic reinforcement was discontinued, and, as we would expect from the principle of extinction, the behavior decreased. But it did not decrease below its high level that had occurred prior to the introduction of extrinsic reinforcement, as would evidently be expected by those who argue that extrinsic reinforcement undermines intrinsic reinforcement.

5. For example, Allen, Turner, and Everett (1970) reported that prior to extinction, the classroom tantrums of a four-and-a-half-year-old boy lasted an average of about five minutes each. The first tantrum that occurred after the teacher began ignoring this behavior was more severe than previous ones and lasted twenty-seven minutes. The next day, only one tantrum occurred; it lasted fifteen minutes. After that, there were no further tantrums.

6. Studies with monkeys and other animals (for instance, by Hutchinson, Azrin, and Hunt, 1968) have shown that aggression toward animate and even inanimate objects can be produced by extinguishing a food-reinforced lever press. This phenomenon has not been studied extensively with humans, in part because of the ethical problems involved in deliberately creating situations that would provoke people to engage in such aggression.

Study Questions on Notes

1. How are extinction and forgetting similar, and how are they different?
2. What is "bootleg reinforcement"? Give an example.

3. How did Kazdin and Polster demonstrate that behavior is more persistent after intermittent reinforcment than after continuous reinforcement?

4. What are two common criticisms or objections to using positive reinforcement? How might you respond to them?

5. What is meant by intrinsic reinforcment? Extrinsic reinforcement?

6. During extinction, behavior may get worse before it begins to decrease. Describe an example of this.

CHAPTER 4

Getting A New Behavior to Occur: an Application of **SHAPING**

"Valerie, walk by yourself to supper"

TEACHING VALERIE TO WALK

An additional problem with Valerie, the self-abusive girl described in Chapter 3, was that she would not walk by herself. She had been taught to walk four years previously, but this behavior had deteriorated to the point that as soon as a nurse let go of her hand she would drop to the floor.

A procedure to teach Valerie to walk by herself to the dining room was devised.

The following three steps summarize that procedure.
1. *Specifying the final desired behavior:* Walking unaided from the TV room to the dining room when told to do so was selected as the final desired behavior. Since this behavior never occurred, however, it was not possible to reinforce it. In order to get it to

occur so that it could be reinforced, it was necessary to reinforce some other behavior first.

2. *Identifying a response that could be used as a starting point in working towards the final desired behavior.* Valerie would sometimes stand up and move from one chair to another (if the two chairs were very close together, about a foot or two apart, and if she was reinforced with food for doing this). The staff decided that this was a good response to begin with, since it was related to the desired behavior of walking to the dining room, in the sense that Valerie moved herself from one location to another.

3. *Reinforcing the starting response; then requiring closer and closer approximations until eventually the desired response occurred.* First, the response of moving two feet, from one chair to another, was reinforced with food. This distance was gradually, increased until, finally, Valerie would walk the entire distance from the TV room to the dining room.

At mealtimes, Valerie's food was placed on a table beside the sofa, behind which (as described in Chapter 3) Valerie was seated on a chair. The sofa was moved far enough back from the wall so that Valerie could walk from her chair to the chair next to the table on which the meal was located. Valerie was then left in the TV room by herself. When the other children had finished their meal in the dining room, Valerie was again placed on the chair behind the sofa, whether or not she had finished her meal.

As can be seen in Figure 4-1, over a period of several days the table was moved farther and farther away from the sofa.

Valerie continued to walk slightly farther each time, until the table was placed under the archway leading out of the TV room. At this point,

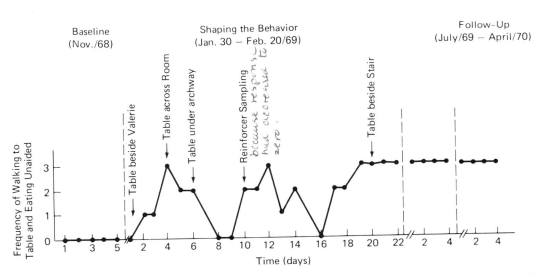

FIGURE 4-1. *Control of Valerie's walking behavior. Each dot on the graph represents the number of times Valerie walked unaided to a table to eat her meal on any given day.*

Valerie missed six meals in a row.* It appeared that the staff might have to revert to an earlier approximation of the final desired behavior. Specifically, it appeared they might have to place the table closer to the couch in order to regain the behavior of walking to the table. ~ regain previous b.h.

On the tenth day of the procedure, however, the staff gave Valerie a few spoonfuls of food before placing it on the table. (When a response has decreased to a zero level of occurrence, it is sometimes helpful to present a small amount of the reinforcer at the beginning of a session. This is termed *reinforcer sampling*.)[1] The same thing was done the next seven days, during which time Valerie usually obtained her meals. On the nineteenth day, reinforcer sampling was discontinued and Valerie obtained all three of her meals. On the twentieth day, the table was placed beside the stairs outside the archway leading to the dining room.

One day, after about two weeks in which Valerie had not missed a meal, she walked past the table with the meal on it, up the stairs, and into the dining room with the other children. This response was highly reinforced with praise and approval by the staff, and Valerie was given her meal in the dining room. Thereafter, Valerie was required to walk by herself to meals, which she continued to do and for which she received a great deal of approval from the staff. We are happy to report that more than five years later Valerie continues to improve and has had no relapses. She has received visits from her parents and has been much more of a joy for the staff and the other children.

SHAPING

Shaping is a procedure used to establish a behavior that is not presently performed by an individual. Since the behavior has a zero level of occurrence, it is not possible to increase its frequency simply by waiting until it occurs and then reinforcing it. Therefore, the teacher begins by reinforcing a response that occurs with a greater-than-zero frequency and at least remotely resembles the final desired response. (Valerie, for example, was first reinforced for walking two feet because this behavior occasionally occurred and because it remotely approximated the behavior of walking the full distance from the TV room to the dining room.) When this initial response is occurring at a high frequency, the teacher stops reinforcing it and begins reinforcing a slightly closer approximation of the final desired response. Thus, the final desired response is eventually established by reinforcing successive approximations of it. For this reason, shaping is sometimes referred to as "the method of successive approximations." Shaping can be defined as the development of a new behavior by the successive reinforcement of closer approximations and the extinguishing of preceding approximations of the behavior.

*However, a psychiatric nurse fed Valerie twice per day so that her good health would be ensured.

The new behaviors that an individual acquires during a lifetime develop from a variety of sources and influences. Sometimes, a new behavior develops when an individual emits some initial behavior and the environment (either the physical environment or other people) then reinforces slight variations in that behavior across a number of trials. Eventually, that initial behavior may be shaped so that the final form no longer resembles it. For example, most parents are not aware that they use the shaping procedure in teaching their children to talk. When an infant first begins to babble, some of the sounds he makes remotely approximate words in his parents' native language. When this happens the parents usually reinforce the behavior excitedly with hugs, caresses, kisses, and smiles. The sounds "mmm" and "daa" typically receive exceptionally large doses of reinforcement from English-speaking parents. Eventually "ma ma" and "da da" occur and are strongly reinforced, and the more primitive "mmm" and "daa" are subjected to extinction. At a later stage, reinforcement is given after the child says "mommy" and "daddy," and "ma-ma" and "da-da" are extinguished.

The same process occurs with other words. First, the child passes through a stage in which very remote approximations of words in her parents' native language are reinforced. She then enters a stage in which "baby talk" (i.e., closer approximations of actual words) is reinforced. Finally, the child is required by her parents and others to pronounce words in accordance with the practices of the verbal community before reinforcement is given. For example, if the child says "wa-wa" at an early stage, she is given a glass of water, which if she is thirsty, reinforces the response. At a later stage, "watah" rather than "wa-wa" is reinforced with water. Finally the child is required to say "water" before water reinforcement will be given.

Of course, this description greatly oversimplifies the way in which a child learns to talk. But it serves to illustrate the importance of shaping in the process by which normal children gradually progress from babbling to baby talk and finally to speaking in accordance with prevailing social conventions.

This discussion illustrates how shaping might be applied by parents, either accidentally or deliberately, to modify the topography (that is, the form) of a behavior—in this case, specific sounds and words that are spoken.[2] Aspects of behavior that we can count and measure might also be influenced by shaping. In Valerie's case, the amount of behavior was shaped: Valerie was reinforced over a number of days for taking more and more steps in walking to the table. The force or intensity of a behavior might also be modified in shaping. Consider a young farm boy whose job it is to pump water out of a well with an old hand pump. When the pump was first installed, it was freshly oiled, the boy applied a certain amount of force to the handle, it moved up and down very easily, and water was produced. Let's suppose, however, that with rain, moisture, and lack of regular oiling the pump has gradually acquired a little rust. Each day, the boy probably applies the approximate amount of force he applied the previous day. When that force is no longer reinforced by the production of water, because of the addition of the small amount of rust that has made the pump handle more difficult to move, the boy would likely apply a little more force and find that it pays off. Over several months, the boy is gradually shaped to press very hard on the first trial, a terminal behavior quite different from the initial behavior of moving the pump handle very easily.

FACTORS INFLUENCING THE EFFECTIVENESS OF SHAPING

1. Specifying the final desired behavior

The first step in shaping is to clearly identify the final desired behavior, which is often referred to as the terminal behavior. In Valerie's case, the final desired behavior was walking unaided from the TV room to the dining room at mealtimes when told to do so. With a definition as specific as this, there was very little possibility that different staff members would develop different expectations regarding Valerie's performance. If different people working with the individual expect different things, or if one person is not consistent from one training session or situation to the next, then progress is likely to be retarded somewhat. A precise statement of the final desired behavior increases the chances for consistent reinforcement of successive approximations of that behavior. The final desired behavior should be stated in such a way that all of the characteristics of the behavior (its frequency, topography, intensity, and so forth) are identified. In addition, the conditions under which the behavior is or is not to occur should be stated, and any other guidelines that appear to be necessary for consistency should be provided.

2. Choosing a starting behavior

Since the final desired behavior does not occur initially, and because it is necessary to reinforce some behavior that approximates it, you must identify a starting point. This should be a behavior that occurs often enough to be reinforced within the session time allowed, and it should approximate the final desired behavior. For example, Valerie's behavior of standing up and moving from one chair to another (if the two chairs were very close together) is something that she did occasionally. Since the terminal behavior was "extended walking" (at least from the TV room to the dining room), it was desirable to start with an approximation of walking—namely, standing up and taking a step or two.

In a shaping program, it is crucial to know not only where you are going (the terminal behavior) but also the level at which the individual is performing at the present time. The purpose of the shaping program is to get the two together, by reinforcing successive approximations from the starting point to the final desired behavior, even though the starting point might be completely dissimilar to the terminal behavior.[3]

3. Choosing the shaping steps

Before initiating the shaping program, it is helpful to outline the successive approximations through which the person will be moved in the attempt to approximate the final desired behavior. For example, suppose the final desired behavior is to teach a child to say "daddy." It has been determined that the child says "daa," and this response is set as the starting behavior. Let us suppose that we decide to go from the initial behavior of "daaa" through the following steps: "da-da," "dad," "dad-ee," and "daddy." To begin with, the child is reinforced on a number of occasions for emitting the initial behavior ("daa"). When this behavior is occurring repetitiously, the trainer moves on to step 2 ("da-da") and reinforces that approximation for several trials. This step-by-step procedure continues until the child finally says "daddy."

We are sure some critical questions have already occurred to you. What is a reasonable step size? How many trials at each step should one reinforce before proceeding to the next step? Unfortunately there is no set of guidelines for identifying the ideal step size. In attempting to specify the behavioral steps from the initial behavior to the terminal behavior, the teacher might imagine what steps she herself would go through. Also, it is sometimes helpful to observe students who can already emit the terminal behavior, and to ask them to emit the initial and subsequent approximations. Whatever guidelines or estimates are used, it is important to try to stick to them and yet be flexible if the trainee does not proceed quickly enough or is learning more quickly than had been expected. Some guidelines for moving through the behavioral program are offered in the following paragraphs.

4. Moving along at the correct pace

There are several rules of thumb to follow in reinforcing successive approximations of a final desired response:

a) Do not move too soon (that is, after too few trials) from one approximation to the next. Trying to go to a new step before the previous approximation has been well established can result in losing the previous approximation through extinction without achieving the new approximation.

b) Proceed in sufficiently small steps. Otherwise, the previous approximation will be lost through extinction before the present approximation has been achieved.

c) If you lose a behavior because you are moving too fast or taking too large a step, return to an earlier approximation where you can pick up the behavior again. (This almost happened in the case of teaching Valerie to walk. Recall that when the table with food on it was placed under the archway, Valerie missed six meals in a row. Perhaps the staff had progressed a little too fast and should have reverted to an earlier approximation. Instead, they gambled that the use of reinforcer sampling would bring about the next approximation. Fortunately, the gamble paid off — but it might not have, and the staff might have lost a good deal of the behavior they had established so painstakingly.)

d) Items (a) and (b) caution against going too fast, and item (c) states how to correct for the bad effects of going too fast. It is also important not to progress too slowly. If one approximation is reinforced for so long that it becomes extremely strong, new approximations are less likely to appear.

These guidelines may not seem very helpful. On the one hand, it is advisable not to move too fast from one approximation to another, and on the other hand, it is advisable not to move too slowly. If we could accompany these guidelines with a mathematical formula for calculating the exact size of the steps that should be taken in any situation and exactly how many reinforcements should be given at each step, the guidelines would be much more useful.[4] Unfortunately, the experiments necessary for providing this information have not yet been carried out. The teacher must observe the behavior carefully and be prepared to make changes in the procedure — changing the size of, slowing down, speeding up, or retracing steps — whenever the behavior does not seem to be developing properly. Shaping requires a good deal of practice and skill if it is to be performed with maximum effectiveness.

PITFALLS OF SHAPING: HOW IT WORKS TO THE DISADVANTAGE OF THOSE WHO ARE IGNORANT OF IT

As with other behavior principles and procedures, shaping can be misused by people who are not aware of it. An example of this can be seen in Figure 4-2: a harmful behavior that might never have occurred without shaping is gradually developed as a result of it. Another example of the misuse of shaping, one that is commonly observed in retarded children, leads to self-destructive behavior. Suppose, for example, that because of an unusual and unfortunate

FIGURE 4-2. *A misapplication of shaping.*

family situation, a small child receives very little social attention when he emits appropriate behavior. Perhaps one day the child accidentally falls and strikes his head lightly against a hard floor. Even if the child is not injured seriously, an overly solicitous parent may come running quickly and make a big fuss over the incident. Because of this reinforcement, and because anything else the child does seldom evokes attention, he is likely to repeat the response of striking his head lightly against the floor. The first few times this occurs, the parent may continue to reinforce the response. Eventually, however, seeing that the child is not really hurting himself, the parent may stop reinforcing it. Since the behavior has now been placed on extinction, the child may *increase the intensity* of the behavior in an attempt to regain the reinforcer. That is, the child may begin to hit his head more forcefully, and the slightly louder "thud" will cause the parent to come running again. If this shaping process continues, the child will eventually hit his head with sufficient force to cause physical injury. It is extremely difficult, if not impossible, to use extinction to eliminate such violently self-destructive behavior. It would have been best never to have let the behavior develop to the point where the child's parents were forced to continue reinforcing it and increasing its strength.

Sometimes, extinction can be carried out in a modified setting and the results can be transferred to other settings. For example, the self-abusive child in the previous example could be placed in a padded room, where he could bump his head harmlessly against the soft floor and walls. Ideally, the room would be equipped with a one-way window so that an adult could rush in and reinforce the child after he has stopped banging his head. The reinforcer would be presented after the child had been nonabusive for a certain period of time—for example, fifteen seconds. This period of time would gradually be increased. When head banging had decreased to zero in the padded room, the child would be allowed to move freely in other rooms and would frequently be reinforced for refraining from head banging.

The problem with this procedure is that it requires transferring the new behavior of non–head banging from a situation (the padded room) in which the old behavior of head banging was weak (i.e., was not reinforced) to a situation (another room) in which the old behavior had been strongly established. The old behavior is more likely to reappear in the other room, where it seems impossible not to reinforce it, and the new behavior may not get a chance to occur at all. As a result, it is very difficult to transfer the new behavior from the one setting to the other. Research has indicated that an effective way to eliminate such extremely self-destructive behavior is through a punishment procedure. We shall therefore return to this example in Chapter 12, in which we take up the topic of punishment.

Many undesirable behaviors commonly seen in retarded children—for example, violent temper tantrums, hyperactivity, serious injury inflicted by one child on another, and voluntary vomiting—are often products of shaping. All of these behaviors can be eliminated by a combination of extinction of the undesirable behavior and positive reinforcement for desirable behavior. Unfortunately, this is often difficult to do, because (1) the behavior is sometimes so harmful that it cannot be allowed to occur even once during the period in which extinction is to take place, and (2) adults who are ignorant of behavior principles often unknowingly foil the efforts of those who are conscientiously attempting to apply these principles.

As in medicine, the best cure is prevention. Ideally, all persons responsible for the care of other persons will eventually be so thoroughly versed in behavior principles that they will refrain from shaping undesirable behavior.

Another kind of pitfall is the unknowing failure of a person to apply shaping when it should be applied. Some parents, for example, are simply not very responsive to their child's babbling behavior. Perhaps they expect too much from the child right from the beginning, and are not inclined to reinforce extremely remote approximations of normal speech. (Some parents, for example, seem to expect their tiny new genius to say "Father!" right off the bat, and are not at all impressed when the child says "da-da.") Or perhaps their personal problems interfere with their devoting the necessary attention to the child. On the other hand, some parents give their children plenty of reinforcement for the wrong things. Perhaps they are so overly concerned about the child's well-being that they provide her with all kinds of reinforcement without ever having to say or do anything for it. For example, they may continue to reinforce remote approximations of speech without ever demanding closer approximations. In other words, although shaping is a process that most parents apply in a more or less desirable fashion, without realizing it, there are some parents for whom this is not true.

Thus, there are many variables that can prevent a physically normal child from receiving the shaping that is necessary to establish normal speech behavior. If a child has not learned to talk by a certain age, he or she may be labeled as retarded or autistic. No one knows how many so-called mentally deficient individuals are in institutions not because of any genetic or physical defects, but simply because they were never exposed to effective shaping procedures. This number could be quite large, for 80 percent of the individuals diagnosed as mentally retarded "have no verifiable or noticeable organic-genetic impairment" (Braginsky and Braginsky, 1971, p. 19).

Regardless of the causes of a child's failure to talk, much progress can usually be made by the use of a shaping procedure. We shall defer a detailed description of developing verbal behavior until other principles applicable to the development of normal verbal behavior have been discussed (see Chapters 7, 8, and 10).

GUIDELINES FOR THE EFFECTIVE
APPLICATION OF SHAPING

1. *Select the terminal behavior*
   a) Choose a specific behavior (such as working quietly at a desk for ten minutes) rather than a general category of behavior (for example, "good" classroom behavior). Shaping is appropriate for changing quality, accuracy, quantity, and timing, as well as for developing new behavior of a different topography (form).
   b) If possible, select a behavior that will come under the control of natural reinforcers after it has been shaped.

2. *Select an appropriate reinforcer*
   See Figure 2-2 and p. 32.

3. *The initial plan*

   a) List successive approximations of the terminal behavior, beginning with the initial behavior. To choose the initial behavior, find a behavior already in the student's repertoire that resembles the terminal behavior most closely and that occurs at least once during an observation period. If your terminal behavior is a complex sequence of activities (such as making a bed) that you have broken down into sequential steps, and if your program amounts to linking the steps together in a particular order, then your program is not best described as shaping, nor is it best developed through a shaping program. Rather, it should be developed by chaining (see Chapter 10).

   b) Your initial steps or successive approximations are usually "educated guesses." During your program, you can modify these according to the student's performance.

4. *Implementing the plan*

   a) Tell the student about the plan before starting.

   b) Begin reinforcing immediately following each occurrence of the starting behavior.

   c) Never move to a new approximation until the student has mastered the previous approximation.

   d) If you are not sure when to move the student to a new approximation, utilize the following rule of thumb: Move to the next step when the student performs the current step correctly in six out of 10 trials (usually with one or two trials less perfect than desired and one or two trials where the behavior is better than the current step).

   e) Don't reinforce too many times at any one step, and avoid under-reinforcement at any one step.

   f) If the child stops working, you have moved up the steps too quickly, the steps are not the right size, or the reinforcer is ineffective:

      (1) First, check the effectiveness of your reinforcer.

      (2) If the student becomes inattentive or shows signs of boredom, the steps may be too small.

      (3) Inattention or boredom may also mean you have progressed too rapidly. If so, return to the previous step for a few more trials and then try the present step again.

      (4) If the student continues to have difficulty, despite "retraining" at previous steps, add more steps at the point of difficulty.

Study Questions

(for examination purposes)

1. Identify the three basic steps in any shaping procedure, as presented at the start of this chapter, and describe them with an example (either the case of Valerie or an example of your own).

2. Explain how shaping involves successive applications of the principles of positive reinforcement and extinction. *successive*

3. What is another name for shaping? *approximation*

4. Outline, according to the three steps in a shaping procedure, how parents might shape their child to say a particular word.

5. What one word characterizes all of the variables plotted on the vertical axis of all the graphs in the book thus far?

6. What do we mean by the topography of a response? Give an example.

7. What do behavior modifiers mean when they talk about the "terminal behavior"?

8. Why bother with shaping? Why not just learn about the use of straightforward positive reinforcement to increase a behavior? *— too complex + overwhelming.*

9. Define shaping. *reinforcing successive approximations of a beh. that has not yet occured*

10. What factors influence the selection of the successive approximations or steps between the initial starting behavior and the terminal behavior? Discuss an example. *the complexity of the ben, the person involved, their intelligence,*

11. How do you know you have enough successive approximations? *Person is able to master each step*

12. How do you know if you are allowing enough reinforced trials to occur at each of the approximations? *The step is learned well — able to progress cont error.*

13. Describe an example of how shaping might be accidentally used to develop an undesirable behavior.

14. Describe an example of how the failure to apply shaping might have an undesirable result. *— not learning to talk like an adult*

15. What are two difficulties in trying to eliminate an undesirable behavior by extinguishing that behavior and applying positive reinforcement for a desirable alternative behavior? (See p. 66.) Give an example from your own experience. *— new beh might not ever occur — undesirable beh may be harmful.*

16. Give an example from your own experience of a terminal behavior that might best be developed through a procedure other than shaping. (See p. 68.) *— might be difficult + progress extinguish*

17. Why is it necessary to avoid reinforcing too many times at any step?

18. Why is it necessary to avoid underreinforcement at any step?

19. How is the procedure of shaping similar to the principle of positive reinforcement? How is it different? *Entails both the reinf + extinction*

20. Why do we refer to positive reinforcement and extinction as principles, and to shaping as a procedure? *— it procedes to use extinction + reinf.*

Study Exercise

(to be practiced by the reader)

Think of a normal child between the ages of two and seven with whom you have had contact (for example, a sister, brother, or neighbor). Specify a realistic behavior that you might try to develop by utilizing a shaping procedure. Outline the starting point you would choose and the successive approximations you would go through.

Self-Modification Exercises

(to be practiced by the reader)

1. Take a close look at many of your own behaviors—for example, sporting skills, personal-interaction skills, love-making skills, and study-skills. Identify at least five specific behaviors of yours that were probably shaped by others, either knowingly or unknowingly. Identify at least five specific behaviors that were probably shaped by the natural environment. Put each of your examples in sentence form, approximately as follows: "I was probably shaped to hit a ping-pong ball with a good chop stroke. That is, after learning basic ping-pong skills, each time I tried a bit of a chop, the ball would fly off the table. Eventually, a slight chop was reinforced by the ball landing on the table and the other person hitting the ball into the net. As the other person learned to return my chops, I was reinforced for putting slightly increasing amounts of chop on the ball. In all cases, the reinforcement was returning the ball to the other side of the table and even greater reinforcement was returning it to the other side of the table such that the other person missed."

2. Select one of your behavioral deficiencies that you listed at the end of Chapter 1. Outline a complete shaping program that you (with a little help from your friends) might use to overcome that deficiency. Make sure that your plan follows the above guidelines for the effective application of shaping. However, do *not* try your plan at this time.

EXTENDED DISCUSSION AND NOTES

1. Recall from Chapter 2 the principle of positive reinforcement: if in a given situation a response is followed immediately by a certain consequence, then that response is more probable when the individual next encounters a similar situation. This implies that the response should be maximally probable in a future situation that is most identical to the one in which reinforcement occurred, and that that situation typically includes sensory cues of the reinforcer. It was this reasoning that led Ayllon and Azrin (1968a) to suggest a procedure of briefly presenting a reinforcer before a response in order to increase the probability of the response occurring, and then presenting the remainder of the reinforcer following the response. Ayllon and Azrin coined the term *reinforcer sampling* to refer to this technique. In their experiment, mental hospital patients earned tokens that could be cashed in for a variety of reinforcers. Reinforcer sampling was used to increase the probability that the individuals would cash in the tokens for particular reinforcing activities.

2. Shaping also appears to be useful in modifying aspects of certain internal behaviors, such as particular types of brain waves and the rate at which the heart beats. Using reinforcement to modify such behaviors, a process called *biofeedback*, has generated a great deal of interest, in part because of its potential medical significance. For example, biofeedback has raised the possibility of effectively applying behavioral

70   (Continued)

methods in the treatment of diseases such as high blood pressure. One problem that has been detected by research on the use of biofeedback in the modification of heart rate, however, is that the changes obtained are typically in the range of only one to six beats per minute, which is of very little or no therapeutic value.

A study by Scott, Peters, Gillespie, Blanchard, Edmunson, and Young (1973) indicated that shaping may be important in overcoming this problem. Three individuals participated in the study—two normal male college students and a psychiatric patient suffering from chronic anxiety and manifesting a moderately elevated heart rate. During daily twenty-minute experimental sessions (each of which was preceded by a twenty-minute "adaptation" period), each man sat in a chair and watched television while his heart rate was recorded. After determining each man's baseline heart rate when he was watching television over a number of sessions, the experimenters wired the equipment in such a fashion that the sound portion of the television program would be on continuously but the video portion would be on only when the individual's heart rate was five beats per minute *above* the baseline rate (for each of the college students) or five beats per minute *below* the baseline rate (for the psychiatric patient). (One of the college students was also reinforced with one cent for every ten seconds that his heart rate was at the specified level, since he had complained about the standard television fare with which he was being presented.) This was shaping step 1. When the individual's heart rate remained at the designated high or low level for three consecutive sessions, the difference between the baseline level and the level required for reinforcement was increased by five beats per minute. This was shaping step 2. Shaping step 3 consisted of again increasing the requirement by five beats per minute, after the successful completion of shaping step 2. The outcome of the shaping procedure was that the heart rate of one of the college students was accelerated to an average of seventeen beats per minute above baseline, that of the other college student was accelerated to an average of sixteen beats per minute above baseline, and the heart rate of the psychiatric patient was decelerated to an average of sixteen beats per minute below his baseline rate. In the next phase of the study, the experimenters permitted each man to view the video portion without having to behave in any specific manner. The heart rates of the two college students quickly returned to baseline levels. That of the psychiatric patient, however, remained at the low level to which it had been shaped. To demonstrate that the shaping procedure was responsible for this man's decrease in heart rate, the experimenters then used the procedure to shape his heart rate back to its original level. Interestingly, the experimenters noted that during the period that this patient's heart rate was decelerated, reports from his ward indicated that "he seemed less 'tense' and 'anxious' " and that "he made fewer requests for medication . . ."

3. For example, in a classic study, Isaacs, Thomas, and Goldiamond (1960) used shaping to redevelop verbal behavior in a catatonic schizophrenic who had been mute for nineteen years prior to training. Using chewing gum as a reinforcer, the experimenter shaped the patient through the behaviors of eye movement towards the gum, facial movement, mouth movements, lip movements, vocalizations, word utterance, and, finally, verbal behavior.

4. In some situations, one's choice of step size might be influenced by

(Continued)

the type of recording apparatus available. Jackson and Wallace (1974) shaped voice loudness in a fifteen-year-old girl (Alice) who was diagnosed as "severely disturbed, withdrawn, and mildly retarded." A major problem was that Alice rarely spoke; when she did, her speech was barely audible (a disorder called aphonia). Jackson and Wallace conducted training sessions that incorporated a voice-operated relay wired to a token dispenser. Alice was shown the tokens and instructed that she could cash them in for books, beauty aids, and a photo album, among other things. However, in order to earn tokens, she had to speak into the voice-operated relay loudly enough to trigger the dispenser. Initially, the relay was set for maximum sensitivity so that very soft speech by Alice would produce tokens. When 80 percent of Alice's responses were loud enough to produce tokens, the dial on the voice-operated relay was changed by one unit, such that slightly louder speech was required. When Alice again performed at the 80-percent level, the sensitivity of the relay was altered by another unit. In this way, Alice's voice loudness was successfully shaped through eleven steps.

Study Questions on Notes

1. What is reinforcer sampling?
2. Describe an example of reinforcer sampling (which was not identified as such) that you read about on p. 18.
3. What is biofeedback? Why is it important to study it?
4. Describe how Scott et al. used shaping to markedly decrease the heart rate of a man suffering from chronic anxiety and manifesting a moderately elevated heart rate.
5. After using shaping to markedly alter the heart rate of three individuals, how did Scott et al. demonstrate that their procedure was responsible for this alteration?
6. What did Isaacs, Thomas, and Goldiamond do?
7. Your choice of step size in a shaping program might be influenced by your apparatus. Briefly describe an example of this.

Developing
Behavioral Persistence
Through the Use of
INTERMITTENT
REINFORCEMENT

"Benny, you must learn to be patient"

SOME PATIENCE FOR BENNY

Benny, an eleven-year-old severely retarded boy, could not wait for various enjoyable ward activities to begin.* Just before meals, juice-and-cookie periods, and visiting times, for example, he would run to the nurses and beg them to start the activities. After a while, the nurses found this rather disrupting. Consequently they decided to teach Benny to sit quietly outside their office door until they came out to initiate the scheduled activity.

Besides being impatient to start activities, Benny loved candy. In developing patient behavior in Benny, the nurses therefore decided to use candy and the activities themselves as reinforcers. The procedure was as

*We gratefully acknowledge Dr. Lynn Caldwell, Department of Rehabilitation Medicine, University of Washington, for providing us with the details of Benny's case.

follows. First, the staff bought a big bag of candy and made sure that Benny had no access to any other candy on the ward. Second, they purchased a kitchen timer—the kind that goes "Ding!" at the end of a set time period from zero to ten minutes. Third, they put a chair just outside the office door half an hour before each activity was to begin. Fourth, they gave Benny the following instructions: "Benny, from now on we are going to play a game with you. Whenever you come to the office to tell us to start some activity we will set the timer, and when it goes 'Ding!' we will look to see where you are. If you are sitting on the chair, then we will give you a candy and let you be first [i.e., the first to participate in the activity]. But if you are not sitting on the chair when the timer goes 'Ding!' then you will not get a candy and you will miss the activity." Benny was given the above instructions one morning after the nurses' coffee break. (How well he understood these instructions is not clear. Nevertheless, he was able to follow some simple instructions, and this was helpful in establishing the desired behavior—although, like the procedures described in the previous chapters, the present procedure might have worked even had he not understood any instructions at all.) Shortly before lunchtime the same day, Benny came running to the office on his regular mission of pestering. Armed with the timer, one of the nurses met him and said, "Benny, sit on the chair." The timer, which was set for a very short period, went "Ding!" almost as soon as Benny was seated. Immediately, all the nurses rushed out of the office and praised him, and one nurse gave him a candy. Moreover, they told him that he would be the first to line up for lunch. This procedure was followed during five additional half-hour periods that day. On each occasion the timer was set at a different value, which varied from twenty seconds to two minutes. Benny never knew when the "Ding!" would occur; it might be after a long, short, or intermediate interval.

The next few days during which there were twelve trials, Benny was out of the chair on three occasions when the "Ding!" occurred. On each of those occasions, he did not receive candy and was not allowed to participate in the activity. On the other occasions, he was seated in the chair and thus received the scheduled reinforcements. Over a period of one week, the range of time intervals used was extended so that the Ding!" occurred from twenty seconds to ten minutes after the chair was placed in front of the office. Benny never knew when the payoff would come, and he developed great persistence in sitting and waiting patiently.

INTERMITTENT REINFORCEMENT

The term *intermittent reinforcement* refers to the maintenance of a behavior by reinforcing it only occasionally (i.e., intermittently) rather than every time it occurs. Benny's sitting behavior, for example, was not reinforced continuously while he was on the chair. Instead, it was reinforced once in a while at unpredictable times. As a result, Benny learned to sit patiently and wait for reinforcement.

To talk about intermittent reinforcement, we must first define *schedule of reinforcement*. A schedule of reinforcement is a rule specifying which occurrences of a given behavior, if any, will be reinforced. One of the two simplest schedules of reinforcement is *continuous reinforcement*. Had Benny received reinforcement each time he sat down on the chair, or had he received reinforcement throughout the entire period he was on the chair, we would say that he was on a continuous-reinforcement schedule.[1] This schedule was incorporated in several of the cases discussed in prior chapters. For example, Charles (Chapter 2) was on a continuous reinforcement schedule for taking his pills, because he received a puff on a cigarette each time he swallowed a pill.

The second of the two simplest schedules of reinforcement is the opposite of continuous reinforcement. It is called *extinction*. As we have seen in Chapter 3, on an extinction schedule no instance of a given behavior is reinforced. The effect is that the behavior eventually decreases to a very low level, or disappears altogether.

Between these two extremes — continuous reinforcement and extinction — lies intermittent reinforcement: one may reinforce certain instances of the given behavior while allowing other instances to go unreinforced. Any rule specifying a procedure for doing this is called an *intermittent*-reinforcement schedule. There are an unlimited number of such schedules. Since each produces its own characteristic behavior pattern, the different schedules are suitable for different types of applications.[2] In this chapter, we will limit our discussion to schedules that (1) appear to be the most useful for increasing and maintaining behavior in various training programs or (2) are useful for interpreting the influence of schedules of reinforcement in daily life. We will illustrate these schedules with examples from everyday life (see, for instance, Figure 5-1), where most behavior is reinforced intermittently (although seldom as a result of well-planned design). In addition, we will examine various uses of the schedules in training programs. Specific reference will be made throughout to Benny's case. In the remainder of Chapter 5, we will discuss eight schedules: fixed-ratio, variable-ratio, fixed-interval, fixed-interval-with-limited hold, variable-interval, variable interval-with-limited-hold, fixed-duration, and variable-duration.[3]

1. The Fixed-Ratio Schedule

On a fixed-ratio (FR) schedule, reinforcement occurs each time a set number of responses of a particular type are emitted. If ten responses are required per reinforcement, we call the schedule an FR 10 schedule; if twenty are required, we call it an FR 20 schedule; and so on. One common example of an FR schedule is paying an in-

FIGURE 5-1. *Examples of people responding on intermittent-reinforcement schedules.*

dustrial worker a certain amount of money for a specified number of completed parts. The student who must do a specified number of problems or read a specified number of pages to complete a homework assignment is also performing under this type of schedule.

Provided that the amount of behavior required for reinforcement has been increased fairly gradually, the characteristic effect of an FR schedule is a high rate of responding followed by a pause (a period of no responding) after each reinforcement and before the person starts working toward the next reinforcement.

The length of this pause depends on the amount of behavior required per reinforcement. If too much responding is required, or if the amount of responding required is increased too rapidly, the pause will be so long that little or no responding will occur. (This breakdown in responding is called *ratio strain*.) There are several reasons for using FR schedules rather than continuous reinforcement in applied training programs:

1. FR generates higher rates of responding than continuous reinforcement (at least partly because less time is spent administering reinforcement).
2. The reinforcer remains effective longer on FR than on continuous reinforcement (because satiation takes place more gradually).
3. Behavior takes longer to extinguish after it has been reinforced on FR than after it has been continuously reinforced.
4. Training on FR helps prepare the behavior for being maintained by the intermittent-reinforcement schedules that often exist outside the training situation for that same behavior, or a similar one; in other words, training on FR teaches "persistence."

We have made use of FR schedules in a task designed to teach picture names to retarded children. In this task, each time the child attended to the teacher (for example, by looking at him), the teacher presented a picture to the child. According to a carefully designed sequence, the teacher sometimes spoke the name of the picture for the child to imitate and sometimes required that the child correctly name the picture. Each correct response was reinforced by the teacher saying "Good!" Correct responses were also reinforced with small, sugar-coated chocolate candies (M&Ms or Smarties), but we have since found that it is better not to reinforce every correct response with a candy (Stephens, Pear, Wray, and Jackson, 1975). Children attend at higher rates, make more correct responses, and learn to name more pictures when correct vocal-imitation and picture-naming responses are reinforced on an FR schedule than when they are continuously reinforced. This is true, however, only if the FR schedule does not require too many correct responses per reinforcement. As the response requirement increases, performance improves at first but then begins to show ratio strain. The optimal response requirement differs for different children. In general, it must be found by trial and error.

Although FR is the appropriate schedule for some behaviors, it is not appropriate for others. Suppose that Benny had received reinforcement on an FR 10 schedule. That is, suppose that he received reinforcement after each tenth time he sat down on the chair. This would have produced a high rate of sitting down, standing up, sitting down, and so on, until he obtained reinforcement. Obviously, this was not the behavior pattern the staff wanted in this particular case. Thus, they did not choose this schedule for Benny.

2. The Variable-Ratio Schedule

A variable-ratio (VR) schedule is like an FR schedule except that the number of responses required to produce reinforcement changes unpredictably from one reinforcement to the next. The number of responses required varies around some mean value. For example, if the mean value is twenty-five, then fifteen responses may be required to produce the first reinforcement, fifty to produce the second, thirty to produce the third, five to produce the fourth, and so on. If an average of fifteen responses are required for reinforcement, we call the schedule a VR 15 schedule; if an average of twenty-five are required, we call it a VR 25 schedule, and so on.

The natural environment contains many common examples of VR schedules. The one cited most often is the "one-armed bandit." Slot machines and other gambling devices are programmed according to VR schedules such that gamblers have no way of predicting how many responses they must make (that is, how many coins they must put in the slot) in order to be reinforced (by hitting the jackpot), although the management can predict that they will lose money over the long run. Nevertheless, such devices maintain rapid and persistent responding by those who are unfortunate enough to have been "hooked" on the schedules of reinforcement they provide. This shows that in our society, at least, certain reinforcement schedules are not always used to the advantage of the person being reinforced.

Frequently, however, it is advantageous to be hooked on a VR schedule. Even after repeated failures to "get a bite," the persistent fisherman continues casting into a school of fish because his casts occasionally result in a catch. The persistent reader reads a large amount of material just to get to the parts she finds entertaining, interesting, or useful. A final example from the natural environment should reflect the common occurrence of VR schedules in everyday life. A door-to-door salesman who averages one sale every ten houses is working on a VR 10 schedule. He can never predict exactly when he will make a sale, although he probably knows that his success rate is one out of ten. Sometimes he makes two or more sales in a row. At other times, he may have to call at twenty or more homes before he makes a sale. Such individuals, as we all know, tend to be very persistent.

Provided that the average amount of behavior required per reinforcement has been increased fairly gradually, the characteristic effect of VR is a high rate of responding.[4] In this respect, it is like FR. Moreover, if the amount of responding required per reinforcement is too large, or if it is increased too rapidly, there will be little or no responding. VR has the same advantages over continuous reinforcement in applied training programs that FR does (see p. 77). In addition, VR has at least two advantages over FR:

1. On VR, unlike FR, there is typically little or no pausing after reinforcement.
2. The amount of behavior required per reinforcement can be increased to a greater extent on VR than on FR, without deterioration of the behavior.

Nevertheless, FR is often used when these advantages are not too important, because it is simpler to administer.

VR was not used with Benny for the same reason that FR was not used: it would have generated a high rate of sitting down, standing up, sitting down, etc., which was not the behavior pattern desired in that particular case.

3. The Fixed-Interval Schedule

On a fixed-interval (FI) schedule, the first instance of a particular behavior after a fixed period of time (measured from some event such as the previous reinforcement or the beginning of a trial) is reinforced. All that is required for reinforcement to occur is that the individual engage in the behavior after the reinforcement has become available due to the passage of time. If one minute must elapse before the behavior can be reinforced, we call the schedule an FI 1-minute schedule, and so on.

To avoid confusion, note these two features of FI: first, by itself the passage of time is not sufficient for reinforcement to occur. The reinforcer is contingent upon the first instance of the behavior that occurs anytime after the passage of a specified interval. Second, a response occurring before the specified interval is up has absolutely no effect on when the reinforcer will occur.

A job that pays by the hour is sometimes cited as an example of an FI schedule, but this is not correct because hourly pay assumes that the individual works during the hour. An FI schedule, however, requires only one response at the end of an interval. If a person is paid weekly, his going to pick up his paycheck can be considered to approximate an FI schedule. It does not make any difference how many times he goes to pick it up before it is ready: if it's not ready, it's not ready, and he will not get it any sooner if he spends all his free time at the pay window. However, at the appointed time when the check is ready or at any time thereafter, if he goes to the pay window, he will receive his monetary reinforcer. Strictly speaking, this example only approximates an FI schedule, because a worker has access to clocks and calendars that tell him exactly when his paycheck will be available.

Provided that the length of the interval has been increased fairly gradually, the characteristic effect of an FI schedule is relatively steady responding just prior to reinforcement, followed by a pause immediately after reinforcement. The length of this pause depends on the length of the FI: the longer the interval, the longer the pause.[5] It also depends on the individual's "sense of timing," especially if this sense is facilitated by clocks or calendars. For example, the worker who is paid by the week is not likely to report for her paycheck a day or even an hour early, because she knows the exact date and time it is due.

Simple FI schedules are not often applied in training programs, mainly because they generate long pauses after each reinforcement and before the person begins working toward the next reinforcement. It was for this reason that Benny's chair-sitting behavior was not reinforced on an FI schedule. On this type of schedule, Benny could have bothered nurses for long periods of time and then sat down and received reinforcement.

4. The Fixed-Interval-With-Limited-Hold Schedule

A fixed-interval-with-limited-hold (FI/LH) schedule is an FI schedule with a slight modification, but one that has a powerful effect on behavior. With FI/LH, as with a simple FI schedule, the behavior is reinforced only if it occurs after a fixed period of time. However, to be reinforced, the behavior must also occur no later than a certain period of time. That is, once a reinforcement is "set up," its availability is not "held" for an indefinite period of time, as it is with a simple FI schedule; rather, it is held for only a limited period (hence, the term "limited hold"). Suppose that a given behavior is reinforced on what is called an FI 5-minute/LH 2-second schedule. This means that for reinforcement to be given, the behavior must occur within two seconds following a time interval of five minutes.

In the natural environment a good approximation of an FI/LH schedule is waiting for a bus. Buses usually run on a regular schedule—for instance, one ever twenty minutes. An individual may arrive at the bus stop early, just before the bus is due, or just after it arrives—it makes no difference, for she will still catch her bus. So far, this is just like a simple FI schedule. However, the bus will wait only a limited time—perhaps two minutes. If the individual is not at the bus stop within this limited period of time, she misses her bus and must wait for the next one.

Provided that the length of the FI portion of the schedule has been increased gradually, the characteristic effect of FI/LH is (1) steady responding and (2) much shorter pauses after each reinforcement and before the person begins working toward the next reinforcement, than with simple FI. If the interval is too large, or is increased too rapidly, the behavior will decrease drastically or will not occur at all, especially if the limited-hold period is very short.

An FI/LH schedule could have been used with Benny, but the nurses decided against it, primarily because another schedule—one that is to be discussed below—offered further advantages. Suppose that the nurses had used an FI 5-minute/LH 2-second schedule with Benny. The boy would have been on the chair a good portion of the five minutes, and the nurses would not have had to monitor his behavior continuously. However, he might still have bothered them for the first several minutes or so of the interval. Furthermore, this schedule would not have taught Benny to sit on the chair for much longer than a five-minute period on each occasion.

Because the material concerning schedules of reinforcement is quite complex, and because in this book we have tried to be consistent in applying the available information concerning schedules of reinforcement, we have decided to divide Chapter 5 into two sections. (As described on pp. 77 and 79 excessively large FR's and VR's produce ratio strain. Section Two of the chapter begins on p. 84.)

Study Questions

(for examination purposes)

1. Describe briefly, point by point, how Benny was taught to sit and wait patiently.
2. Define and give an example of each of the following:
   a) intermittent reinforcement
   b) schedule of reinforcement
   c) continuous reinforcement
   d) extinction
3. What are the two simplest schedules of reinforcement?
4. Name the schedules of reinforcement mentioned in Chapter 5, section one.

5. Explain what an FR schedule is. Give two examples of FR schedules in everyday life (at least one of which is not in the text).

6. What is the characteristic effect of an FR schedule?

7. Describe what happens if an FR schedule is too large, or if its size is increased too rapidly.

8. What is ratio strain?

9. Explain why FR was not used in teaching Benny to sit and wait patiently.

10. Explain what a VR schedule is. Give two examples of VR schedules (at least one of which is not in the text).

11. Describe how a VR schedule is similar to an FR schedule. Describe how it is different.

12. What is the characteristic effect of a VR schedule?

13. Describe what happens if a VR schedule is too large, or its size is increased too rapidly.

14. Which schedule is most advantageous in training programs—FR, VR, continuous reinforcement? Justify your selection.

15. State two advantages of VR over FR in training programs.

16. State two possible applications of VR in training programs.

17. Explain why VR was not used in teaching Benny to sit and wait patiently.

18. What is an FI schedule? What is its characteristic effect?

19. Explain why simple FI schedules are not often applied in training programs.

20. Explain what an FI/LH schedule is, and give two examples from everyday life (at least one of which is not in the text). (Hint: Think of behaviors that occur at certain fixed times, such as arriving for meals, plane departures, and cooking.)

21. Describe how an FI/LH schedule is similar to a simple FI schedule. Describe how it differs.

22. What is the characteristic effect of an FI/LH schedule?

23. Describe what happens if the FI portion of an FI/LH schedule is too large, or is increased too rapidly.

24. Explain why FI/LH was not used in teaching Benny to sit and wait patiently.

EXTENDED DISCUSSION AND NOTES

1. In current usage, continuous reinforcement means reinforcement of each discrete occurrence of a response. But current usage derives mainly from basic research in operant behavior (as represented in, for example, the *Journal of the Experimental Analysis of Behavior*). This research has concentrated mainly on measuring behavior in terms of the rate of discrete responses (for example, the rate of lever pressing), and has tended to neglect the duration of behavior (for instance, the amount of time a lever is held down). Although neglected in basic re-
(Continued)

(Continued)

search, duration is a more meaningful property than rate for some socially significant behaviors dealt with in applied research (as represented in, for example, the *Journal of Applied Behavior Analysis*). It seems appropriate to regard continuous reinforcement of such behaviors to mean, literally, continuous presentation of the reinforcer throughout the period in which the behavior occurs.

2. The effects of different reinforcement schedules have been studied extensively with animals—especially pigeons, rats, and monkeys—but, unfortunately, not very much with humans. The classic authoritative work on this topic was written by Ferster and Skinner (1957); it deals mainly with pigeon experiments. The research on schedules of reinforcement with humans that has been done, however, suggests that human behavior patterns generated by various reinforcement schedules are quite similar to those of other animals (see, for example, Long, Hammock, May, and Campbell, 1958; Ellis, Barnett, and Pryer, 1960; Orlando and Bijou, 1960).

3. For a very clear and comprehensive discussion of reinforcement schedules, see Reynolds (1975).

4. Kale, Kaye, Whelan, and Hopkins (1968) trained three withdrawn, chronic schizophrenic patients to emit spontaneous greetings (e.g., "Hello, Mr. – – –!") by using cigarettes as reinforcers. The reinforcement schedule was gradually thinned from continuous reinforcement to a high VR schedule. Nevertheless, the response of greeting continued to occur at a high rate. Moreover, it continued to occur at a high rate even when cigarette reinforcement was discontinued completely (although it was perhaps being maintained by the social interaction it produced).

5. A recent analysis suggests this may be true even with intervals of several months duration. Weisberg and Waldrop (1972) examined the rate at which the U.S. Congress passed bills during legislative sessions from 1947 to 1968. This rate exhibited a fixed-interval pattern. It was extremely low during each three to four month interval after commencement, followed by an increase in the rate of bills passed until the time of adjournment.

Study Questions on Notes

1. What would be the difference between a continuous-reinforcement schedule for a child's jumping and a continuous-reinforcement schedule for a child's sitting?
2. Who wrote the classic authoritative work on schedules of reinforcement, and what is the title of their book?
3. What potential natural reinforcement may have been involved in the Kale et al. experiment?
4. The pattern of responding shown by U.S. congressmen is typical of what schedule? Describe three of your behaviors under similar long-term control.

CHAPTER 5 SECTION TWO

More About Increasing and Maintaining Behavior Through the Use of
INTERMITTENT REINFORCEMENT

1. The Variable-Interval Schedule

A variable-interval (VI) schedule is like an FI schedule except that the time that must elapse before reinforcement becomes available changes unpredictably from one reinforcement to the next, instead of being constant. The interval varies around some mean value. For example, if the mean value is five minutes, then two minutes may be required to elapse before a response will produce the first reinforcement, fifteen minutes may be required to elapse before a response will produce the second reinforcement, five minutes after that before a response will produce the third reinforcement, and so on. The average amount of time required before a response will produce reinforcement is designated in the abbreviation of the schedule. For example, if this average interval is five minutes, we call the schedule a VI 5-minute schedule.

In the natural environment an approximation of a VI schedule is telephoning a friend whose line is busy. To make the example fit better, let us assume that the friend will not go out and that he will not receive any other calls. Note that this satisfies the definition of VI in three ways: (1) as long as the line is busy, we will not get through to him any faster no matter how many times we dial; (2) however, reinforcement (getting through) may be obtained any time after he hangs up and the line is no longer busy; (3) we cannot predict how long this will be (sometimes he has lengthy phone conversations, sometimes short ones), and, thus, we must keep dialing until we get through.

Provided that the average amount of time prior to the availability of reinforcement has been increased fairly gradually, the characteristic effect of VI is fairly uniform responding. This may seem to give it an advantage over FI, which, as we already noted, produces a pause—the length of which depends on the length of interval—following reinforcement. However, with VI, pausing is still present but is spread more uniformly throughout the interval. Hence, this advantage of VI may be more apparent than real. Partly for this reason, simple VI, like simple FI, is not often used in training programs. Had Benny's chair-sitting behavior been reinforced on VI, he probably would have been on the chair for only very short periods of time—perhaps just long enough to see whether reinforcement had been "set up" yet—and would likely have spent the rest of the time bothering the nurses.

2. The Variable-Interval-With-Limited-Hold Schedule

A variable-interval-with-limited-hold (VI/LH) schedule is a simple VI schedule with the same kind of modification that transforms a simple FI schedule into an FI/LH schedule. With VI/LH, as with a simple VI schedule, the behavior is reinforced only if it occurs after a certain interval, which varies unpredictably from one reinforcement to the next. However, in order to be reinforced, the behavior must also occur no later than a certain period of time following the availability of reinforcement. That is, once a reinforcement is set up, its availability is held for only a limited period of time. If it is not obtained within that limited period, it is "lost" and reinforcement cannot be obtained until the end of the next interval. For example, suppose that a given behavior is reinforced on what is called VI 5-minutes/LH 2-seconds. This means that the behavior is reinforced only when it occurs within two seconds after the end of intervals varying in duration around a mean of five minutes.

There are many more examples from the natural environment of VI/LH schedules than there are of simple VI schedules. Telephoning a friend whose line is busy, given above as an example of a VI schedule, more accurately approximates a VI/LH schedule. The friend may leave shortly after he finishes his phone call, or he may receive another call. In each case, if we do not call during one of the limited periods in which the line is free and the friend is at home, we miss the reinforcement of talking to our friend and must wait another unpredictable period before we again have the opportunity to gain this reinforcement.

Watching television programs, movies, and sporting events are other examples of behavior reinforced on a VI/LH schedule. Occasionally, at rather unpredictable intervals, something reinforcing happens and maintains our watching behavior. The limited-hold aspect is present in that the viewer will miss a reinforcer if he is not attending when it occurs (although instant replays may alter this situation somewhat). Just as a compulsive gambler is "hooked" on VR, so the television addict is tightly controlled by VI/LH, in which reinforcement is not only unpredictable but also (for many programs) rather infrequent. As with other schedules (especially VR), VI/LH schedules may work to the disadvantage of people exposed to them (as when a student "wastes" too much time watching television when she could be more productive by studying). The persistence developed by VI/LH can also be desirable, however. The patience of a fisherman hanging a line in the water is rewarded on VI/LH, because schools of fish swim near his bait at varying intervals.

Provided that the average length of the VI portion of the schedule has been increasing gradually, the characteristic effect of VI/LH is steady responding with very little pausing. In this respect, it has an advantage over FI/LH, which typically produces pauses before the person begins working toward the next reinforcement. Moreover, VI/LH is usually no less convenient to apply than FI/LH, and thus is used quite often in preference to that schedule. However, with VI/LH, as with FI/LH, if the average length of the interval is too large or is increased too rapidly, the behavior will decrease drastically or will not occur at all—especially if the limited-hold period is very short.

VI/LH, like FI/LH, can be used effectively in any situation in which it is not convenient to monitor the behavior continuously. A mother wishing to maintain appropriate playing-quietly-by-herself behavior in her child might use VI/LH by occasionally checking on the child and presenting reinforcement when she is engaging in the desired behavior. A timer set at varying intervals could be used to remind her to check on the child. This would necessitate only occasional interruptions of her household chores. An added benefit might be that looking in on her child for a few seconds and presenting reinforcement (for instance, by playing with her for a few minutes) if she is engaging in the desired behavior might also help reinforce her housekeeping behavior.

Another useful application of VI/LH is to reinforce attentive behavior in a classroom. This is also done often with the aid of a timer that makes a distinctive sound at the end of a preset interval. Generally, each student is reinforced—for instance, with a point representing some amount of free time, or by early dismissal of class—if he is attentive and in his seat when the interval has elapsed. Any student who is not attentive when the interval has elapsed misses that opportunity for reinforcement. Hence, the limited hold of this VI/LH schedule is the length of time it takes the teacher to look over the class.[1]

Benny was reinforced on a VI/LH schedule whose limited hold was a tiny fraction of a second. To receive reinforcement, he had to be on the chair at the exact moment the "Ding!" occurred and the nurse looked toward the chair. Since Benny could never know when this would happen (because different times were used on different trials), he had to be on the chair almost continuously after the announcement of an activity in order to avoid missing reinforcement. Accordingly, this is what he did, even though he sometimes had to sit on the chair for as long as ten minutes before reinforcement occurred. Had the nurses wished to do so, they could have gradually increased the VI part of the schedule so that Benny would have had to sit for even longer periods. However, it would still have been necessary to include some short and intermediate intervals; otherwise (as with FI), Benny would have learned that he could bother the nurses for the first few minutes without losing the opportunity to obtain reinforcement.

3. The Fixed-Duration Schedule

On a fixed-duration (FD) schedule,[2] reinforcement occurs after the behavior has been engaged in for a certain continuous period of time. If ten continuous seconds of the behavior are required per reinforcement we call the schedule an FD 10-second schedule; if twenty are required, we call it an FD 20-second schedule; and so on.

Parents commonly use (or attempt to use) FD schedules: "Practice the piano for an hour and then you can go out and play"; or, "Study your homework assignment for two hours and then you can watch TV." A worker who is paid by the hour is also (presumably) on an FD schedule. Sometimes the physical environment provides FD schedules. For example rubbing two sticks together rapidly for a certain continuous period produces fire; directing a steady stream of water on the fire for a certain continuous period extinguishes it. Another example is that to melt solder, one must hold the tip of the soldering iron on the solder for a continuous fixed period of time. If the tip is removed, the solder cools quickly and the person has to start over again and apply heat for the same continuous period.

Provided that the amount of behavior time required for reinforcement has been increased fairly gradually, the characteristic effect of an FD schedule is that the behavior occurs continuously for long periods of time. As with FR schedules, however, a pause occurs immediately after reinforcement and before the person begins working toward the next reinforcement. The length of this pause depends on the time requirement of the FD schedule: the longer the time requirement, the longer the pause. Moreover, if the time requirement is too large or is increased too rapidly, the behavior will decrease drastically or will not occur at all. (FD has not been studied as much as the schedules described above. Thus, these statements about its effects should be taken with some caution.)

FD schedules are useful only when the target behavior can be measured conveniently and accurately and reinforced on the basis of its duration. One should be very careful not to assume that this is the case for any target behavior. Presenting reinforcement contingent upon a child's studying his homework or practicing the piano for an hour *may* work satisfactorily. On the other hand, it may reinforce sitting at the desk or in front of the piano more than it reinforces studying or practicing. This is particularly true for something like studying, where it is difficult for the parent or teacher to observe whether the desired behavior is occurring (the child may be daydreaming, or reading a comic book hidden in his text). Practicing the piano is easier to monitor because the parent or teacher can hear whether the child is doing his lesson appropriately.[3]

The most common use of FD schedules in training programs is with target behaviors that one wishes to occur steadily throughout a fixed period of time. Eye contact is one such behavior that is commonly reinforced on an FD schedule in training programs with retarded and autistic children. Many such children do not make eye contact with others, and any attempt by an adult to initiate this behavior causes them to quickly avert their eyes from the adult. Eye contact is an important behavior to establish because it seems to be prerequisite to further social development.

Sitting attentively at a desk in a classroom is another behavior that is commonly reinforced on an FD schedule. This behavior is similar to what the nurses wished to establish in Benny. Thus, the nurses could have used an FD schedule. They did not, however, because it would have required continuous monitoring of Benny's behavior (preferably with a stopwatch). This was not convenient because the nurses had other duties to perform while Benny was sitting in the chair.

4. The Variable-Duration Schedule

A variable-duration (VD) schedule is like an FD schedule except that the amount of continuous time the behavior must be engaged in to produce reinforcement changes unpredictably from one reinforcement to the next. The amount of time required varies around some mean value. For example, if the mean value is twenty-five seconds, then fifteen continuous seconds of engaging in the behavior may be required to produce the first reinforcement, fifty to produce the second, thirty to produce the third, five to produce the fourth, and so on. If an average of fifteen continuous seconds of the behavior are required for reinforcement, we call the schedule a VD 15-second schedule; if an average of twenty-five seconds are required, we call it a VD 25-second schedule; and so on.

Some of the above examples of FD schedules from the natural environment might be thought of more appropriately as VD schedules. Rubbing two sticks together, for example, does not always require exactly the same length of time to produce fire (unless exactly the same conditions—such as the size, shape, and dryness of the sticks—are present each time this is done). As with many basic schedules, it is difficult to find common examples that precisely fit the definition of a VD schedule. One approximation is that of waiting in a ticket line. This example satisfies the definition of a VD schedule in two respects: (1) the amount of time one must wait in line for a ticket varies with the length of the line when one enters it, the speed of the ticket seller, and other factors; and (2) if one steps out of line (i.e., ceases to engage in appropriate waiting behavior), then one has to start again at the end of the line to obtain the reinforcer (the ticket). The example is not perfect, however, because the length of the line and how fast it is moving give some indication of how long one must wait for a ticket; so, this time is not completely unpredictable. For another example of a VD schedule, see Figure 5-2.

Provided that the average amount of time required for the behavior to be reinforced has been increased fairly gradually, the char-

FIGURE 5-2. *Example of a variable-duration schedule.*

acteristic effect of a VD schedule is that the behavior occurs continuously for long periods of time. In this respect, it is like FD. Moreover, if the time requirement is too large or is increased too rapidly, the behavior will decrease drastically or will not occur at all. Typically, however, we would expect less pausing after reinforcement in a VD schedule than in an FD schedule. (VD, like FD, has not been studied as much as some of the other schedules discussed here, and so it is difficult to make very definite statements about its effects.)

A VD schedule can be used effectively with any target behavior for which an FD schedule is appropriate. It is not as convenient to use as an FD schedule, and so it is not used as often. The nurses did not use a VD schedule with Benny for the same reason they did not use FD: it would have required continuous monitoring of his behavior, which was not convenient because of their other duties.

PITFALLS OF INTERMITTENT REINFORCEMENT: HOW IT WORKS TO THE DISADVANTAGE OF THOSE WHO ARE IGNORANT OF IT

The most common pitfall of intermittent reinforcement often traps not only the unitiated, but also those with some knowledge of behavior modification. It involves what may be described as inconsistent use of extinction. For example, a parent may at first attempt to ignore a child's tantrums. But the child persists, and in despair the parent finally "gives in" to the child's obnoxious demands for attention, candy, or whatever. Thus, the child obtains reinforcement on a VR or VD schedule, and this leads to further persistent tantruming in the future. Many times, parents and staff say that they had to give in to the child's demands because "extinction was not working." However, the resulting intermittent reinforcement produces behavior that is even more persistent and hence takes much longer to extinguish than behavior that has been continuously reinforced.

In our work, we have encountered cases in which children have screamed until exhausted and then, as soon as they've rested, done the same thing again. (This is called spontaneous recovery; see p. 51.) Eventually, even such severe tantrums can be eliminated by extinction, but this requires a good deal of time and patience. We suspect that such persistent undesirable behavior would not occur in the first place were it not for the inadvertent application of intermittent reinforcement.

GUIDELINES FOR THE EFFECTIVE USE OF INTERMITTENT REINFORCEMENT

To use intermittent schedules effectively in generating and maintaining desired behaviors, it is important to observe the following rules.

1. Choose a schedule that is appropriate to the behavior you wish to strengthen and maintain. For example, for the reasons pointed out above, FR, VR, FI, and VI, were not appropriate for Benny's sitting behavior, whereas VI/LH was.

2. Choose a schedule that is convenient to administer (but, of course, remain consistent with the first rule). For example, although VD and VI/LH were appropriate for Benny's sitting behavior, the latter was much more convenient to administer than the former.

3. Use appropriate instruments and materials to determine accurately and conveniently when the behavior should be reinforced. For example, if you are using a ratio schedule, make sure that you have a counter of some sort—be it a fancy wrist counter (as used for keeping golf scores), a string of beads, or simply pencil and paper. Similarly, if you are using an interval or duration schedule, make sure you have an accurate timer appropriate to your schedule. If you are using a variable schedule, make sure you have arranged to follow a sequence of random numbers that vary around the mean you have chosen.

4. The frequency of reinforcement should initially be high enough to maintain the desired behavior, and should then be decreased gradually until the final desired amount of behavior per reinforcement is being maintained. Recall that for Benny, the average interval was at first very short, and was then increased gradually. To take another example, suppose you wanted to maintain a particular behavior on FR 100. First, continuously reinforce the behavior for awhile; then put it on FR4 for awhile, then FR 10; and so on, until the desired performance is achieved. Always remain at each stage long enough to insure that the behavior is strong. If you increase the requirement too rapidly, the behavior will deteriorate and you will have to return to an earlier stage (possibly continuous reinforcement) in order to recapture it. This is similar to the shaping procedure described in Chapter 4.

5. If possible, inform the individual, in language he can understand, of the procedure you will be using with him.

Study Questions

(for examination purposes)

1. Explain what a VI schedule is. Give two examples of VI schedules that occur in everyday life (at least one of which is not in the text).

2. Describe how VI is similar to and how it differs from FI.

3. What is the characteristic effect of a VI schedule?

4. Explain why VI schedules do not have much application in training programs.

5. Explain what a VI/LH schedule is. Give two examples of VI/LH schedules that occur in everyday life (at least one of which is not in the text).

6. Describe how a VI/LH schedule is similar to and how it differs from a simple VI schedule.

7. What is the characteristic effect of a VI/LH schedule?

8. Describe what happens if the VI portion of a VI/LH schedule is too large or is increased too rapidly.

9. What practical advantage does VI/LH have over FI/LH?

10. State two possibe applications of VI/LH in training programs.

11. Explain how VI/LH was used to teach Benny to sit and wait patiently.

12. Explain what an FD schedule is. Give two examples of FD schedules that occur in everyday life (at least one of which is not in the text).

13. Explain why FD might not be a very good schedule for reinforcing studying behavior.

14. State two possible applications of FD in training programs.

15. Explain why FD was not used to teach Benny to sit and wait patiently.

16. Explain what a VD schedule is. Give two examples of VD schedules that occur in everyday life (at least one of which is not in the text).

17. Describe how a VD schedule is similar to and how it differs from an FD schedule.

18. What is the characteristic effect of a VD schedule?

19. Explain what happens if a VD schedule is too large or is increased too rapidly in size.

20. For what type of target behaviors are VD schedules useful?

21. Explain why VD might not be a very good schedule for reinforcing study behavior.

22. State two possible applications of VD schedules in training programs.

23. Explain why a VD schedule was not used to teach Benny to sit and wait patiently.

24. Explain what sort of instruments and materials you might use, and how you would use them, to implement each of the following schedules:
    a) FR   e) FI
    b) VR   f) FI/LH
    c) FD   g) VI
    d) VD   h) VI/LH

25. Describe how intermittent reinforcement works to the disadvantage of people who are ignorant of its effect. Give an example.

26. How is the appropriate method for adjusting an individual to a high FR or FD schedule similar to applying the shaping procedure?

Study Exercises

(to be practiced by the reader)

1. The schedule during the latter few days of Benny's program was a VI 5-minute/LH "zero-second" schedule. Assume that a new staff member has been given the task of ringing the timer to indicate to the other nurses when they should check Benny to see if he's sitting on his chair. Prepare a list of time intervals and appropriate instructions for the new staff member. The program should be applied for a maximum of ten minutes per trial, three trials per day.

2. Assume that the following behaviors have been established:
   a) dishwashing behavior of roommate or spouse
   b) dusting behavior of teenage son or daughter
   c) completion of a mathematics assignment by a student
   You are now faced with the task of maintaining them. Following the
   guidelines for the effective use of intermittent reinforcement, describe
   in detail the best schedule to use and how you might apply it in order
   to maintain the above behaviors.

Self-Modification Exercise

(to be practiced by the reader)

Assume that you have been assigned a 400-page book to read during the
next few days. Select an appropriate reinforcer for yourself, and identify the
best schedule on which to dispense the reinforcer. Describe the reasons for
your selections, and outline the mechanics of how you might implement the
program and complete it successfully.

EXTENDED DISCUSSION AND NOTES

1. Wolf, Hanley, King, Lachowicz, and Giles (1970) used this method,
which they called the "timer-game," to increase the in-seat behavior of
sixteen low-achieving children in a remedial class. The authors noted,
"The timer-game was an effective technique for decreasing out-of-seat
behavior. . . . It was also practical since it did not require continuous
monitoring by the teacher. The teacher needs to observe only the out-
of-seat behavior that occurred when the timer rang."

The timer-game was not uniformly effective for all the children.
But one child whose out-of-seat behavior remained high when her in-
seat behavior earned points only for herself showed good improvement
when her in-seat behavior also earned points for the four students who
sat closest to her. Speculating about this, the authors remarked, "The
peer points condition resulted in more control over Sue's out-of-seat
behavior than the individual points condition. Exactly what the peers
contributed to the effect must await further analysis. Our impression
was that they provided a number of consequences and other functions
for Sue. For example, if she stood up, she was immediately reminded to
sit down. If she broke her pencil, which she often did, one of the four
peers would volunteer to sharpen it for her. If she went to the lavatory,
she was reminded to hurry. However, the extent of their attending behavior was not determined."

2. The terms "fixed-duration schedule" and "variable duration schedule" are not in standard use. In fact, there are no standard terms denot-
ing these two schedules, apparently because behaviors whose important measurable property is duration have not received much attention
in basic research (see note 1 of Chapter 5, Section One). Stevenson and
Clayton (1970) used the term "response duration schedule" in reference
to a procedure in which reinforcement occurred when a lever was held
down for a continuous fixed time. But we prefer the term "fixed-

(Continued)

duration schedule" for this type of schedule because we can thereby distinguish it from the type we call a "variable-duration schedule." Moreover, these schedules may be applied to an entire activity—not just a single response. Because fixed-duration and variable-duration schedules have not been studied as extensively as the other schedules described in this book, the statements we make about them are somewhat more speculative than those we make about the other schedules.

3. There is evidence that when FR and FD both appear to be applicable, the former schedule is preferable. Semb and Semb (1975) compared two methods of scheduling workbook assignments for elementary school children. In one method, which they called "fixed-page assignment," each child was instructed to work until he finished fifteen pages. In the other method, "fixed-time assignment," each child was instructed to work until the teacher told him to stop. The amount of time he was required to work was equal to the average amount of time he spent working during the fixed-page condition. In both methods, each child received free time if he correctly answered at least eighteen of twenty randomly selected workbook frames; otherwise, he had to redo the entire assignment. On the whole, the children completed more work and made more correct response under the fixed-page condition than under the fixed-time condition.

Study Questions on Notes

1. Might it be better to reinforce a child for dusting the living-room furniture for a fixed period of time, or for a fixed number of items dusted? Explain your answer.

2. Describe Wolf et al.'s "timer-game."

3. Is it accurate to say that Sue (in the Wolf et al. study) received bootleg reinforcement? Why or why not? (Hint: Check note 2 in Chapter 3.)

CHAPTER 6

TYPES OF INTERMITTENT REINFORCEMENT
to Decrease Behavior

"Tommy, a little less talking out, please"

DECREASING TOMMY'S TALKING OUT

Tommy, an eleven-year-old boy classified as trainable mentally retarded, was judged by his teacher to be the most disruptive student in his special education classroom.* He frequently engaged in inappropriate talking and other vocalizations during class. The behavior was troublesome not so much because of its nature, but because of the high rate at which it occurred. A program was therefore undertaken, not to elminate it, but rather to reduce it to a less bothersome level.

The undesirable behavior, "talking out," was given the following precise behavioral definition: "talking to the teacher or classmates without the teacher's permission; talking, singing, or humming to oneself; and

*This case study is based on Dietz and Repp (1973).

making statements not related to the ongoing class discussion." A practice teacher located in the back of the room recorded Tommy's talk-outs during one fifty-minute session per day. (A second trained observer also recorded Tommy's talk-outs, to insure the accuracy of the observations.)

In phase 1 of the program, the behavior was recorded for ten sessions. It was found that Tommy averaged about one talk-out every nine minutes (or about .11 per minute). In phase 2, Tommy was told the definition of a talk-out and instructed that he would be allowed five minutes of free play time at or near the end of the day if at the end of the fifty-minute session he had made three or fewer talk-outs (i.e., less than about one every seventeen minutes). At the end of each session, Tommy was told by the teacher whether he had met the requirement, but during the session he was never told the number of talk-outs recorded.

This procedure was quite effective. During phase 2, which lasted fifteen sessions, Tommy averaged about one talk-out every fifty-four minutes (.02 per minute). Moreover, he never exceeded the upper limit of three per session.

In the third and final phase, the above reinforcement schedule was removed and Tommy was told that he would no longer receive free time for low rates of talk-outs. Over the eight sessions of this phase for which data were taken, his rate of talking out increased to an average of one every thirty-three minutes (.03 per minute). Although this rate was much higher than the rate during the treatment procedure (phase 2), it was still a great deal lower than the rate before the procedure was introduced (phase 1). Thus, the treatment had a beneficial effect even after it was removed.

DIFFERENTIAL REINFORCEMENT OF LOW RATES

If reinforcement occurs only when responding is occurring at a low rate, responding will subsequently tend to occur at a low rate. This phenomenon is called *differential reinforcement of low rates*. Tommy's case illustrates one way that low-rate behavior can be differentially reinforced. In that case, an interval was specified (fifty minutes) and reinforcement occurred at the end of the interval if it contained fewer than a specified number of responses (three talk-outs).

This method, like those discussed in Chapter 5, involves a schedule of intermittent reinforcement. The schedule is called "DRL," which stands for "Differential Reinforcement of Low Rates." There are several types of DRL schedules. The type used with Tommy is useful when two conditions hold: (1) some of the behavior is tolerable, but (2) less of it is better. In Tommy's case, the teacher felt that three talk-outs per session would not be too disruptive; no doubt, she would have preferred none at all, but she did not wish to impose too stringent a requirement on Tommy. Therefore, Tommy could earn his five minutes of free time by making three, two, one, or zero talk-outs during any given session.[1]

Sometimes, however, the behavior you want to reduce is not only tolerable but desirable — as long as it does not occur at too high a rate. For example, a student who always volunteers the correct answer deprives his classmates of the chance to respond to the teacher's questions. Naturally, we would not wish to eliminate this child's behavior; we would hope, rather, to reduce it to a more appropriate level. We might do this by placing the behavior on the following type of DRL schedule: any target response that occurs after five minutes of the previous target response is immediately reinforced; any target response that occurs within five minutes of the previous target response is *not* reinforced. This is called a "DRL 1-response/5-minute schedule."[2] This type of schedule requires that responses be emitted in order for reinforcement to occur. On the type of schedule used with Tommy, the individual need not respond at all in order to obtain reinforcement.

Eating is a particularly good example of behavior that is desirable at a moderate rate but that often occurs too rapidly. Some overweight people eat their meals so rapidly that they finish a normal portion well before the end of a normal mealtime. As a result, they perhaps do not experience a "full" or "satisfied" feeling until long after they have passed the point of satiation. In such cases, it might be beneficial to reinforce eating bites of food on a DRL schedule. Meals would then be eaten at a slower rate, which would tend to promote less eating (see Stuart and Davis, 1972, pp. 89–90).

Another use of DRL would be to reinforce slow speech in a student who speaks too rapidly. The student would be asked questions (such as "How are you?" or "Where do you live?") for which standard responses are reinforced — but only if they encompass a certain minimum time period whose length is determined by what the teacher regards as a normally acceptable rate of speech.

DIFFERENTIAL REINFORCEMENT OF ZERO RESPONDING

The type of DRL schedule used with Tommy might have specified an upper limit of zero rather than three talk-outs per fifty-minute period. This schedule is used frequently enough to merit a special name — DRO (pronounced "D–R–Oh"), which stands for "*Differential Reinforcement of Zero Responding*."[3] Had this schedule been used with Tommy, it would have been called a "DRO 50-minute schedule."

DRO is frequently used when one wishes to eliminate a behavior. For example, a person can eliminate tantruming by placing it on a DRO schedule. A good schedule for this purpose might be DRO 15-seconds. The procedure might involve resetting a stopwatch to zero each time a tantrum occurred and allowing it to "tick off" seconds when the tantrum stopped. Reinforcement would occur when a continuous fifteen seconds had elapsed with no tantruming. When the nonoccurrence of the behavior is under good control of this contingency, the schedule should be increased—for example, to DRO 30-seconds. The size of DRO should continue to be increased in this fashion until (1) the behavior is occurring very rarely or not at all and (2) a minimum amount of reinforcement is being given for its nonoccurrence.[4]

PITFALLS OF DIFFERENTIAL REINFORCEMENT OF LOW RATES: HOW IT WORKS TO THE DISADVANTAGE OF THOSE WHO ARE IGNORANT OF IT

DRL is used commonly and unknowingly by parents, teachers, and others to decrease the frequency of behavior that in actuality they would like to maintain at a high rate. Consider what happens when a child starts performing well in school—by giving correct answers to questions, for example. At first, the teacher is quite impressed and enthusiastically reinforces the behavior. But as the rate of the behavior increases, the teacher gradually becomes less impressed. This is "obviously a bright child," and so one expects a high rate of good behavior from her. Thus, the reinforcement gradually decreases, perhaps to zero, as the rate of the behavior increases. Eventually, the child learns that she obtains more reinforcement if she performs at a low rate, because the teacher is more impressed with good behavior when it occurs infrequently than when it occurs frequently. Many kids breeze through school showing only occasional "flashes of brilliance" instead of developing to their full potential. To avoid this type of inadvertent DRL schedule, teachers should precisely define the behavior they want to maintain at a high rate. They should then make sure they reinforce this behavior on an appropriate schedule, whether or not they happen to be "impressed" with it on any particular occasion.

GUIDELINES FOR THE EFFECTIVE USE OF DIFFERENTIAL REINFORCEMENT OF LOW RATES

DRL and DRO schedules are intermittent-reinforcement schedules similar to those discussed in Chapter 5. The main difference is that DRL and DRO are used to reduce behavior, whereas the schedules in Chapter 5 are used to strengthen and maintain it. Similar guidelines for effective usage apply to all types of schedules:

1. Choose a schedule that is appropriate for the behavior you want to reduce. For example, one would not typically apply DRO to a behavior one did not wish or need to eliminate completely.

2. Use appropriate timing devices to determine accurately and conveniently when reinforcement should occur. For some DRL and DRO schedules, a stopwatch is almost essential; for others, a simple egg timer or an ordinary clock will do.

3. The frequency of reinforcement should initially be high enough to maintain the nonoccurrence of the undesirable behavior, and should then be decreased gradually. Some individuals, particularly those who understand instructions, may be able to sustain a relatively low frequency from the beginning. Tommy, for example, did quite well even though he was reinforced, at most, only once every fifty minutes. Other individuals may initially require more frequent reinforcement.

4. If possible, inform the individual, in language she can understand, of the procedure you will be using with her.

Study Questions

(for examination purposes)

1. Describe briefly, point by point, how Tommy's talking out in class was reduced.
2. Explain what a DRL schedule is. Give an example of a DRL schedule that occurs in everyday life.
3. Describe the type of DRL schedule that is useful when both of the following conditions hold: (1) some of the behavior is tolerable, but (2) the less of it the better.
4. Describe the type of DRL schedule that is useful when the behavior you want to reduce is desirable as long as it occurs at a specified rate.
5. Give two examples (at least one of which is not in the text) of how DRL would be useful in treating a behavior problem.
6. Explain what a DRO schedule is. Give an example of a DRO schedule that occurs in everyday life.
7. Give two examples (at least one of which is not in the text) of how DRO might be useful in treating a behavior problem.
8. Describe how DRL works to the disadvantage of people who are ignorant of its effects. Give an example.
9. Explain how DRL and DRO differ from the intermittent-reinforcement schedules discussed in Chapter 5.
10. What happens if the frequency of reinforcement on DRL or DRO is too low or is decreased too rapidly?

Study Exercises

(to be practiced by the reader)

1. For each of the two types of DRL schedules cited in study questions 3 and 4, describe two possible applications in training programs with retarded children. Describe in detail how you would program and administer DRL in these situations.
2. Describe two possible applications of DRO in programs of early-childhood education. Describe in detail how you would program and administer DRO in these situations.
3. Explain what sort of instruments and materials you might use, and how you might use them, to implement DRL and DRO.

EXTENDED DISCUSSION AND NOTES

1. The terminology for DRL schedules is considerably less standardized than that for most of the schedules discussed in Chapter 5. Ferster and Skinner (1957, p. 459), for example, used the term *drl* to refer generally to any modification of a schedule (for example, FI) such that reinforcement occurred on that schedule only when the response rate was below some specified value. Later, Sidman (1960, p. 124) used the term *DRL* to designate a schedule in which reinforcement was contingent upon a response separated by a certain minimum time interval from the previous response. This latter usage has now come to be widely accepted in basic research (although Morse [1966, p. 93] has questioned using schedule names that designate the expected behavioral effect—in this case, low rates). Both of the above uses imply that reinforcement is contingent upon responding, although at a low rate. In applied research, at least, the term *DRL* has been expanded by Deitz and Repp (1973) to include schedules in which reinforcement occurs following a period of time containing fewer than a specified number of responses— even if no response has occurred during that period. This expanded usage has been adopted in this book.

2. This type of DRL schedule corresponds more closely to the most common use of the term DRL in basic research. See Reynolds (1975, p. 92) for the manner in which a DRL schedule specifying any maximum number of responses in a given time period can be represented diagrammatically.

An interesting application of this type of DRL was reported by Poole and Yates (1975). They treated a twenty-four-year-old male university student who experienced an excessively frequent urge to urinate, a problem that interfered seriously with his studying and his social life. During a three-week observation period, the young man urinated an average of 34.4 times per day. During treatment, he was placed on a DRL schedule from 9:00 A.M. to 9:00 P.M. For the remaining twelve hours of each day, he could urinate as often as he desired. Over the first three weeks, the DRL was one hour. Over the next twenty-five weeks, the DRL was gradually increased to four hours. This schedule was highly successful in reducing the frequency of urinating to an ac-

(Continued)

ceptable rate. This low rate also generalized to the twelve-hour period in which the DRL was not in effect, and was maintained twenty-four hours per day during a one-year follow-up period. This study is also noteworthy in that no reinforcers were utilized other than the natural reinforcement gained by controlling the frequency of urinating.

3. Sometimes, the O in *DRO* is said to stand for *other* responding. Whether you think of it as standing for *zero* or *other* responding seems to make little practical difference. The distinction lies in whether you want to think of the schedule as reinforcing no responding of a particular type (for instance, no talking out), or whether you prefer to think of it as reinforcing any behavior other than the specified response (for instance, anything other than talking out). The term *omission training* has also been used to refer to a DRO procedure (see Uhl and Garcia, 1969). In other words, a reinforcer is presented only if a particular response is omitted during a given time period.

4. In a basic experiment with pigeons, Zeiler (1971) compared DRO with extinction as response-elimination procedures. Two responses were reinforced until they occurred at a high rate. One response was then placed on extinction, and the other was reinforced on a DRO 30-second schedule. The behavior on DRO decreased more quickly than the extinguished behavior.

Weiher and Harmon (1975) applied DRO to reduce the head banging of a fourteen-year-old retarded child. The boy's head was a mass of scar tissue as a result of his self-destructive behavior, and, consequently, he was kept in restraints. Prior to the DRO program, the boy was fitted with a padded cap that allowed freedom of movement but prevented injury. During observation sessions in which the boy wore the protective cap, he banged his head at a rate of approximately fifteen "thumps" per minute. Training sessions were then initiated, again with the boy wearing the protective cap in order to prevent injury. During the first seven sessions, reinforcement (a half-teaspoon of applesauce dispensed through a baby's bottle) was presented on a DRO 3-seconds for head banging. Sessions were conducted twice per day and varied in duration from several minutes to twenty-five minutes. During the next few sessions, the DRO was gradually increased and then made variable. By the fiftieth session, the DRO varied from fifteen to ninety seconds. The results were highly successful in eliminating this dangerous behavior. As a result of this treatment, the boy was able to enter training programs designed to establish a variety of useful skills.

Not all uses of DRO have proved so successful. Repp, Deitz, and Deitz (1975) noted two important differences between "successful" and "unsuccessful" studies of DRO reported in the applied literature: (1) the unsuccessful studies used larger starting values for the DRO schedule than did the successful studies; (2) the successful studies used DRO starting values that were approximately equal to the mean intervals between instances of the target behaviors prior to the introduction of the DRO schedule.

Repp *et al.* (1976) successfully used DRO to reduce behaviors such as hair twirling, hand biting, thumb sucking, and disruptive behavior in retarded individuals.

(Continued)

Study Questions on Notes

1. How does the use of the term DRL adopted in this text differ from the use of that term by Sidman?

2. What does the O in DRO stand for? Explain.

3. Compare the DRL schedules for Tommy's talk-outs and the university student's frequent urges to urinate, in terms of the following: the behavior; its initial frequency; its final frequency; the reinforcer; and the duration of the program.

4. If you wanted to decrease a behavior, would you apply an extinction program or a DRO schedule. Justify your choice. (Hint: There are two points to be made.)

5. What are two differences between the successful and unsuccessful attempts to apply DRO?

6. Compare and contrast DRO with FD.

CHAPTER 7

Doing the Right Thing at the Right Time and Place is a Matter for

STIMULUS CONTROL

"Now, Girls, Let's Sit Quietly and Watch TV"

LEARNING TO SIT QUIETLY AT THE RIGHT TIME AND PLACE

The residents of Cedar Cottage spent a good deal of time in the TV room.* At times, they would watch TV, wander around, play with each other, or play with the staff. Occasionally, they would sit quietly. Although the staff generally approved of the children mingling and doing what they pleased in the TV room, there were occasions when it was desirable for them to sit quitely—such as during staff discussions with visitors, and staff meetings. Although the children did sit quietly on occasion, this behavior usually did not occur when the staff desired it. This was clearly a situation,

*Cedar Cottage is a self-contained residence for thirty severely and profoundly re-tarded girls located at The Manitoba School. This case study was taken from Martin (1972).

then, in which the desired behavior (sitting quietly) was in the children's repertoire but did not occur at the desired times.

The procedure for developing appropriate quiet behavior at the right times consisted primarily of two contingencies. First, a distinctive green light was turned on at specific times during the day, and a staff member would announce, "Okay, children, the light is on. Everyone sit down and be quiet." The light was left on for about fifteen minutes. Immediately following the announcement, a second staff member would take those who were standing or moving around and guide them to a seat in the TV room. Another staff member would then walk around the room and reinforce, with praise, tokens, and/or candy, those children who were sitting quietly. Reinforcement was presented on a variable-interval two-minute schedule (approximately) with a very short limited hold (approximately fifteen seconds). This was the first contingency. While the light was on, those residents who got up from their seats and were extremely noisy were immediately presented with a verbal "No! The light is on" and were taken to a time-out room for a brief period (usually from two to five minutes). (Time-out is discussed in more detail in Chapter 12. In general, a time-out room is a small, usually empty room. A child placed in such a room loses the opportunity of earning positive reinforcement in other rooms.) This was the second contingency. After several weeks of this procedure, the green light became a powerful controlling cue for sitting quietly in the TV room. If the light was turned on at any time of the day, the children would immediately sit down and be quiet. When the light was turned off, the children would move about and become noisier. The strong control exerted by the light was inadvertently tested by the staff one night during the evening meal. On this occasion, the residents were particularly noisy. Frustrated by the situation, one of the nurses decided to bring in the green light from the TV room. When the light was turned on, not only did the residents immediately become quiet, but the six residents who had been taught to serve in the dining room sat down and refused to serve the remainder of the meal until the light was turned off.

STIMULUS CONTROL

A *stimulus* is any physical event or object in the environment. Books, sounds, pens, people, trees, and shoes are all stimuli. Certain responses occur in the presence of some stimuli and not others. This is called *stimulus control*.[1] Consider the behavior of picking up a telephone receiver and saying "Hello." For most people in our culture, this behavior occurs in the presence of the stimulus provided by the phone ringing; it does not occur in the absence of the stimulus. This means that a telephone ringing (the stimulus) *controls* the behavior of picking up the receiver and saying hello (the response).

The procedure by which we learn to emit appropriate behavior in the presence of the "right" stimuli, and not in the presence of the "wrong" stimuli, is called *stimulus-discrimination training*. Basically, this procedure involves reinforcing a response in the presence of one stimulus and not reinforcing the response (in other words, extinguishing it) in the presence of other stimuli. For example, in the presence of the stimulus of a ringing telephone, if we respond by picking up the phone and saying "Hello," we are reinforced by having someone answer. (However, the reinforcement schedule may be intermittent. For instance, the caller may hang up without speaking, or the caller may be someone with whom we do not wish to talk.) In the presence of the stimuli of a nonringing phone, if we respond by picking up the receiver and saying "Hello," we are not reinforced by having someone answer.

One of the authors recently had the opportunity to watch his two-year-old son learn to answer the telephone. On several trials when the phone rang and it was known that Grandma was phoning, the boy was reinforced by the conversation with Grandma. However, on several occasions thereafter, the boy picked up the phone and said "Hello" even though it had not rung. On those occasions, there was no reinforcement. Eventually, he learned to pick up the receiver and say "Hello" only when the phone rang. In more general terms, a behavior is likely to occur in the presence of stimuli that were present when previous instances of that behavior were reinforced; a behavior is not likely to occur in the presence of stimuli that were present when previous instances of that behavior were extinguished.

From the above example, and from casual observation, it can be seen that any situation in which behavior occurs can be analyzed in terms of three sets of events: (1) the stimulus conditions that exist just prior to the occurrence of the behavior; (2) the behavior itself; and (3) the consequences of the behavior. The stimuli that exist just prior to a response can be placed in one of the two general classes— S^Ds and S^Δs. If an event is a stimulus in the presence of which the occurrence of a specified response will be reinforced, then that event is called an S^D (pronounced "ess-dee") for that response. That is, an S^D is a signal that a particular response will pay off. If an event is a stimulus in the presence of which a specified response will not be reinforced, then that event is called an S^Δ (pronounced "ess-delta") for that response. Thus, an S^Δ is a signal that a particular response won't pay off.

The symbol S^D is an abbreviation for the term *discriminative stimulus*. Δ is the Greek letter D. Thus, there are two types of discriminative stimuli: S^Ds, which are associated with reinforcement, and S^Δs, which are associated with extinction or nonreinforcement. Through discrimination training, individuals learn to emit responses in the presence of S^Ds and learn not to emit them in the presence of S^Δs. In our example of a child learning to respond to the telephone, the stimulus of a phone ringing is an S^D for the response of answering the phone because that response will be reinforced when the phone is ringing. The stimulus of a phone in view but not ringing is an S^Δ for the response of answering the phone because that response will not be reinforced when the phone is not ringing. This can be diagramed as follows:

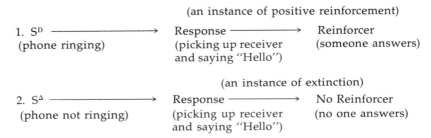

In the case study at the beginning of this chapter, the green light on in the TV room was the S^D for sitting quietly, since the children were reinforced when they sat quietly in its presence. The green light off was the S^Δ for sitting quietly, since when the light was off the children were not reinforced for sitting quietly. This may be diagramed as follows:

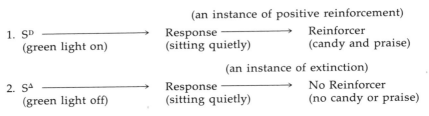

A phrase that is frequently used in connection with the type of diagram shown above is *contingency of reinforcement*. According to Skinner (1969, p. 7), an "adequate formulation of the interaction between an [individual] and [his or her] environment must always specify three things: (1) the occasion upon which a response occurs, (2) the response itself, and (3) the reinforcing consequences. The interrelationships among them are the 'contingencies of reinforcement.' "[2] Thus, extinction is a contingency of reinforcement; an FI schedule is a contingency of reinforcement; and any arrangement among stimulus, response, and consequences is a contingency of reinforcement.

Since the 1930s, behavioral psychologists have been studying the effects of certain contingencies of reinforcement on the behaviors defined by those contingencies. Prior to that time, psychologists studied the environment (the independent variables) and behavior (the dependent variables) as separate events, and regarded the environment as influencing behavior in a reflexive sense. Of all of Skinner's contributions to psychology, possibly the most important is his discovery of how the interrelations between behavior and the environment (in other words, contingencies of reinforcement) as independent variables affect future behavior as the dependent variable.

It is an interesting exercise to take any situation in which we find ourselves and examine the stimulus control of some of our behaviors.[3] Consider the typical awakening-in-the-morning scene for most of us. Stimuli indicating morning—such as daylight in the window, specific configurations on clocks, and the sound of an alarm clock—are typically S^Ds for the behavior of rising and getting dressed. The call to breakfast is likely an S^D for entering the dining area and eating. The cues associated with having just eaten breakfast are likely S^Ds for washing, brushing one's teeth, and combing one's hair. Pressure on the bladder and distention of the bowels are S^Ds for going to the toilet.

Our culture and physical environment set up stimuli as S^Ds and S^Δs for our behavior, but we are not always "appropriately" controlled by those S^Ds and S^Δs. Suppose that a child finishes the main course at mealtime and demands of his mother, "Gimme dessert!" instead of asking, "Please may I have my dessert?" Let us suppose, further, that the parents decide that when the child has finished his main course, only a polite request for dessert ("Please may I have my dessert?") will be reinforced. In other words, the empty plate in that situation is an S^D by definition in that it is a stimulus signaling that a particular response (such as asking "Please may I have my dessert?") will be reinforced. Although the parents have set up that stimulus as an S^D, it may take several trials (and perhaps some instructions by the parents) before the child finally emits the appropriate behavior. Thus, stimuli may be set up as S^Ds by one's parents (or peer group), but they do not necessarily control one's behavior. In many situations, the appearance of a lady standing beside a door with an armful of groceries is an S^D for someone to open the door for her, and that behavior is likely to be reinforced with social approval. The sight of a hitchhiker is an S^D to stop and be reinforced by the hitchhiker's gratitude and companionship.

Examples of this sort could be cited at length. Although many of the stimuli in these examples are S^Ds by definition, in that appropriate responses emitted in their presence would be followed by reinforcement, these stimuli frequently do not actually control the behavior of the individuals of concern. It is therefore helpful to distinguish between stimuli that are S^Ds of S^Δs only by definition and those that function as controlling stimuli for some behavior. Controlling stimuli are sometimes referred to as *effective* S^Ds and S^Δs, whereas S^Ds and S^Δs that are such by definition but do not control the behavior are often called *ineffective*. Some examples of ineffective S^Ds and S^Δs are shown in Figure 7-1.

The failure of one individual to respond to the discriminative stimuli provided by another can be a major source of difficulty in a variety of interpersonal situations. For example, husbands and wives often provide each other with ineffective S^Ds and S^Δs. Even though a spouse may not be "in the mood" for love-making, the partner may not respond to the subtle cues provided. Individuals often experience certain moods: they may be preoccupied with other matters, they may feel somewhat tired, depressed, or excited, and so forth. Sometimes these private behaviors are signaled very obviously, and sometimes the signals are not so obvious. When other individuals do not respond to the S^Ds and S^Δs provided, unpleasant interactions frequently follow. A comment, a glance, a touch, or a smile may mean far more or far less than was intended by the individual making the comment or doing the glancing, touching, or smiling. Misinterpretations occur between lovers, parents and children, friends, and employers and employees. It is often extremely helpful to analyze these situations in terms of the problems of ineffective stimulus control, for at least one of the individuals in such situations has not learned to respond appropriately to the S^Ds, and S^Δs provided.[4] Some of the reasons for inappropriate responses to S^Ds and S^Δs are discussed later in this chapter.

The above examples of ineffective stimulus control might be described as instances of *failure to discriminate*. Additional difficulties arise from *failure to generalize*. These difficulties will be discussed in Chapter 11.

FACTORS DETERMINING THE EFFECTIVENESS OF STIMULUS CONTROL

1. Choosing distinct signals

If it is important to develop stimulus control of a particular behavior, it is desirable to identify controlling S^Ds that are very distinctive. For example, in the case of the parents who wanted to teach their child to ask, "Please may I have my dessert?" in response to the stimulus of the empty plate following the main course, it would be desirable for the parents to do a number of things designed to make that particular stimulus distinctive. For instance, one of the parents might run to the child, wipe the empty plate clean, and say, "Boy, do you ever have a clean plate; you ate everything! Would you like your dessert now?" If, on the other hand, the parents sometimes provide the dessert when a few pieces of food are left on the plate, sometimes when

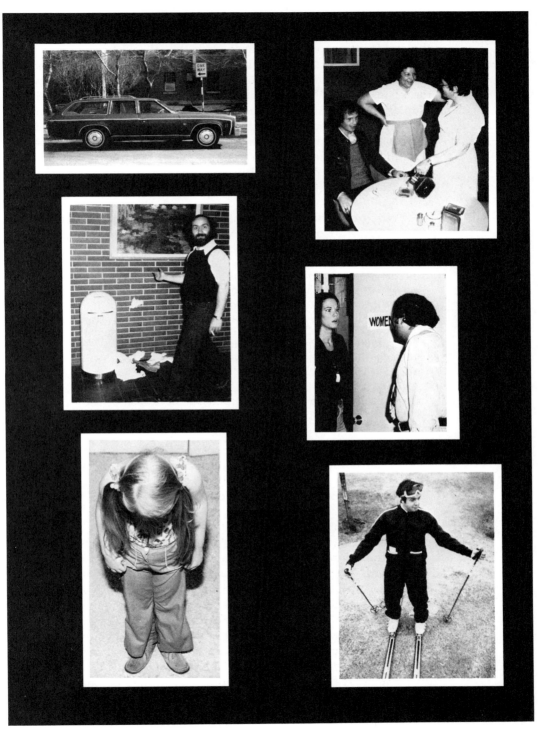

FIGURE 7-1. *Examples of ineffective S^D s and S^Δ s.*

the plate has some gravy and a piece of bread sitting at the side, or sometimes when the plate has a lot of a particular item on it because the child did not want that item, then the stimulus that they wish to function as an S^D for the desirable response is much more difficult to discriminate from other stimuli (namely, having slightly more food on the plate), and the discrimination training is likely to go more slowly. Similarly, some of the misunderstandings between lovers, friends, and others might be averted if the stimuli that were meant as S^Ds were made much more distinctive and described to the other person. (Techniques that help people present clearer discriminative stimuli to indicate their needs and feelings to others are collectively called *assertive training*. These techniques are discussed in Chapters 14, 15, and 16.)

When considering a stimulus that you are setting up as an S^D for the behavior of another person, you might ask yourself the following questions:

1. Is the stimulus different from other stimuli along more than one dimension? That is, is it different in location, size, color, and sensory modality (vision, hearing, touch, and so on)?
2. Is the stimulus one that can be presented primarily on occasions when the desired response should occur, so that confusion with the occurrence of the stimulus on other occasions is avoided?
3. Is the stimulus such that there is a high probability of the person attending to it when it is presented?
4. Have you thought about undesirable responses that might be controlled by the chosen stimulus? If some undesirable response follows the stimulus, it will interfere with the development of new stimulus control with the desired response.[5]

Careful attention to these questions will increase the chances that your stimulus control is effective rather than ineffective.

2. Minimizing the opportunities for error

Let us return to the example of a child learning to answer a phone when it rings, but not if it doesn't ring. The response of picking up the phone if the phone has not been ringing is a response to an S^Δ. This kind of response is typically referred to as an "error." Stimulus control can be developed much more effectively when the teacher attempts to minimize the possibility of errors on the part of the student. For example, if a parent is trying to teach a child to appropriately answer the phone, the parent might move the phone out of reach if the phone is not ringing and add verbal prompts of this sort: "Now remember, we don't answer telephones when they are not ringing. We only answer them just after they've begun to ring." Then, as soon as the phone rings (perhaps a phone call from a friend, made specifically for training purposes), the parent can immediately place the phone in front of the child and say, "Hey, the phone is ringing. Now you should answer it. Right?"

At this point you might be thinking, "But often we want to teach people to respond to subtle cues. Why should we then maximize distinctive signals and do funny little things to minimize errors?" Let us simply reply that choosing distinctive cues and minimizing errors will lead to more effective stimulus control than might otherwise occur. In Chapter 8, we will discuss techniques for gradually introducing discriminations involving very subtle cues. For the moment, it is important to keep in mind that efforts to choose distinctive signals and to minimize errors will lead to the development of effective stimulus control more quickly and with much less frustration for the student (and the teacher too) than attempts to develop discriminations that involve very subtle cues.[6]

3. Maximizing the number of trials

As we mentioned in Chapters 2 and 3, instances of positive reinforcement and extinction have the effects, respectively, of increasing and decreasing behaviors after several repetitions (even before any really obvious behavior change would be noticeable to a casual observer). Likewise, effective stimulus control is developed after a person reinforces the desired behavior in the presence of S^Ds on a number of trials and alternatively presents the S^Δs on a number of trials in such a way that erroneous responding is minimized. In general, it is well accepted that a number of reinforced trials are necessary for the development of consistent behaviors in the retarded and other behaviorally deficient individuals. What many people forget is that this is true for all of us when we are acquiring new discriminations. In the previous example of a husband and wife, one of whom is "not in the mood," it is important for that partner to realize that the other partner may not learn to respond to subtle cues, or even obvious cues, with just one or two trials. (In fact, some learning theorists have hypothesized that one-trial discrimination learning never occurs.[7]) After a number of instances of reinforcement for correct responding to the S^Ds, those S^Ds will likely control the response on several subsequent trials, even though reinforcement may no longer be forthcoming or may come on an intermittent basis.

PITFALLS OF STIMULUS CONTROL: HOW IT WORKS TO THE DISADVANTAGE OF THOSE WHO ARE IGNORANT OF IT

Any effective method can be misapplied, and stimulus control is no exception. An example of this is the case, observed by one of the authors, of a seven-year-old retarded boy who banged his head against hard surfaces unless an adult was with him and holding his hand. As soon as the adult dropped the child's hand and moved away, the child would immediately dive to the floor and begin banging his head hard enough to cause considerable bleeding. This behavior occurred only when the child was standing on a hard floor or on concrete. It did not occur when he was standing on a rug or on grass. The reason for this is easy to see. No one would come running and give him attention if he banged his head on a soft carpet or on grass, since he did not injure himself when he did that. Of course, the staff had no choice but to give him attention when he banged his head on hard surfaces. Otherwise, he would have seriously injured himself.* The staff had thus inadvertently taught the boy the following discrimination:

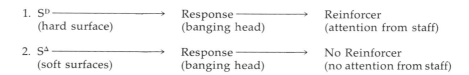

1. S^D ——————————→ Response ——————————→ Reinforcer
   (hard surface)   (banging head)   (attention from staff)

2. S^Δ ——————————→ Response ——————————→ No Reinforcer
   (soft surfaces)   (banging head)   (no attention from staff)

There are numerous examples of situations in which people inadvertently teach others to respond inappropriately to particular cues. If they were aware of what they were doing, they would not teach those discriminations. Behavioral episodes of the following sort are common in many households with young children: Terry, a three-year-old boy, is playing with the adjustment dials on the TV set. Mother says quietly, "Terry, please leave those dials alone." Terry continues to fiddle with the dials. A few minutes later, Mother hollers a little louder and a little less politely, "Terry, get away from that TV set." Terry continues to fiddle with the dials, screwing up the color, the contrast, and the horizontal focusing. A minute or two later, Mother says, this time loudly and with a threatening look, "Terry, for the last time get away from the TV set before I come and spank your bum." Terry finally moves away from the TV set and Mother says, "Now that's better Terry. Mommy loves you much better when you do what I tell you; why didn't you do that in the first place?" It is probably obvious to you that Mother has just reinforced Terry for responding only to her third-level threats. The discrimination Terry is learning is that of waiting until Mother is really angry and threatening before attending to her requests.

Consider another behavioral episode that many of you will recognize. At a neighborhood party for a half-dozen or so couples, Jack gets a little drunk and begins to "hustle" one of the other wives.

*The procedures that were used to treat this problem successfully are described in Chapter 12.

Jack's wife, Brenda, gives him a couple of stern glances. Jack continues to hustle. A little later, Brenda looks at Jack with her hands on her hips and says, "Jaaack!" Jack continues to hustle. Finally, Brenda takes Jack aside, gives him a stern lecture, and threatens to go home, following which Jack stops hustling and attends more to Brenda. After some discussion, Brenda expresses her confidence in Jack and shows him some affectionate attention. Question: What discrimination is being developed in Jack?

If you feel that you have to tell an individual something many times before he or she responds, or that nobody listens to you, or that others are not doing the right thing at the right time and place, you should closely examine your interactions with these individuals for instances of misapplication of stimulus control.

GUIDELINES FOR EFFECTIVELY DEVELOPING STIMULUS CONTROL

1. *Choose distinct signals.* Specify the S^Ds and at least one S^Δ. (In other words, specify conditions under which the behavior should and should not occur).
2. *Select an appropriate reinforcer.* See Figure 2-2 and p. 32.
3. *Develop the discrimination.*
   a) Arrange for the student to receive several reinforced trials in the presence of the S^D.
      (1) Specify clearly the S^D–desirable response–reinforcer sequence.
      (2) To teach the student to remember to act at a specific time, present additional cues for correct performance just before the action is to occur rather than after he has performed incorrectly.
      (3) To teach the student to act in a particular way under one set of circumstances but not under another help him identify the cues that differentiate the circumstances for the behavior and use instructions where appropriate.
      (4) Stimulus control over the child's behavior will not develop if he is not attending to the cues; therefore, use dramatic gestures to emphasize the cues.
      (5) Keep verbal cues constant initially.
      (6) Post the rules in a conspicuous place, and review them regularly.
   b) When the S^Δ is presented, make the change from the S^D very obvious, and follow the rules for extinction for the behavior of concern. Stimulus control is maintained by such things as geographical location of training place; physical characteristics and location of furniture, equipment, and people in the training room; time of day of training; and sequence of events that precede and accompany training. A change in any of these may disrupt stimulus control.
4. *Weaning the person from the program* (discussed in more detail in Chapter 11).
   a) If the behavior occurs in the right place at the right time at a desirable

rate during a dozen or so of the opportunities for the behavior, and if it is not occurring in S^Δ situations, it might be possible to gradually eliminate contrived reinforcers and maintain the behavior with social approval.

b) Look for other natural reinforcers in the environment that might maintain the behavior once it is occurring in the presence of S^Ds and not in the presence of S^Δs.

c) Plan periodic assessments of the behavior after the program is terminated in order to ensure that it is occasionally being reinforced, and that the desired frequency of the behavior in the presence of S^Ds is being maintained.

Study Questions

(for examination purposes)

1. What is the difference between a stimulus and a discriminative stimulus?
2. What is the difference between stimulus control and stimulus-discrimination training?
3. Shaping and stimulus-discrimination training are similar in that they both involve successive applications of reinforcement and extinction. In what two ways are they dissimilar?
4. What is a synonym for an effective S^D?
5. For any two stimuli that have been set up as an S^D and an S^Δ, but whose relationship to the behavior is best described as ineffective stimulus control, what would be the behavior in the presence of these stimuli?
6. Define and give an example of an $S^{D.}$
7. Define and give an example of an $S^{\Delta.}$
8. What are "contingencies of reinforcement"? Explain.
9. Identify examples of S^Ds and S^Δs as follows: two S^Ds from Table 2-1; two S^Ds from Table 2-2; two S^Δs from Table 3-1; and two S^Δs from Table 3-2.
10. What questions might you ask yourself when you are considering the selection of a stimulus to be set up as an S^D for the behavior of another person? (See p. 110.)
11. For each of the questions that you asked yourself in the preceding question, provide an example from your own experience.
12. What do we mean by an error in discrimination training?
13. Consider the task of teaching a child to discriminate the proper placement of a knife, fork, and spoon at a table setting. There are a number of things that one might do, before and during training, to minimize the possibility of errors. Describe three such things.
14. Describe an example of how ignorance of stimulus control may work to one's disadvantage.

Study Exercises

(to be practiced by the reader)

1. Identify five S^Ds that controlled your behavior during the past day or two. Clearly identify the general situation, the controlling S^D, the behavior controlled, and the reinforcement contingency.
2. Identify five situations in which you presented an S^D that controlled the behavior of some other person. Write the situations clearly as in the previous exercise.
3. Describe five situations in which you presented an S^Δ to some other person. Label the situations clearly, as in exercises 1 and 2, and indicate whether or not the S^Δ controlled the behavior appropriately.
4. Briefly describe a situation in which someone close to you has not been doing the things that you like him or her to do, and you suspect the problem is that you are not presenting clear-cut S^Ds and S^Δs. Describe how you might develop better stimulus control over the desired behavior in that person.

Self-Modification Exercises

(to be practiced by the reader)

1. Choose an excessive behavior of yours that you might like to decrease. For that behavior, carefully monitor those situations in which the behavior occurs and does not occur over a two- or three-day period. Clearly identify the controlling S^Ds and, if possible, some controlling S^Δs for the behavior. Such information will prove to be extremely helpful if you should decide later to set up a self-control program after completing this book.

2. On the basis of the material you have read thus far in this book, describe in detail how you might set up specific control of your study behavior so as to improve your learning of the discriminations that are necessary in mastering the remainder of the material in this book. (Hint: consider stimulus control, reinforcement, extinction, incompatible behaviors, and schedules of reinforcement.)

3. Select one of the behavioral inappropriatenesses that you listed at the end of Chapter 1. Describe in detail the stimuli currently controlling the behavior. Describe in detail the stimuli that you would like to control the behavior.

EXTENDED DISCUSSION AND NOTES

1. A more technical definition is offered by Rilling (1977, p. 433): "*Stimulus control* is observed when a change in a particular property of a stimulus produces a change in some response characteristic, as in the rate or probability with which a response occurs. For example, the onset of a light is said to control behavior if responding occurs at a higher

(Continued)

(Continued)

(or lower) rate in the presence of the light than in its absence." Thus, technically speaking, it is not necessary for a particular response to occur only in the presence of a particular stimulus in order to say that the stimulus controls the response; it is necessary only for the behavior that occurs in the presence of the stimulus to be in some manner different from the behavior that occurs in the absence of that stimulus.

2. Although we have adopted Skinner's use of the term "contingency," other authorities use the term differently (see, for example, Blackman, 1974; Powers and Osborne, 1976; Reynolds, 1975). They distinguish between "dependencies" and "contingencies" as follows: a *dependency* exists when a reinforcer has been scheduled to follow a response such that the presentation of the reinforcer depends on the occurrence of the response; a *contingency* exists when a reinforcer closely follows a response, but the relationship is accidental. According to Skinner both of these relationships would be contingencies. However, Skinner has differentiated between the two types of contingencies, in arguing that many superstitious behaviors (such as rain dancing) are due to accidental contingencies (such as rain occurring after a rain dance). In our view, the meaning of contingency that we have adopted in this text is by far the more popular interpretation.

3. Often, behaviors that appear perplexing to the uninformed are easy to understand to an individual knowledgeable about stimulus control. For example, some children may be little angels with one parent and little monsters with the other. Relatives, outside viewers of the situation, and often the parents themselves find it difficult to comprehend the Dr.-Jekyll-and-Mr.-Hyde behaviors of the children. Such contrasts are easily understood in terms of stimulus control. To illustrate, let's consider an experiment by Redd and Birnbrauer (1969). In this study, two adults worked with the same retarded children, but at different times. One adult provided candy, ice cream, or sips of Coke along with much praise when the children played cooperatively with other children. The second adult provided the same reinforcers, but did so on a time basis, which was independent of the children's behavior. That is, the second adult provided the reinforcers on a noncontingent basis with respect to the children's responses. This meant that behaviors other than cooperative play would be reinforced at least as often, if not more often, than cooperative-play behavior. The result was that the adults gradually acquired stimulus control over the play behavior of the children: whenever the first adult appeared, the children showed a great deal of cooperative-play behavior (which was the behavior reinforced in that adult's presence); when the second adult was present, the cooperative-play behavior of the children occurred at a much lower level. Thus, it is clear that different individuals can become S^Ds, and S^Δs, for completely different behaviors of others. In the presence of particular adults, children generally emit the behavior that those adults are likely to reinforce. If a child is a "monster" in your presence, check the reinforcement contingencies that you are applying.

4. In some situations, individuals in our culture hope that others will respond to particular stimuli as S^Ds, however, there may not be any reinforcers to make the particular stimuli function as S^Ds. For example, government officials and many private citizens would like litter baskets to function as S^Ds for the general public such that the public would deposit their litter rather than being litterbugs. Accordingly, governments,

(Continued)

stores, and various other organizations have placed litter baskets and litter bags in a variety of locations, along with instructions for individuals to deposit their litter. Often, however, there is no reinforcement for individuals who respond (although there may be an occasional punisher in the form of a fine for being a litterbug). The obvious result is that a number of individuals do not respond in desired ways to litter bags and trash cans. This was clearly demonstrated in an interesting experiment by Burgess, Clark, and Hendee (1971), who evaluated procedures to control littering by children in two movie theaters in Seattle, Washington. Their study clearly indicated that providing litter bags with instructions on how to use them, providing extra trash cans, and showing a special antilitter film before the feature film in the theaters had relatively little effect on the littering behavior of the children. Only when given reinforcement for returning the bags full of litter (either ten cents or a free movie ticket) did the children respond appropriately.

5. This difficulty was taken into consideration by Goldiamond (1965) in an interesting study in which he helped a husband and wife overcome their quarreling behavior. By utilizing reinforcement and counseling procedures, they wished to develop desirable stimulus control over pleasant interaction. One of the stimulus situations chosen as an S^D for pleasant interaction was the bedroom. However, the bedroom controlled an undesirable behavior in the sense that it was a scene of frequent quarreling in the past. The problem was therefore to find a stimulus that would change the appearance of the room completely, and yet be easy to apply and withdraw. The solution was to install a yellow night light, which markedly altered the perceptual configuration of the room. The night light was turned on as an S^D only when both individuals felt amorous; it was kept off on all other occasions. Eventually, desirable stimulus control was developed in the bedroom (and other locations too), and communication between the husband and wife improved greatly.

6. Procedures to develop discriminations in which the S^D and the S^Δ are presented alternately for set periods of time, and in which responses to the S^D are reinforced and responses to the S^Δ are extinguished, are called *traditional discrimination-training procedures.* Eventually, after many errors, the individual learns to discriminate and responds primarily to the S^D. Terrace (1963) demonstrated that discriminations could be taught with minimal errors, or none at all. In an experiment on training pigeons to peck at a plastic response key when it was illuminated with red light, and to not peck when it was illuminated with green light, he initially presented the S^D for a few trials and reinforced an appropriate response by the pigeons. The S^Δ was then presented very briefly (so briefly that the pigeons did not have a chance to respond) and in a completely different form from what it would eventually be. Over a number of trials, the form of the S^Δ was gradually changed and its duration increased so that eventually the S^D and S^Δ were alternating for equal periods of time. Since the pigeons made very few or no errors, this approach has been called the *errorless discrimination-training procedure.*

In a study with severely retarded girls, McDonald, Martin, Williams, and Hardy (1973) demonstrated that errorless discrimination-training procedures were superior to traditional procedures in teaching the girls to recognize their names. Each girl taught by the traditional discrimination-training procedure was presented with her name and one other name in randomly alternated positions and was asked to identify her own name. Correct pointing (pointing to one's own name) was reinforced, and incorrect pointing (pointing to the other name) was extinguished. The girls in the errorless discrimination-training group were initially presented with their names and a blank card. Over a number of trials of alternating the position of the cards, more and more printing was presented on the blank card; eventually, girls were discriminating their own names from other names. The girls taught by the errorless procedure performed better during training, and they retained their behaviors more effectively during a five-month follow-up.

7. To this, you might say, "That can't be right; I know I've sometimes learned to respond correctly in just one trial." It is true that the behavior that follows a particular stimulus may occur correctly after just one trial. However, that is not the typical discrimination development that we have been describing. An example of the sort of situation that you are thinking of in which a discrimination seems to develop in one trial might be putting money in a cigarette machine and receiving no cigarettes. After pounding on the cigarette machine (showing the frustration that we talked about in Chapter 3), you are likely to find another cigarette machine, complain to the manager, or emit some other appropriate behavior. However, you are not likely to put more money in the offending machine at that time. This type of situation has been labeled *discriminated extinction.* In other words, you are discriminating a situation in which further responding on your part will be extinguished, and you are making this discrimination after one trial. The important thing to keep in mind, however, is that you have undoubtedly had similar experiences (or observed similar experiences had by others) in very similar situations. If we were to combine all of these situations, your discrimination would probably be seen to have developed over several trials. Alternatively, if we were to take a vending machine and a lot of money to a primitive culture, we would probably not observe the phenomenon of discriminated extinction in one trial. The point here is that when you observe the development of a discrimination in one trial, it is important to carefully evaluate the prior learning history of the individual before concluding that one-trial discrimination learning is common, or that the individual is a genius.

Study Questions on Notes

1. How does the technical definition of **stimulus control** differ from the simplified definition given in the text? Give examples in order to illustrate the difference.

2. Explain how different authorities have used the terms "contingency" and "dependency."

3. How might you explain the behavior of a child who is usually a "perfect angel" with one parent and a "holy terror" with the other? Briefly outline an experiment supporting your explanation.

4. What is an important inference about cultural control to be drawn from the littering study by Bergess et al.? Explain.

5. What is discriminated extinction? Explain in terms of S^Ds and S^Δs.

(Continued)

6. There are several things to consider when choosing a stimulus to be developed as an S^D. How were two of these considerations exemplified in the case of marriage counseling discussed by Goldiamond?

7. How would you go about using traditional discrimination training to teach a child to discriminate between the colors red and blue? How would you go about using Terrace's discrimination training for the same purpose? In each case, describe the general setting, procedures for each trial (stimuli, responses, consequences), and pretest and post-test for assessing the student's performance.

CHAPTER 8

Developing Appropriate Behavior With FADING

"Peter, what's your name?"

TEACHING PETER HIS NAME

Peter possessed an extensive mimicking repertoire (he could repeat many of the words other people said) but had little other verbal behavior.* He would mimic many words, even when it was not appropriate. For example, when asked "What's your name?" he would reply "Name." Sometimes he would repeat the entire question, "What's your name?" This was a problem of stimulus control in which questions (stimuli) evoked mimicking responses rather than appropriate answers.

*This case is taken from Martin, England, Kaprowy, Kilgour, and Pilek, (1968), and utilizes procedures first described by Risley and Wolf in a paper presented to the American Psychological Association in 1964 (and reprinted in Ulrich, Stachnik, and Mabry, 1966; pp. 193–198).

Using the following procedure, a university student, Veronica, taught Peter to respond appropriately to the question "What's your name?" First, Veronica identified an effective reinforcer. Since Peter had previously been taught to work for plastic tokens that could be exchanged for treats such as candy and popcorn, Veronica decided to use the tokens as reinforcers.

Peter sat at a small table in a quiet room, and Veronica sat across from him. In a very soft whisper, Veronica asked "What's your name?" then, very loudly and quickly and before Peter could respond, she shouted "PETER!" Of course, Peter mimicked the word "Peter," and Veronica reinforced this with "Good boy!" and a token. You may wonder how this could represent any progress, since the boy was still only mimicking the student. However, over several trials Veronica began asking the question "What's your name?" more loudly and began supplying the answer "Peter" more quietly. In each case, she continued to reinforce the correct response—"Peter." Eventually, Veronica asked loudly "What's your name?" and simply mouthed the word "Peter." Nevertheless, the boy responded with the correct answer, "Peter." Over several trials, Veronica ceased even mouthing the correct answer, but Peter still responded correctly to the question "What's your name?"

FADING

Fading is the gradual change of the stimulus controlling a response, such that the response eventually occurs to a partially changed or completely new stimulus. In the case described above, Peter would at first say his name only when it was said to him. Through a fading process, the stimulus control over the response "Peter" was gradually transferred from the stimulus "Peter" to the stimulus "What's your name?"

In any situation in which a stimulus exerts strong control over a response, fading can be a very useful procedure for changing the stimulus control. The discovery and development of fading techniques have led to some dramatic changes in educators' views regarding the learning process. At one time, it was felt that people had to make mistakes while learning in order to know what not to do. However, errorless transfer of a discrimination can occur, and it has at least three advantages over procedures involving trial and error. First, errors consume valuable time. Second, if an error occurs once, it tends to occur many times, even though it is being extinguished. (Remember from Chapter 3 that during extinction, "things may get worse before they get better.") Third, the nonreinforcement that occurs when errors are being extinguished often produces emotional side effects such as tantrums, aggressive behavior, and attempts to escape from the situation.

We have used fading procedures in many learning situations in our programs with retarded and autistic individuals.[1] In teaching students to name an item of clothing—a shirt, for example—teachers might proceed according to the following instructions:

1. Point to your shirt and say "shirt." Keep doing this until the student consistently mimics "shirt" a number of times, and immediately reinforce each correct response. (This assumes that you have a student who is able to mimic this particular word. It also assumes that the student has been trained to look at any item you point to.)

2. When the student consistently mimics "shirt," present the stimulus that you want to control the response, and at the same time gradually fade out the stimulus "shirt." That is, you might say, "What's this? Shirt" while pointing to the shirt. In response, the student usually mimics "shirt." Over several trials, gradually decrease the intensity of the stimulus "shirt" to zero, so that the student eventually responds with the answer "shirt" to the stimulus of someone pointing at his shirt and asking "What's this?" Again, each appropriate response is to be reinforced.

In this way, children can be taught to name a variety of objects. We have also used fading to teach other behaviors—for example, tracing, copying, and drawing circles, lines, squares, triangles, numerals, and letters of the alphabet. To teach a student to trace a circle, the teacher might begin with a large number of sheets on each of which is a heavily dotted circle. The teacher places a pencil in the student's hand, says "Trace the circle," and then guides his hand so that the pencil traces the circle by connecting the dots. Immediately after this, of course, the student receives a reinforcer. After several such trials, the teacher fades out the pressure of her hand as a cue controlling the student's tracing, by:

1. lightly holding the student's hand for several trials;
2. touching her fingertips to the back of the student's hand for several trials;
3. pointing to the item to be traced;
4. finally, simply giving the instruction, "Trace the circle." (Steps 1, 2, and 3 are always accompanied by this instruction.)

Once the teacher has taught the student to trace, she can teach him to draw or copy, by fading out the dotted cues that guide the tracing. For example, the teacher might use a sheet on which there are several dotted circles. The circles progress from a heavily dotted circle on the left to a circle with very few dots on the right. The teacher points to the most heavily dotted circle and instructs the student, "Trace the circle here." The desired response is reinforced, and the procedure is repeated for each of the more lightly dotted circles. On subsequent steps, the dots can be faded out completely so that the student will draw a circle in the absence of dots. It is then a simple matter to fade in the instruction "Draw a circle" to this newly acquired response. The instruction "Copy a circle," said while the teacher points to a circle, can also be faded in and come to control the response. Teaching the student to copy many different figures in this fashion will eventually enable him to adequately copy figures that he has had little or no experience copying.

Thus far, we have talked of fading in a rather restricted sense— that is, in the sense that fading can be used to change stimulus control when a specific response occurs to a rather specific stimulus (such as in the example in which the specific response "Peter" was brought under the control of specific stimulus "What's your name?"). Fading can also be used to maintain appropriate behaviors when the general situation changes. For example, in one of the authors' programs with autistic children, we wanted to have a group of autistic boys respond appropriately in a classroom setting (Martin et al, 1968). But these boys were very disruptive, especially in a group situation. This being the case, we could not at first place them in a classroom setting. Thus, we decided to first obtain the desired behavior from each child in an individual situation, and then fade in the classroom setting.

Our initial training sessions were conducted in a small room in which there were several chairs and tablet-arm desks. Two or three teachers (university students) worked individually with two or three students in a one-to-one ratio. The procedures involved eliminating tantrums through extinction, and reinforcing sitting attentively, appropriate verbal behavior, drawing, copying, and other desirable behaviors. Each child's desk was placed against the wall in such a fashion as to make it difficult for him to leave the situation.

Within one week, the children learned to sit quietly, attend to the teacher, and mimic words in verbal training. Stimulus control was established between the general training situation and the children's attentiveness. But our goal at that time was to teach the children to sit quietly in a regular classroom situation with one teacher at the front of the class. If we had switched immediately to this situation after the first week, however, much inattentiveness and disruptive behavior would no doubt have occurred. Therefore, over a period of four weeks, we gradually changed from one small room with three students and three teachers to a standard-size classroom with seven students and one teacher. This fading occurred along two stimulus dimensions.

One dimension was the physical structure of the room. We moved the children from the small room to the regular large classroom. However, we did so by first placing the three tablet-arm desks against the wall of the regular classroom, just as we had done in the small room. The three chairs that the teachers sat in were also moved to the regular classroom. The rest of the classroom was empty. Over several days, the tablet-arm desks were gradually moved away from the wall and toward the center of the room until, finally, the three desks were side by side. Additional desks and furnishings were added one at a time until the children were finally sitting in desks in a normally furnished classroom.

The second dimension was the number of children per teacher. Fading along this dimension was carried out at the same time that fading along the first dimension took place. At first, one teacher worked with one student for several sessions. The teacher then worked with two students, alternating questions between them for several sessions. In this fashion, the student/teacher ratio was gradually increased until only one teacher worked with as many as seven children in a classroom situation.

It can be seen from this case that fading procedures can be useful in generalizing the results of training in a controlled, relatively simple situation to the more complex settings that exist in society at large.[2] The problem of generalizing the results of behavior modification to the "real world" will be discussed in more detail in Chapter 11.

Extreme care should be taken to avoid confusing fading with shaping. Both are procedures of gradual change. However, as described in Chapter 4, shaping involves reinforcement of slight changes in a behavior so that it gradually comes to resemble the target behavior. The stimulus situation generally stays about the same, and the behavior changes from an initial behavior (not necessarily resembling the target) to the final target behavior. Fading, on the other hand, involves reinforcement of a specific response in the presence of slight changes in a stimulus so that the stimulus gradually comes to resemble the stimulus that you wish to control that particular response. Thus, *shaping involves the gradual change of a response while the stimulus stays about the same; fading involves the gradual change of a stimulus while the response stays about the same.*

USING FADING PROCEDURES TO TEACH VERBAL SKILLS TO SEVERELY RETARDED AND AUTISTIC CHILDREN

Because of the importance of language skills in our culture, we would like to indicate in some detail the potential use of fading procedures in this area. We are not going to describe a completely self-contained, highly detailed training program for the development of language. Such programs are described elsewhere (see, for example, Kent, 1974). Rather, we would like to talk about some procedures that relied heavily on fading and were used successfully to develop extensive verbal skills in severely retarded and autistic children.

The first step in many verbal-training programs involves the use of reinforcement procedures to teach motor and sound imitations. Let us suppose that this has already been accomplished. One can then use a fading procedure to teach the student to imitate words. For example, to teach the student to mimic "cat," present the following cue: "Say 'cat.' Caa ... tuh." Wait until the student mimics "caa" before presenting the stimulus "tuh." Reinforce the student immediately after he correctly imitates the last sound (in this case, "tuh"). Continue doing this, and at the same time gradually fade out the stimulus "tuh." (One reason for fading out "tuh" before fading out "caa" is that over several trials, "caa" will become a strong stimulus for evoking "tuh." Moreover, the response "tuh" is followed more immediately by reinforcement, and should therefore be easier to maintain as some of its stimulus support is gradually removed.)

Now you have the student responding with "caa ... tuh" to the stimulus "Say 'cat.' Caa." The next step is to fade out the "caa." You will then have a student who responds with "caa ... tuh" to the stimulus "Say 'cat.' "

After reinforcing this last behavior a number of times to make sure it is strong, you can now teach a new word by using the same procedure. Keep giving the student occasional practice with words that have been learned, in order to make sure that they remain strong.

But, you may ask, shouldn't the student be taught next to say "cat" instead of "caa ... tuh"? This is perhaps a reasonable approach, but it may be better not to bother with it at this stage. Over a number of trials in the natural environment, the student will very likely begin running the sounds of words together and then pronouncing them just like everyone else. Even if this does not happen, it may be better to teach a large number of words that are pronounced imperfectly than to spend a great deal of time teaching a few words perfectly. Being able to communicate would seem to deserve priority over impeccable pronounciation.

When the student imitates a number of sounds and words, he can then be taught to name a variety of objects. In many cases, the object the teacher wishes to teach the individual to name will not be readily available. In our verbal-training programs, therefore, we use literally hundreds of pictures that have been purchased from educational supply companies or cut out of magazines and catalogues and pasted on pieces of cardboard. We then use fading to teach the student to name the pictures. One picture at a time is taught, but it is always alternated, over trials, with a picture the student has already learned. This ensures that the student is actually naming the picture and not just repeating the same word. After the student has been taught several words, we find that the fading procedure is often no longer necessary. The student learns to respond with the name of the object after he has simply been told what it is.

Teaching an individual with limited verbal behavior to name objects does not proceed easily. It requires tremendous patience: often, it appears that no progress is occurring, or even that ground is being lost. Remember, however, that even a normal child requires several years to learn to talk in a rudimentary fashion. Our experience has been that one can often see good progress with even severely retarded individuals after three to six months of one one-hour sessions per day—especially if the individual is quite young.

When the student can name a number of objects, training may proceed in a variety of directions. Regardless of the particular direction the teacher decides upon, fading procedures can be very helpful. Consider the following use of fading to teach an eight-year-old autistic boy to count objects.* Danny had participated in a token-reinforcement program in which he earned poker chips that could be exchanged for food, candy, and other goodies. He had increased his attention span and had learned to identify and recite the numerals 1 through 10. To teach Danny to count up to ten objects, the teachers developed a detailed training procedure that utilized fading. Danny was required to complete ten consecutive correct trials at each of six steps before progressing to the next step. Whenever Danny made an error on any step after step 1, he was moved back to the previous step and again required to complete that step correctly on ten consecutive trials in order to advance. After Danny had progressed successfully through all six steps for a given numeral, he was returned to step 1 for the next numeral. The steps were as follows:

Step 1. Danny received a sheet of white paper with a numeral printed on the upper right-hand corner and a corresponding number of circles drawn on the paper (see Figure 8-1A). A trial began with the teacher pointing to the numeral, such as 5, in the upper right-hand corner of the page and asking, "Danny, what number is this?" Danny consistently identified the numeral 5 correctly, to which the teacher responded, "Good boy Danny. Put five circles on the paper." Danny then filled the outlined circles with circles cut from orange felt and received approval and a token. If Danny responded incorrectly, the teacher said "no" and demonstrated the correct response. After ten consecutive correct trials, Danny was moved to step 2 of the training procedure for that particular numeral.

Step 2. The procedure remained the same as in step 1, except that the outlines of the circles were finer (see Figure 8-1B).

Step 3. The procedure was the same as in step 1, except that the outlines of the circles were now broken lines (see Figure 8-1C).

Step 4. The procedure was the same as in step 1, except that the paper on Danny's desk was now blank, with only the numeral printed in the top right-hand corner (see Figure 8-1D).

Step 5. The procedure was the same as in step 1, except that the sheet of pa-

*This case is taken from Murrell, Hardy, and Martin (1974), and is paraphrased by permission of the publisher.

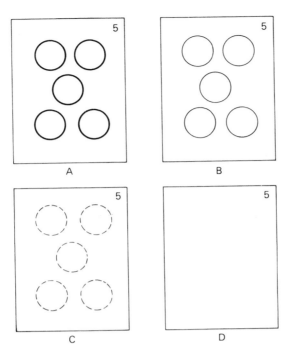

FIGURE 8-1. *The stimulus sheets used in Danny's fading program.*

per was not placed on Danny's desk. Instead, at the start of the trial Danny was shown the appropriate numeral cut from felt material and asked, "Danny, what number is this?" When Danny correctly identified the numeral, such as 5, the teacher said, "Good boy, Danny. Now place five circles on your desk." After correctly doing this, he received reinforcement. As in all previous steps, Danny had to complete ten consecutive trials correctly before moving on to the next step.

Step 6. The procedure was the same as in step 5, except that Danny was required to place the appropriate number of orange circles in the teacher's hand rather than on the desk. Following Danny's correct identification of the numeral, such as 5, the teacher held out her hand and said, "Good boy, Danny. Now give me five circles." On the first trial of step 6, the teacher held her hand on the desk. During the second through the fifth trials, the teacher gradually raised her hand off the desk and held it in midair directly in front of Danny. During the last few trials, Danny was taking the correct number of circles from a pile and placing them in the teacher's hand.

After Danny completed ten consecutive trials in step 6, the numeral was considered learned. He was then taught to count the next numeral, proceeding through the same six steps. In this way, Danny learned to count objects for all of the numerals 1 through 10. Danny made only six errors in the entire training program. You can see how fading was utilized in several different ways in this program.

FACTORS INFLUENCING THE EFFECTIVENESS OF FADING

1. Choosing the target stimulus control — should occur in the natural environment.

It is important to select the target stimulus (the stimulus you want to eventually control the behavior) such that the occurrence of the response to that particular stimulus is likely to be maintained in the natural environment. Many fading programs make the error of stopping with a target stimulus control that does not include some aspect of a stimulus that the student will frequently encounter in the natural environment. Consider Danny's case. It would have been easy for the teachers to stop training after step 5, for Danny was clearly counting out the correct number of circles and placing them on his desk when asked to do so. However, classroom observation indicates that a more natural occurrence is for a teacher to approach a student, hold out her hand, and ask him to give her a specific number of objects. The training program was therefore carried on through step 6. Moreover, the teachers conducted further training with Danny: following step 6, he was asked to count out other items (such as bingo chips, wooden blocks, and puzzle pieces of varying sizes, shapes, and colors) under the training procedure utilized in step 6.

2. Choosing the starting stimulus control

It is important to select an initial stimulus that reliably evokes the desired behavior. In Danny's training program, the teacher knew that Danny would place a felt circle on the heavy outline of a circle if there was only one such outline on the piece of paper in front of him. Therefore, that was the starting stimulus control selected to teach Danny to count. In the task of teaching Peter his name, Veronica knew that Peter would mimic the last word of a question if that word was spoken loudly. Therefore, the starting stimulus control with Peter was the question, "What's your name?" said very softly and followed quickly by the shouted answer, "Peter!"

The stimuli that are presented to insure the occurrence of a response are sometimes referred to as prompts. In order to carefully identify the stimulus dimensions to be faded, it is helpful to distinguish among *verbal prompts,* which are verbal hints or cues, *gestural prompts,* certain motions the teacher makes without touching the student, *environmental prompts,* in which the environment is altered in a manner that will evoke the desired behavior, and *physical prompts* (also called *physical guidance),* in which she touches the student to guide him. The teacher may provide any or all of these stimulus dimensions in order to ensure the correct response. For example, suppose that the teacher wishes to develop appropriate stimulus control of the instruction "Touch your head" over the response of the student touching his head. The teacher might initiate training by saying, "Touch your head. Raise your hand and put it on your head like this," while touching his own head. In this example, "Raise your hand and put it on your head like this" is a verbal prompt, the teacher's action of putting his hand on his head is a gestural prompt. Selecting several kinds of prompts that, together, reliably produce the desired response will minimize errors and maximize the success of the fading program.[3]

3. Choosing the fading steps

When the desired response is reliably occurring to the prompts given at the onset of the training program, the prompts can then be gradually removed over trials. The steps through which the prompts are to be eliminated should be carefully chosen. Unfortunately, effective use of fading is, like effective use of shaping, still somewhat of an art. It is very important to monitor the student's performance closely in order to determine the speed at which fading should be carried out. If the student begins to make errors, then the prompts have been faded too quickly or through too few fading steps. It is then necessary to backtrack until the behavior is again well established before continuing with fading. On the other hand, if too many steps are introduced or too many prompts are provided over a number of trials, the student might become overly dependent on the prompts. Consider the example of teaching a child to touch his head when asked to do so. If the teacher spends a great many trials providing the prompt of touching her own head, the child may become dependent on it and attend much less to the instruction "Touch your head."

PITFALLS OF FADING: HOW IT WORKS TO THE DISADVANTAGE OF THOSE WHO ARE IGNORANT OF IT

Just as other behavior principles can be applied unknowingly by those who are not familiar with them, so can fading be misused. However, it appears to be more difficult to inadvertently misuse fading because the necessary gradual change in cues rarely occurs by chance.

The case of the child who banged his head on hard surfaces (described in Chapter 7) might be an example of the effects of the misuse of fading. On p. 65, we mentioned that shaping might produce such behavior. It is also possible that fading is responsible for it. Suppose that the child initially began attracting attention by hitting his head on soft surfaces, such as grass. At first, this behavior may have caused adults to come running to see if the child had injured himself. When they eventually learned that no injury resulted from this behavior, they ceased providing it with attention. The child may then have progressed to hitting his head with the same force but on slightly harder surfaces, such as carpeted floors. For awhile, this perhaps increased the amount of attention elicited from adults, but this amount of attention may eventually have decreased when the adults learned that the child did not injure himself in this way. Only when the child graduated to hitting his head on surfaces such as hard floors and even concrete, which caused real and serious self-injury, did the adults give him continued attention. Note that throughout this example there was a gradual change in the stimulus (the type of floor surface) evoking the undesired behavior; eventually, the behavior was evoked by the most undesirable stimulus possible.

GUIDELINES FOR THE EFFECTIVE APPLICATION OF FADING

1. _Choosing the target stimulus control_. Specify very clearly the conditions in the presence of which the target behavior should eventually occur.
2. _Selecting an appropriate reinforcer._ See Figure 2-2 and p. 32.
3. _Choosing the starting stimulus control and the fading steps._
   a) Specify clearly the conditions under which the desired behavior now occurs — that is, what people, words, physical guidance, and so forth, are necessary, at present, to evoke the desired behavior.
   b) Specify clearly the dimensions (such as color, people, and room size) that you will fade in order to reach the desired stimulus control.
   c) Outline the specific fading steps to be followed, and the rules for moving from one step to the next.
4. _Putting the plan into effect._
   a) The fading of cues should be so gradual that there are as few errors as possible. However, if an error occurs, move back to the previous step for several trials and provide additional prompts.
   b) When the desired stimulus control is obtained, review the guidelines in previous chapters for weaning the student from the program (a topic that is discussed in more detail in Chapter 11).

Study Questions •

(for examination purposes)

1. Define fading and give an example of it.
2. Why is it advantageous to establish stimulus control without errors?
   errors take up time
   make it harder to learn

3. Identify three stimulus dimensions along which fading occurred in the examples cited in the first two sections of this chapter.

4. Describe an example from this chapter in which the training situation remained constant but a specific dimension was faded.

5. Describe an example from this chapter in which the general training situation was faded but the specific training stimuli remained relatively constant.

6. Describe how you might use fading to teach your pet to perform a trick. Describe how you might use shaping to teach your pet to perform another trick. Drawing from your example, clearly distinguish between fading and shaping.

7. Assume that you have an eighteen-month-old child who will imitate the word "chip." Describe in detail how you might use fading to teach your child to correctly identify a chip (i.e., a potato chip) when you point to it and ask "What's that?"

8. Describe two ways in which fading was used in the program through which Danny learned to count. — *physical guidance* , *visual guidance*

9. What do we mean by *target stimulus control*? Give an example.

10. What do we mean by *starting stimulus control*? Give an example, and explain what the target stimulus control would be for your example.

11. What are the four major categories of prompts? Give examples from this chapter. *physical , verbal , gestural , environmental*

12. How many reinforced trials should occur at any given fading step before the stimuli of that particular step are changed? (Hint: What suggestions were made in the examples in this chapter?) *(5-10)*

Study Exercises

(to be practiced by the reader)

1. Suppose that a two-year-old child has reached the stage where he is beginning to "explore" the surrounding neighborhood. The child has already learned some speech, and you wish to teach him to answer the question, "Where do you live?" Outline a fading program with which you could teach the answer to this question: indicate what you would use as a reinforcer, the number of trials you would have at each fading step, and so forth.

2. Assume that you must teach a severely retarded child, or a very young normal child, to eat with a spoon. Outline a program in which you would use all four of the major categories of prompts. Describe how each of the prompts would be faded.

3. Suppose that the official temperature scale has been switched recently from Fahrenheit to Celsius (i.e., centigrade). The government has assigned you the job of designing an effective program for teaching citizens to respond knowledgeably to the Celsius scale. You have been given complete freedom to work with the radio and television weather announcers. Describe a plan that would accomplish this task. Include a precise statement of your target stimulus control, your starting stimulus control, and the fading steps you would use.

Self-Modification Exercise

(to be practiced by the reader)

A self-modification exercise in Chapter 7 required you to list the current stimulus control and the target stimulus control of one of your behavioral inappropriatenesses. Indicate in detail how you might use fading to transfer the stimulus control in order to overcome your behavioral inappropriateness. (Cite the guidelines for the effective application of fading that you would follow.)

EXTENDED DISCUSSION AND NOTES

1. In addition, fading has been used cleverly by Meyerson and Michael (1964) to diagnose the level of hearing of children who were presumed to be moderately retarded. These authors wanted to determine if the behavioral problems of the children were due to poor hearing or to other conditions. The authors first designed an experimental testing room in which two small levers were placed directly below two light bulbs, each arranged on a console so that it was difficult to press both levers simultaneously. The children were taught to press the lever underneath the light bulb that was lit. When they did so, they were reinforced with candy, toys, and other items. The children soon learned to press the lever under the light that was lit, and to switch to the other lever when that light bulb went off and the opposite light bulb went on. The schedule of reinforcement was then changed to VR 8. The next step in the program consisted of presenting a loud sound (one that was approximately in the middle of the frequency range of normal hearing) each time the light bulb on the left was illuminated. When that light went off and the opposite light was illuminated, the sound terminated. Fading was then introduced: over a number of alternations of the two lights, during which the loud tone was presented whenever the left light was illuminated and was not presented whenever the right light was illuminated, the intensity of the lights was gradually diminished until they were not presented at all. The result of this fading procedure was that the children learned to press the left lever when the tone was presented and to press the right lever when there was no sound. The children were finally ready to be tested for their hearing. Over a number of trials, the intensity of the sound was gradually changed. In other trials, the frequency of the sound was changed as well. At the point where the children's lever pressing no longer correlated with the presence or absence of the tone, Meyerson and Michael knew that they had encountered a hearing deficiency. Thus, by using a fading technique Meyerson and Michael were able to determine that some of the children had been diagnosed as moderately retarded due to brain damage when in fact their behavioral handicaps were due at least in part to poor hearing.

2. An interesting example of generalizing the results of training was reported by Conrad, Delk, and Williams (1974). The problem concerned an eleven-year-old American Indian girl who interacted normally with

(Continued)

selected friends, siblings, and her parents but would not speak in the classroom. According to school officials and written records, the child had been totally mute in the classroom for the entire five years of her school attendance. Thus, the behavior of answering questions was in her repertoire, but it was not under the desired stimulus control. Training sessions consisted of reinforcing the girl (initially with candy, and later tokens exchangeable for candy) for answering questions about flash cards. This behavior occurred in settings that were gradually faded into the classroom according to the following steps:

Session 1: conducted in the girl's home on the reservation, with her mother and a mental health worker (male tribal member) present; consisted of initial instructions in the girl's Indian language.

Sessions 2 and 3: conducted in the home by the mental health worker, but with the mother absent.

Sessions 4 and 5: conducted in a psychology clinic on the reservation, with the mental health worker and a classmate present.

Sessions 6–9: conducted in the clinic, with the mental health worker, classmate, and teacher present.

Session 10: conducted in the classroom, with five classmates and the teacher present.

Sessions 11 and 12: conducted in the classroom with the entire class and the teacher present.

In a one year follow-up the girl was still responding satisfactorily to the teacher in classroom situations.

3. An interesting example of combining a variety of prompts was reported by Mahoney, VanWagenen, and Meyerson (1971) in their description of a program to train normal and retarded children to walk to the toilet. They utilized verbal prompts (the instruction "Let's go potty"), environmental prompts (toys placed near the entrance to the toilet, and an auditory signal presented concurrently with the verbal prompts), and guidance (taking the child by the hand). These prompts were faded out as the children learned to approach the toilet on their own. For a description of the detailed fading steps, see Mahoney et al.

Study Questions on Notes

1. Describe how the Meyerson-Michael procedure might be adapted so as to test for red-green color blindness in severely retarded children who have very little speech.

2. Does the program you designed for the previous question use the same general classes of prompts utilized by Mahoney et al. in their toilet-training program?

3. What two general dimensions were faded in the case of the eleven-year-old American Indian girl who would not speak in the classroom?

CHAPTER 9

Developing
and Maintaining
Behavior With
CONDITIONED
REINFORCEMENT

*"Johnny, would you like to
cash in your pegs?"*

JOHNNY'S TOKEN-REINFORCEMENT PROGRAM

As a beginning teacher at the St. Amant Centre, Nickie Martin was confronted with a classroom of ten rowdy, retarded children.* In the midst of
this "bedlam," she was faced with the problem of consistently applying
positive reinforcement to each child for desirable behavior while con-
tending with the disruptive behavior of others.

　　The solution she adopted involved, in a sense, teaching each child to
reinforce his or her own good behavior. Nickie worked with each child individually while an aide temporarily "baby-sat" with the other children.

*This case study is based on an unpublished progress report submitted by Nickie Mar-
tin, Joseph Pear, and Garry Martin to the St. Amant Centre, an institution for retarded
children in Winnipeg, Manitoba.

Seating the first child, Johnny, at a table, she placed before him a board containing five rows of five holes in each. A wooden peg was placed in the hole at the top left-hand corner, and all the other holes were covered with tape. When Johnny attended by looking at her, she immediately said, "Good boy, Johnny! Cash in your peg." Taking the child's hand, she guided him to remove the peg and give it to her. Immediately following this action, Johnny was given a small candy, a potato chip, or some other agreeable item. Over a number of trials, the guidance was faded out so that eventually Johnny would hand Nickie the peg, upon request, without any assistance.

In the next step, there was no peg in the board. But near the board was a small jar of pegs. When Johnny attended to her, Nickie said, "Johnny, take a peg," and then guided his hand into the jar and helped him put the peg in the board. Then she said, "Johnny, cash in your peg," and presented reinforcement when he complied. Over several trials, the guidance for taking the peg was faded out; eventually Johnny would take the peg and put it in the board on request, as well as remove it and hand it to Nickie for reinforcement when told to cash it in. The interval between these two instructions was then gradually increased, so that Johnny would sit for some time with the peg in the board. If he manipulated the peg when not instructed to do so, it was taken forcefully from his hand and he was ignored for five seconds.

Let us pause for a moment and review the behavior sequence that had thus far been established. Johnny would sit quietly until Nickie said, "Johnny, take a peg." He would then reach into the jar, take a peg, and place it in the board. After waiting a brief period, Nickie would say, "Johnny, cash in your peg." He would then take the peg out of the board and hand it to her. The entire sequence would then be reinforced with something he liked, such as a bite of candy, or potato chip.

After the above chain had been established, it was a relatively simple matter to teach Johnny to collect several pegs before cashing them all in for reinforcement. Recall that in the first phase of the procedure, all holes except the one in the top left-hand corner were covered with tape. In the next phase, Nickie uncovered the hole immediately to the right of that one and taught Johnny to place two pegs in the board. She did this by instructing him twice to take a peg and then asking him to "cash in" his pegs for reinforcement. Eventually, Johnny would collect five pegs, place each in its appropriate hole, and return all of them for reinforcement when given the corresponding instruction.

At this point, you may be saying, "So what? Perhaps this is a good way to teach a manual-dexterity task, but how does it solve the problem we started with? How does it help us cope with a classroom full of boisterous kids?" The answer is that once all the children had been trained in the above manner, Nickie's job of managing reinforcers for each child was greatly facilitated. First, she could administer reinforcement immediately simply by telling the child to take a peg. Second, simply by noting the number of pegs in each child's board, she could easily monitor the number of reinforcements each child received and thus maintain an adequate amount of reinforcement for each. Adequate reinforcement was insured in three ways: (1) each child worked at his or her own level (for some children, merely attending to the teacher earned reinforcers; for others, complex verbal responses to questions were required); (2) children who might earn fewer reinforcers were not required to collect as many pegs to cash in for goodies as were children capable of earning more reinforcers; (3) Nickie alternated trials among the children in such a manner as to insure that each child received reinforcement frequently enough to maintain the behaviors of sitting attentively and responding appropriately. Thus, the number of pegs in each child's board served as S^Ds to control Nickie's behavior.

Of course, the pegs were reinforcing mainly because they could be cashed in for something else that was reinforcing. That is, the "value" of the pegs was strengthened by other reinforcers, which were called *back-up reinforcers*. In order to maintain the reinforcing value of the pegs, Nickie had to let each child cash in his pegs for a back-up reinforcer after he had earned a specified number of pegs. Although the procedure greatly facilitated the task of administering reinforcement to each child in a group situation, the problem remained of having to interrupt the class to provide back-up reinforcement to children who had earned the required number of pegs. Nickie solved this problem by instituting two daily "store-time" periods. During one half-hour period in the morning and one half-hour period in the afternoon, the children were allowed to buy back-up reinforcers. The available back-up reinforcers were consumable (such as popcorn, potato chips, and candy), activity (such as helping the teacher clean up the classroom and participating in a game), manipulative (such as a toy or puzzle), and possessional (such as wearing a favorite hat). Any reinforcer that could be administered during store-time was used. The price of each reinforcer (that is, the number of pegs required to buy it) differed for different children. The more desirable the reinforcer to a particular child (as determined by how many times in the past he selected it), the higher its price. Also, the more pegs a child could earn, the more he had to pay. Some children spent all their pegs during each store-time. Others saved for days in order to purchase more expensive items. It can be seen that in addition to enabling Nickie to efficiently manage the task, the peg system she established taught the children concepts they would later find useful when they learned how to use and save money.

CONDITIONED REINFORCEMENT

If a stimulus indicates that reinforcement is forthcoming, then that stimulus itself becomes reinforcing. In the above example, pegs become reinforcing to the children because a child could receive back-up reinforcement if he had enough pegs but would not receive it if he did not have enough.

A stimulus is called a *conditioned reinforcer* if it is not originally reinforcing, but acquires reinforcing power through association with a stimulus that *is* reinforcing. The pegs Nickie used in her class were not originally reinforcing to the children. No child would have worked very hard, if at all, to get pegs for their own sake. The children worked hard because the pegs could be cashed in for very strong back-up reinforcers. Another example of conditioned reinforcement is praise, which seems to acquire its reinforcing power from its association with various kinds of reinforcing events. For example, when Nickie said, "Good boy, Johnny," this verbal stimulus was associated with the same back-up reinforcers with which the pegs were associated.

Reinforcers such as popcorn and candy are usually reinforcing in themselves. Some children just "naturally" like them. Stimuli such as these are called *primary reinforcers.** Back-up reinforcers can be, but need not be, primary reinforcers. Conditioned reinforcers can also serve as back-up reinforcers. For example, money is quite effective as a back-up reinforcer for a valid check or for poker chips on a gambling table. But money is a conditioned reinforcer, not a primary reinforcer, because no one would work for money if it could not ultimately be exchanged for items that are more reinforcing, such as food, clothing, shelter, transportation, and entertainment.

Conditioned reinforcers that can be accumulated and exchanged for other reinforcers are called *tokens.* A behavior modification program that uses tokens is called a *token system* or a *token economy.* Just about anything that can be accumulated can be used as the medium of exchange in a token system (see figure 9-1). Pegs are a good example. In some token systems individuals earn plastic discs (such as poker chips), which they can retain until they are ready to cash them in for back-up reinforcers (see Martin et al., 1968). In other token systems they are paid with "paper money," on which is written the amount earned, the individual's name, the name of the employee who paid him, the date, and the task the individual performed to earn the token (see Logan, 1970). In still others, individuals receive points, which are recorded on a chart beside their name or in notebooks they keep with them (see Phillips, 1968). Superficially at least, this last system seems similar to the old, familiar procedure whereby teachers award stars to children for good performance. But this longstanding procedure, as commonly practiced, is not really a token system in the strict sense, because of the absence in it of clearly specified, consistently administered, and effective back-up reinforcers.

Tokens constitute one type of conditioned reinforcer, but stimuli that cannot be accumulated can also be conditioned reinforcers. A common example, as mentioned above, is praise. A mother who expresses her pleasure at her child's good behavior is simultaneously disposed to smile at the child, hug him, play with him, and give him a treat or a toy. Praise is normally established as a conditioned reinforcer during childhood, but it continues to be maintained as one for adults. This is because when people praise us, they are generally

---

*Another name for primary reinforcer is *unconditioned reinforcer* (that is, a stimulus that is reinforcing without being conditioned).

FIGURE 9-1. *Examples of tokens.*

more likely to favor us in various ways than when they do not praise us.[1]

Although it is normal for praise to become a conditioned reinforcer, this does not hold true in the case of some behaviorally handicapped people. Perhaps for them, no one ever associated praise with effective back-up reinforcers. Indeed, this may be one reason for their behavioral handicaps. Praise is used so commonly as a reinforcer in our society that any individual for whom it is not reinforcing cannot be expected to acquire very many socially desirable behaviors. It would seem that such an individual would almost necessarily become behaviorally handicapped—no matter what the "innate potential" for her intellectual and other social development might be. Of course, if her "innate potential" is not very great to begin with, she may emit socially desirable behavior so rarely that people in her natural environment seldom or never praise her. Thus, her lack of contact with praise precludes it from becoming a conditioned reinforcer, which makes it even more difficult for her to develop socially desirable behaviors.

It follows that those working with behaviorally handicapped people should ensure that praise becomes a conditioned reinforcer for them. In training programs, this is typically done by praising desirable behavior just prior to presenting other types of reinforcement (recall Nickie's "Good boy, Johnny! Take a peg."). The praise then serves as immediate feedback that is reinforcing because it signals that something nice is about to happen.

Before closing this section we might briefly mention the principle of *conditioned punishment,* which is very similar to that of conditioned reinforcement. Just as a stimulus that signals reinforcement becomes reinforcing itself, so a stimulus that signals punishment becomes punishing itself. "No!" and "Stop that!" are examples of stimuli that become conditioned punishers, because they are often followed by punishment if the individual continues to engage in the behavior that provoked them. Moreover, punishing tokens as well as reinforcing ones are possible. The demerit system used in the military is an example of a punishing-token system. There are, however, problems associated with the use of punishment (see Chapter 12).

FACTORS INFLUENCING THE EFFECTIVENESS OF CONDITIONED REINFORCEMENT

1. The Strength of the Back-up Reinforcers.

The reinforcing power of a conditioned reinforcer depends in part upon the reinforcing power of the back-up reinforcer on which it is based. For example, suppose that Nickie had used only potato chips as a back-up reinforcer. In that case, the pegs would have been effective reinforcers only with children for whom potato chips were an effective reinforcer. Pegs would not have been reinforcing with any child who had "had his fill" of potato chips, was very thirsty, or just was not fond of potato chips.

2. The Variety of Back-up Reinforcers

The reinforcing power of a conditioned reinforcer depends in part on the number of different back-up reinforcers available for it. This factor is related to the one above in that if there are many different back-up reinforcers available, then at any given time at least one of them will probably be strong enough to maintain tokens at a high reinforcing strength for any individual in the program. A conditioned reinforcer that is based on a number of different back-up reinforcers is called a *generalized reinforcer*. Thus, the pegs in Nickie's classroom were generalized reinforcers. Money is another example of a generalized reinforcer because it can be exchanged for an almost unlimited variety of reinforcers. This is why it can keep people occupied day after day in its pursuit.

3. The Schedule of Pairing with the Back-Up Reinforcer

In Chapter 5, we saw that behavior is more persistent if reinforcement does not follow every occurrence of the target behavior. Likewise, conditioned reinforcement is more effective if back-up reinforcement does not follow each occurrence of the conditioned reinforcer. For example, the children in Nickie's program had to earn a certain number of tokens before they were given back-up reinforcement.

4. Extinction of the Conditioned Reinforcer

For a conditioned reinforcer to remain effective, it must continue to be associated with a suitable back-up reinforcer(s). Had Nickie discontinued store-time in her program, the children would eventually have stopped working for the pegs. Ceasing to provide back-up reinforcement for a conditioned reinforcer is called *extinction of a conditioned reinforcer* and is similar to the procedure described in Chapter 3 for extinguishing a response.

PITFALLS OF CONDITIONED REINFORCEMENT: HOW IT WORKS TO THE DISADVANTAGE OF THOSE WHO ARE IGNORANT OF IT

People who are unfamiliar with the principle of conditioned reinforcement may unknowingly misapply it in various ways. One very common misapplication occurs when an adult scolds a child for behaving inappropriately, but (1) does not provide any type of "back-up punishment" (see Chapter 12) along with the scolding, and (2) does not reinforce desirable alternative behavior. The scolding, no doubt, is given in the expectation that it will be punishing, but often this is not the case. Indeed, the attention that accompanies such negative verbal stimuli may even be highly reinforcing, especially for behaviorally handicapped individuals, who often do not receive much attention from adults. In this way, scoldings and other negative verbal stimuli (such as "No!") can become conditioned reinforcers, and the individual will behave inappropriately in order to obtain them.

Indeed, even stimuli that are normally punishing can become conditioned reinforcers through association with powerful primary reinforcers. The classic example is the parent who spanks a child for misbehavior and then "feeling guilty" from the ensuing piteous crying, immediately hugs the child and gives her ice cream or some other tasty treat. The possible outcome of this unthinking procedure is that the child will develop a "liking for lickings"; that is, the spanking could become a conditioned reinforcer that would maintain, not eliminate, the misbehavior it follows.

Extinction of a conditioned reinforcer can be unknowingly applied with unfortunate results by those who are unfamiliar with this aspect of conditioned reinforcement. An example of this is a teacher who awards stars for good behavior but fails to use effective back-up reinforcers. The result is that the stars eventually lose whatever reinforcing power they may have had when they were first introduced.

GUIDELINES FOR THE EFFECTIVE USE OF CONDITIONED REINFORCEMENT

The following guidelines should be observed in applying conditioned reinforcement.[2]

1. A conditioned reinforcer should be a stimulus that can be easily managed and administered in the situation in which you plan to use it. For example, pegs were ideally suited for the children in Nickie's classroom. For more advanced individuals moving freely in a large environment, other items may be more appropriate.

2. As much as possible, use the same conditioned reinforcers that the individual will encounter in the natural environment. For example, Nickie did not just tell Johnny to take a peg when he behaved appropriately; she always said, "Good boy, Johnny! Take a peg." Because "Good boy" was followed by the instruction "Take a peg," and because pegs were backed up by powerful reinforcers, "Good boy" also became reinforcing. Now, when Johnny hears "Good boy" in the natural environment (for instance, from his parents), he will be more likely to continue to engage in the behavior that evoked this stimulus.

   Carrying this rule still further, it is desirable in training programs to transfer control from artificial-token systems (such as pegs) to the monetary-token system used in the natural environment. Of course, this goal would have to be approached through gradual steps in a carefully planned long-range program. Such a program might consist of moving from pegs to different-colored plastic chips (the different colors representing different values), to play money, and finally to real money with which the individuals could make purchases at the local store or canteen. Along the way, of course, the individuals would have to be taught some basic arithmetic so that they could correctly count change.

3. In the early stages of establishing a conditioned reinforcer, back-up reinforcement should be presented as quickly as possible after the presentation of the conditioned reinforcer. Later the delay between conditioned reinforcement and the back-up reinforcement can be gradually increased, if desired.

4. Use generalized conditioned reinforcers wherever possible; that is, use many different types of back-up reinforcers, not just one. This way, at least one of the back-up reinforcers will probably be strong enough at any given time to maintain the power of the conditioned reinforcer.

5. The number of tokens that each individual in a token system should be required to pay for a given back-up reinforcer should be directly related to the strength of the back-up reinforcer for that individual. In other words, charge each individual more for the reinforcers she finds more desirable. This will ensure efficient use of the back-up reinforcers. (Note that because various back-up reinforcers differ in their value for different individuals, some individuals will be charged more for the same back-up reinforcer. This should not cause any problems if the following rule is observed.)

6. When the program involves more than one individual (as was the case in Nickie's classroom), avoid destructive competition for conditioned and back-up reinforcers. If one person receives reinforcement to the detriment of another, this may evoke aggressive behavior in the second individual and/or his desirable behavior may extinguish. This rule implies in particular that one should avoid making an issue out of the fact that one individual is earning more conditioned and back-up reinforcement than another. Of course, people differ in their abilities, but the bad effects of these differences can be minimized by designing programs such that each individual earns a good deal of reinforcement for performing at his own level.

7. Let an individual sample back-up reinforcers that she is unwilling to buy with her tokens. *Reinforcer sampling,* as this is called, will increase the reinforcing value of the tokens because it adds to the number of back-up reinforcers that an individual might actually purchase.* (The rationale here

---

*Reinforcer sampling was discussed in Chapter 4, note 1, with reference to Ayllon and Azrin (1968a).

is similar to the one that prompts companies to distribute free samples of a new product.) In some cases, individuals may work for tokens and then refuse to exchange them for any back-up reinforcement. In these cases, as well as less extreme ones, an effective reinforcer-sampling procedure might be to expose the individual to the back-up reinforcer for a short period of time and then require her to cash in some tokens in order to retain the reinforcer for a longer period. For example, a child may be given a toy to play with for one minute and then be required to pay five tokens in order to retain it for five minutes. Or she may be taken to a movie theater, and then be required to pay ten tokens in order to go inside to watch the movie.

8. Prevent unauthorized acquisition of tokens. Sometimes individuals in token economies steal tokens from each other or sell items or favors for tokens. Seldom, if ever, are these the kinds of behaviors we want to reinforce. Close monitoring can be effective in checking such infractions (see Chapter 12). Another solution is to individualize the tokens so that only the individual who earned them can exchange them for back-up reinforcement. For example, each individual might receive as tokens plastic chips with his name on them. Another method is to make out checks for the appropriate amount of reinforcement.

9. In addition to these eight rules, one should follow the same rules for conditioned reinforcers that apply to any positive reinforcer (see Chapter 2). Additional details for establishing token economies are described in Chapters 22, 23, and 24.

Study Questions

(for examination purposes)

1. Describe briefly, point by point, how Johnny was taught to exchange pegs for back-up reinforcement.
2. Describe briefly, point by point, four *essential* features of a token system.
3. Explain how Nickie's peg system facilitated her job of managing reinforcers for the children.
4. How did Nickie insure adequate reinforcement for each child?
5. How did Nickie avoid having to frequently interrupt the class in order to provide back-up reinforcement?
6. How did Nickie determine how many pegs each child would have to pay for each back-up reinforcer?
7. Explain what a conditioned reinforcer is. Give and explain two examples.
8. Explain what a back-up reinforcer is. Give two examples.
9. Explain what a primary reinforcer is. Give two examples.
10. Which of the reinforcers in Figure 2-2 are primary reinforcers and which are conditioned reinforcers? Defend your answer.
11. Explain why money is a conditioned reinforcer.

12. Conditioned reinforcers that can be accumulated and exchanged for other reinforcers are called _____.

13. Explain in two or three sentences what a token system is. Describe the different media of exchange used in various token systems.

14. Give two examples of stimuli that are conditioned reinforcers but not tokens. Explain why they are conditioned reinforcers.

15. Why is it important for those working with the behaviorally handicapped to insure that praise becomes a conditioned reinforcer for them?

16. Explain what a conditioned punisher is. Give and explain two examples.

17. Explain what a generalized reinforcer is. Explain why a conditioned reinforcer that is a generalized reinforcer is more effective than one that is not.

18. Explain what extinction of a conditioned reinforcer is.

19. A conditioned reinforcer is more effective if back-up reinforcement follows every occurrence of it. True or false?

Self-Modification Exercise

(to be practiced by the reader)

Self-modification exercise 2 in Chapter 2 required you to complete the reinforcer questionnaire for yourself. Self-modification exercise 2 in Chapter 4 required you to outline a detailed shaping program to overcoming one of your deficiencies. Now select several reinforcers from you reinforcer questionnaire and describe how they might be used in a plausible token system to carry out your shaping program from Chapter 4.

EXTENDED DISCUSSION AND NOTES

1. Even the mild murmur "mmm-hmm," if used as an expression of interest or approval, can have measurable reinforcing effects. As described in detail in Chapter 2, note 5, Greenspoon (1951) demonstrated this in a classic experiment in which he instructed college students to "free-associate" and then said "mmm-hmm" contingent upon the emission of plural nouns. The frequency of plural nouns increased even for those students who appeared (on the basis of testing) not to have been aware of the reinforcement contingency. Moreover, the frequency of plural nouns decreased when Greenspoon extinguished this behavior by withholding "mmm-hmm."

2. The development of a token system that will be used to effectively alter a small number of behaviors of one or two individuals is one thing. The development of a detailed token system that will be used to manage many behaviors of many individuals is something else. The guidelines described in this chapter, if used in conjunction with the guidelines for the effective application of the other behavioral principles and procedures discussed in this book, are probably sufficient to help a teacher, parent, or whomever, to design a simple token system for one

(Continued)

(Continued)

or two behaviors of one or two individuals. However, you should not try to develop a large-scale token system just on the basis of these guidelines. In Chapters 22, 23, and 24, we will describe many additional details that require attention in the design of a large-scale token economy. In addition, entire books have been written on how to develop token economies in specific settings. Ayllon and Azrin (1968b) described procedures for developing a token economy on a ward in a mental hospital. Cohen and Filipczak (1971) outlined in detail a token economy for improving the behavior of boys in the National Training School for Boys in Washington, D.C. More recently, Stainback, Payne, Stainback, and Payne (1973) and Walker and Buckley (1974) described easy-to-follow step-by-step procedures for designing token economies appropriate for classroom settings. Welch and Gist (1974) presented guidelines for developing a token economy in sheltered workshops. In addition to these "how-to-do-it" manuals for the design of full-scale token economies, there are a number of research reports that have investigated the effectiveness of token economies. For excellent reviews of these studies, see Kazdin and Bootzin (1972) and Kazdin (1975, 1977). Moreover Patterson (1976) edited a book concerned with solving the routine problems of token-economy operation.

CHAPTER 10

Getting
A New Behavior
to Occur With
BACKWARD CHAINING

"Giselle, will you make the bed for me, please?"

TEACHING GISELLE TO MAKE A BED

Giselle was an institutionalized severely retarded girl with an IQ of 32.*
One summer, one of the authors and his co-workers decided that it would
be a good idea to teach bedmaking to some of their charges. Giselle was
chosen as one of the pupils for this task, mainly because she would follow
some simple instructions.

Before beginning the bedmaking training, the staff conducted a test
to see what Giselle could do without any training at all. They piled the
sheets, blanket, bedspread, and pillow on top of one bed and asked Gi-

---

*This example is taken from Martin, England, and England (1971), and is paraphrased
with permission of the copyright holders, Division 22, American Psychological Association, Inc.

selle to make the bed next to it. Under these conditions, Giselle knew enough to move the materials to the unmade bed, but not much else. She grabbed everything in one big lump, piled it on the bed, and moved it around a little. It was clear that Giselle could not make a bed, at least under the test conditions.

Making a bed consists of a complex sequence of responses that must be followed, one response at a time, in the proper order. It was apparent that before any progress could be made, these steps would have to be specified. Therefore, the entire process of bedmaking was divided into the following twenty sequential units or steps:

1. putting on the bottom sheet such that it covers all or nearly all of the mattress
2. tucking in the bottom sheet at the head of the bed
3. tucking in the bottom sheet at the foot of the bed
4. tucking in the sides of the bottom sheet
5. placing the top sheet on the bed
6. pulling the top sheet up to the head of the bed
7. straightening the top sheet
8. tucking in the foot of the top sheet
9. putting the (folded) blanket on the lower right-hand corner of the bed
10. unfolding the blanket from the corner such that it covers the bottom half of the bed
11. pulling the top layer of the blanket up such that the blanket covers the whole bed
12. tucking in the foot of the blanket
13. placing the spread on the bed
14. finding the rounded corners of the spread
15. placing the rounded corners at the foot of the bed
16. pulling the spread up from the foot of the bed such that it covers the bottom half of the bed
17. pulling the spread up from its halfway position such that it covers the whole bed
18. pulling the spread back for the pillow
19. putting the pillow at the head of the bed
20. pulling the spread over the pillow

The training procedure, which was carried out by a nurse, involved teaching the last step first, then teaching the next to the last step, and so on, working backwards in a fashion that is called *backward chaining*. The nurse made the bed completely except for step 20. She then told Giselle, "Pull the spread over the pillow." Immediately after making this request, she physically guided Giselle through the proper motions, giving additional verbal prompts along the way. This was followed with "Good girl, Giselle!" and the presentation of a plastic token as reinforcement. (Giselle had already been taught how to use tokens to buy back-up reinforcers.) The nurse repeated the step several times, each time giving Giselle less physical guidance. Each correct response was reinforced, and each incorrect response was followed by the verbal stimulus "no!" and a brief period in which Giselle was ignored.

When Giselle had performed step 20 correctly on three consecutive trials without physical guidance or verbal prompts, the nurse introduced step 19. She made the bed completely except for the last two steps. She then told Giselle, "Put the pillow on the bed" and physically guided her through the motion. She then told her, "Now pull the spread over the pillow," which Giselle did readily and without prompting. The nurse said, "Good girl, Giselle!" and presented her with a token after the completion of this step (step 20). Over trials, the physical guidance for step 19 was faded out, just as it had been faded out for step 20. Steps 19 and 20 were repeated until Giselle performed both correctly, without physical guidance, in three consecutive trials. In this fashion, Giselle was taught to perform steps 18, 19, and 20; then steps 17, 18, 19, and 20; and so on, until she had mastered the entire twenty-step sequence. Even though Giselle was severely retarded, within fifteen half-hour sessions of this procedure she had learned to make the bed completely.

STIMULUS-RESPONSE CHAINING

A stimulus-response chain is a sequence of discriminative stimuli (S^Ds) and responses (Rs) in which each response produces the S^D for the next response; the entire sequence is typically followed by a reinforcer. What Giselle had acquired in learning to make a bed was such a sequence of stimuli and responses. The first stimulus (S^D_1) for the entire sequence (completed in a forward fashion) was the instruction "Make the bed"; this was the instruction that was given in the presence of a completely unmade bed. The response (R_1) to that stimulus was "putting the bottom sheet on the bed." The bottom sheet on the bed was the stimulus (S^D_2) for "tucking in the bottom sheet at the head of the bed" (R_2). The bottom sheet tucked in at the head of the bed was the stimulus (S^D_3) for "tucking in the bottom sheet at the foot of the bed" (R_3). And so on, until the bed was completely made at which point Giselle received praise and a token. The reason for calling this procedure a stimulus-response chain can be seen by writing it out as follows:

$$S^D_1 - - R_1 - - S^D_2 - - R_2 - - S^D_3 - - R_3 - - \ldots . - - S^D_{20} - - R_{20} - - S^+$$

The stimulus-response connections are the "links" that hold the chain together. As the saying goes, "A chain is only as strong as its weakest link." Similarly, if any response is so weak that it fails to be evoked by the S^D preceding it, the next S^D will not be produced and the rest of the chain will not occur. The chain will be "broken" at the point of its weakest link. The only way to "repair" the chain is to strengthen the weak stimulus-response connection by means of an effective training procedure.

The symbol "S⁺" at the far right of the above diagram symbolizes the positive reinforcer that follows the last response in the chain. It designates the "oil" that one must apply regularly in order to keep the chain "rust-free" and strong.

One major method of teaching a stimulus-response chain is called *backward chaining*. Students often find this method strange, apparently because they think that it teaches an individual to perform the chain backwards, as the name suggests. Actually, this is not true. There is a very good rationale for using backward chaining. Consider the example of teaching Giselle to make a bed. Backward chaining was the method used in that program. The response of step 20— "pulling the spread over the pillow"—was reinforced in the presence of the stimulus "pillow on the bed." On the basis of the principle of conditioned reinforcement, the sight of "pillow on the bed" became a conditioned reinforcer for the response immediately preceding it, "putting the pillow on the bed." This response, in turn, was reinforced (by the conditioned reinforcing stimulus "pillow on the bed") in the presence of stimulus "spread pulled back for the pillow." Therefore "spread pulled back for the pillow" became a conditioned reinforcer for the response immediately preceding it, "pulling the spread back for the pillow." And so on. Thus, when backward chaining is used, the reinforcing power of the positive reinforcer (presented at the end of the chain) is transferred "down the line" to each S^D as it is added to the chain. This makes for very efficient use of positive reinforcement to establish a strong chain.

Backward chaining has also been used in teaching various dressing, grooming, and verbal behaviors to retarded individuals. In order to teach a boy to put on a pair of slacks, for example, we break down the task into the following nine steps:

1. taking the slacks from the dresser drawer
2. holding the slacks upright with the front facing away from the individual
3. putting one leg in the slacks
4. putting the other leg in the slacks
5. pulling the slacks to the knees
6. pulling the slacks to the thighs
7. pulling the slacks all the way up
8. doing up the button or snap
9. doing up the zipper

When we teach an individual this chain, we start with the last step first. The trainer helps the individual put on the slacks so that all the steps are completed except for step 9. The individual is then taught to do up the zipper. When he can do this, he is taught to do up the button (step 8), which is the S^D for doing up the zipper. When he can make both responses, the slacks are pulled down to his thighs. He is then taught to pull them all the way up (step 7), which is the S^D for the response at step 8. The training proceeds in this backward fashion, with one step being added at a time, until the individual can perform all nine steps.

An interesting and often useful feature of chaining is that it is possible to break down any link into a sequence of smaller stimuli and responses. Suppose that an individual has difficulty performing step 9 in the above procedure. That step can be made easier if we break it down into a chain of its own that can also be taught by the method of backward chaining.

No doubt because backward chaining resembles a reversal of the natural order of things, forward chaining is used more often in everyday situations outside the behavior modification setting. Among the many examples that could be cited, consider the way the child is taught to pronounce a multisyllable word such as "milk." He is first taught to say "m," then "mi," then "mil," and finally "milk." However, one of the authors recently taught the same chain in a backward fashion to his eighteen-month-old son. The child first learned "k," then "lk," then "ilk," and finally "milk." For relatively short chains such as this, we suspect that it doesn't make much difference whether forward or backward chaining is used, but for long chains we usually prefer the backward method. (Whether we are correct on these points has yet to be determined by experimental research.)

Another example of backward chaining is teaching answers to questions. Martin et al. (1968) taught autistic children to answer the question "Where does milk come from?" in the following way. The teacher began by pointing to some milk, or a picture of milk, and saying, "Where does milk come from? Milk comes from a COW." Since the students had extensive verbal-imitation training, they would usually mimic "cow." The teacher immediately reinforced this response. Then the teacher faded out the words of the required response over several trials. That is, the teacher said, "Where does milk come from? Milk comes from $A - -$," to which the students generally responded, "a cow." The next step was "Where does milk come from? Milk comes $FROM - -$," to which the students generally said, "from a cow." The teacher continued reducing the size of the prompt: "Milk comes $- -$"; "Milk $- -$." Finally, the only stimulus that remained was the question "Where does milk come from?"

Backward chaining might be used effectively in all sorts of everyday situations in which the typical method is forward chaining. For example, it would certainly be an easy matter to analyze a golf swing in terms of a chain of steps. No doubt, this is already done to some extent: a golf pro is likely to examine how you grip the club, how you approach and stand by the ball, how you transfer your weight on the backswing, how you begin your downswing, how you hit the ball, and how you follow through. He might also divide any of these steps into a finer chain. But, would he use backward chaining to teach the entire sequence? Probably not. It would be interesting to teach a novice to hit a golf ball by starting with the proper position at the end of the follow-through and then proceeding backwards one step at a time until the entire sequence was acquired.

FACTORS INFLUENCING THE EFFECTIVENESS OF BACKWARD CHAINING[1]

1. Identify the components of the final sequence

The behavioral sequence you wish to develop must be broken down into individual components, and the proper order of the sequence must be kept. As with the selection of shaping steps (discussed in Chapter 4), the selection of chaining steps or components is somewhat subjective. The components should be simple enough to be learned without great difficulty. If you wanted to teach a severely retarded child to brush her teeth, for example, it would be a mistake to consider the task in terms of the three gross steps of putting toothpaste on the brush, brushing, and rinsing. In order for the child to master the chain, each of these steps would have to be subdivided into even smaller steps. The components should also be selected so that there is a clear-cut stimulus or set of stimuli signaling the completion of each component. This will facilitate the development of those stimuli as conditioned reinforcers for preceding responses and as S^Ds for subsequent responses throughout the chain. For example, in utilizing backward chaining to teach a child appropriate handwashing behavior, you might select putting water in the sink as one of the components. It would be important to specify a particular level of water, and perhaps even make a mark (at least temporarily) approximately halfway up the sink, in order to provide a very clear stimulus that terminates the end of this particular component (which you might define as "holding the water taps until the water level reaches the halfway mark").

2. Develop each component to a high level before proceeding to the next component

In the case of teaching Giselle to make a bed, step 20, the final component, which consisted of pulling the spread over the pillow, was developed to a high degree before Giselle was taught step 19 (and step 19 was followed immediately by step 20). This is extremely important, for two reasons. First, research has indicated that a weak behavioral component in a chain will weaken all of the components preceding it. As we suggested earlier, a chain is only as strong as its weakest link. Second, it is important that a behavioral component be under effective stimulus control of the preceding S^D. For example, in step 20 of teaching Giselle to make a bed, the preceding S^D was the appearance of a bed that was completely made except that the spread was pulled down from the pillow. Training on step 20 continued until Giselle's behavior of pulling the spread over the pillow was under very good stimulus control of the preceding S^D. This means that the preceding S^D was closely associated (in Giselle's case) with the stimuli provided when bedmaking was completed. In turn, those stimuli were closely associated with a terminal reinforcer. This means that the preceding S^D will become a more effective conditioned reinforcer and will reinforce preceding components.

3. Always complete the components that have been taught

In every trial during training, the student should be required to complete all of the components learned previously, in the order in which they were taught. This provides more opportunities for pairings of preceding stimuli with subsequent stimuli in the chain. The more often these pairings occur, the greater the possibility that the stimuli in the chain will become, and remain, effective conditioned reinforcers and S^Ds. This requirement also insures that the student always completes a trial successfully, since it denies the previously learned components the opportunity to weaken.

4. When teaching long chains, add supplemental reinforcers at various components

The bedmaking program for Giselle consisted of twenty components. Following completion of the entire chain, Giselle received a token. Since the procedure was backward chaining, only the stimuli associated with the final component were paired with the token. Thus, the stimuli provided by the completion of the first component (the component that starts the chain) were never paired with the token. In other words, stimuli from early components were never paired with the major reinforcer provided for the completion of the chain. Research has indicated that early components in a chain can be strengthened if they are occasionally paired with a major reinforcer during the performance of the chain. For example, in the bedmaking program for Giselle, step 7, straightening the top sheet, could occasionally lead to a token (as well as providing the stimuli for Giselle to perform the next step). Intermittent pairings of each component with powerful reinforcers (such as the reinforcer provided for the completion of the chain) will help strengthen those components and keep them strong. This is especially true of the early components in very long chains.

PITFALLS OF CHAINING: HOW IT WORKS TO THE DISADVANTAGE OF THOSE WHO ARE IGNORANT OF IT

Just as relatively simple undesirable responses are often established inadvertently through the thoughtless administration of positive reinforcement, so also are undesirable chains. For example, Steven, a little boy in one of our programs, always used to say "ple-ap" when asked to say "apple." Clearly, the boy had learned to make the correct imitative responses for the word, but for some reason or other he had chained them together in the wrong order. Once strengthened, this inappropriate chain continued to be maintained, because adults in Steven's immediate environment "understood what he meant" and gave him apples when he said "ple-ap." However, incorrect syllable chains do not promote optimal verbal development, so we replaced this inappropriate chain with the correct one. The teacher first taught Steven to imitate "ap" and "ple" separately. Then, using fading, she would say very softly, "Steven, say 'apple.'" Quickly and loudly, before Steven could say "ple-ap," the teacher said "ap." As soon as he said "ap," she said "ple" and reinforced the correct imitation of the last syllable. Over trials, the prompt "ap-ple" was gradually softened (faded out) and the instruction "Steven, say apple" was gradually made louder (faded in). Eventually, Steven correctly imitated the verbal stimulus "apple" without prompting.

Probably the most common kind of undesirable chaining occurs when an inappropriate response precedes an appropriate response that is reinforced; both responses are thereby strengthened together. A good example of this type of chaining is the distracting habit exhibited by some speakers of prefacing each remark with "uh." A similar though somewhat more serious example is the making of bizarre facial expressions prior to each utterance.

Sometimes, the application of other behavior modification procedures results in accidental undesirable chaining. Here is an example from our experience. A father resolved to change from using punishment (spankings) to using positive reinforcement to teach his infant son the meaning of "No." Whenever the boy touched a dangerous object (such as a light plug) or a fragile one (such as the stereo), the father said "No" in a firm tone. This caused the boy to stop touching the object (because in the past he had been spanked for continuing to do so when his father said "No"), whereupon the father immediately rewarded him with praise and hugs. One day, the father noticed that the boy had developed a consistent behavior pattern that one might suspiciously call a "game." It seemed to be played in this way: (1) touch an object in view of Dad; (2) if Dad says "No," stop touching the object, run to Dad, and get praise and hugs; (3) repeat with other objects, and get more praise and hugs. Thus, it appeared that the child had acquired the following chain:

S^D	R	S^D	R	S^+
(Dad's presence.)	(Child touches object.)	(Dad says "No.")	(Child stops touching object and runs to Dad.)	(Dad gives child praise and hugs.)

The father, who happened to be a behavior modifier, was not totally unprepared for the development of this undesirable chain and was able to change the game appropriately. Can you guess how?

The self-control problems that plague many people provide several other examples of undesirable behavioral chains. Consider the problem of overeating. Although there are undoubtedly a variety of possible reasons for overeating, one of the more frequent causes is the inadvertent development of undesirable behavioral chains. For example, it has been observed that some overweight people eat very rapidly.[2] An examination of the behavioral chains involved suggests the following components: loading food on to the utensil, placing food in the mouth, reloading utensil while chewing the food, simultaneously swallowing the food while raising the next load of food to the mouth, placing food in the mouth, and so forth. This behavioral chain has been successfully broken by extending the chain and introducing delays. A more desirable chain might be the following: loading food on to the utensil, placing food in the mouth, putting down the utensil, chewing the food, swallowing, waiting three seconds, reloading the utensil, and so on. In other words, in the undesirable chain the person gets ready to consume the next mouthful before even finishing the present one. A more desirable chain separates these components and introduces brief delays.

Another undesirable behavior chain that is manifested by some overweight people consists of watching TV until a commercial comes on, going to the kitchen during the commercial, getting a snack, and returning to the TV (a very powerful reinforcer in itself). Another example, one that is commonly observed in homemakers who eat excessively consists of preparing a snack, taking the snack to the telephone, calling a neighbor or relative, and eating the snack while talking on the telephone (again, thereby supplementing the reinforcement value of the food itself). There are a variety of procedures for solving such self-control problems, and these are discussed more fully in Chapter 25. The point to remember here is that undesirable behaviors are frequently unintentionally developed behavioral chains.

GUIDELINES FOR THE EFFECTIVE USE OF BACKWARD CHAINING[3]

One should observe the following rules when developing stimulus-response chains.

1. Identify the units of the chain that are simple enough to be learned without great difficulty by the individual to whom you are teaching the chain.
2. The units must be taught in the proper sequence. Otherwise, poor stimulus control will develop, in that when one step is completed it will not necessarily be a discriminative stimulus for the next step but rather may control some other step (as when a young child learns to count incorrectly—for example, 1, 2, 4, 3).
3. Make sure that a given step has been mastered before you teach the next step. Otherwise, the task may be too difficult for the individual you are teaching and his behavior may extinguish because of the lack of sufficient reinforcement.
4. To expedite learning, use the fading procedure to teach each unit in the chain. (See the examples in this chapter of teaching bedmaking and question answering.)
5. If you are using backward chaining, make sure that each time the student responds he performs the entire set of components learned up to that point. He should fulfill this requirement in order to receive the reinforcer at the end of the chain.
6. Make sure that the reinforcement provided at the end of the chain conforms to the guidelines for the effective application of positive reinforcement given in Chapter 2. The more effective this terminal reinforcement is, the more stable the chain of responses will be. This does not mean, however, that once a chain is developed it must be reinforced in order to be maintained. After Giselle had been taught to make a bed, for example, bedmaking could be viewed as a single response, which could, if desired, be put on any intermittent-reinforcement schedule.

Study Questions

(for examination purposes)

1. Why was the bedmaking program for Giselle divided into twenty steps? Why not eighteen steps? Why not twenty-two steps?
2. What is backward about backward chaining?

3. In the bedmaking program with Giselle, what were the criteria for deciding that a particular component was learned and for introducing a new component?

4. In the training program with Danny (Chapter 8), what were the criteria for deciding that a particular step was learned and for moving to the next step? Why were the criteria for Danny's program and Giselle's program different?

5. Describe or define a stimulus-response chain, and give an example other than the examples in this chapter.

6. Why do you suppose a behavioral chain is called a chain?

7. In a chain, a given stimulus is both an S^D and a conditioned reinforcer. How can this be? (Explain with an example.)

8. What is a problem encountered in forward chaining that is not encountered in backward chaining? (Hint: The problem involves the terminal reinforcer.)

9. In the behavioral chain of driving a car, accelerating it, and changing gears (assume that you have a four-speed transmission), how is the chain of the driver who has a tachometer (and uses it) different from the chain of the driver who does not have a tachometer?

10. What are two major differences between chaining and shaping?

11. In what major respect are fading and chaining different, and in what major respect are they similar?

12. What are the details of the backward chain Nickie developed when token-training Johnny (Chapter 9)?

13. When learning poetry, individuals frequently have more problems remembering a new line after completing an earlier line than remembering the words in a particular line. Why do you suppose this is? (Hint: Examine the factors influencing the effectiveness of chaining.)

Study Exercises

(to be practiced by the reader)

1. Describe how you might use backward chaining to teach a child to lace his shoes.

2. Describe how you might use backward chaining to teach a child to tie a knot.

3. Describe how you might use backward chaining to teach a child to tie a bow.

4. Try out your programs in the above three questions and see how they work.

Self-Modification Exercise

(to be practiced by the reader)

Identify a behavioral deficiency of yours that might be amenable to a backward-chaining procedure. Describe in detail how you might use the guidelines for the effective use of backward chaining to overcome this deficiency.

EXTENDED DISCUSSION AND NOTES

1. There has been very little applied research on the variety of factors that might be important in the development and use of chaining with humans. However, there has been a good deal of basic research on factors influencing the development and maintenance of chains of behavior in lower organisms (see Kelleher and Gollub, 1962; Kelleher, 1966). The suggestions made in our discussion of the factors influencing the effectiveness of backward chaining have been abstracted primarily from basic research studies.

2. An excellent analysis of behavior principles, including chaining, that are involved in the problem of overeating was made by Ferster, Nurnberger, and Levitt (1962). However, the "eating styles" of obese individuals has not received extensive attention from researchers. Interested readers should consult an excellent report by Mahoney (1975), who stresses the importance of recognizing some of the unexamined assumptions of the behavior modification approaches to weight control.

3. Although we have emphasized backward chaining in this chapter, there are actually three main strategies for developing a behavioral chain: backward chaining, forward chaining, and total task presentation. Forward chaining proceeds in a fashion opposite to that of backward chaining. For example, in a 20-step training program, the teacher would reinforce the student for performing step 1 to some satisfactory mastery criterion; then for performing steps 1 and 2 to criterion; then steps 1, 2, and 3, and so on, until all 20 steps in the chain were mastered. In the total task presentation strategy, a student is prompted through all of the steps in a chain on each trial. In a 20-step training program, this student would be taught and helped to perform all 20 steps on each trial. As his performance improved on the steps, help would be gradually eliminated. (Also, see the example on p. 125 concerning teaching a child to imitate "cat"). Examples of the application of all three strategies to develop behavioral chains can be seen in a paper by Martin, Kehoe, Bird, Jensen, and Darbyshire (1971).

CHAPTER 11

Transferring A Behavior From One Setting to Another Through GENERALIZATION

"Let's improve our posture"

SANDRA, SARAH, SIGRID, AND SUSAN LEARN GOOD POSTURE

Many severely and profoundly retarded individuals are rather conspicuous in public because of their bizarre walking, standing, and sitting postures. Whether due to biological defects, early-childhood deprivation and injury, or inadvertent reinforcement by the attention they tend to evoke, such bizarre postures clearly are not advantageous. First, and most important—as any physiotherapist can tell you—poor posture is simply not conducive to good physical health and growth. Second, and most unfortunately—as any social psychologist can tell you—people are often rejected, ridiculed, and stigmatized for no better reason than that they "look funny." Posture is, of course, an important aspect of appearance. It might be desirable to change society's negative attitude toward those who appear different, but until this can be done, it would be well to help retarded individuals to look as "normal" as possible in the eyes of the public. These individuals already have enough social prejudice against them without unnecessarily compounding it by their manner of carrying themselves.

These considerations led psychology graduate student Rae Lowther to set up a special classroom for the teaching of good posture in Cedar Cottage, a residence for severely and profoundly retarded young women at The Manitoba School.* Because the class was set up on an experimental basis, only four residents—the ones showing the very worst postures—were chosen to participate in it. Their names, for the purpose of this report, were Sandra, Sarah, Sigrid, and Susan. All were profoundly retarded. Their chronological ages ranged from 22 to 25, and their mental ages ranged from "unmeasurable" to 2 years. Only sitting postures were worked on in this early stage of the experiment.

Rae knew that by using behavior modification procedures, she would probably not find it too difficult to establish good posture in the experimental classroom. But she also realized that it would be pointless to form this new behavior if it did not subsequently occur more readily in other situations as a result of the classroom training. Therefore, she selected two other situations—the day hall and the dining room—in which to test for improvement in posture that would be attributable to the posture training being given in the classroom. She also decided that should these tests indicate that the behavior did not generalize satisfactorily across situations, she would attempt to discover how such generalization could be increased.

The classroom contained four chairs for the residents, which were arranged in a semicircle around the teacher's chair. A board for holding small pegs was attached to one side of each resident's chair. Just prior to the study, the residents were trained to accept pegs as token reinforcers that could later be exchanged for desired items such as candy, cookies, and Coke.

Two classroom sessions were conducted each weekday, one in the morning and one in the afternoon. Each session lasted for thirty minutes. Alternating trials among the residents, Rae modeled the correct posture and verbally instructed the resident whose turn it was. A red stimulus light was switched on as soon as the resident showed the correct behavior. The light remained on until a required duration of engaging in the behavior had elapsed, and reinforcement was then presented. An incorrect trial—one in which the resident did not engage in the behavior within a given time period or did not engage in it long enough—led to a sharp "No!" from Rae, who then turned off the light if it had been on. Rae used shaping, fading, and other standard procedures, and obtained a high level of correct performance.

The classroom was connected to an observation room by a one-way window. There, two observers kept accurate records of the sitting posture of each resident during trials and between trials.

Over a number of sessions, all of the residents eventually reached 100-percent-correct trial performance. Rae then began intermittently rein-

*This case study is based on Lowther, Martin, and Nicholson (1977).

forcing good posture between trials while continuing the above procedure during trials. About twenty-five days after the beginning of training, all of the residents were still showing 100-percent-correct performance during trials. Moreover, Sandra, Sigrid, and Susan were showing good posture between trials. Sarah was showing good posture about 70-percent of the time between trials.

Observers then began systematically recording the four students' postures in the day hall and the dining room before and after each classroom session. They found that very little or no generalization occurred from the classroom to these other settings. Posture in the day hall and dining room was terrible, even though it was excellent in the classroom. Rae attempted to find out exactly what she had to do in order to obtain satisfactory generalization.

The first thing she tried was simply entering the day hall and modeling good posture while sitting in one of the chairs. She did this for fifteen minutes twice a day—just before and just after classroom sessions—for six days. All four residents showed immediate improvement in the day hall, but this improvement was temporary for all but Sandra, who continued to perform well even when Rae was not in the day hall. In the dining room, virtually no improvement occurred with any of the four residents.

Since satisfactory generalization was temporary for all but Sandra, Rae turned to another tactic. Prior to each classroom session, she modeled the desired posture and also delivered verbal instructions and social reinforcement in the day hall. Moreover, she presented reinforcement on VI schedules at other times throughout the day when the residents were in the day hall. In order to do this, Rae constructed five VI schedules, ranging from VI 15 minutes to VI 35 minutes. Each day, Rae drew one of these at random, entered the day hall according to schedule, and reinforced the four residents' good posture with smiles, praise, coversation, and physical contact. She ignored poor posture. Sandra, Sigrid, and Susan showed immediate, large, and lasting improvement in the day hall. In addition, their posture improved in the dining room (although to a lesser extent), even though Rae was never present in that setting! Sarah, however, who had shown the poorest improvement all along, showed a little improvement in the day hall and none in the dining room. Nevertheless, Rae was very encouraged that the experimental program had proved so successful for three of the four residents on whom it was tried. The generalization data for Susan (who was representative of the three successes) and Sarah, whose posture improved only a little, are shown in Figure 11-1.

The general success of the program was that Sandra, Sigrid, and Susan maintained good posture in numerous situations after their formal training was concluded. They held their heads up on most occasions and readily made eye contact with anyone who approached them. They slouched and sprawled very infrequently. Staff members were instructed to continue to reinforce good posture as often as possible.

Considering that the four residents had shown the very worst posture—because of biological defects, early childhood deprivation and injury, and many years of nothing more than custodial care—and considering that they were so profoundly retarded, Rae's experimental posture-training program appears to have been very successful overall. It seems, moreover, that such a program could be applied advantageously to many

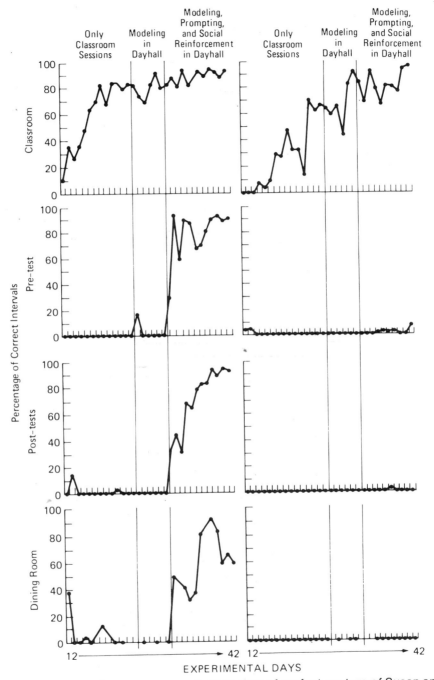

FIGURE 11-1. *Summary generalization data of perfect posture of Susan and Sarah, as observed in the dining room, during the inter-trial intervals in the classroom, and during the pretests and posttests in the day room. Adapted from Lowther, Martin, and Nicholson (1977).*

residents. But although the amount of generalization ultimately obtained was quite satisfactory on the whole, the study showed that this result is not something that can be taken for granted. Rather, generalization must be carefully built into any program for which success is important enough not to be left to chance.

GENERALIZATION

When establishing a behavior in the presence of a particular stimulus or situation causes the behavior to occur more readily in the presence of another stimulus or situation, we say that the behavior has *generalized* from the first to the second stimulus or situation. *Stimulus generalization* occurs when behavior becomes more probable in the presence of one stimulus or situation as a result of having been strengthened in the presence of another stimulus or situation. In the above study, for example, Rae Lowther was concerned with the generalization of good posture from the classroom situation to the day hall and the dining room.

Generalization is the opposite of discrimination. As explained in Chapter 7, when a behavior occurs in the presence of one stimulus or situation more readily than in the presence of another, we say that the individual has *discriminated* between the two stimuli or situations. The four residents in the above study, for example, initially discriminated between situation 1 — the classroom — and situations 2 and 3 — the day hall and the dining room — in that their postures were excellent in situation 1 and terrible in situations 2 and 3.

There are many examples of generalization in everyday life. Consider a case that is familiar to many parents: An infant learns to say "doggie" to a hairy, four-legged creature with floppy ears and a friendly bark. Later, the infant sees a different kind of dog and says "doggie." This is an instance of generalization because a previously reinforced response ("doggie") was emitted in the presence of a new stimulus (a new kind of dog). Still later, the infant sees a horse and again says "doggie." This is another instance of generalization, even though the response in this case is incorrect — proving that not all instances of generalization are favorable and illustrating why it is necessary to teach discriminations, as described in Chapter 7.

Looking back through the previous chapters, one can see that generalization is an important consideration in every training program. For example, it was desirable for Charles (Chapter 2) to take his pills from nurses other than Ms. Peabody. Likewise, it was desirable for Peter (Chapter 3) to decrease his tantruming in situations other than the classroom. Unfortunately, Peter failed to generalize and continued to tantrum when back on the ward. These and similar examples illustrate that failure to obtain generalization is a major problem facing behavior modifiers. How do we solve the problem?

Before answering that question, we must make it clear that there are two levels of generalization to be concerned with in any training program. One is generalization to different stimuli within a given training program. An example of this is teaching a child to say "dog" to different pictures of dogs, "horse" to different pictures of horses, and so on. The child in this example is being taught to generalize the response "dog" to many different members of the stimulus class "dog," to generalize the response "horse" to many different members of the stimulus class "horse," and so forth. Incidentally, note that the child is also being taught to discriminate between stimulus classes so that he will not say "dog" when the stimulus is a horse, or "horse" when it is a dog.[1]

The second level of generalization to be concerned with is generalization from the training situation to the natural environment. Continuing with the above example, this level of generalization would be demonstrated if the child correctly identified dogs and horses whenever he saw them outside of the training situation.

The first level of generalization is relatively easy to obtain: just reinforce the response in the presence of different members of the stimulus class to which you want the response to generalize (while, of course, extinguishing the response to inappropriate stimuli). But the second level of generalization usually poses quite a problem. Not that it is especially difficult to obtain *temporary* generalization: just make the training situation very similar to the natural environment. The problem is to obtain *long-lasting* generalization.[2] As we have seen, if the behavior is not reinforced in the natural environment, the behavior might extinguish in that situation. That is, the individual might discriminate between the training situation and the natural environment. It is therefore very important that the behavior modifier consider the following factors when programming for generalization.

FACTORS INFLUENCING THE EFFECTIVENESS OF GENERALIZATION

1. The similarity between the training and test situations

The initial occurrence of generalization depends critically on the physical similarity between two stimuli or situations. The more similar they are, the more initial generalization (and hence the less discrimination) there will be between them. In Rae Lowther's study, there apparently was little physical similarity between the classroom and the day-hall situations. That is, there was little physical similarity until the teacher entered the day hall and modeled the correct posture. This made the day-hall situation similar to the classroom situation, and generalization between the two situations therefore occurred (even though this generalization was only temporary).

Thus, the first effort of the behavior modifier attempting to program generalization should be to make the final stages of the training situation similar to the test situation in as many ways as possible. (By "test situation," we mean either the natural environment or some other situation to which we want generalization to occur.) Other things being equal, the best way to do this is to train in the test situation.

2. The reinforcement contingencies in the test situation

Besides physical similarity, generalization from one stimulus or situation to another (if it is to be long-lasting) depends critically on whether the behavior will be reinforced in the presence of the second stimulus or situation. Initially, when Rae Lowther entered the day hall she did not reinforce good posture in that situation. Recall from Chapter 7 that reinforcing a behavior in the presence of a particular stimulus or situation and not reinforcing it in the presence of another is the method for establishing a discrimination between the two stimuli or situations. This explains why generalization of good posture from the classroom to the day hall was only temporary for Sigrid and Susan when the teacher merely modeled good posture in the day hall. To obtain long-lasting generalization from the classroom to the day hall, Rae had to reinforce the behavior in the latter as well as the former situation.

But why, you will probably ask, did Sandra — unlike the other three residents — show strong and long-lasting generalization to the day hall when good posture was not reinforced in that situation, and, indeed, even when the teacher was not present there? We have to admit that in the present state of knowledge of behavioral psychology, we cannot answer that question adequately. Of course, we can make some educated guesses. Perhaps Sandra had an unknown source of reinforcement for good posture. Or perhaps for Sandra good posture, once it had been "reinforcer sampled," was "self-reinforcing" (that is, no external reinforcement was required to maintain it). Or perhaps, as a last-resort explanation, Sandra simply had more of an innate (that is, inborn) tendency to generalize than did the other three residents.[3] But these guesses are of little importance. The important point, to reiterate, is that reinforcing a behavior in a situation outside the original training situation will maintain the generalization to that second situation.

Although Rae was able to generalize good posture by reinforcing it in the day hall, it is obvious that this solution would be impractical in many situations. No behavior modifier could follow all her students around and reinforce the target behaviors everywhere it was desirable for them to occur. It would be a full-time job to do this for just one individual. Short of this extremely impractical measure, there are four general approaches to the problem of achieving lasting generalization by managing contingencies in the test situation.

a. NATURAL CONTINGENCIES OF REINFORCEMENT. The first approach is to make use of the reinforcement the natural environment already provides for the target behavior. In most cases, such contingencies are probably operating at least to a minimal extent; otherwise, the target behavior would probably be useless to your student and therefore not worth establishing.

Talking is an obvious example of behavior that is heavily reinforced in most natural environments. Yet a child may not learn to talk because of what are, at least for him, deficient shaping contingencies in his environment. Nevertheless, after speech has been established in a training situation, it continues unabated in the natural environment because of the natural contingencies of reinforcement for it there. Indeed, it sometimes seems necessary only to establish vocal imitation and a few object naming responses in order for the natural contingencies of reinforcement to take over and develop very functional speech behavior.

Many fears can be overcome permanently if the natural contingencies are allowed to take over after the individual has been gradually induced to engage in the previously feared activity. Such activities often provide their own sources of reinforcement once they are no longer feared. For example, playing with other children is a behavior that might gradually be shaped in a very shy child. Once this behavior is strongly established, however, the behavior modifier probably will not have to worry about reinforcing it further. The other children will take care of that themselves in the course of their play, for, indeed, that is what social play is all about.

This approach to the problem of lasting generalization has been called *trapping*, because it involves developing behavior that in a sense falls into the "behavioral trap" represented by the contingencies in the natural environment (Baer and Wolf, 1970). The approach requires the behavior modifier to carefully tailor the target behavior to fit these contingencies after he or she has realistically appraised them. For example, the behavior modifier should gradually adjust the target behavior to an intermittent schedule that provides reinforcement less frequently than does the natural environment. It would be unwise to expect the target behavior to survive the transition to less frequent reinforcement at the same time that it is making the transition to a physically less similar situation. On the other hand, a transition to more frequent reinforcement will help overcome the tendency of the individual to discriminate between the natural environment and the training situation. (An example of behavioral trapping is shown in Figure 11-2.)

b. CHANGING THE PEOPLE IN THE NATURAL ENVIRONMENT. A second approach to the problem of achieving lasting generalization is usually more difficult than the first. It involves actually changing the contingencies in the natural environment so that they will maintain the behavior established in the training situation. This is illustrated in the case study at the beginning of this chapter, in which the staff members were instructed to reinforce good posture in the day hall in order to help effect generalization to that situation. Later, the staff members were instructed to reinforce good posture in many other natural settings as well.

In following this second approach, it is necessary to work with people in the natural environment—ward staff, parents, teachers, neighbors, and others who have contact with the target behavior. The behavior modifier must teach these individuals how to appropriately reinforce the behavior (if it is desirable) or how to extinguish it (if it is undesirable). The behavior modifier must also occasionally reinforce the appropriate behavior of these individuals—at least until it comes into contact with the improved target behavior, which will then, ideally, reinforce their continued application of the appropriate procedures.[4]

As an example of this second approach, consider the case of a child living at home who has little behavior in her repertoire except tantruming. Possibly this is her sole means of gaining attention and other reinforcers from her parents. There is little doubt that more desirable behaviors could be established in a training situation, but such behaviors would not be maintained in the home situation unless the contingencies operating there were changed. A behavior modifier called in on this case might therefore adopt the following plan.

In a training situation designed to teach the child to play with toys rather than tantrum, he would first adjust the desired behavior to an appropriate schedule—for instance, VI/LH with infrequent reinforcement (since it will not be practical for the parents to give frequent reinforcement in the home environment). Having accomplished this, the behavior modifier would begin generalization training in the home environment.

The behavior modifier would show the mother how to keep accurate records of the child's desirable and undesirable behavior. At first, the mother, with the help and prompting of the behavior modifier, would frequently reinforce the child for playing nicely with her toys in the living room. Gradually, she would decrease the frequency of reinforcement in order to have more time for activities that did not involve the child. She would use a kitchen timer, or similar device, to remind herself to reinforce the child. Throughout this procedure, the behavior modifier would frequently reinforce the mother for appropriately managing and recording the child's behavior. Then he would quickly fade out of the situation by visiting less and less frequently to check the mother's records. (But he would not fade out too fast; if the program deteriorated, he would temporarily stop the fading process and spend enough time in the training situation to correct mat-

FIGURE 11-2. *An example of behavioral trapping.*

ters.) Ideally, the mother's behavior of appropriately reinforcing the target behavior would eventually be maintained by the child's good play behavior and her decreased whining, crying, and tantruming.[5]

c. USING SCHEDULES OF REINFORCEMENT IN THE TEST SITUATION. In some test situations, it is possible to utilize schedules of reinforcement in such a way that the generalized behavior can be maintained for long periods of time. Consider an interesting study by Kale, Kaye, Whelan, and Hopkins (1968). These authors first used prompting and fading to teach three schizophrenic patients in a mental hospital how to appropriately greet staff members whom they encountered on the ward. Whenever the patients greeted a staff member correctly, the staff member responded and provided a good deal of praise along with cigarette reinforcers. When the greeting responses were well established, the schedule of reinforcement was gradually changed over several weeks to a variable-ratio schedule (for one of the patients, the schedule was as high as a VR 20). Next, the patients were reinforced only with praise for greeting the staff appropriately: they were not supplied with cigarette reinforcers. However, the greeting response did not generalize to a second staff member until the training procedure was repeated with five new staff members. The program then produced persistent greeting behavior (at least toward the first two of the staff members), which was maintained during a three-month follow-up. Although no additional follow-up data were recorded, the results imply that proper use of schedules of reinforcement might help bring about generalization.

d. GIVING THE CONTROL TO THE INDIVIDUAL. In recent years, a rapidly growing area within behavior modification has been concerned with helping individuals (primarily adults) to apply behavior modification to themselves. This area, which has been referred to as self-management, self-modification, and behavioral self-control, has produced several books containing easy-to-follow "how-to-do-it" procedures that help individuals manage their own behavior. (This area is discussed more fully in Chapter 25.) It seems clear that individuals can rearrange their environment in order to change their behavior, and in general develop good self-control.

3. The number of training situations in which the behavior was reinforced

A third factor influencing generalization to a new stimulus or situation is the number of other stimuli or situations in the presence of which the behavior has been reinforced during training. In the study conducted by Rae Lowther, when good posture was reinforced only in the classroom, none of the four residents showed any generalization to the dining room. But when good posture was reinforced both in the classroom *and* in the day hall, three of them generalized to the dining room, even though good posture was not explicitly reinforced in that situation.[6] Of course, when good posture was later reinforced in the dining room, generalization to that situation became even stronger.

PITFALLS OF GENERALIZATION: HOW IT WORKS TO THE DISADVANTAGE OF THOSE WHO ARE IGNORANT OF IT

Without generalization, learning would be of very limited value. No matter how perfectly a person learned something, he would have to learn it all over again every time the situation changed even slightly. (Just imagine how annoying it would be to have spent much time learning a skill only to discover that you no longer possessed it after moving to a new city to begin a job that depended on that skill.) But generalization has its disadvantages too, in that a behavior learned in a situation in which it is appropriate may then emerge inconveniently in a situation in which it is inappropriate.

A conspicuous example of this problem among retarded individuals lies in the area of greetings and displays of affection. Of course, it is highly desirable for these behaviors to occur under appropriate circumstances, but when an individual walks up to and hugs a total stranger, the result can be less than favorable for a number of obvious reasons. The solution to this problem is to teach the individual to discriminate between situations in which different forms of greetings and expressions of affection are appropriate and situations in which they are inappropriate.

The opposite type of problem should also be noted. For example, the suppression through punishment of displays of affection may cause an individual to be cold and withdrawn in situations that warrant affectionate behavior. Perhaps this sort of generalization is at the root of certain so-called emotional disturbances. Again, the solution is to teach the individual when and how to express emotional behavior such as affection, as well as when not to do so.

Another example of inappropriate generalization may be the destructive competitiveness demonstrated frequently by some individuals and occasionally by all of us. Such behavior may stem in part from the strong reinforcement given in our culture for winning in sports and in achieving high grades in our educational system. As a wise person once remarked, "It may be true that wars have been won on the playing fields of Eton, but they have also been started there."

Another example of the failure to recognize the factors controlling generalization is seen in the typical study habits of students. Frequently, students cram for exams the night before the examination. They memorize certain verbal chains in response to certain prompts and questions. What they frequently fail to consider is the importance of bringing their knowledge of the material under broader stimulus control than just one or two questions, that is, they do not program for generalization. A great many people have had the same experience with learning a second language. One of the authors was among the many who took a second language during four years of high school. At the end of that time, he was clearly incapable of speaking the language. He had a certain repertoire for answering questions on French exams, translating English articles into French, and translating French articles into English, but this repertoire had not been brought under the stimulus control of a typical conversational setting.

Another pitfall of generalization occurs in the interaction between parents and their children. In various social situations, such as restaurants, parents frequently do not present the same stimuli to their children, or provide the same contingencies of reinforcement, that they present at mealtimes in the home situation. Consequently, the children frequently do not generalize their table manners and good behaviors that occur at home to the restaurant or other social settings. It is not uncommon to hear the parents lament, "I thought I taught you how to be a good child, and now look at you." We hope that after reading this book and performing the study questions and study exercises, the same parents will do a much better job of programming generalization. (If not, you will probably hear us lament, "I thought I taught you how to be a good behavior modifier, and now look at you.")

GUIDELINES FOR EFFECTIVE GENERALIZATION PROGRAMMING

To ensure strong and lasting generalization from the training situation to the natural environment, the behavior modifier should observe the following rules as closely as possible.[7]

1. Choose target behaviors that are clearly useful to the individual, as these are the behaviors that are most likely to be reinforced in the natural environment.
2. Teach the target behavior in a situation that is as similar as possible to the natural environment in which you want the behavior to occur.
3. Establish the target behavior successively in as many situations as is feasible, starting with the easiest and progressing to the most difficult.
4. Gradually reduce the frequency of reinforcement in the training situation until it is less than that occurring in the natural environment.

5. When changing to a new situation, increase the frequency of reinforcement in order to offset the tendency of the individual to discriminate the new situation from the previous training situation.

6. Make sure that sufficient reinforcement for maintaining the target behavior occurs in the natural environment. This rule requires especially close attention in the early stages of transferring the target behavior from the training situation to the natural environment. Add reinforcement as necessary, including reinforcement to those people (such as parents and teachers) who are responsible for maintaining the target behavior in the natural environment, and then fade out this reinforcement slowly enough to prevent the target behavior from deteriorating.

Study Questions

(for examination purposes)

1. Briefly describe the main conclusions to be drawn from Rae Lowther's study on generalization.

2. In some cases, letting people "do their own thing" can have unpleasant consequences. How is this exemplified in the case of Sandra, Sarah, Sigrid, and Susan?

3. What was the training situation and what were the test situations with Sandra and the other girls? (One word for each is all that we're concerned with.)

4. Why is it that Rae could be quite confident that her reprimand "No" was not a reinforcer for Sarah and the other girls?

5. What was the tactic that Rae applied unsuccessfully in the day hall in trying to produce generalization? What tactic did she try that worked?

6. Would it have been easier to remember the girl who showed the poorest posture generalization if her name had been, say, Judy instead of Sarah? (Hint: Explain on the basis of stimuli controlling your generalization.)

7. Carefully explain the difference between stimulus generalization and stimulus discrimination.

8. In a sentence each, describe three main factors influencing the effectiveness of generalization.

9. In a sentence each, describe four main types of reinforcement contingencies that will influence generalization in the test situation.

10. What do we mean by behavioral trapping?

11. Did Kale et al. utilize schedules of reinforcement in the training situation or the test situation in order to improve generalization?

12. Describe two examples of pitfalls of generalization.
13. Describe two examples of pitfalls of generalization that are not discussed in the text.

Study Exercises

(to be practiced by the reader)

1. Describe a recent situation in which you generalized in desirable ways. Clearly identify the behavior, the training situation, and the test situation.
2. Describe a recent situation in which you generalized in an undesirable way (in other words, the outcome was undesirable). Again, identify the behavior, training situation, and test situation.
3. Choose one of the cases described in the previous chapters in which there was no effort to program generalization. Outline a specific plausible program for producing generalization in that case, taking into account the factors influencing the effectiveness of generalization training.

Self-Modification Exercise

(to be practiced by the reader)

Consider the behavior deficiency for which you outlined a shaping program at the end of Chapter 4. Assuming that your shaping program will be successful, discuss what you might do to program long-lasting generalization. (See the factors influencing the effectiveness of generalization that were discussed earlier in this chapter.)

EXTENDED DISCUSSION AND NOTES

1. A *stimulus class* is a set of stimuli, all of which have some characteristic in common. For example, look around the room you are in and list the objects you see that are red. These objects constitute the stimulus class that we might label "red objects." Although these objects are different in many respects, they all have in common the color red (defined physically in terms of a particular wavelength). When an individual can appropriately identify all red objects, we say that that individual has the *concept* "red." Stated differently, if an individual emits an appropriate response to all of the members of a particular stimulus class, and does not emit that response to stimuli that do not belong to the class (for instance, in the example above the individual does not include green objects, blue objects, etc.), then the individual generalizes to all of the members within a stimulus class (or concept), and discriminates be-

(Continued)

172

tween stimulus classes (for instance, between all red objects and all blue objects), and we say that the individual is showing conceptual behavior (Keller and Schoenfeld, 1950, p. 155). For a more detailed discussion of conceptual behavior, see Whaley and Malott (1971, pp. 171–192).

2. Baer, Wolf, and Risley (1968) described some dimensions of applied behavior analysis. One of the dimensions they discussed was generality. They suggested, "A behavioral change may be said to have generality if it proves durable over time, if it appears in a wide variety of possible environments, or if it spreads to a wide variety of related behaviors" (p. 96). The first two types of generality mentioned in the above quotation are what we have described as lasting generalization. The third type of generality, behavior spreading to a wide variety of related behaviors, is sometimes called response generalization. It would take place if, for example, improvement of articulation of specific words in a clinical setting led to improvement in the articulation of other untreated words. This type of behavioral effect has been referred to as an "avalanche" effect by Patterson, McNeal, Hawkins, and Phelps (1967), and as those authors suggest, little is known about such effects. The spread of improvements to related behaviors may be caused by a complex set of events. For example, Patterson et al. described a reinforcement program that improved the behavior of a child in a classroom situation. As a result, the child became much less obnoxious to his peers, and his interaction with the peer group occurred much more frequently. This interaction, in turn, appeared to result in the strengthening of a large number of socially adaptive behaviors. Perhaps because of the complexity of response generalization, perhaps because the desirable target behaviors are usually incorporated into the program design, and perhaps for other reasons, behavior modifiers have tended not to describe detailed procedures for developing response generality (Keeley, Shemburg, and Carbonell, 1976).

3. It is often mistakenly thought that behaviorists do not believe that individual differences in behavior can be due to genetic factors. Actually, the behavioristic position is generally that such explanations should be proposed only as a "last resort," in the sense that the job of the scientific psychologist is first to thoroughly check out possible environmental explanations before saying something like, "Well, the reason this individual behaves differently from others must be genetic." The noted behaviorist Murray Sidman expressed this position quite clearly when he observed that there is little point in investigating presumed genetic causes of behavioral differences as long as "psychologists are not yet capable of stating unequivocally whether or not the variability [i.e., differences between individuals] in their data stems from inadequate experimental control, insufficient understanding of the [behavioral] processes involved, or from factors [e.g., genetic] that lie outside their sphere of competence" (1960, p. 180).

4. Martin (1972) discussed the importance of reinforcing the behavior of the behavior modifier. Psychiatric nurses and nursing attendants who used behavior modification procedures to improve the behavior of retarded individuals did so much more consistently when their own behavior was reinforced in a structured staff-incentive program. For a more recent discussion of factors important in maintaining staff behaviors in residential treatment programs, see McInnis (1976).

(Continued)

(Continued)

5. For a review of programs in which parents have been taught the use of behavior modification to manage the behavior of their children in the home, see O'Dell (1974).

6. Another example of this factor was reported by Stokes, Baer, and Jackson (1974). They utilized prompting and shaping techniques to teach four institutionalized retarded children to greet the teacher with a hand-waving response. After training had been completed by one teacher, the greeting response did not generalize when the children were approached by any one of the twenty other institutional staff members. However, three of the four children showed high levels of generalization to other staff members after receiving additional training from a second teacher. The fourth child, who did not receive training from the second teacher, nevertheless showed generalization of hand waving after receiving additional training from the first teacher.

7. For a thorough review of the current technology of generalization see Stokes and Baer (1977).

Study Questions on Notes

1. What do we mean by "stimulus class"? By "conceptual behavior"?
2. Describe how you might teach the concept *wet* to a child.
3. Describe how you might teach the concept *honesty* to a child.
4. Is love a concept? Explain your answer in behavioral terms.
5. How will the authors judge whether or not you are showing appropriate conceptual behavior in response to the stimulus class *positive reinforcer?*
6. What are the three types of generality discussed by Baer, Risley, and Wolf?
7. How is a behavioral "avalanche" different from a behavioral "trap"?
8. "Genetic explanations for behavioral deficiencies should be proposed only as a 'last resort.' " Briefly discuss.
9. Which factor influencing the effectiveness of generalization is exemplified by Stokes et al.?

CHAPTER 12

Eliminating Inappropriate Behavior Through **PUNISHMENT** and Positive Reinforcement

"James, don't hurt yourself"

ELIMINATING JAMES'S SELF-ABUSE

James was a seven-year-old institutionalized hydrocephalic retarded boy.* He had a moderate understanding of speech, and he could follow a few simple instructions. His was a very pathetic case, however, for he had to spend most of his waking hours strapped in a specially constructed chair-table arrangement.

The reason for this degrading confinement was that James was a chronic head banger. Only if he was holding on to the hand of an adult, or was on a soft surface such as grass or a carpet, was it safe to allow him

*This report is based on an unpublished case study by Pauline Kaprowy and Joseph Pear at the St. Amant Centre, an institution for retarded children in Winnipeg, Manitoba.

175

out of his chair. If the adult released his hand while he was standing on a hard surface, James would immediately "dive" to the floor and begin banging his head. Unless stopped, he would continue until he was bleeding profusely.

We have already discussed how this behavior had most likely been reinforced by the attention it evoked from adults; attention was a strong positive reinforcer for James. A number of procedures had been tried in an effort to eliminate the behavior, but all had failed. The behavior modification personnel at the hospital were familiar with studies such as those by Risley (1968) and Lovaas and Simmons (1969), which had shown that self-destructive behavior can be suppressed by punishing it with electric shock. Therefore, the behavior modification staff met with the hospital's medical director and other senior personnel responsible for James's care, and discussed the possibility of applying shock in an attempt to eliminate James's head banging.

Electric shock is not a pleasant thing.* But neither was James's present condition. Previous episodes of head banging had left an ugly scar on the child's head, and life to James meant little more than days spent strapped in a chair that protected him from himself. At the meeting between the behavior modification staff and the senior hospital personnel, the feeling of the participants was summed up by one senior official who said, "Almost anything is worth a try. If we don't do something soon, one of these days that boy is going to kill himself."

The following day, the behavior modification personnel secured a two-foot-long cylinder-shaped device that contained six flashlight batteries at one end and shock electrodes at the other. This device is commonly known as a cattle prod. Since that name has misleading and unpleasant associations, however, we shall refer to the device simply as the "shocker."

At first, the behavior modifiers, Pauline and Brenda, worked with James for about one hour daily in a small room. They stood a few feet from each other and instructed James to walk back and forth between them. One staff member held various objects, which she instructed James to take and carry to the other staff member. Each time he correctly followed the instruction, he was rewarded immediately with candy and lavish praise and hugs. But each time he attempted to dive to the floor, two brief shocks were applied to the bare skin on his leg. This proved to be quite punishing, in that soon he was walking back and forth without any sign of diving.

Over trials, the distance between the staff was gradually increased, until finally they were in different rooms. When James could walk back and forth between the two rooms without banging his head, the program was moved to the ward. Since this was a place where, from past experience, head banging was very probable, the distance between the two staff members was decreased to just a few feet again. Gradually, it was increased to the entire length of the ward. At this point, only one staff member was needed to work with James.

*Any behavior modifier contemplating the use of electric shock should consult a qualified electrical technician and follow appropriate safety guidelines, such as those given by Butterfield (1975).

During each one-hour daily session, Pauline instructed James to run various "errands" for her. These "errands" consisted mainly of getting objects from various rooms and taking them to Pauline, and taking other objects from Pauline to the various rooms. Sometimes James was instructed to go to the main desk and ask the nurse in charge for a Kleenex or some other item.

At all times, Pauline was careful to keep the shocker available, but out of James's view. Otherwise, James would easily have learned that head banging would not be punished when the shocker was out of sight.

Soon, James would never bang his head when Pauline was around. The staff on the ward were extremely impressed to see James roaming the ward, freely and safely, under Pauline's watchful eye. None of them had ever seen James behave that way. But although this represented a remarkable improvement in the boy's behavior, it was, of course, not good enough. The child still banged his head when Pauline was not around. In fact, it appeared that in her absence his head banging was a bit worse then it had been before the program began.[1]

To solve this problem, Pauline had to play, temporarily, an unusual role in the program. Hiding behind doors and around corners, she would watch James while other staff members dressed him, bathed him, took him to his meals, and generally took care of him. Whenever he began to bang his head, she would quickly come out from her hiding place and apply the shock. Meanwhile the other staff members were instructed to copiously reinforce James for not banging his head.

Of course, Pauline was sometimes busy with other activities and could not watch James. On these occasions, Pauline was on call so that if James began to bang his head, a staff member would tell him, "I'm going to call Pauline." If he did not stop, Pauline was called to the scene, whereupon she applied the shocker. After a few instances of this, the threat "I'm going to call Pauline" was usually enough to stop the head banging.

Still, this was a good deal less than satisfactory. Pauline could not always be on call. Therefore, the head nurse and other supervisory personnel of each shift were authorized to use the shocker. The shocker was kept at the main desk, and all of the staff were instructed that they should immediately call a supervisor whenever James started to bang his head. To guard against possible misuse of the shocker, all staff members met with behavior modification personnel to discuss the use of the shocker, and a set of rules for applying the program were circulated and discussed.

James's initial reaction to being shocked by someone other than Pauline appeared to be surprise and anger. But his head banging on the ward was greatly suppressed by this procedure.

At about this time, James started attending the special-education classes that were conducted at the institution. His teacher was trained in the use of the shocker, and in the use of positive reinforcement. James worked well in the classroom and soon became one of the better students.

James's head banging decreased tremendously as a result of the program, and, consequently, he was allowed to move about the ward on his own. He quickly learned to play with other children—something he had never done before. At first, the ward staff were so impressed that they gave James a great deal of social attention for doing things without banging his head. But as the novelty of James's new repertoire wore off, it appeared that he received less and less attention. Perhaps for this reason there was some regression: James began banging his head again, although not nearly as frequently as before. Most of these head bangings occurred in the playroom—a place in which James did not particularly like to be.

To offset the problem of lack of reinforcement, James was put on a DRO schedule. The staff were asked to give James a token for each five-minute period he spent in the playroom without banging his head. To prevent James from losing the tokens, the staff did not give them to him directly. Rather, the tokens, which could be linked together to form a chain, were hung on the wall in a place where James could easily see them.

When James had earned seven tokens, he could leave the playroom and go for a walk with one of the staff members. If no staff member was free when James had earned his seven tokens, he was allowed to play by himself in the hall. Since he did not like to be in the playroom, either of these alternatives was reinforcing to him.

A specially constructed data sheet was hung on the door of the playroom, and the attendant was instructed to record on it the number of times James banged his head and the number of tokens he received for not banging his head. The behavior modification personnel checked the data sheets daily and provided feedback to the attendants on their application of James's program. Thus, data sheets were as much a means of controlling staff behavior as a means of controlling James's behavior.

The daily instances of James's head banging eventually decreased to a very small number. Although the shocker still had to be used occasionally, even after the program had been in effect for several months, James's behavior improved greatly. He could run about and play with other children and no longer had to be confined to his chair.

THE PRINCIPLE OF PUNISHMENT

Like the principle of positive reinforcement (described on pp. 18–19,) the principle of punishment has two parts: (1) if in a given situation somebody does something that is followed immediately by a certain consequence, then (2) that person is less likely to do the same thing again when he next encounters a similar situation. Such consequences are called punishers. In James's case, shock was a punisher for his head-banging behavior. As with positive reinforcement, many repetitions of punishment of a particular response may be necessary before that response will noticeably decrease in frequency or probability. As we all know, it is unpleasant to be punished, and there are a number of potentially harmful effects from punishment procedures, which we will enumerate later. For these reasons, it is very important that any punishment program be designed so that it is maximally effective with the least amount of discomfort. A number of factors influence the effectiveness of punishment.[2] Let us turn to them now.

FACTORS INFLUENCING THE EFFECTIVENESS OF PUNISHMENT

1. Maximizing the conditions for a desirable alternative response

To decrease some undesirable response, it is maximally effective to concurrently increase some alternative desirable response. This means that you should identify some desirable response that will compete with the undesirable behavior to be eliminated. You should also attempt to identify powerful S^Ds that control the desirable behavior and present these in order to increase the likelihood that the behavior will occur. To maintain the desirable behavior, you should also have effective positive reinforcers that can be presented on an effective schedule. For James, the desirable alternative that was initially prompted and reinforced was simply walking back and forth between two staff members and not banging his head.

When consulted by individuals who are thinking about using a punishment procedure to decrease an undesirable behavior in someone else, we have always recommended that they first design effective positive-reinforcement and stimulus control programs for desirable alternative behaviors. Thus, if you are considering developing and using a punishment program to decrease someone's undesirable behavior, we strongly urge you to first review and apply the information in the earlier chapters concerning positive reinforcement and stimulus control (see Figure 12-1).

2. Minimizing the causes of the response to be punished

In order to maximize the opportunity for the desirable alternative behavior to occur anyone attempting a punishment program should first minimize the causes of the punished behavior. This implies two things. First, one should try to identify the current stimulus control of the punished behavior. In James's case, it was clear that he banged his head on the floor (1) in the presence of staff members, and (2) if the floor had a hard surface. These stimuli were therefore removed in the initial training program: two behavior modification personnel, rather than staff members, conducted the initial training sessions, and an alternative setting with a carpet on the floor was used. Second, it is necessary to attempt to identify existing rein-

FIGURE 12-1. *An example of the reinforcement of a desirable alternative behavior.*

forcers for the undesirable behavior. If the behavior is occurring, it is likely that occasional reinforcers are maintaining it. In James's case, it seems clear that occasional attention from the staff for head banging was the most likely reinforcer maintaining the undesirable behavior. This contingency was completely removed at the onset of the program.

It is interesting to note that in many situations in which someone is emitting undesirable behavior, careful attention to these two factors may yield some desirable alternative behavior that competes so strongly with the behavior to be decreased that punishment will never have to be used. However, there are situations in which punishment procedures appear to be necessary and justified, and, therefore, additional factors must be considered.

3. Selecting a punisher

It is very important that the punisher be effective. Some stimuli may seem to be punishing when in fact they are not. For example, a parent may say "No! Naughty boy! Stop that!" to a child who is engaging in an undesirable behavior. The child may immediately cease the undesirable behavior and emit some other, desired behavior, which will continue to receive the attention of the adult. The adult might then conclude that the verbal reprimand was an effective punisher. However, if the adult were to keep track of the frequency of that undesirable behavior in the future, she would likely find that the verbal reprimand was not a punisher, but in fact a reinforcer. The child may have stopped temporarily, because now that he has the attention of the adult it is likely that he can emit other behavior that will maintain her attention, at least for a short time. In other words, the verbal reprimand may function as an S^D for subsequent desirable behaviors of the child, regardless of the effects of the verbal reprimand as a punisher or a reinforcer on the preceding undesirable behavior. Several studies indicate that verbal reprimands often function as positive reinforcers, and that the long-term frequency of the undesirable behavior that evoked the reprimand is therefore likely to increase.[3] This is not to say that verbal reprimands or threats are never punishing. However, the situations in which they are effective seem to be those in which they are consistently backed up by a strong punisher.

In order to be effective, the punishing stimulus should be fairly intense. Frequently, individuals start with a weak punisher in the belief that they can increase its strength if it is not effective. Many parents have experienced the following situation. A child emits some undesirable behavior, which is followed by a mild reprimand by the parent. The behavior reoccurs, and the parent provides a stronger reprimand, perhaps coupled with a frown. The behavior is repeated, and the parent severely scolds the child. The behavior is repeated, and the child receives a scolding and a mild slap. The behavior is repeated until finally the parent delivers a severe spanking. There are two problems here. One is that the undesirable behavior may be very harmful or dangerous; if that behavior consists, for example, of running out in the street and playing in the traffic, then the long-term consequences of allowing it to occur many times are potentially disastrous. The second problem is that the severe punisher, the spanking, may have lost a good deal of its effectiveness by the time it is applied. Gradually increasing the intensity of a punisher is not nearly as effective as introducing the punisher in its final form on the first occasion (Azrin and Holz, 1966).

The punisher selected should be one that can be presented immediately following the undesirable behavior. The punisher should also be one that can be presented in a manner such that it is in no way paired with positive reinforcement. This requirement often presents difficulties in situations in which the punisher is delivered by an adult and the student being punished receives very little adult attention. If a student has received a lot of loving attention from an adult during a period of time prior to the occurrence of the undesired behavior, and the adult immediately presents a strong verbal reprimand following the undesirable behavior, then the verbal reprimand might be slightly punishing. On the other hand, if that reprimand is the only adult attention that has been received by the student for an extended period of time, then that reprimand is a form of adult attention and may in fact be reinforcing.

Shock is a drastic form of punishment, one that should be used only when no other recourse is available for eliminating a serious behavior.[4] It seemed to be required in James's case, but less extreme punishers will be quite adequate in most cases that call for punishment. As with selecting an effective reinforcer for a particular individual, it sometimes requires a little imagination to discover an effective punisher. This can be illustrated by the case of Ricky, a retarded boy who occasionally bit or scratched other children.* The injuries he inflicted were so severe that in order to protect the other children, the staff made Ricky wear a special face mask (resembling a catcher's mask) that prevented him from biting, and special heavy cloth mittens that prevented him from scratching. Both the face mask and the mittens were tied on so that Ricky could not remove them.

The behavior modification personnel at the institution decided to tackle Ricky's biting first and deal with his scratching later. They reasoned that the probable reinforcement for biting (and scratching) was the attention that it evoked when staff members came running to rescue the injured child. Extinction by withholding this reinforcer was out of the question, since it would likely result in many serious injuries. Some form of punishment seemed called for, but the behavior modification personnel did not wish to increase Ricky's discomfort unnecessarily. By observing him, they noted that he appeared to dislike having his face mask put on. Thus, the idea occurred to them: Why not try the face mask as a punisher?

Thereupon, the following procedure was specified: Ricky will no longer be required to wear his face mask unless he bites. Immediately after a bite, the face mask will be put on for ten minutes. He will be given plenty of social attention for "not biting" when the face mask is off. The procedure worked very well, and soon Ricky no longer bit other children.

Because this procedure worked so well in the case of biting, a similar procedure was tried for scratching. It was decided that Ricky would no longer be required to wear his mittens unless he scratched. Immediately after a scratching episode, the mittens would be put on him for ten minutes. But this time the strategy failed. Rather than decreasing, scratching occurred very frequently, and it appeared to be increasing when the behavior modification personnel called a halt to the procedure. It seemed that the mittens were not punishing and may in fact have been reinforcing. The next idea that occurred to the behavior modifiers was this: If the face mask worked as a punisher for biting, why shouldn't it also work as a punisher for scratching? But before following through on this idea, the behavior modifiers had to answer one further question: What do we do if Ricky scratches while he has the face mask on? It was decided that in this case, and this case only, shock would be applied.

The results of this procedure were quite effective. Ricky's scratching gradually decreased in frequency. The number of times he scratched when the face mask was on decreased very quickly to zero,

*This report is taken from an unpublished case study conducted by Brenda Geisbrecht and Joseph Pear at the St. Amant Centre, Winnipeg, Manitoba.

because of the stronger punishment for this behavior. An added feature that contributed to the success of the procedure was that Ricky was reinforced on a DRO schedule, similar to that used for James, for engaging in behavior other than biting and scratching.

Another type of punishment is the response-contingent withdrawal of positive reinforcement. A common example would be sending a misbehaving child away from the dinner table. Here, food (presumably a positive reinforcer) has been withdrawn from the child as a result of her misbehavior. A disadvantage of this procedure is that it removes the child from the situation for a longer period of time than might be necessary, and thus prevents some of the learning that could occur in the situation. In one of our programs, a somewhat milder version of this method was used with a retarded girl who ate too rapidly. Food was a powerful reinforcer for this child. Therefore, whenever the child was eating too rapidly, a staff member gripped the child's wrist tightly for a few seconds so that she could not get the food to her mouth. This delay in reinforcement was aversive enough that the child soon slowed to a normal rate of eating. Of course, the staff lavished the child with praise when this occurred.

The most extreme form of withdrawal of positive reinforcement is the elimination of all possible sources of it. This is referred to as "time out from positive reinforcement," or more simply, *time-out*. This may be accomplished in several ways. One method is to turn away from the individual and ignore him for a brief period. In another method, the individual who is to receive this punisher is actually placed in a "time-out room," a small room that is typically completely bare of furniture. Since there is nothing in the time-out room to entertain the individual, the procedure effectively eliminates almost all sources of positive reinforcement. The period of detention in the time-out room should not be very long; about five minutes is usually quite effective if the principles of punishment are adhered to closely.[5] However, the individual should not be let out if he is engaging in undesirable behavior (such as tantruming) when the detention period has elapsed. Otherwise, the undesirable behavior will be reinforced. To prevent this, the staff should wait until the undesirable behavior has stopped for a short time—say, ten seconds.[6]

There are certain problems with the use of a time-out room. Obviously, it would not be feasible to use this procedure with a severe head banger unless the room was well padded. Another problem, one that we encountered in one of our programs, was the case of a retarded girl who defecated and smeared her feces while in the time-out room. We guessed that the reinforcement for this behavior came from two sources: (1) the child enjoyed smearing her feces, and (2) she enjoyed the warm shower the staff give her after she engaged in this behavior. We found it difficult to extinguish the behavior in the time-out room and elsewhere. Therefore, we decided to give the child a shower, as before, whenever the behavior occurred. But it was to be a cool shower, not a warm shower. This contingency quickly reduced the undesirable behavior to zero.

4. Delivering the punisher

Punishment will be most effective when the punisher is presented immediately following the undesirable behavior. If the punisher is delayed, some more desirable behavior may occur prior to the punisher and this desirable behavior may be affected by the punisher to a much greater extent than the prior undesirable behavior. The classic example of this is the mother who asks her husband, as he returns home from work, to spank their son, who has been bad earlier in the day. This request is doubly disastrous: not only does the child receive punishment, even though he may now be engaging in good behavior, but the father is punished for coming home from work. We do not mean to imply that delayed punishment is completely ineffective. Most human beings are adept at bridging rather large times gaps between their behavior and its consequences. Even so, immediate punishment is much more effective than delayed punishment.

The punisher should be delivered after *every* instance of the undesirable behavior (see, for example, Kircher, Pear, and Martin, 1971). Occasional punishment is not nearly as effective as punishment that follows every instance of the undesirable behavior. This implies that if the teacher is unable to detect most instances of the behavior to be punished, he should have serious doubts about the value of implementing a punishment procedure.

The delivery of the punishment should in no way be paired with positive reinforcement. Such a pairing weakens the punisher. Worse, it may completely offset the effects of punishment and cause an increase in the undesirable behavior. In addition, the person administering the punishment should remain calm when doing so. Anger and frustration on his part may reinforce the undesirable behavior and/or inappropriately alter the intensity of the punishment. A calm, matter-of-fact approach ensures that a punishment program will be followed as it has been designed, and that the person administering the punishment will be less likely to apply a punisher at inappropriate times (i.e., when angry or annoyed) rather than immediately following an occasion of undesirable behavior.

PITFALLS OF PUNISHMENT: HOW IT WORKS TO THE DISADVANTAGE OF THOSE WHO ARE IGNORANT OF IT

Punishment is a tricky endeavor. Its use should be approached with caution, since it has a number of potential drawbacks, undesirable side effects, and pitfalls.

Strong punishment tends to elicit undesirable emotional behavior. Experiments with animals show that painful stimuli cause them to attack other animals—even though these other animals had nothing to do with inflicting the painful stimuli (Azrin, 1967). If this finding also applies to humans, then we should not be surprised to observe individuals who have just been punished attacking other individuals.[7] Clearly, such behavior is a very undesirable side effect of punishment.

Strong punishment can produce other undesirable emotional side effects, such as crying and general fearfulness. Not only are these side effects unpleasant for all concerned, they frequently interfere with desirable behavior—especially if it is of a complex nature.

Any stimulus that is associated with a punishing stimulus tends to become punishing itself.[8] Such a stimulus is called a conditioned punisher. For example, if you are trying to teach a child to read, and if you punish her whenever she makes a mistake, anything associated with this situation—such as printed words, books, the person who delivers the punishment, the type of room in which the punishment occurs—will tend to become punishing. The child may attempt to escape or avoid these stimuli. Thus, instead of helping the individual to learn, punishment may drive her away from people, objects, and events associated with the learning situation.

Punishment does not establish any new behavior; it only suppresses old behavior. In other words, punishment does not teach an individual what to do; at best, it only teaches what not to do. For example, the main defining characteristic of the retarded is that they lack behavior that nonretarded people have. The primary emphasis for these individuals, then, should be on establishing new behavior rather than on merely eliminating old behavior. Reinforcement is required for the accomplishment of this task.

Children often model or imitate adults. If adults apply punishment to children, the children are apt to do the same to others. Thus, in punishing children we may inadvertently be providing a model for them to follow in showing aggression towards others (Bandura, 1965, 1969).

Punishment may become addictive to the user. Because it results in quick suppression of undesirable behavior, it can tempt the user to rely heavily on it and neglect the use of positive reinforcement for desirable behavior. However, the undesirable behavior may return after only a temporary suppression; or, some other undesirable behavior could occur. Like any other addict, the person "hooked" on administering punishment may resort to progressively heavier doses, thereby creating a vicious circle with disastrous side effects.

Before closing this section, we must emphasize that punishment should be used only as a last resort. It is far too easy to devise a punishment procedure when a reinforcement procedure is indicated instead. An example of this in one of our programs was the case of a retarded girl who refused to eat. The child would fight off attempts by the attendant to put food in her mouth. Finally, she had to be force-fed. Because food did not appear to be an effective reinforcer for this child, someone suggested that the only thing that would work would be to punish her refusals of food. But closer analysis revealed that this was not the case. Food might very well have been a powerful reinforcer for this child, but by refusing it she eventually received not only food but also the attention and physical contact that came with force feeding. Acting upon this analysis, we shaped and maintained the child's eating by (1) turning away for a brief period when she refused the food, and (2) giving her plenty of attention and contact, first for approximations to eating and finally for accepting the food. Clearly, this was a case in which punishment was *not* called for and in which it could have done real damage by making the eating situation aversive to the child. The use of positive reinforcement created a very pleasant situation in which the child ate her food *and* received the attention and physical contact that she desired.

We have discussed extensively the large number of pitfalls lying in wait for those who try to use punishment without being familiar with its principles. At least as serious are the many instances in which punishment is applied by people who are not aware that they are applying it. A common example of this is criticizing or ridiculing a person for inadequate behavior. Since criticism and ridicule are generally punishing, they will likely suppress future instances of that behavior and tend to drive the individual away from the person administering them. Yet the inadequate behavior that is criticized and ridiculed may be an approximation to more adequate behavior. Suppressing it could destroy the individual's opportunity to obtain the adequate behavior through the use of shaping. In everyday language, the individual becomes "discouraged" and "gives up" in his "attempt" to develop adequate behavior. In addition, because he will attempt to escape from and avoid the person administering the criticism and ridicule, that person will have lost a great deal of his potential reinforcing effectiveness.

Another example of someone applying punishment without being aware of it is the person who says, "That was good, but. . . ." Suppose a teenager helps a parent with the dishes and the parent replies, "Thanks for helping, but the next time don't be so slow." We are sure that on the basis of the previous material you can describe a much more effective and pleasant way for the parent to react.

As you can see, the use of punishment can cause difficulties. In our view, punishment should be applied only in conjunction with positive reinforcement for a desirable behavior, and only for the purpose of eliminating undesirable behaviors that cannot be reduced in other ways. We do not recommend its use by individuals who are not familiar with the factors influencing its effectiveness, or with its potentially harmful side effects.

GUIDELINES FOR THE EFFECTIVE APPLICATION OF PUNISHMENT PROCEDURES

Punishment is clearly aversive for the one being punished, it is a lot of work and no fun for the punisher, and the results are frequently setting-specific and may or may not be permanent (depending on other factors). In addition, the rules for the effective use of punishment are probably violated more than those for any other principle. Therefore, if you propose a punishment procedure (even one involving a mild punisher), you owe it to yourself and the person being punished to do an effective job. Otherwise, leave it completely alone and use only positive reinforcement.

1. *Selecting a response.* Punishment is most effective with a specific behavior (such as jumping on the arm of the chair) rather than a general category of behavior (such as wrecking furniture).
2. *Maximize the conditions for a desirable (nonpunished) alternative response.*
   a) Select a desirable alternative behavior that competes with the behavior to be punished such that the alternative behavior can be reinforced. If possible, select a behavior that will be maintained by the natural environment after the termination of your reinforcement program.
   b) Provide strong prompts in order to increase the likelihood that the desirable alternative behavior will occur.
   c) Reinforce the desirable behavior with a powerful reinforcer on an appropriate schedule.

3. *Minimize the causes of the response to be punished.*
   a) Try to identify and eliminate many or all of the stimuli controlling the undesirable behavior, at least early in the training program.
   b) Try to eliminate any possible reinforcement for the undesirable behavior.
4. *Select an effective punisher.*
   a) Choose an effective punisher that can be presented immediately following the undesirable behavior.
   b) The punisher should be one that will in no way be paired with positive reinforcement following the undesirable behavior.
   c) Select a punisher that can be presented following every instance of the undesirable behavior.
5. *Delivering the punisher.*
   a) The punisher should be presented *immediately* following *every* instance of the response to be decreased.

b) The individual administering the punisher should do so in a calm and matter-of-fact manner.

c) The person doing the punishing should also be associated with a lot of positive reinforcement for alternative behaviors, so that the person does not become a conditioned punisher.

d) Take care not to pair punishment with reinforcement.

6. In all programs involving punishment, careful data should be taken on the effects of the program. The conditions under which the program should be applied must be clearly stated, written down, and adhered to.

Study Questions

(for examination purposes)

1. How were reinforcement, shaping, schedules of reinforcement, and tokens used in the program for eliminating James's self-destructive behavior?

2. How do we identify stimuli as punishers or reinforcers?

3. How did Pauline attempt to maximize the conditions for a desirable alternative response with James during the early part of the program for eliminating his self destructive behavior,

4. In the program for eliminating James's self destructive behavior, how did Pauline try to minimize the probability that the response to be punished would occur during the initial training program?

5. What are the problems with gradually increasing the intensity of the punishing stimulus over successive applications of that stimulus?

6. How would you determine if a verbal reprimand was a punisher for a particular child?

7. In the subsection "Selecting a punisher," we described a sequence (involving a potential reprimand) of events and behaviors that might be characterized as a behavioral chain. What was that sequence?

8. What is a common example of the response-contingent withdrawal of positive reinforcement that is applied as punishment by parents to their children?

9. In the subsection "Delivering the Punisher," we suggested that if the teacher is unable to detect most instances of a behavior to be punished, then he should have serious doubts about the value of implementing a punishment procedure.

a) From the information in this chapter, what reasons can you cite to support this suggestion?

b) What alternative means of managing the situation are availabe to the teacher?

10. What are four concerns of the teacher in regard to delivering the punisher?
11. Briefly cite seven pitfalls of the application of punishment.

Study Exercises

(to be practiced by the reader)

1. Consider the behavior of speeding (driving a car in excess of the speed limit) in our culture.
   a) Briefly outline the current contingencies with respect to speeding.
   b) Compare the current contingencies for speeding with the guidelines for the effective application of punishment procedures. Identify those guidelines that either were simply not attended to or were flagrantly violated by the lawmakers and law enforcers.
2. Consider the behavior of littering the highways in your area. Repeat the analysis that you applied in study exercise 1.

Self-Modification Exercise

(to be practiced by the reader)

Choose a behavior of yours that you would like to decrease. With the help of a friend, describe in detail a punishment program that would likely decrease your behavior. (Make the program as realistic as possible, but do not apply it.) Your punishment program should be consistent with all of the guidelines for the effective application of punishment.

EXTENDED DISCUSSION AND NOTES

1. This finding is closely related to a phenomenon reported by Reynolds (1961). In a basic experiment, pigeons were reinforced according to a VI schedule for pecking a plastic disc in the presence of a particular stimulus, and they were reinforced on the same VI schedule for responding in the same chamber in the presence of a different stimulus. The two stimuli alternated. After the performance was relatively steady in the presence of both stimuli, Reynolds decreased the reinforcement frequency in the presence of one stimulus, thereby causing a decrease in the response rate there. The result of this action was an increase in responding in the presence of the other stimulus, even though the reinforcement frequency in the presence of that stimulus had remained the same. This was termed *behavioral contrast* by Reynolds. Another study on contrast that is even more similar to the situation described for James was reported by Brethower and Reynolds (1962). In this study, the pi-
(Continued)

geons were reinforced for responding in the presence of a green light on a VI schedule, and also for responding in the presence of a red light on a VI schedule, the schedule and lights alternating within the experimental chamber. When a condition was added such that responses in the presence of the green light also produced an electric shock, the performance in the presence of the green light decreased and there was a corresponding increase in the rate of responding to the red light.

2. Azrin and Holz (1966) summarized the results of their research on punishment that had been conducted during approximately the preceding five years. They outlined a number of influences on the effectiveness of punishment, and a review of the literature since that time suggests that none of their major conclusions have been refuted. Much of the material in this chapter is based on their work.

3. The potential reinforcing value of reprimands was demonstrated nicely in a study by Madsen, Becker, Thomas, Koser, and Plager (1970). A teacher was instructed to increase her use of the reprimand "Sit down!" when the children were actually out of their seats. As a consequence of the teacher saying "Sit down!" more often, the children's out-of-seat behavior increased.

4. Even in cases where electric-shock punishment may appear warranted, one should always search the literature for alternatives. A very dramatic example of an alternative treatment concerns what may have been the life-saving treatment of a six-month-old baby (Sajwaj, Libet, and Agras, 1974). Sandra was admitted to the University Hospital in Charleston, South Carolina because of a failure to gain weight that was associated with the constant bringing up of food without nausea (ruminating). She was underweight and undernourished, and death was a distinct possibility. Preliminary observations indicated that a few minutes after being given milk, Sandra would begin ruminating and would continue for about twenty to forty minutes until she had apparently lost all the milk she had previously consumed. Now considering the seriousness of the problem (Sajwaj, et al. cited statistics indicating that one in six or seven babies with rumination die), a program of electric-shock might appear to have been warranted. Indeed, Sajwaj et al. cited several studies demonstrating the effectiveness of shock punishment in eliminating rumination. However, for several reasons outlined by Sajwaj et al., the authors were reluctant to utilize shock. Instead, they utilized lemon juice as a punisher. During treatment, Sandra's mouth was filled with lemon juice immediately after staff members detected the vigorous tongue movements that reliably preceded her rumination. After sixteen feedings with lemon juice, the rumination had decreased to a very low level. To ensure that the improvement was due to the treatment program, Sajwaj et al. suspended the use of lemon juice for two feedings. The result was a dramatic increase in rumination. The lemon-juice therapy was reintroduced and again led to a dramatic decrease in rumination. Following additional treatment Sandra was discharged to foster parents, who maintained the treatment until it was no longer necessary. Five months later, Sandra was returned to her natural parents, a much improved little girl.

5. Bostow and Bailey (1969) successfully applied time-outs of two minutes duration (plus an additional fifteen seconds of quiet behavior at the end of that time) for disruptive and aggressive behaviors of two

retarded patients in a state-hospital ward setting. In another study, White, Nielsen, and Johnson (1972) compared the effectiveness of time-out durations of one minute, fifteen minutes, and thirty minutes in controlling deviant behaviors in a group of twenty institutionalized retarded individuals. They found that one-minute time-outs were not as effective in general as fifteen- and thirty-minute time-outs, but there was little difference between the two longer time-out intervals. Thus, excessively long time-outs do not necessarily increase the effectiveness of the time-out as a punisher. For additional discussion of a variety of time-out studies, see MacDonough and Forehand (1973).

6. A detailed set of guidelines for the application of time-out in an institutional setting has been prepared by the Research Unit staff at The Manitoba School, and is available upon request from Dr. Glen Lowther, Medical Superintendent, The Manitoba School, Portage la Prairie, Manitoba, Canada.

7. Some authors cite aggression as a side effect of a punishment program; others cite punishment programs that have had desirable suppressing effects without producing aggression. Examples of the former are Foxx and Azrin (1972) and Pendergrass (1972), who both reported temporary aggressive behaviors of both adults and children exposed to punishment procedures. On the other hand, Johnston (1972), in an excellent review of punishment, reported that many studies in applied settings not only did not observe undesirable side effects, but did observe increases in desirable behaviors as a consequence of a punishment program.

8. This was demonstrated very clearly in an experiment by Lovaas, Schaeffer, and Simmons (1965) with autistic children. In the first part of the experiment, the children were reinforced with candy for pressing a lever, and they demonstrated very high lever-pressing rates. On several occasions, immediately following a lever press the experimenter said "No!" which had practically no effect on the rate of lever pressing. The severely disturbed children were then given a training session in which their extreme self-stimulation and tantruming behaviors were followed by a "No!" and a brief electric-shock punisher. After several pairings of the word "No!" with the shock in these sessions, the children were again given an opportunity to press a lever for candy reinforcement. When their lever pressing was occurring at a high rate, the experimenter said "No!" and the presentation of this verbal stimulus now had a very strong suppressing effect on the lever pressing.

Study Questions on Notes

1. What is "behavioral contrast"?
2. How are the two examples of behavioral contrast reported by Reynolds different?
3. How did Madsen et al. demonstrate that reprimands can actually be reinforcing?
4. Describe in three or four sentences the "lemon-juice therapy" reported by Sajwaj et al.

(Continued)

(Continued)

5. The longer the time-out, the more effective the punishment. Right? (Discuss.)

6. Punishment does not produce aggression. Right? (Discuss.)

7. Briefly describe how Lovaas et al. demonstrated that a stimulus paired with punishment will itself become punishing. What is such a stimulus called?

CHAPTER 13

Establishing A Desirable Behavior By Using **ESCAPE** and **AVOIDANCE** Conditioning

"Scotty, would you like to play with your new toy?"

A NEW TOY FOR SCOTTY

Scotty was a seven-year-old institutionalized severely retarded boy, diagnosed as having Down's syndrome, who habitually beat his head with his hands.* This self-destructiveness was so severe that Scotty spent twenty-four hours a day in a crib with his hands tied to his waist and a modified football helmet on his head. Because of the severity of the problem, the staff psychologist designed a behavioral procedure involving electric-shock punishment (similar to procedures described in Chapter 12). This quickly eliminated Scotty's head beating in the training situation. But what about other situations?

*This case study was described in Whaley and Malott (1971). For the original report, see
  Whaley and Tough (1970).

The psychologist realized that it would not be safe to let the boy run freely on the ward until some desirable alternative behavior to head beating was developed. To accomplish this, staff members placed Scotty in a highchair and put a large metal truck on the tray in front of him. An electric timer wired to the truck measured how long the boy touched the truck. Since Scotty engaged in this activity hardly at all, it was clear that special procedures would be required to get him to do so. Before describing these procedures, we should emphasize that prior to being implemented they were reviewed and approved by the Ethical Review Committee of the institution. This committee also monitored the program throughout the time that it was in effect. (As we shall point out in Chapter 29, all behavior modification programs should be subject to appropriate ethical controls. This is especially critical when aversive events such as shock are to be used.)

At the beginning of the program, Scotty was given trials in which a mild electric shock was presented through electrodes attached to his leg; simultaneously, a buzzer sounded. When Scotty touched the truck, the buzzer and the shock turned off automatically. At first, it was necessary to prompt Scotty by guiding his hand to the truck when the buzzer and shock came on. After about a dozen trials, however, he did this himself immediately upon the presentation of the two stimuli. After each trial, Scotty's hand was taken from the truck, if necessary, before a new trial was begun.

This procedure is called *escape conditioning* because Scotty escaped the shock (that is, he removed or terminated it) by placing his hand on the truck. When he escaped consistently, the escape procedure was changed to what is called *avoidance conditioning.* To keep the buzzer off and prevent shock from occurring, Scotty had to keep his hand on the truck. The instant he removed it the buzzer sounded, and three seconds later shock occurred. By keeping his hand on the truck continuously, Scotty could avoid shock altogether.

Although at the beginning of the program Scotty practically never touched the truck, during the subsequent avoidance procedure he kept his hand on it almost continuously for up to several hours—depending on how long the session lasted. During that time, he did not beat his head. The next step was to teach Scotty to touch another toy. The truck was replaced with a toy tiger stuffed with metal shavings so that it could be used, as was the truck, to electrically record the amount of time Scotty held his hand on it. As with the truck, Scotty kept his hand on the toy constantly and did not beat his head.

Gradually, Scotty began to grasp and manipulate the toy tiger. At times, he was observed to even hug and kiss it. The shocker was then disconnected, although the buzzer remained operative. Since Scotty never released the toy long enough to learn that the shock would no longer occur, it appeared that the shock contingency was no longer necessary. Next, the buzzer was disconnected. Nevertheless, the boy continued to hold the tiger about as much as before.

Other stuffed animals were then faded in. Occasionally, it was necessary to present a short booster session with shock, but this quickly reestablished the desired behavior and thus was required very infrequently.

The psychologist therefore decided that the time had come to let Scotty roam the ward freely with a stuffed toy. The boy clutched the toy wherever he went and did not beat himself.

Perhaps some readers will think it cruel to make a child so dependent on a toy through the use of electric shock. Actually, the child was much better off with this tendency than without it. No longer did he have to be restrained in his bed twenty-four hours a day. He could run, play, and learn social interaction and other vital skills. At first, he was extremely dependent on his toy; in fact, once when he was accidentally deprived of it he beat his head ferociously. But over the space of about a year, he gradually became less and less dependent on it. Eventually, he did not beat his head even when he did not have his toy with him.

ESCAPE AND AVOIDANCE

Two principles were used in Scotty's case: escape conditioning and avoidance conditioning. The principle of escape conditioning states that there are certain stimuli whose removal immediately after the occurrence of a response will increase the likelihood of the response. In the escape procedure used with Scotty, the removal of shock following the response of touching the truck increased the probability that Scotty would touch the truck each time shock was presented.

Note that escape conditioning is similar to punishment in that both procedures involve the use of some sort of aversive event, such as shock. However, escape conditioning is just the opposite of punishment. In the punishment procedure, the likelihood of future behavior is *decreased* as a result of *presenting* a punisher following past instances of the behavior. In the escape-conditioning procedure, the likelihood of a behavior is *increased* as a result of terminating or *removing* a punisher following past instances of the behavior.[1]

Escape conditioning has the disadvantage that the aversive stimulus must be present in order for the desired response to occur. For example, when Scotty was on the escape procedure shock had to be presented before he would touch the toy. Therefore, escape conditioning is generally used not as a terminal contingency but rather as preparatory training for the introduction of avoidance conditioning. Thus, Scotty was given avoidance conditioning after he had acquired escape behavior.

In avoidance conditioning, a response prevents the occurrence of a punisher. This increases the probability of occurrence of the response if it is low, and maintains that probability at a high level. Thus, the principle of avoidance conditioning states that a behavior will increase in frequency if it prevents a punisher from occurring. During the avoidance procedure with Scotty, touching a toy prevented shock from occurring. When Scotty took his hand off the truck, the buzzer sounded and shock occurred three seconds later.

The sound of the buzzer when Scotty removed his hand from the toy was a *warning stimulus*: it signaled the occurrence of shock three seconds later. Other names for warning stimulus are *conditioned aversive stimulus* and *conditioned punisher*. Eventually, Scotty would keep his hand on the toy just to avoid the sound of the buzzer, and it was thus possible to dispense with the shock altogether. This type of avoidance conditioning, which includes a warning signal that enables the individual to discriminate a forthcoming punisher, is called *discriminated avoidance conditioning*.[2] Finally, the buzzer itself was disconnected and the behavior was maintained without either buzzer or shock—except, as we mentioned, for an occasional booster session as new toys were faded in.

How was it possible to eventually maintain the behavior of toy touching without shock or the buzzer? There are two probable answers. First, it is in the nature of an avoidance procedure that when the behavior occurs regularly, the punisher does not occur. Therefore, when the procedure no longer applies, regardless of what the individual does, it takes quite some time for him or her to discover that performing the behavior is not what keeps the punisher from occurring. Second, after Scotty began holding the toy, he probably came in contact with *positive* reinforcers that tended to maintain the behavior apart from the termination of the shock. After all, normal kids enjoy hugging stuffed animals, and it seems reasonable to suspect that this activity became reinforcing for Scotty too. Also, other people may have frequently praised Scotty for the nice way he was playing with his toys. Thus, two things—the tendency for an avoidance response to be very resistent to extinction and the availability of positive reinforcement for desirable behavior—probably account for the fact that Scotty continued to hold stuffed animals long after this behavior no longer prevented shock from occurring.

You may also wonder why Scotty eventually ceased beating his head, even when he did not have his toy with him. The answer would seem to be related to why he beat his head in the first place. This behavior was probably reinforced by the attention Scotty received for it. Moreover, because he had to be severely restrained, he had no opportunity to learn to obtain attention in other ways. However, when he could move about freely without beating his head, more desirable behaviors could occur and be reinforced with attention. Eventually, these more desirable behaviors took precedence over the gruesome one of head beating.

Although escape conditioning seems to be less frequent than avoidance conditioning in our society, there are examples of escape conditioning with which we are all familiar (see Table 13-1).

TABLE 13-1. *Examples of escape conditioning.*

AVERSIVE SITUATION	ESCAPE RESPONSES BY INDIVIDUAL	REMOVAL OF AVERSIVE SITUATION	LONG-TERM EFFECTS
1. A child sees an adult with a bag of candies. The child begins to scream, "candy, candy, candy."	To terminate the screaming, the adult gives the screaming child a candy.	The child stops screaming.	In the future, the adult is more likely "to give into" the screaming child (and the child is more likely to scream when she sees a candy bag, because of the positive reinforcement she gains for doing so).
2. Child A slaps (and continues to slap) child B. Child B cries loudly.	An adult removes child A from the vicinity of child B.	The slapping ceases.	Child B is likely to cry more quickly in future situations in which she is slapped.
3. A retarded child has had shoes put on her that are too tight and are pinching her toes.	The child makes loud noises in the presence of an adult and points to her toes.	The adult removes the shoes (and perhaps puts on larger shoes).	The child is more likely to make loud noises and point to her sore feet (or to other areas of pain) more quickly in similar situations in the future.
4. An adult frowns at a child and says, "Pick up that paper you threw on the floor."	The child picks up the paper.	The adult stops frowning.	The response of picking up the paper (or obeying the adult) is likely to occur more quickly in future situations in which the adult frowns while giving instructions.
5. A staff member in an institution comes upon a pile of smelly feces on the floor.	The staff member walks away without cleaning it up.	The staff member does not have to clean up the feces, and escapes the aversive smell.	In the future, the staff member will likely walk away from feces on the floor.

Avoidance conditioning influences us every day. Unfortunately, it is common in the classroom, where children may be required to give the right answer in order to avoid the teacher's ridicule or anger and to avoid a poor mark. Our legal system is based entirely on avoidance conditioning. We pay our taxes to avoid going to jail. We put money in parking meters to avoid getting a ticket. We pay our parking fines in order to avoid a court summons.

Like punishment, escape and avoidance conditioning involve aversive stimulation. They therefore suffer from much the same disadvantages as punishment (see Chapter 12). Aversive stimuli can produce undesirable emotional behaviors, such as aggression and general fearfulness, which, among other things, interfere with the learning process. Moreover, any stimulus associated with punishment tends to become aversive itself. Thus, an individual will tend to avoid or escape any situation or person associated with the use of punishers. Clearly, this does not further an individual's social, emotional, and intellectual development.

It is encouraging to note that Scotty did not show any of these side effects of aversive stimulation. He evidenced no hesitation in going to experimental sessions. In fact, he showed a great deal of affection toward the person who worked with him, such as by approaching him with outstretched arms when spotting him among a group of people. Nevertheless, escape and avoidance, like punishment, should generally be thought of as last-resort procedures: they should not be used if positive reinforcement will do the job.

PITFALLS OF ESCAPE AND AVOIDANCE: HOW THEY WORK TO THE DISADVANTAGE OF THOSE WHO ARE IGNORANT OF THEM

Often, people inadvertently use escape and avoidance conditioning to establish behaviors they probably would rather not see established.

Children often learn to escape and avoid punishment in ways that are not particularly desirable. An everyday example is the child who desperately promises "I'll be good; I won't do it again" in order to escape or avoid a spanking for some infraction of parental authority. When such pleas are successful, the pleading behavior is strengthened and thus increased in frequency under similar circumstances, but the undesirable behavior the parent meant to decrease has probably been affected very little or not at all. Verbal behavior having little relation to reality may be increased while the undesirable target response may persist in strength.

Prisoners frequently learn to make the "right" verbal statements in order to obtain early parole, but all too often it is merely their verbal behavior that has been modified, not their antisocial tendencies. Apologies, confessions, and the "guilty look" characteristic of transgressors in all walks of life can be traced to similar contingencies. Lying or misrepresenting the facts is another way to avoid punishment, if one can get away with it.

Behaviors more harmful than inappropriate verbal behavior can also result from unintentional escape or avoidance contingencies. For example, we have observed some retarded children who bite themselves after doing something they have been told not to do. What causes this? It is quite possible that this behavior has been strengthened because adults are less likely to punish a child who appears to be punishing himself.

Another pitfall of escape and avoidance is the inadvertent establishment of conditioned aversive stimuli, to which an individual then responds in such a way as to escape or avoid them.[3] By their excessive use of punishment, some teachers transform themselves, their classroom, and the learning materials they use into conditioned aversive stimuli. All too frequently, this situation produces individuals who avoid teachers, school, and books, and who therefore fail to advance academically. Clearly, this is a most unfortunate consequence of escape and avoidance conditioning.

Another pitfall of escape conditioning is that in many situations it maintains undesirable behaviors by the teacher. This can easily be seen in the first example in Table 13-1.

GUIDELINES FOR THE EFFECTIVE APPLICATION OF ESCAPE AND AVOIDANCE

The following rules should be observed by any person who applies escape and avoidance.

1. Given a choice between maintaining behavior on an escape or an avoidance procedure, the latter is to be preferred. There are two reasons for this. First, in escape conditioning the punisher must be present prior to the target response, whereas in avoidance conditioning the punisher occurs only when the target response fails to occur. Second, in escape conditioning the target response does not occur when the punisher is not present, whereas in avoidance conditioning responding decreases very slowly when the punisher may no longer be forthcoming.
2. The target behavior should be established by escape conditioning before it is put on an avoidance procedure. Avoidance behavior is usually easier to establish if escape behavior is established first, as was done in the case of Scotty.
3. During avoidance conditioning, a conditioned punishing stimulus should signal the impending punisher. This enhances conditioning by providing a "warning" that failure to respond will result in aversive stimulation. An example from the natural environment is the printed word "VIOLATION" on a parking meter, which indicates to the motorist that he may receive a parking ticket if he does not put a coin in the meter. The buzzer served a similar function for Scotty, indicating that shock would occur three sec-

onds after he removed his hand from the toy. (Presumably, although the authors of the study don't say whether this was so, if Scotty placed his hand back on the toy within three seconds, the buzzer would shut off and shock would be prevented. Similarly, putting a coin in a parking meter removes the "VIOLATION" sign and prevents a ticket.)

4. Escape and avoidance conditioning, like punishment, should be used cautiously. Because these procedures involve aversive stimuli, they can result in harmful side effects, such as aggression, fearfulness, and a tendency to avoid or escape any person or thing associated with the procedure.

5. Positive reinforcement for the target response should be used in conjunction with escape and avoidance conditioning. Not only will it help strengthen the desired behavior, it will also tend to counteract the undesirable side effects mentioned above.

6. As with all the procedures described in this text, the individual concerned should be told—to the best of his or her understanding—about the contingencies in effect. However—again, as with all these procedures —instructions are not necessary for escape and avoidance conditioning to work.

Study Questions

(for examination purposes)

1. How is escape conditioning similar to the punishment procedure? How is it different?

2. In what two ways is escape conditioning different from positive reinforcement? In what way are they similar?

3. What are two differences between escape conditioning and avoidance conditioning?

4. How are conditioned positive reinforcers and conditioned punishers similar, and how are they different?

5. Give two other names for "conditioned punisher."

6. What two factors probably account for the observation that Scotty eventually continued to touch the toy even without the application of a shock or the buzzer?

7. Explain in behavioral terms, with an example of your own, why individuals frequently reinforce the undesirable behavior of other individuals. (Hint: See the first example in Table 13-1.)

8. Explain how escape conditioning might maintain an adult's behavior of responding inappropriately to a child's extreme social withdrawal.

9. Why should escape- and avoidance-conditioning procedures be considered only as a last resort?

10. Briefly describe at least three pitfalls of escape and avoidance. (If possible, use examples other than those in the text.)

11. Why is an avoidance procedure generally preferred to an escape procedure? *— the aversive stim isn't experienced.*

Study Exercises

(to be practiced by the reader)

1. Construct a chart similar to Table 13-1 in which you present five examples of avoidance conditioning that have influenced your behavior. Present each example in terms of the categories of situation, warning signal, response, consequences, and long-term effects.
2. Successful avoidance behavior means that an individual has been conditioned to respond (probably to a warning signal) in such a way as to avoid the occurrence of a punisher. This means that the avoidance behavior might persist even if (for whatever reasons) the environment has changed such that the punisher will no longer be presented, regardless of the individual's behavior. Why is this so? Give two examples from your own experience.

Self-Modification Exercise

(to be practiced by the reader)

Identify a fear or anxiety reaction that you experienced recently. Describe your reaction and its stimulus control in some detail. Is your reaction best analyzed as positively reinforced, avoidance, or escape behavior? Justify your analysis with reference to behavioral principles and procedures.

EXTENDED DISCUSSION AND NOTES

1. Unfortunately for the student striving for a clear understanding of behavioral psychology, a variety of technical terms are used in reference to punishing or aversive events. To make matters worse, there are often rather subtle differences in the manner in which different authorities define these different terms. For example, Skinner uses the term "negative reinforcer," which he defined and distinguished from "positive reinforcer" as follows:

> Events which are found to be reinforcing are of two sorts. Some reinforcements consist of *presenting* stimuli, of adding something—for example, food, water, sexual contact—to the situation. These we call *positive* reinforcers. Others consist of removing something—for example, a loud noise, a very bright light, extreme cold or heat, or electric shock—from the situation. These we call *negative* reinforcers. In both cases the effect of reinforcement is the same—the probability of response is increased. (Skinner, 1953, p. 73)

(Continued)

(Continued)

Thus, negative reinforcement is equivalent to what this text refers to as escape conditioning (that is, increasing the probability of a response by making the removal of a particular type of stimulus—which is called a punisher, an aversive stimulus, or a negative reinforcer—contingent on that response). However, there is disagreement among behaviorists on the logical validity of distinguishing between positive and negative reinforcement. Most notably, Michael (1975) has argued against the distinction on the basis that it is logically meaningless to distinguish between cases in which a stimulus is removed and cases in which a stimulus is presented. The removal of one stimulus (for example, extreme cold or heat) always logically implies the presentation of another stimulus (in this case, a more moderate temperature), and vice versa. Thus, instead of distinguishing between presenting and removing stimuli, Michael would speak only of events involving changes in the stimuli present in a situation. Such stimulus-change events are reinforcing when they increase the probability of responses they follow, and they are punishing when they decrease the probability of responses they follow. Thus, Michael would get rid of the distinction between positive and negative reinforcement, but would retain the distinction between reinforcement and punishment.

The manner in which we defined punishment in Chapter 12 is consistent with Michael's defintion of that term (as well as with that of other writers, such as Azrin and Holz, 1966). However, Skinner's definition of punishment is different. He does not define it in terms of its effect in reducing behavior. Rather, he defines punishment as the presentation of a negative reinforcer or the removal of a positive reinforcer following a response. According to this definition, in order to say that presenting or removing a particular stimulus constitutes punishment, it is necessary to first show that that stimulus is a negative or positive reinforcer, respectively.

2. Two less common types of avoidance conditioning are not described in this chapter. One type does not involve a warning signal. This type of avoidance is known most commonly as Sidman avoidance (after Murray Sidman, who studied this type of avoidance extensively with lower organisms); it is also known as timed avoidance. An interesting experiment was conducted with Sidman avoidance by Hefferline, Kennan, and Harford (1956). In this experiment, individual normal adults sat in a chair and listened to music. Attached to their thumbs were tiny wire electrodes that measured extremely small thumb twitches. The individuals were instructed to listen to the music through earphones, and were told the music might occasionally be interrupted by noise. (Other individuals were given somewhat different instructions, but for our purposes their results will not be described.) During the first few minutes, the music continued uninterrupted and Hefferline et al. recorded the number of thumb twitches. Then, during an experimental period, thumb twitches affected music and noise according to an escape/Sidman-avoidance procedure. When the noise was superimposed on the music, a thumb twitch would enable the individual to escape from the noise for fifteen seconds. Subsequent thumb twitches during that time (without any warning signal) would continue to postpone the noise for fifteen-second intervals. Under these conditions, the rate of the thumb twitching increased greatly—to the extent that the individuals were able to listen to the music without interruption. (An interesting sidelight to this experiment was that the individuals were completely unaware—that is,

(Continued)

they were unable to verbalize the fact—that they had been conditioned to thumb-twitch in the fashion described above.)

A third type of avoidance, one that may or may not involve a warning stimulus, has been referred to as passive avoidance. With this type of program, individuals avoid punishing consequences by not making a response (that is, by remaining passive). For example, beekeepers instruct others that they can avoid being stung by a bee if they remain perfectly still when in the vicinity of a buzzing bee.

3. Many phobias (extreme and unreasonable fears) can be attributed to some sort of unfortunate escape and/or avoidance conditioning that has occurred in the patient's history. For example, Lubetkin (1975) reported a case of brontophobia and astraphobia (abnormal fear of thunder and lightning) that was "traced to the patient's early childhood years in Europe during W.W. II in which she was exposed to highly traumatizing daily bombings and firings." The phobia was so intense that during thunderstorms she "would go to the basement of her home and suffer in terror until the storm subsided." A very interesting treatment was used in this case. The patient was given training on how to relax, and was taken to a local planetarium that had been contracted to provide highly realistic presentations of lightning and thunderstorms. The patient relaxed, and then signaled the projectionist to start the show. There were approximately eight three-minute presentations of the storm per visit. The phobia was markedly alleviated after only eight visits by the patient to the planetarium. (The procedure used in this case is related to treatments that are described in more detail in Chapters 14 and 26.)

unable to escape + avoid.

Study Questions on Notes

1. What is the difference between the definition of a punisher in this text and Skinner's definition of a negative reinforcer?

2. Why did Michael recommend that we dispose of the term "negative reinforcer"? Discuss.

3. What is Sidman avoidance conditioning?

4. Briefly describe two situations in which you were influenced by Sidman avoidance conditioning.

5. How is the Hefferline et al. experiment related to the Greenspoon experiment described in Chapter 2, note 5?

6. What is passive avoidance?

7. Describe a situation in which you responded on a passive-avoidance schedule with a warning stimulus.

8. Describe a situation in which you responded on a passive-avoidance schedule with no warning stimulus.

9. What are brontophobia and astraphobia? (No, they're not dinosaurs!)

CHAPTER 14

Procedures Based On
RESPONDENT CONDITIONING

The principles and procedures described in the previous pages of this book are mainly those of operant conditioning. The basic tenet of operant conditioning is that a behavior is increased or decreased by its consequences. As we have seen, consequences that cause a behavior to increase are called reinforcers, and those that cause it to decrease are called punishers. However, some behavior modification procedures do not seem to fit the model of operant conditioning. Rather, these procedures seem to be described more accurately in reference to another type of conditioning. This type of conditioning has several names: it is variously referred to as *Pavlovian* conditioning, *classical* conditioning, or *respondent* conditioning.*

*The content of this chapter has forced us to write it in a style that is somewhat more technical than that of the previous chapters. This may cause hardship for some who are primarily interested in practical rather than general and theoretical information. However, those who are so inclined can omit this chapter without seriously distorting the continuity of the text.

Respondent conditioning (as we shall call it here) is based on the fact that certain stimuli automatically elicit certain responses apart from any prior learning or conditioning experience. These "automatic" stimulus-response relationships are called *unconditioned reflexes*. Examples of such reflexes are shown in Figure 14-1.

The reflexes in Figure 14-1 are unconditioned in the sense that the stimuli elicit the responses without prior conditioning (in other words, they are inborn). For each of the responses in Figure 14-1, there are stimuli that do not elicit them. For example, assume that a particular stimulus (such as the sight of food) does not presently elicit a particular response (such as salivation) in a particular individual (such as a baby who has not yet eaten that particular type of food). The principle of respondent conditioning states that if that stimulus (the sight of food) is followed closely in time by a stimulus (food in the mouth) that does elicit the response (salivation), the former stimulus (the sight of food) will also tend to elicit the response (salivation) in the future.[1]

STIMULUS ⟶ RESPONSE ELICITED

Food in the mouth ⟶ Salivation

Lemon juice in the mouth ⟶ Salivation and puckering of the lips

Cinder in the eye ⟶ Tears

Pepper in the nose ⟶ Sneezing

Painful jab ⟶ Emotional responses (such as an increased rate of heartbeat and the secretion of adrenalin into the blood)

FIGURE 14–1. *Some unconditioned reflexes.*

The diagrams in Figure 14-2 illustrate the main difference between respondent- and operant-conditioning procedures. The upper box in Figure 14-2 shows that respondent conditioning occurs when one *stimulus* is followed closely in time by another *stimulus* that elicits a particular response. The result of this temporal pairing of these two stimuli is that the first stimulus comes to elicit the same response that the second stimulus elicits. The lower box shows that operant conditioning occurs when a *response* is followed closely in time by a particular type of *stimulus*. The result depends on whether the stimulus is reinforcing or punishing: if it is reinforcing, the response will tend to occur again; if it is punishing, the response will tend not to occur again. To follow the parenthetical examples in Figure 14-2, the reader should consider the case of an infant or young child who has had little experience with different types of food.

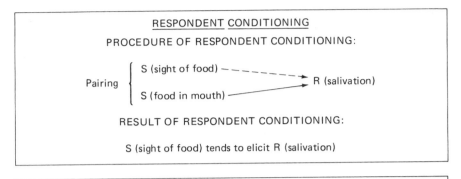

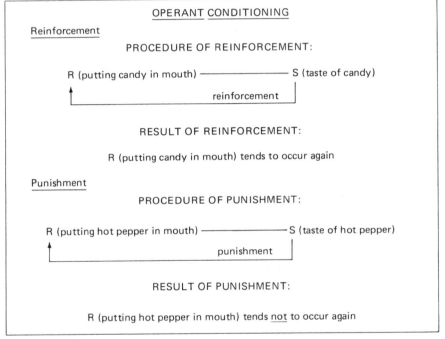

FIGURE 14-2. *Respondent and operant conditioning compared.*

At this point you may be asking, "Until this chapter, you were talking about behaviors that were controlled mainly by their consequences; now you seem to be talking about behaviors that are controlled only by antecedent stimuli, without any mention of consequences. Does this mean there are two different kinds of behaviors?" The answer to this seems to be yes. As we mentioned in earlier chapters, behaviors that are controlled by consequences have sometimes been referred to as "voluntary" behaviors. More technically, they are called *operant behaviors,* because they operate on the environment to generate consequences (and are in turn controlled by those consequences). However, some of our behaviors seem to be reflexive (that is, elicited by prior stimuli quite apart from the consequences of the behaviors). These are called *respondent behaviors.* Examples of such behavior are presented in Figure 14-1. It seems that many components of our emotional reactions (that is, certain aspects of fear, anger, love, hate, and so forth) are of this sort.

Any behavioral sequence is likely to include both respondent and operate conditioning. In some situations, we might select certain stimuli and responses from a sequence in order to study respondent conditioning. Or, we might examine that same sequence somewhat differently and study operant conditioning. Consider the behavior sequence shown in Figure 14-3. As you can see the sound of the bell in Figure 14-3 appears to be involved in both respondent and operant conditioning.

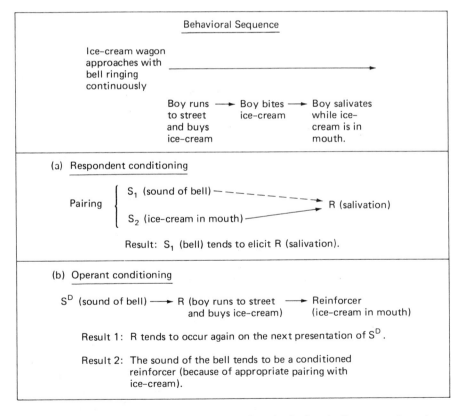

FIGURE 14-3. *A behavioral sequence that includes both operant and respondent conditioning.*

Another example of a behavioral sequence that involves both respondent and operant conditioning might be as follows: Suppose that a small child runs to pet a large dog. Never having had any reason to fear dogs, the child shows no fear now. Suppose, however, that the dog playfully jumps at the child and knocks him down. Quite naturally, the child will begin crying because of the pain and surprise of this rough treatment. Now what will happen the next time the child sees that dog or one that resembles it? Of course, the child will probably start crying and showing other types of fear behavior. Thus, a stimulus (sight of dog) that previously did not elicit a particular response (crying and other types of fear behavior) comes to do so because it was paired with a stimulus (suddenly being knocked down) that did elicit that response.

It is important to note that in this example, the child's experience with the dog will have two important effects on his behavior. First, as we mentioned, the child will have a fear reaction (consisting of trembling, crying, the secretion of adrenalin into the blood, and an increased rate of heartbeat, among other things) whenever he sees a dog that resembles the one that knocked him down. This fear reaction to dogs is, as we mentioned, a response that has been respondently conditioned. Second, any behavior (such as looking over a back-yard fence) that leads to the sight of a dog resembling the one that knocked him down will likely decrease in frequency. Moreover, the child will tend to avoid or get away from such dogs. In other words, those dogs will have become conditioned punishers for the child. In Chapter 12, we stated that a stimulus that is not punishing can become punishing if it is paired with a stimulus that is punishing. Some psychologists would theorize that the sight of the dog has become a conditioned punisher because it elicits fear as a result of respondent conditioning, and that the fear so elicited is aversive.[2]

It is evident that the same procedure that will cause a stimulus to elicit fear will also cause that stimulus to be a conditioned punisher. This is illustrated in Figure 14-4.

It is not always possible to discuss a behavioral sequence just in terms of operant conditioning. For example, it might be said that the child in the preceding example had been punished for approaching dogs by having been knocked down by a dog. Although this might explain why the child no longer approaches dogs, it does not explain why he experiences fear (which can be measured in terms of internal bodily reactions, such as increased level of adrenalin in the blood and an increased rate of heartbeat) when he sees a dog. It therefore appears that it is necessary to add the principle of respondent conditioning to our list of basic behavioral principles.

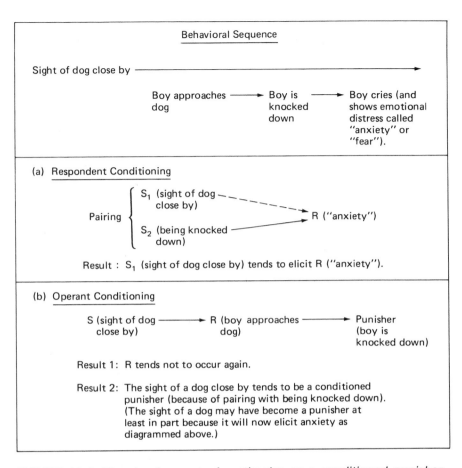

FIGURE 14-4. *The development of a stimulus as a conditioned punisher. Some psychologists would theorize that in this example, the sight of the dog has become a conditioned punisher because it elicits anxiety as a result of respondent conditioning.*

The behavior modification procedures described in subsequent pages of this chapter seem to be based in large measure on respondent conditioning. This is not to say that they do not also involve operant conditioning, or that respondent conditioning was not operating in some of the procedures described previously in this book. Both types of conditioning are present and probably interact in virtually all behavior modification procedures. Although this complicates the description of behavior modification procedures, it probably does not hinder the practice of behavior modification. Indeed, as we have seen repeatedly throughout this book, increasing the number of principles that are applied to a behavior problem generally increases the likelihood that the treatment will be successful.

APPLICATIONS OF RESPONDENT CONDITIONING

Aversion Therapy

Certain kinds of positive reinforcers can be very troublesome. People who find pastries and other sweets overly reinforcing tend to eat too many fattening foods and become overweight. Similarly, people who find cigarettes, alcohol, and other harmful commodities overly reinforcing tend to overindulge in these reinforcers to the detriment of their health and well-being. People who obtain sexual reinforcement in socially unacceptable ways — for instance, by seducing children — tend to endanger others, by exposing them to potentially harmful experiences, and themselves, by risking imprisonment and other social sanctions.

Aversion therapy has been developed largely as an attempt to counteract the power of undesirable reinforcers (those that tend to be overindulged in or that harm others). Before describing some of the methods of aversion therapy, we should caution the reader that their safe and effective use requires special expertise. These procedures, as the label aversion therapy implies, involve the use of aversive stimulation. As we have seen in Chapter 12, there are serious dangers in the use of aversive stimulation. It should therefore be used only by qualified experts who know when and how it is most likely to be effective, and how to guard against potentially harmful side effects.

Basically, aversion therapy involves the repeated pairing (that is, over a number of trials) of an undesirable reinforcer with an aversive event. The rationale is that the undesirable reinforcer should then become less reinforcing, because it will come to elicit a response similar to that elicited by the aversive stimulus.

For example, in the treatment of alcoholism a person may be given a drug that will make him nauseous. Just before the drug takes effect, he is given a sip of an alcoholic beverage. Thus, the sight, smell, and taste of the drink is followed immediately by nausea. (See, for example, Lemere and Voegtlin, 1950.) This pairing of alcohol with nausea is repeated over a number of sessions. Eventually, alcohol itself should tend to elicit nausea, which would tend to cause the individual to avoid alcohol. How well the therapy works in any given case probably depends, at least in part, on other treatment factors and on operant processes operating in the natural environment — such as whether the client receives social reinforcement for his subsequent choosing of nonalcoholic over alcoholic beverages at parties, restaurants and bars.* This proposition is in accord with the statement at the beginning of this chapter that respondent- and operant-conditioning principles are probably never manifested independently of each other; they interact, and behavior modifiers should utilize their potential interaction whenever possible. Having made this point, we now continue with our emphasis on the respondent-conditioning aspects of aversion therapy.

Electric shock is frequently used as an aversive stimulus in aversion therapy. The main reasons for its use are that (1) it is relatively easy to administer, (2) it can be delivered instantly, (3) its intensity and duration can be precisely controlled, (4) it can be used on repeated trials in a single session, and (5) it is aversive to virtually everyone.

In one commonly used procedure (cf. Feldman and MacCulloch, 1965), a client is shown slides of the undesirable reinforcer. As she looks at each slide, such as a picture of very fattening food (assuming that she is being treated for obesity) a painful shock is delivered through electrodes attached to her arm or leg. The slide is removed at the same time that the shock terminates, so that relief from shock is associated with the absence of the undesirable reinforcer. In fact, many behavior therapists maintain that a slide showing a desirable alternative reinforcer (such as nutritious, nonfattening food in this example) should be presented at the same time that the shock ceases. Thus, the undesirable reinforcer is paired with shock, and the desirable alternative reinforcer is paired with relief from shock. This modified form of aversion therapy is called aversion-relief conditioning.

Symbolic representations (such as pictures, slides, and filmstrips) of the undesirable reinforcers, rather than the actual reinforcers themselves, are commonly used in aversion therapy. This is largely a matter of convenience. Hundreds of slides or filmstrips dealing with a wide variety of troublesome reinforcers can easily be stored in the therapist's office. Moreover, it is relatively easy to make new slides or filmstrips appropriate to individual cases. These stimuli can then be presented at specified intervals and for specified durations, and can be associated with the onset or termination of the aversive stimulus in a precisely controlled manner. Moreover, their use precludes various problems that would arise if the actual undesirable reinforcers were used during therapy. To give an extreme example, one obviously would not use real children to decondition a child molester. It is generally acceptable, however, to use pictures of children in various poses.

In many cases, aversion therapy is conducted not only in the absence of the actual undesirable reinforcers, but even in the absence

*For a review of the behavioral treatment of alcoholism, see Nathan (1976).

of *external* representations of those reinforcers. Instead, *internal* representations are used. Most people can visualize internal pictures called images. Moreover, these internal images need not be merely visual; they can also be auditory (i.e., one can imagine various sounds), tactile (i.e., one can imagine touching or being touched), kinesthetic (i.e., one can imagine making various movements), and so forth. In short, all the sensations evoked by the physical world can be represented in one's imagination.

The use of images or imaginary stimuli is illustrated in a case reported by Lesser (1967). The client was a young man who wished to eliminate his drug habit, which involved injections of morphine several times per week. Before the initiation of aversion therapy, several nonaversive conditioning procedures were tried. For example, by means of assertive training (described later in this chapter), the client's social skills were improved so that he would have some desirable alternative forms of reinforcement. These procedures were only partially successful, and it was therefore decided to use aversion therapy to associate anxiety with the paraphernalia and process of drug administration. Prior to treatment, the client was instructed to vividly imagine going through a sequence of five steps while, for two of the steps, he picked up and held the equipment that he used when actually giving himself an injection. During each step of the sequence, the client was given a shock as soon as he signaled to the therapist that he had a clear image of that step. The shock continued until the client had (1) ceased to visualize that step, which he indicated to the therapist by saying "stop," and (2) dropped any of the equipment he had been holding during that step. The client was given the sequence three times per session, and received two sessions per week. For the first sixteen sessions, shock was given during every step. Thereafter, it was given intermittently. A ten-month follow-up indicated that the client continued to successfully avoid "hard" drugs following treatment.

You might wonder whether this case actually illustrates only the process of punishment, and not that of respondent conditioning. Indeed, the procedure that was used does seem very similar to that of punishment. There are, however, some basic differences. First, the client was instructed by the therapist to engage in the behavior that was followed by shock. Thus, if punishment was the critical process that was operating, it would seem that attending therapy sessions and following the therapist's instructions would have ceased before the actual drug-taking behavior was eliminated. Second, shock did not occur contingent on the actual drug-taking behavior. Rather, it was paired with stimuli (such as the injection equipment and the imagined situation and actions accompanying injections) that were involved in the drug-taking behavior. Finally, after aversion therapy had been in effect for eight sessions, the client took drugs on one occasion. The procedure had therefore not, at least at that time, sufficiently punished the behavior so as to eliminate it completely. Nevertheless, the client reported that he did not get the "good feeling" he had experienced on previous occasions when he took drugs. It therefore appears that the main effect of aversion therapy in this case was to reduce the reinforcing effect of the drug rather than to directly punish the drug-taking behavior.

Covert Sensitization

The preceding case was presented primarily to illustrate the use of imagery in aversive conditioning. The stimuli that were imagined related to experiencing the undesirable reinforcer (the effects of the drug). These stimuli were paired with electric shock, which is, of course, a very real aversive stimuli. A commonly used procedure called *covert sensitization* (Cautela, 1966), however, involves having the client imagine both the undesirable reinforcer and the aversive stimulus. This procedure is so named because the pairing of the stimuli occurs only in the client's imagination (in other words, it is "covert") and the anticipated result of this covert pairing process is that the undesirable reinforcer becomes aversive (that is, the client becomes "sensitized" to it). One use of the procedure is with clients who wish to give up smoking (as described by Irey, 1972). For example, during a particular trial the client might be instructed to vividly imagine lighting a cigarette after dinner in a restaurant, inhaling, and then suddenly becoming so violently ill that he vomits all over his hands, his clothes, the table cloth, and the other people at the table. He continues to vomit and then, when the contents of his stomach are empty, to gag while the other people in the restaurant stare at him in amazement and disgust. In short, the scene is made extremely realistic and aversive. When the maximum degree of aversiveness is felt, the client is instructed to imagine turning away from his cigarette and immediately beginning to feel better (as in aversion-relief conditioning). The scene concludes with the client washing up in the bathroom, without his cigarettes, and feeling tremendous relief.

From this brief survey of aversion-therapy procedures it can be seen that a number of possibilities are available. All involve the basic process of reducing the reinforcing value of a stimulus by pairing it with an aversive stimulus. The procedures differ mainly in two ways: (1) the stimulus that is paired with the aversive stimulus may be the actual stimulus whose reinforcing power the client wishes to reduce or eliminate, or it may be a pictorial or imaginary representation of that stimulus; (2) the aversive stimulus may be an overt physical event such as electric shock, or it may be imaginary. Probably the relative effectiveness of the procedures varies to a large extent with particular types of clients and problems.

Convenience and greater control over stimulus presentations are factors that often favor the use of pictures or images over the use of the actual undesirable reinforcer. Images have the added advantage of providing a wider variety of stimuli and situations (it would clearly be impractical to have a client actually vomit in a real restaurant, for example). It might be argued that images of an undesirable reinforcer are so far removed from the natural environment that their use is not likely to produce generalization to that environment. On the other hand, if the client has a "good imagination," then making those images aversive might generalize to the natural environment just as readily as would making the actual undesirable reinforcer aversive (since many of the covert stimuli in both cases may be identical).

Regardless of the type of stimuli that are used, there are several general guidelines that qualified therapists typically follow in applying aversion therapy:

1. During conditioning trials, the onset of the stimulus to be made aversive (that is, the undesirable reinforcer) is generally followed 0.5 to 1.0 seconds later by the aversive stimulus. The pairing continues for a few seconds, and then the two stimuli terminate at approximately the same time.
2. The client is encouraged to experience the undesirable reinforcer (or its symbolic representations) as fully as possible while also experiencing the aversive stimulus. The aversive stimulus must be strong enough to transmit its effects to the undesirable reinforcer, rather than the other way around.
3. The termination of the aversive stimulus is usually paired with a stimulus that the client wishes to have as a positive reinforcer that will replace the undesirable reinforcer.
4. Reinforcement is normally arranged in the natural environment so as to follow instances when the client chooses the desirable alternative reinforcer over the undesirable reinforcer.
5. Occasional "booster" aversion-therapy sessions may be required to maintain the low reinforcing value of the undesirable reinforcer after the conclusion of therapy. Follow-ups should be conducted periodically to determine whether booster sessions are necessary and to evaluate the effectiveness of the treatment.

Systematic Desensitization

As explained above, aversion therapy works primarily by causing an undesirable reinforcer to become aversive, or at least less reinforcing. Often, however, the opposite type of problem is encountered: a stimulus that the client wishes to be reinforcing, or at least neutral, elicits a strong aversive reaction. The little boy who was knocked down by a dog in the example at the beginning of this chapter may continue long afterwards to have a strong fear of dogs. It would, of course, be unfortunate if this fear prevented him from enjoying dogs who posed no real threat to him. Many people have fears that are so intense that they are virtually incapacitated by them. For example, a person might have such an intense fear of heights that he cannot walk up a single flight of stairs or look out of a second-story window without experiencing acute anxiety. Or, to take another example, a person might be so terrified of crowds that she cannot bear to go into public places. Surprising as it may seem, trying to convince these people that their fears are irrational often has no beneficial effect. Indeed, they usually know that their fears have no rational basis, and would like to control them but cannot do so because the fears are automatically elicited by specific stimuli. Such intense, irrational, incapacitating fears, which are called *phobias*, generally require treatment by professional psychologists or psychiatrists.

One method that has proved quite effective for treating phobias, and that appears to be based in large part on respondent-conditioning procedures, was developed by Wolpe (1958) (for the history of this method, see Chapter 28). Wolpe originally hypothesized that if a response incompatible with fear could be made to occur in the presence of a stimulus that normally produced fear, then the incompatible response would inhibit the occurrence of fear on subsequent presentations of that stimulus. In other words, opposite responses to a given stimulus tend to reciprocally inhibit each other. Wolpe referred to this process as *reciprocal inhibition*. Wolpe hypothesized that a reasonable treatment for phobias was to identify responses that were opposite to fear and to teach the client to engage in those responses in situations that normally produced fear. The three classes of responses that he used to inhibit fear were relaxation, assertion responses, and sexual responses. The fear-antagonistic behavior that Wolpe found most suitable to his purpose was relaxation, and the term used to describe his therapy that incorporates relaxation is *systematic desensitization*.

A procedure for training people to completely relax their muscles had previously been developed by Jacobson (1938), and Wolpe (1958, 1969) adapted this procedure for use with his clients who experienced debilitating fears. In general, the relaxation procedures require a client to alternately tense and then relax a set of muscles so that they are more deeply relaxed following the tensing than before. The client is taught to apply this tension-relaxation exercise to muscles of all major areas of the body (such as arms, neck, face, and shoulders). By following the appropriate procedures during several training sessions, many individuals can eventually learn to relax deeply in a matter of minutes. (A more detailed description of this procedure is given in Chapter 26.)

Systematic desensitization first involves teaching the client to readily induce deep-muscle relaxation. In addition, by interviewing the client thoroughly, the therapist obtains a detailed description of all of the stimuli and situations that are related to the debilitating fear or anxiety that the client experiences. Thus, the therapist identifies not only those stimuli that elicit the most intense anxiety, but also related stimuli that elicit lesser degrees of anxiety. The client then rates these stimuli on a 100-point scale in which a rating of 0 indicates that the stimulus elicits the least amount of anxiety and a rating of 100 indicates that it elicits the greatest amount of anxiety. The anxiety-eliciting stimuli or situations are then arranged in a hierarchy, with those that elicit the least anxiety at the bottom and those that elicit the most anxiety at the top. The following hierarchy might be constructed for a client who is terrified of riding in crowded elevators:

9. Being pressed against the wall in an elevator that is filled to capacity.
8. Being in an elevator that is three-fourths full.
7. Being the only passenger in an elevator.
6. Being in an elevator that has four people in it.
5. Being in an elevator that has two people in it.
4. Standing outside an elevator door while waiting for the elevator to arrive.
3. Walking toward an elevator twenty feet away.
2. Walking toward an elevator from the front door of the building in which it is located.
1. Walking to an appointment on the top floor of a tall building that has an elevator.

Note that although the client in this hypothetical example is most afraid of being in an elevator that is filled to capacity, he is also more frightened of being the only passenger in an elevator than of being in an elevator with several other people. This illustrates that it is important to construct a hierarchy that is valid for the particular client. A hierarchy that is valid for one client may not be valid for another, even though both may have the same general type of phobia. (For an example of a more complex hierarchy from an actual case, see Table 26-1, pp. 389–390.)

After the therapist has taught the client how to induce self-relaxation and has constructed a hierarchy of anxiety-eliciting stimuli (or several hierarchies, if the client has more than one type of debilitating fear), therapy begins. While relaxing on a couch, the client is instructed to clearly imagine the first scene in the hierarchy. If the client experiences any anxiety whatsoever while visualizing the scene, he signals this to the therapist by raising one finger (this minimal signaling response is used so that the client does not disrupt his relaxed state). If no anxiety has been signaled, then the therapist, after about seven to ten seconds, signals the client to relax and to stop imagining the scene. Following approximately fifteen to thirty seconds of relaxation, the client is again requested to imagine the scene. After two successes of imagining a scene (with a fifteen- to thirty-second period of relaxation after each presentation), the therapist then instructs the client to clearly imagine the next scene in the hierarchy. At the first indication of anxiety, the therapist immediately instructs the client to cease imagining the scene. Then, after the client is again completely relaxed, the therapist instructs him to imagine the previous scene. If no anxiety is experienced with that scene, the next scene in the hierarchy is attempted again. In this manner of alternately imagining scenes and then relaxing without imagining them, the client gradually proceeds through the least anxiety-eliciting to the most anxiety-eliciting scenes. At each step, relaxation counteracts the anxiety elicited by that scene.[3] When the client finishes the last scene in the hierarchy, he can generally encounter the actual feared situations without undue distress.[4] No doubt, the positive reinforcement he then receives helps to maintain his continued interactions with the stimuli that previously elicited intense, debilitating fear.

Here are some of the guidelines that many therapists follow when using systematic desensitization.

1. Before beginning desensitization, they ensure that:
   a) the client has been properly trained to induce self-relaxation;
   b) all anxiety-eliciting stimuli have been indentified, and ranked in a valid hierarchy;
   c) the client can form clear images. If he cannot (which is very rare), special training in forming images may be required before therapy can begin.
2. During desensitization sessions:
   a) they are very careful to present the scenes in such a manner that they elicit the absolute minimum amount of anxiety. If the client is taken too rapidly through the hierarchy, or if he is not sufficiently relaxed, the desired result might not be obtained. Indeed, there is the danger that the opposite effect might occur: the client might be made even more fearful of the anxiety-eliciting stimuli than he already is.
   b) they are careful not to present reinforcement (for instance, by saying "good") when the client imagines a scene without reporting anxiety. Such reinforcement might tend to prevent the client from reporting anxiety when he experiences it.
3. After the client has successfully progressed through the hierarchy, the therapist should (if possible) arrange for positive reinforcement to occur on at least the first few occasions that the client interacts with the stimuli to which desensitization was directed.
4. Follow-ups should be conducted to ensure that the treatment remains effective over a long period of time. If a relapse occurs, booster sessions should be given.

FIGURE 14–5. *An example of a failure to identify all anxiety-eliciting stimuli prior to desensitization (guideline 1b, p. 217).*

Assertive Training

Another technique that many writers consider to be within the respondent-conditioning orientation is that of assertive training. In an important text on assertive training, Lange and Jakubowski (1976, p. 38) define *assertion* as follows: "Assertion involves standing up for personal rights and expressing thoughts, feelings, and beliefs in direct, honest, and appropriate ways which respect the rights of other people." As we mentioned earlier in this chapter, Wolpe originally included assertive responses as one class of responses that could be used to reciprocally inhibit fear and anxiety.[5] Wolpe considered assertive training to be especially appropriate in certain social situations in which anxiety occurred. Examples might be situations in which a person shows meek, submissive behaviors when a more assertive reaction is called for (such as speaking up instead of letting others trample all over you), or awkward behavior in situations that call for a certain amount of social grace (such as asking someone for a date).

Although Wolpe assumed that the teaching of assertive behavior counter-conditioned the anxiety in a Pavlovian sense, it seems that the behavior changes that occur in a client during assertive training might be due largely to operant-conditioning procedures. Rimm and Masters (1974, p. 93) have suggested that "by far the most commonly used assertive training technique is *behavior rehearsal*. This technique requires that the client and therapist act out relevant interpersonal interactions. Part of the time, the client plays himself with the therapist assuming the role of a significant person in the client's life such as a parent, employer, or spouse." It would seem that this "role playing" serves several functions. It helps the therapist determine what behaviors need to be changed in the client so that he can evoke favorable reactions from the people in his environment. It also provides the therapist with the information necessary to re-create relevant S^Ds for the client so that behavior appropriate to them can be modeled and reinforced in their presence as he plays the role of himself. Also, it is possible that by playing the roles of significant people in his environment, a client learns how to better predict their reactions to his behavior (even as it is said that an actor, as he becomes increasingly involved in the role of the character he is portraying, comes to really "know" that character), and hence to adjust his own behavior accordingly. Thus, although assertive training appears to be in the historical tradition of respondent-conditioning procedures, it seems reasonable to interpret the behavior of the client and the therapist during assertive training largely in terms of operant-conditioning principles.[6] Examples of assertive training from this viewpoint are given on pp. 232–3, 244–5 and 251–2.

The following general guidelines for assertion therapists are paraphrased slightly from Lange and Jakubowski (1976, p. 5):

1. Teach the differences between assertion and aggression, nonassertion, and politeness. (Extreme care should be taken to avoid confusing assertion with aggression.)
2. Help people to identify and accept their own personal rights as well as the rights of others.
3. Reduce existing emotional and cognitive (see Chapter 27) obstacles to acting assertively.

4. Use active practice to develop assertive skills: arrange for the client to be reinforced for acting assertively in appropriate situations both during role-playing and in the natural environment.

Other Respondent-Conditioning Applications

Most respondent-conditioning procedures presently in use involve the establishment or elimination of aversive reactions to specific stimuli. It would be a mistake, however, to think that this exhausts the possibilities. Therefore, this chapter concludes with two examples of other uses of respondent conditioning.

One example is a treatment for chronic constipation that was developed by Quarti and Renaud (1964). Defecation, the desired response in cases of constipation, can be elicited by administering a laxative. However, reliance on such drugs to achieve regularity is not the healthiest solution because of the undesirable side effects that often result. Quarti and Renaud therefore had their clients present themselves with a distinctive electrical stimulus—a mild, nonpainful electric current—immediately prior to defecating. Defecation was initially elicited by a laxative, and then the amount of the drug was gradually decreased until defecation was elicited by the electrical stimulus alone. Then, by applying the electrical stimulus at the same time each day, several of the clients were also able to get rid of the electrical stimulus, because the natural-environment stimuli characteristically present at that time each day acquired control over the behavior of defecating. Thus, these clients achieved regularity without the continued use of artificial stimulation.

The second example of a respondent-conditioning procedure that does not involve conditioning or counter-conditioning of aversive states is a treatment for enuresis (bed-wetting). One possible explanation for enuresis, a problem that is rather common in young children, is that pressure on the child's bladder when he is asleep and has to urinate does not provide sufficient stimulation to awaken him. A device that seems to be effective for many enuretic children consists of a buzzer connected to a special pad under the bottom sheet on the child's bed (see, for instance, Mowrer, 1938; Wickes, 1958). The apparatus is wired so that the buzzer sounds and awakens the child as soon as the first drop of urine makes contact with the pad. Eventually, in many cases the child will awaken before he urinates—apparently because the response of waking up has been conditioned to the stimulus of pressure on the bladder. Naturally, the procedure should be supplemented with reinforcement to the child when he goes to the toilet at night so that this behavior will occur instead of bed-wetting.[7]

Some general guidelines for using respondent conditioning are as follows:

1. Identify a stimulus (S_1) that reliably elicits the response that you desire to condition.
2. Identify a stimulus (S_2) that does not presently elicit the response, but that would be convenient or desirable to have elicit the response.
3. Repeatedly pair the two stimuli by presenting S_2 first and quickly (within 0.5 to 1.0 seconds) following it with S_1.
4. Gradually decrease the number of trials during which S_1 is presented, but continue to present S_2 so that it alone will eventually elicit the response.
5. If possible, positively reinforce the desired response.

A CAUTIONARY NOTE

Chapters 2–12 of this book described basic principles and procedures of operant conditioning, along with guidelines for their application. Chapter 13 presented information on escape and avoidance conditioning, and Chapter 14 has presented information on aversion therapy (including covert sensitization), systematic desensitization, and assertive training. Chapters 15–26 describe additional information for designing and executing behavioral programs. We believe that mastery of the material in Chapters 2–12 and 15–26 will enable the reader to effectively design, implement, and maintain a variety of behavior modification programs. We do not make such a claim for the material in Chapters 13 and 14. Additional information and guidance is necessary before the reader attempts to carry out programs involving escape or avoidance conditioning, aversion therapy (including covert sensitization), systematic desensitization, and assertive training. Chapter 26 provides information for carrying out a self-desensitization program.

Study Questions

(for examination purposes)

1. What is the basic tenet of operant conditioning?
2. Give five examples of unconditioned reflexes (two of which are not in the text). Describe both the stimulus and the response.
3. State the principle of respondent conditioning. Clearly describe and diagram three examples of respondent conditioning (one of which is not in the text).

4. By using diagrams and examples, distinguish between respondent and operant conditioning.

5. Explain how respondent conditioning and operant conditioning can interact to cause an individual to escape or avoid a particular stimulus. Use diagrams and examples to clarify your explanation.

6. For what general type of problem is aversion therapy used? Give three examples (one of which is not in the text).

7. Why should aversion therapy be used only by competent professional practitioners?

8. Describe the basic procedure and rationale of aversion therapy. Give an example of aversion therapy.

9. State three reasons that electric shock is frequently used as an aversive stimulus in aversion therapy.

10. State why slides showing undesirable reinforcers are frequently used in aversion therapy.

11. Describe the basic procedure and rationale of aversion-relief conditioning. Give an example of aversion-relief conditioning.

12. Describe the basic procedure and rationale of covert sensitization. Give an example of covert sensitization.

13. For what general type of problem is systematic desensitization used? Give an example.

14. Explain why relaxation is used in systematic desensitization.

15. Explain how a hierarchy of aversive situations is constructed in systematic desensitization.

16. In one page or less, summarize the basic procedure of systematic desensitization.

17. Who developed systematic desensitization?

18. Briefly describe a respondent-conditioning procedure for treating constipation.

19. Describe a respondent-conditioning procedure for treating enuresis.

20. Define assertive training.

EXTENDED DISCUSSION AND NOTES

1. The physiologist Pavlov (1927) was the first scientist to study this type of conditioning. One of his procedures was to sound a tone (by striking a tuning fork) just before placing food powder in the mouth of one of the dogs he used as experimental subjects. Pavlov noted, of course, that the food (which he called an *unconditioned stimulus*) elicited salivation (which he called an *unconditioned response* to the food). However, he noted that the result of pairing the tone with the food was that eventually the tone (which he called a *conditioned stimulus*) would also elicit salivation (which he called a *conditioned response* to the tone).

Pavlov believed that all learned behavior was based on this general conditioning procedure. That is, he believed that any learned response was a response to a conditioned stimulus (CS). The CS had ac-

(Continued)

quired the ability to elicit the conditioned response (CR) because that CS had been paired with an unconditioned stimulus (US) that elicited an unconditioned response (UR) that was similar to the CR.

Skinner (1935) was the first to clearly distinguish between this type of conditioning, which he called *respondent conditioning,* and the type he called *operant conditioning.*

The terms *classical* and *instrumental* conditioning, which were coined by Hilgard and Marquis (1940) in an early influential book on learning, are frequently used synonyms for respondent and operant conditioning, respectively.

2. This theoretical description of how an interaction between respondent and operant processes can result in escape behavior, avoidance behavior, and punishment was first formulated systematically by Mowrer (1960). The theory is called *two-factor theory* because it is based on two principles of conditioning. It should be noted that this theory is not accepted by some learning theorists (such as Herrnstein, 1969).

3. In addition to respondent conditioning, Pavlov discovered respondent extinction: If the CS is presented repeatedly without being followed by the US, eventually the CS will no longer elicit the CR. It has been argued by some behavior therapists that relaxation and anxiety hierarchies are unnecessary components of the desensitization procedure. Addressing this issue as a learning theorist, Rachlin (1976, p. 195) noted that in systematic desensitization, "a new CR [relaxation] is learned which can transfer to CS's other than the one originally used. Simple [respondent] extinction tends to be too narrowly focused, too weak to overcome strong conditioning, and too easily overcome by reconditioning with the original US or even with other CS's [that still elicit the anxiety reaction]."

4. The great majority of data supporting the effectiveness of systematic desensitization comes from surveys of reported case histories. This data is often difficult to interpret because the case histories frequently involve procedures other than systematic desensitization, utilize subjective verbal reports from clients as the major source of information and do not have adequate baseline or follow-up data. Nevertheless, the information on case histories is impressive. Wolpe (1958) originally claimed 90-percent of 210 clients to be either cured or much improved after an average of thirty-one treatment sessions. Sessions were typically one week or several days apart. For more thorough reviews of these and other data, see Paul (1969a, 1969b) and Kazdin and Wilcoxon (1976). The latter authors pointed out that although systematic desensitization appears to be very effective, it is not clear that its effectiveness is due to the reasons Wolpe and others theorized.

5. It appears that Salter (1949) was the first person to describe assertive-training procedures in detail. However, assertive training did not appear to gather acceptance as a behavior-therapy technique until Wolpe (1958, 1969) emphasized it. Rimm and Masters (1974) have outlined several plausible reasons why the writings of Wolpe on assertive training have had greater impact than those of Salter (pp. 82–83).

6. This position also appears to have been expressed by Rimm and Masters (1974, p. 94) who stated, "The assertive procedures described in this chapter incorporate several well-established principles borrowed from the operant literature (for example, the use of successive approximations). Clinical experience strongly suggests the appropriateness of these extrapolations."

7. Another use of respondent conditioning might be in reducing high blood pressure. Whitehead, Lurie, and Blackwell (1976) found that a sequence of sounds became a CS for lowered blood pressure when it was followed by tilting a client fifteen degrees head-down from the horizontal, which is a US for lowered blood pressure. The usual behavior modification method for reducing high blood pressure is an operant-conditioning procedure (also called a *biofeedback* procedure). However, Whitehead et al. reported a preliminary observation that clients seemed to perform better on the biofeedback procedure if they were also exposed to the respondent-conditioning procedure for reducing blood pressure.

Study Questions on Notes

1. In Pavlov's experiment with dogs, what was:
    a) the unconditioned stimulus?
    b) the unconditioned response?
    c) the conditioned stimulus?
    d) the conditioned response?
2. Diagram the US, the UR, the CS, and the CR in Pavlov's experiment with dogs. (Hint: See the diagram of respondent conditioning in Figure 14-2.)
3. For the example of an infant who learned to salivate at the sight of food, identify the US, the UR, the CS, and the CR.
4. For the example of the child who learned to fear dogs because he was knocked down by a dog, identify the US, the UR, the CS, and the CR.
5. Using Pavlov's terminology, state the principle of respondent conditioning and give an example.
6. Using Pavlov's terminology, state the principle of respondent extinction and give an example.
7. Explain how respondent conditioning might be useful in reducing high blood pressure.

PART III

Some Preliminary Considerations to Effective Programming Strategies

CHAPTER 15

"Short-Cut" Tactics Involving Existing Forms of Stimulus Control:

INSTRUCTION, MODELING, GUIDANCE and SITUATIONAL INDUCEMENT

Consider the following general categories of behavior problems:

1. A desired behavior occurs too infrequently (behavioral deficit).
2. An undesired behavior occurs too frequently (behavioral excess).
3. A desired behavior never occurs (behavioral deficit).
4. A desired behavior occurs, but in the presence of inappropriate stimuli and not in the presence of appropriate stimuli (behavioral inappropriateness).

Thus far, what basic procedures for dealing with such problems has this book given you? For category 1 you will probably answer "reinforcement." For category 2 you will probably say, "extinction, reinforcement of alternative behavior, DRL, DRO, and punishment." For category 3 you will probably reply, "backward chaining and shaping." And for category 4 you will probably respond, "stimulus-discrimination training and fading."

A perfect score—very good! (Of course, we gave you some modeling just in case you needed it—but more about that later.) Before rushing ahead with a program based on the above techniques, let's reflect on whether there might not be some faster or easier way to

228
Some
Preliminary
Considerations
to Effective
Programming
Strategies

achieve your objective. Specifically, what we have in mind is looking for stimuli that already control the desired behavior and, if possible, devising a strategy that incorporates them. Such use of existing forms of stimulus control can be conveniently discussed under the headings of instruction, modeling, physical guidance, and situational inducement.

INSTRUCTION

Instruction is the presentation of verbal stimulation, such as spoken or printed words, in order to control behavior. Obviously, its use as a behavior-control technique dates back to the time that people first started communicating with each other. "There's a dinosaur headed this way" or, more simply, "Dinosaur!" might be one example of a primitive instruction to run for safety. Today, almost everyone frequently uses instruction without fully appreciating what a powerful behavior modification procedure it is.[1] Powerful instructional control has been demonstrated quite humorously numerous times on the popular television program "Candid Camera." For example, in one stunt the signs "MEN" and "WOMEN" were placed on two adjacent telephone booths. The result was that some people stayed out of the booth designated for the opposite sex even when it was unoccupied and they had to wait in line to use the phone in the other booth.

Although instruction can be a powerful behavior modification technique, its exclusive use may also contribute to unresolved behavior problems. Hence, the complaints of many parents: "I don't know how many times I've told that kid――― (insert "to pick up his clothes"; "to mow the grass"; "to do his homework"; "to come home at a decent hour"; "not to track mud into the house"; "not to play his stereo so loud"; "not to stay on the phone so long"; "not to slam the door"; etc.) but he never listens." To the behavior modifier, it is no mystery that such instruction is not effective: in the past, the parent probably has not consistently reinforced appropriate responses and extinguished inappropriate responses to instructions.[2]

Perhaps at least partly as a reaction to the general public's tendency to overrely on instruction, behavior modifiers have sometimes been guilty of the opposite sin. This was especially true when behavior modification was just getting its bearings as a technology. This can be illustrated by an experience of one of the authors when he was a graduate student in the 1960s. While doing his M.A.-thesis research at an institution for retarded people, he decided to demonstrate the effectiveness of positive reinforcement to some of the other students. A retarded girl named Shirley who was working in the kitchen generally piled all the plates, dishes, cups, and utensils in

229
Instruction,
Modeling,
Guidance and
Situational
Inducement

one particular area after drying them. The author decided to use so-cial approval to reinforce putting the plates and dishes in one area and the cups and utensils in another area. After each meal, the author faithfully stood around the kitchen ignoring Shirley when she put everything in one pile, but smiling and nodding his approval when she put the articles in appropriate separate piles. Very little progress occurred over several meals, and the author could see that the training process was probably going to be anything but rapid. At about this time, one of the nurses came into the kitchen and asked the author what he was trying to do. After he told her, she immediately said, "Oh, if that's all you want, that's simple. Shirley, from now on, put the plates and dishes here and the cups and utensils over there." From then on, Shirley did just that. The moral is obvious: if you want someone to do something, first try telling him. It may not always work, but when it does, it takes much less time and effort than painstakingly waiting for the behavior to occur before you reinforce it. Of course, reinforcement should be applied just the same in order to ensure the maintenance of the behavior at a high level.

An even more flagrant failure to use instruction has been noted in more than one university professor we know of who teaches behavior modification. These individuals rely exclusively on extinction when they are busy and do not wish to be disturbed by students. They simply ignore any student who tries to talk to them. This has the desired effect, in that the verbal behavior of students trying to talk to them usually extinguishes. But putting a "PLEASE DO NOT DISTURB" sign on their office door would probably achieve the same effect more quickly and create less hostility in the students. An interesting example of how added instructions may improve responding to a reinforcement program was reported by Glynn and Thomas (1974). They were asked to devise a reinforcement program that would help a teacher of a class of thirty-four third graders. Nine of the children posed special problems of inattention and poor in-seat behavior. These children frequently argued, shouted, hit and kicked other kids, banged furniture, and left the classroom without permission. Glynn and Thomas decided to study the children during an oral and written language lesson from 9:30 to 10:20 every morning, and to take a baseline of "on-task" behavior of these children. On-task behaviors were (1) *during teacher instruction,* to remain silently in one's seat, and look at the teacher; and (2) *during work periods* to write a story, draw a picture, or perform any other activity prescribed by the teacher. During ten days of baseline observations, the nine problem children were on task just less than half the time (overall average: 49.6 percent). The teacher then introduced an interesting system to the children. This system included self-assessment and self-recording of desirable behavior, as well as self-determination and self-administration of reinforcement. The children were each given a

230
Some
Preliminary
Considerations
to Effective
Programming
Strategies

ten-by-twelve-inch card with several rows of squares on it, one row for each day of the week, and the definitions of on-task behaviors were explained to them. The children were told that a "beep" would be heard several times throughout the lesson, and that if a child considered herself to be on-task at the moment of the beep, she should place a check in one of the squares. The children were then told that at the end of the lesson they would be able to cash in each check for one minute of free play time in a nearby reinforcer room that contained a variety of games and toys. A noise generator was set to emit beeps at an average rate of once every three minutes. Data were taken by observers who recorded the on-task behavior of the nine problem children without their knowledge. These data showed that the procedure led to an increase in the on-task behavior of the nine problem children to an overall average of 69.8 percent (approximately a 20-percent improvement over baseline). After ten days of this procedure, the conditions were changed back to baseline for an additional ten days, during which the average on-task behavior of the nine problem children dropped to 50.78 percent.

Although this self-control program led to some improvement, the problem children still spent 30 percent of their time in off-task behavior during the program. Glynn and Thomas identified two possible causes. First, the schedule of beeps may have been too high (that is, once every three minutes, on the average, may have been too infrequent). Second, the children often appeared confused when the teacher changed from one task to another. Thus, when a "beep" occurred they may have had difficulty in deciding whether they were on-task. To overcome this possible confusion, the teacher decided to strengthen the instruction used to designate the appropriate task. She made a large chart, on one side of which was printed in big red letters:

LOOK AT THE TEACHER
STAY IN YOUR SEAT
BE QUIET

On the other side, in green letters, was:

WORK AT YOUR PLACE
WRITE IN YOUR BOOKS
READ INSTRUCTIONS ON THE BLACKBOARD

The self-control system was then reinstituted, but with two changes. First, the schedule of beeps was changed to an average of once every two minutes. Second, the instruction chart was used by the teacher to cue the desired on-task behavior. The children were asked to mark themselves on-task only if they were "doing what the chart says" when a beep occurred. These changes led to an increase

231

Instruction,
Modeling,
Guidance and
Situational
Inducement

in the on-task behavior of the nine problem children to 91.11 percent. Although it is not possible to isolate the relative contributions of the new schedule of beeps and the added instructions to the improved performance, the author's casual observations indicated that the instructional chart eliminated the confusion about self-recording that the children had shown in the earlier phase.

Here are some general guidelines for the effective use of instruction.

1. Instruction should be within the understanding of the individual to whom it is applied.
2. Instruction should specify the behavior to be engaged in.
3. Instruction should specify contingencies involved in complying (or not complying) with it, and these contingencies should be applied consistently.
4. Complex instruction should be broken down into easy-to-follow steps.
5. Instruction should be sequenced so that it proceeds gradually from very easy to more difficult behavior for the individual being treated.
6. Instruction should be delivered in a pleasant, courteous manner.
7. Use fading as necessary to phase out instruction if you want other stimuli that are present to take control of the behavior.

MODELING

Modeling is a procedure whereby a sample of a given behavior is presented to an individual in order to induce him to engage in a similar behavior. Like instruction, it can be quite powerful. You may convince yourself of this by performing the following simple experiments:

1. For an entire day speak only in a whisper, and note how often people around you also whisper (this is a good experiment to try when you have laryngitis).
2. Yawn conspicuously in the presence of other people, and note their frequency of yawning.
3. Stand looking into a window of an empty department store for an hour, and note how many people stop and also look in the window.

In each case, compare the data obtained with data obtained under comparable circumstances when the behavior is not being modeled.

Like instruction, modeling is in such common use by the general public that few people (other than behavior modifiers) think of it as a behavior modification procedure.[3] Parents, for example, use it rather unsystematically, but quite effectively in many cases, to teach language and other behavior to their children. Behavior modifiers use

232
Some
Preliminary
Considerations
to Effective
Programming
Strategies

it in much the same way, although more systematically, to teach a variety of behaviors, as described in Chapter 8.

Modeling often involves having an individual observe a peer who is performing appropriately. For example, consider the case of an extremely withdrawn nursery-school child who almost never interacts with other children. This behavior problem could be treated with shaping. A method that can perhaps produce faster results, however, is to have the child observe several instances of another child joining in the activities of a group of children. The group should be responding to the model in a reinforcing manner (for example, by offering her play material, talking to her, and smiling). To insure that the modeling occurs under opportune circumstances and in a suitable fashion, it may be necessary to instruct certain children to perform as models and to instruct the children in the group to behave in a conspicuously reinforcing manner to the models. It is sometimes convenient and effective to film or video-tape a number of such episodes for viewing by socially withdrawn children.* The presentation of modeling scenes through film, videotape, and other media is called symbolic modeling. Studies show that this type of modeling can sometimes be as effective as the real thing (see, for instance, Masters and Driscoll, 1971).

Modeling is frequently used with adults who possess highly developed behavioral repertoires. The following excerpt from a therapy session illustrates this.** The client being treated was a male college student who had difficulty asking for dates over the telephone. In the excerpt, the client is rehearsing asking for a date. Note how the therapist combines instruction and shaping with modeling.

Client: By the way (pause) I don't suppose you want to go out Saturday night? *antecedent*

Therapist: Up to actually asking for the date you were very good. However, if I were the girl, I think I might have been a bit offended when you said "By the way." It's like your asking her out is pretty casual. Also, the way you phrased the question, you are kind of suggesting to her that she doesn't want to go out with you. Pretend for the moment I'm you. Now, how does this sound: "There's a movie at the Varsity Theater this Saturday that I want to see. If you don't have other plans, I'd very much like to take you." *— modeling*

Client: That sounded good. Like you were sure of yourself and liked the girl too.

Therapist: Why don't you try it.

Client: You know that movie at the Varsity? Well, I'd like to go, and I'd like to take you Saturday, if you don't have anything better to do. *antecedent*

Therapist: Well, that certainly was better. Your tone of voice was especially good. But the last line, "if you don't have anything better to do," sounded like you don't think you have much to offer. *— shaping*

*See O'Connor (1969) for a detailed description of the effective use of this procedure.
**The excerpt is from Rimm and Masters (1974, p. 94).

233

Instruction,
Modeling,
Guidance and
Situational
Inducement

Client: I'd like to see the show at the Varsity, Saturday, and, if you haven't made other plans, I'd like to take you.

Therapist: Much better. Excellent, in fact. You were confident, forceful and sincere. *+ ve reinforcement.*

Here are some general guidelines for the effective use of modeling.

1. The complexity of the modeled behavior should be suitable for the behavioral level of the client.
2. Combine instructions with modeling.[4]
3. Reinforcement should be given for correct imitation of the modeled behavior.[5]
4. The modeling episode should be sequenced from very easy to more difficult behavior for the individual being treated.
5. The modeling scenes should be as realistic as possible.[6]
6. Use fading as necessary so that stimuli other than the model can take control over the desired behavior.

PHYSICAL GUIDANCE

Physical guidance is the application of physical contact to induce an individual to go through the motions of the desired behavior. Some familiar examples of guidance are a dance instructor leading a pupil through a new dance step; a golf instructor grasping the novice's arms and moving them through the proper swing and follow-through; and a parent holding a child's hand while teaching her to cross the street safely. Guidance is always only one component of a teaching procedure. Both the dance instructor and the golf instructor will also use instruction (they will tell the student what to do and give her "pointers"), modeling (they will demonstrate the appropriate physical postures and motions), and reinforcement for correct responses or approximations to them (such as "Excellent!" or "Much better!"). Likewise, the parent teaching her child to cross the street safely will use instruction (for example, by saying, "Look both ways") and modeling (for example, by looking both ways in an exaggerated manner).

Some uses of guidance in behavior modification programs were given in Chapter 8—for example, using guidance and fading to teach a child to touch his head upon request. Guidance is generally used in procedures for teaching instruction following and model imitation, so that instruction and modeling can then be used to establish other behaviors. For example, in one procedure for teaching instruction following, a child is placed in a chair opposite the teacher. At the beginning of a trial the teacher says, "Johnny, stand up" and then lifts

234

Some
Preliminary
Considerations
to Effective
Programming
Strategies

the child onto his feet. Reinforcement is then presented immediately, as though the child himself had performed the response. Next, the teacher says, "Johnny, sit down," and grasping the child's shoulders the teacher gently but firmly presses him down on the chair. Again, immediate reinforcement is presented. The process is repeated over numerous trials while guidance is faded out (see Kazdin and Erickson, 1975). After this set of instructions is learned, the behavior modifier teaches another set (such as "Come here" and "Go there"), using a similar procedure. Less and less fading may be required to teach successive instructions, until eventually even fairly complex instruction-following behavior can be taught with little guidance.

As in teaching instruction following, the teacher who uses guidance to teach model imitation starts with a few simple imitations (such as touching one's head, clapping one's hands, tapping the table, standing up, and sitting down) and adds new imitations as the previous ones are learned. This can involve teaching instruction following and model imitation at the same time, depending on the verbal stimuli presented. For example, the individual will learn to follow an instruction to imitate behavioral displays if the teacher says "Do this" while modeling the behavior. This might facilitate the development of generalized imitation, whereby the individual imitates completely new behavior at the first opportunity to do so.[7]

Another common application of guidance is in helping individuals to overcome fears. For example, helping a person who is terrified of water might involve gradually leading her by the hand into the shallow end of a swimming pool and supporting her while she floats. The least fear-provoking aspects of a situation should be introduced first, and the more fear-provoking aspects later in a very gradual manner. One should never try to force an individual to do more than she feels comfortable doing.[8] The more fearful the person is, the more gradual the process should be. (Note that this process extends systematic desensitization—see pp. 214–218—to the natural environment. For this reason it is sometimes called *in vivo desensitization*.) In the case of a very fearful individual one may have to spend many sessions simply sitting with her on the edge of the pool.

Some general guidelines for the effective use of guidance are as follows.

1. Reinforcement should be given immediately after the successful completion of the guided response.
2. Guidance should be sequenced gradually from very easy to more difficult behavior for the individual being treated.
3. The stimuli you want to eventually control the behavior should be conspicuously present during guidance.
4. Use fading as necessary so that other stimuli can take control over the behavior.

Largely because of our similar histories of reinforcement and punishment, there are numerous situations and occasions in our society that control similar behavior in many of us. The interiors of certain public buildings, such as churches, museums, and libraries, tend to suppress loud talking. Parties tend to evoke socializing and jovial, carefree behavior. Catchy melodies prompt humming and singing, and strident march music tends to incite participation in a foot-stamping parade. The assorted stimuli associated with Christmas induce cheerfulness, friendliness, and gift buying.

We use the term *situational inducement* to refer to the deliberate use of situations and occasions to control behavior. Such techniques, like others we have discussed, no doubt predate recorded history. Ceremonious gatherings involving singing and dancing probably served to strengthen "togetherness" in ancient tribes, just as they do today in almost all cultures. Monasteries and convents have been used for centuries to promote asexual religious behavior by providing an environment conducive to reading religious texts and meditating, and by restricting opportunities for the sexes to interact.

Supermarkets and department stores use many situational features to induce buying. Among these are the attention-evoking manner in which the products are displayed, and pictures showing the products in an attractive way. Fine restaurants provide a relaxing atmosphere so as to optimize eating behavior. If the restaurant becomes crowded and people are waiting for tables, fast music may be played to induce rapid eating.

Examples of situational inducement can also be found in the home. Many people have unusual objects in their living room that function as "conversation pieces." If the conversation lags when guests are present, a rare decorative vase may stimulate someone to initiate a new line of conversation with a remark such as, "Oh, where did you get that beautiful Ming vase?" or, "I saw one just like it on my recent trip to China." Such fragile conversation pieces tend also to induce undesirable handling behavior, especially in children. When this happens, the host may use situational inducement by quickly handing the potential offender something less expensive, such as a toy or a drink.

Situational inducement has been used in a number of imaginative and effective ways in behavior modification programs to help increase or decrease target behaviors, or to bring them under appropriate stimulus control. Examples can be conveniently discussed under four somewhat overlapping categories: (1) rearranging the existing surroundings; (2) moving the activity to a new location; (3) relocating people; and (4) changing the time of the activity.

236
Some
Preliminary
Considerations
to Effective
Programming
Strategies

Rearranging the Existing Surroundings

An interesting example in the first category occurred in a case reported by the well-known behaviorist Israel Goldiamond (1965). Goldiamond was consulted by a married couple who were having a problem in their relationship. When the couple were together in the house, the husband could not refrain from screaming at his wife over her once having gone to bed with his best friend. One of the goals that was decided upon, therefore, was to replace screaming with civilized conversational behavior. Goldiamond reasoned that the husband's screaming had probably come under the control of the S^Ds in the home environment and that one way to weaken the behavior in that situation would be to change those S^Ds. He therefore instructed the couple to rearrange the rooms and furniture in the house to make it appear considerably different. The wife went one step further and bought herself a new outfit. Goldiamond then provided for the reinforcement of civilized conversation in the presence of these new S^Ds which were not associated so strongly with screaming (how he did this is explained more fully below). It was important to do this as quickly as possible, because if screaming occurred too often in the presence of the new S^Ds, it would become conditioned to them just as it had been conditioned to the old S^Ds.

Another example of rearranging the existing surroundings is altering the furniture and other items in one's room in order to promote better and more persistent studying behavior. One might, for example, improve the lighting, clear one's desk of irrelevant material, move the bed as far as possible from the desk, and have the desk facing away from the bed. Better yet, if possible, one should not even have the bed in the same room as the desk because the bed is an S^D for sleeping. In order to prevent nonstudy behaviors from being conditioned to the new stimuli, one should engage only in studying behavior when in the rearranged environment (see Goldiamond, 1965).

Letter writing is a behavior that is difficult to maintain because it involves a long delay of reinforcement (it takes at least several days to get a return letter). One way to strengthen your tendency to write, however, is to place before you a picture of the person to whom you are writing. This is another example of rearranging stimuli to control behavior. (Other examples are shown in Figure 15–1).

Moving the Activity to a New Location

The second category of situational inducement is illustrated by another part of the procedure Goldiamond used in the case of the husband who screamed at his wife. The spouses were instructed that immediately after rearranging the furniture at their home, they were

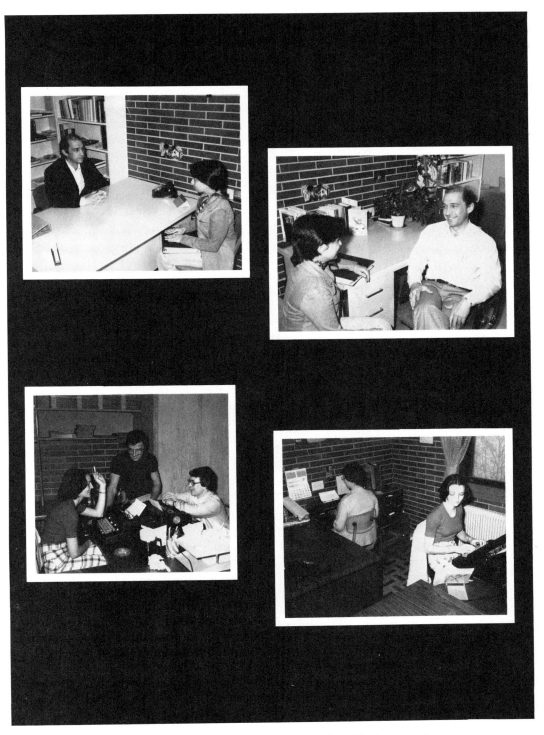

FIGURE 15-1. *Examples of situational inducement.*

238

Some
Preliminary
Considerations
to Effective
Programming
Strategies

to go to a place that would induce civilized conversation. It was hoped that this behavior would continue until they returned home, and would then come under the control of the new S^{D}s in the home. To quote from Goldiamond's report (1965, p. 856):

> Since it was impossible for [the husband] to converse in a civilized manner with his wife, we discussed a program of going to one evening spot on Monday, another on Tuesday, and another on Wednesday.
>
> "Oh," he said, "you want us to be together. We'll go bowling on Thursday."
>
> "On the contrary," I said, "I am interested in your subjecting yourself to an environment where civilized chit-chat is maintained. Such is not the case at a bowling alley."
>
> I also asked if there was any topic of conversation which once started would maintain itself. He commented on his mother-in-law's crazy ideas about farming. He was then given an index card and instructed to write "farm" on it and to attach a $20 bill to that card. The $20 was to be used to pay the waitress on Thursday, at which point he was to start the "farm" discussion which hopefully would continue into the taxi and home.

Changing the location of the activity is one approach to problems relating to studying. The student using this approach should select a special place that is conducive to studying and that has distinctive stimuli that are not associated with any behavior other than studying. A reserved carrel in a university library is ideal for this purpose, although any other well-lit, quiet area with adequate working space would be suitable. Depending on the extent of appropriate study behavior in the student's repertoire, it may be necessary to combine relocating the activity with some of the basic procedures discussed in Part II of this text. For severe deficiencies, behavior incorporating good study skills should first be shaped and then placed on either a low-duration or a low-ratio schedule in the special studying area. The value of the schedule should then be gradually increased so that the behavior will eventually be maintained at the desired level. Appropriate reinforcement (such as coffee with a friend) should be arranged to occur immediately after the schedule requirement has been met. Should one experience a tendency to daydream or to engage in other nonstudy behavior while in the studying area, one should do a little more productive studying and then leave immediately so that daydreaming does not become conditioned to the stimuli in the studying area (see Fox, 1962). Similarly, the husband in the above-mentioned case reported by Goldiamond was instructed to go to the garage and sit on a specially designated "sulking" stool

239
Instruction,
Modeling,
Guidance and
Situational
Inducement

whenever he was in the house and felt a tendency to sulk—this being a behavior that was threatening the recently strengthened conversational behavior after screaming had been eliminated.

Relocating People

The third category of situational inducement was not illustrated in Goldiamond's case study. The procedures used in that case were effective; therefore, a separation of the spouses was not necessary. Although relocating the participants is generally a measure of last resort when dealing with individuals who wish to maintain their respective relationships, it is sometimes the most practical tactic in other circumstances. If you just cannot get along with Sam Jones, and there is no particular reason for you to associate with him anyway, then why try to change his behavior and/or yours in order to make the two of you more compatible? Both of you will probably be happier respecting each other from a distance.

Classroom teachers of small children often change seating arrangements in order to relocate pupils whose close proximity leads to various types of disruptions. This is usually much easier than designing and carrying out reinforcement and/or punishment programs in order to eliminate undesirable interactions, and the end result may be just as effective, or more so.

Changing the Time of the Activity

The final category of situational inducement involves taking advantage of the fact that certain stimuli and behavioral tendencies change predictably with the passage of time. For example, two sexual partners may find that sexual activity is better for them in the morning than at night when one of them is "too tired." Changing the time of an activity has been used effectively in weight-control programs. People who cook for their families sometimes put on excess weight by "nibbling" while preparing meals and then sitting down for a full-course dinner. Rather than foregoing dinner with one's family, a partial solution to this problem is to do the preparation, except for the actual cooking, shortly after having eaten the previous meal, while the tendency to eat is still relatively weak (see Ferster, Nurnberger, and Levitt, 1962).

Situational inducement covers a very broad set of procedures. Its use, therefore, is considerably less straightforward than that of the other methods discussed in this chapter. In short, a good deal of imagination is typically required if it is to be used effectively. We suggest the following guidelines:

240
Some
Preliminary
Considerations
to Effective
Programming
Strategies

1. Insofar as this is practical, arrange for the individual of concern to be exposed to locations and environmental arrangements that already control the target behavior in the desired way, and to avoid locations and arrangements that do not have this control.

2. Determine whether it is necessary or desirable to extend the behavior to situations that do not presently exert desirable control over the behavior, and, if it is, take appropriate steps to bring this about.

3. Make sure that undesirable behavior never occurs in the presence of situations introduced to control the desirable behavior.

Study Questions

for examination purposes

1. What basic procedures discussed in the first thirteen chapters of this text might be used to:
   a) increase an infrequent behavior?
   b) decrease an excessive behavior?
   c) develop a behavior that never occurs?
   d) get a desired behavior to occur in the presence of appropriate stimuli?

2. A teacher of a second-grade class complains to you, "When I tell the children to stay in their desks and work, they never listen to me." Describe the contingencies that are likely operating with respect to that instruction from the teacher to the kids in the class.

3. Explain (in terms of your past experiences with S^Ds, S^Δs, reinforcement, and extinction) why the tone of voice of someone giving you instructions might determine whether you will follow the instructions appropriately.

4. Can you think of any humorous examples from your experience that demonstrate instructional control of behavior?

5. Discuss critically the attitude a number of early behavior modifiers had towards instruction.

6. In regard to the Glynn and Thomas study on added instruction in a classroom situation:
   a) what two examples of stimulus control were Glynn and Thomas measuring during the first baseline?
   b) what was the schedule of reinforcement during the first self-control phase?
   c) did the first self-control phase include a token system? Why or why not?
   d) explain how the added instructions related to the four questions one should ask when selecting an S^D (see p. 110).

7. State and discuss a major implication of the Glynn and Thomas study.

241

Instruction,
Modeling,
Guidance and
Situational
Inducement

8. Describe two recent situations in which you were influenced by modeling to emit a behavior.

9. Describe the specific steps you might go through in using modeling to overcome the extreme withdrawal behavior of a nursery-school child who never interacts with other children. Identify the basic principles and procedures being applied in your program.

10. Describe an example of modeling that appears in Chapter 8.

11. In the dialogue between the client and the therapist concerning the client's difficulty in asking for dates, briefly describe:
    a) how modeling was involved.
    b) how instructions were involved.
    c) how shaping was involved.

12. What is meant by symbolic modeling? Describe how this might be involved in teaching a child to fear snakes.

13. What is meant by physical guidance? How does it differ from gestural prompting? (See pp. 128–9.)

14. Identify a behavior that you were recently influenced to perform as a result of instructions, modeling, and physical guidance. Describe how each tactic was involved.

15. What do we mean by the term situational inducement? Which term given previously in this book has essentially the same meaning? (See p. 128.)

16. What are the four proposed categories of situational inducement?

17. Give an example from the text of each of the four categories of situational inducement.

18. Give an example from your own experience of each of the four categories of situational inducement.

19. State a difference and a similarity between moving the activity to a new location and relocating people.

20. For each of the following examples, identify the category of situational inducement in which it might best be placed and indicate why.
    a) On Saturday afternoon, an exercise buff can't seem to "get up the energy" to lift his weights. In order to increase his likelihood of weight-lifting, he places the weights in the center of the den (where he usually exercises), turns on the TV to the Saturday afternoon wrestling matches, and opens his *Muscle Beach* magazine to the Mr. America centerfold.
    b) It is said that Victor Hugo, the famous writer, controlled his work habits in his study by having his servant take his clothes away and not bring them back until the end of the day (Wallace, 1971, pp. 68–69). *rearranging surrounding.*
    c) In order to quit drinking, an alcoholic surrounds himself with AA members and stops seeing his old drinking buddies. *relocating people.*
    d) Another exercise buff has decided to jog a mile every night before going to bed. Alas, "the road to hell [or perhaps to heart attack] is paved with good intentions." Late nights, good TV, wine with dinner, and other events take their toll. Three months later, our "exercise buff" is still fat and out of shape because of many missed jogging nights. He therefore changes the routine and begins jogging each day immediately upon arriving home and before eating dinner. *Changing timeof activity*
    e) After many interruptions while working on this book at the university, the authors began working at one of their homes. *moving activity to new location*

242
Some
Preliminary
Considerations
to Effective
Programming
Strategies

21. According to the proposed guidelines for the use of the instruction, modeling, and physical guidance:
    a) what behavioral principle is used with all three procedures?
    b) what two other behavioral procedures are likely to be used with all three procedures?

Study Exercises

(to be practiced by the reader)

1. Outline a program that a parent might follow to teach a two-year-old child to respond consistently to the instruction "Please bring me your shoes." Indicate how your program might use instructions, modeling, and guidance, and how it follows the guidelines for the effective application of each.

2. Select two behaviors from the following list:
    a) doing the dishes immediately after a meal
    b) getting up when the alarm rings
    c) feeling happy
    d) cleaning up your bedroom twice per week
    e) doing some exercises daily
    f) decreasing your cigarette smoking
   For each behavior, describe how you might influence the behavior by combining at least three of the following tactics: modeling, guidance, rearranging the existing surroundings, moving the activity to a new location, relocating people, and changing the time of the activity. Make your suggestions highly plausible in regard to the situation.

Self-Modification Exercise

(to be practiced by the reader)

Identify one of your behaviors that you would like to modify (a deficiency, an excess, or an inappropriateness). Describe a plausible program you might use to successfully modify that behavior. Include in your program at least five of the following procedures, and indicate how each is involved: instructions, modeling, guidance, rearranging the existing surroundings, moving the activity to a new location, relocating people, and changing the time of the behavior.

EXTENDED DISCUSSION AND NOTES

1. One reason that instruction is not commonly regarded as a behavior modification technique is that it has been, and still is, used effectively by those whose orientation is <u>mentalistic</u> rather than behavioristic. Par-
(Continued)

(Continued)

ticularly in formal education, it is often held that instruction involves "transmitting" or "communicating" knowledge, ideas, and concepts from the "mind" of one individual (the teacher) to that of another (the student). From a behavioristic point of view, however, even the teaching of complex verbal concepts is no different, *in principle*, from instructing someone to engage in a manual skill, such as driving a car. Consider, for example, the following statement by Skinner (1974, p. 121):

> Much of education is instruction in verbal behavior. The student is told how to "use words" rather than how to use an accelerator or brake. In neither case is he given knowledge; he is told how to behave. The instruction given by a labeled picture often works very quickly; the viewer knows at once what the object is called and what the label means. A definition is a seemingly more internal form of instruction, but its effect is simply that one verbal response is now used interchangeably with another.

2. That instruction alone is not always effective has been empirically demonstrated numerous times. O'Leary, Becker, Evans, and Saudargas (1969) found that rules did not alter disruptive classroom behavior, whereas token reinforcement for desirable behavior decreased the undesirable behavior. Phillips (1968) reported on a token system used in Achievement Place, a residential unit for "predelinquents" (boys who were judged guilty of minor offenses and deemed likely to advance to more serious crimes). One of his findings was that instructions (for example, "Stop that kind of talk") did not effectively reduce aggressive statements (such as "I'll kill you") by the boys. However, aggressive statements were markedly reduced when fines (the loss of tokens) were charged for them. In another study conducted with boys at the same residential unit, Bailey, Wolf, and Phillips (1970) found that giving them a number of classroom rules to follow (such as "Do not talk without permission" and "Do not look out the window") did not effectively decrease the specified undesirable behaviors. However, the undesirable behaviors were markedly reduced when the boys could earn tokens for engaging in them less than 10 percent of the time. + instruction

3. Historically, learning by imitation has been given an important place in a number of different psychological theories, not just behavioristic ones. In Freudian (psychoanalytic) theory, for example, a male child typically develops certain "male" behavior patterns through identification with his father, whereas a female child develops female behavior patterns through identification with her mother. Thus, for example, the absence of a strong male figure with whom to identify could (in theory) lead to feminine traits—even homosexuality—in a boy who identifies excessively with the mother. Gestalt psychologists considered imitative learning to be innate in higher species, and attempted to show, for example, that chimpanzees could learn to solve problems by watching other chimpanzees solve them. More behavioristically oriented psychologists, however, have tended toward the view that imitation is itself a learned behavior.

There are several processes by which imitative behavior might be learned. First, an individual is frequently reinforced when he performs the same actions that another individual performs; hence, other people's actions tend to become S^Ds for engaging in similar actions. (For example, a child who watches someone open a door to go outside receives the reinforcement of going outside when he performs the same action.) Second, to the extent that other people are reinforcing to us, their actions

(Continued)

acquire conditioned reinforcing properties; hence, we receive conditioned reinforcement when we perform the same actions. A third possibility is that once we have learned to imitate simple responses, we can then imitate more complex behaviors, provided that these are composed of the simpler responses. (For example, once an individual has learned to imitate "al," "li," "ga," and "tor" as single syllables, or as units of various words, she can then imitate the word "alligator" the first time she hears it [Skinner, 1957]). A fourth possibility is that imitative behavior is not just a set of separate stimulus-response relationships, but is itself an operant class of responses. In other words, it is possible that once a person is reinforced for imitating some behaviors, he will then tend to imitate other behaviors, even if they contain no elements in common with the imitative behaviors that were reinforced.

Regardless of theoretical orientation, there is no doubt that model imitation is an important factor in human behavioral development. Exactly how, and under what conditions, it influences behavior is an important practical question that is receiving intensive experimental study. Experimental psychologist Albert Bandura and his co-workers have contributed greatly to our understanding of this important aspect of human behavior. (For a review of Bandura's and others' studies in this area, see Bandura, 1969.) Modeling has also been used effectively as a therapy technique (for reviews, see Bandura, 1971; Rachman, 1972).

4. That instruction combined with modeling can be more effective than modeling alone is illustrated in a case study reported by Foy, Eisler, and Pinkston (1975). The patient was a fifty-six-year-old carpenter who experienced chronic difficulties in complying with what he felt were the unreasonable demands of others (such as his foreman or supervisor) "until he released anger in a verbally abusive and often assaultive manner." The study consisted of four phases: (1) baseline; (2) modeling alone; (3) modeling plus focused instruction; and (4) follow-up evaluation.

During the baseline sessions, the therapist role-played several different work-related scenes with the patient. For example, the patient would ask the therapist, playing the role of the supervisor, for a raise, to which the therapist would reply, "I'm not sure that you deserve a raise." Or the therapist, playing the role of the foreman, would blame the patient for a mistake that was not his fault. The patient's subsequent behavior was measured with respect to four categories: (1) hostile comments; (2) irrelevant comments; (3) compliance with unreasonable demands; and (4) a request for the other person to change his behavior.

During the modeling-alone sessions, the patient was shown a video-tape in which the therapist modeled desirable behavior—which was defined as increased requests and decreased compliance, hostile comments, and irrelevant comments. No specific instruction was given to the patient other than "to pay attention to how the model behaves during each scene and then to practice responses to the same situation before viewing the next modeled scene." Over sessions, the patient showed considerable improvement in the behaviors assessed during the baseline.

During the modeling-plus-instruction sessions, the patient was instructed: (1) on the first three sessions to focus on how the model responded without making hostile comments; (2) on the next three sessions to focus on the model's refusing to comply with unreasonable

(Continued)

(Continued)

requests; (3) on the next three sessions to focus on how the model avoided making irrelevant comments; (4) on the final three sessions to notice how the model requested the other person in the scene to change his behavior. In each case, the target behavior improved when instruction was added to the modeling procedure. The follow-up phase showed that the improvements were maintained over a period of six months.

5. For example, Lovaas, Berberich, Perloff, and Schaeffer (1966) used reinforcement to establish vocal imitations in retarded children. They then showed that when reinforcement was given to the children only when they did not imitate correctly, the number of correct imitations decreased. Moreover, Gibson, Lawrence, and Nelson (1977) demonstrated that modeling, instructions, and feedback for teaching social responses to developmentally disabled adults were more effective than modeling alone, or instructions and feedback alone.

6. This rule follows, of course, from the principle of stimulus generalization, discussed in Chapter 11.

7. Generalized imitation occurs when an individual, after learning to imitate a number of behaviors (perhaps with some shaping, fading, guidance, and reinforcement), learns to imitate a new response on the first trial without reinforcement. An example of the study of generalized imitation with severely retarded children is the classic experiment by Baer, Peterson, and Sherman (1967). They used shaping, guidance, and fading with reinforcement to teach a severely retarded child to imitate the teacher when the teacher said "Do this" and simultaneously modeled some behavior. After seven responses (such as raising the left arm and tapping the table with the left hand) were learned, one of the children correctly imitated tapping the arm of the chair when that response was first modeled, even though that response was not reinforced. This was an example of generalized imitation.

8. Not all behavior therapists agree with this view. For example, if a client has a strong fear of something (such as looking out from high places), some therapists encourage the client to form very vivid images of specific situations that cause the fear (looking down from the top of a very tall building, feeling dizzy, feeling more and more anxious, and so forth). It is assumed that this approach will extinguish the anxiety reactions of the client to the scenes imagined in the therapist's office, and that the results will hopefully generalize to the real world. This approach of having a client imagine himself in a very fearful and anxiety-producing situation is called *implosive therapy* (Stampfl and Levis, 1967). However, the literature does not indicate this to be a generally highly successful approach (Morganstern, 1973, 1974), and we would not recommend its use. Also, even an implosive therapist presumably would not throw a fearful nonswimmer into twenty feet of water; he would have him only imagine being thrown in.

Study Questions on Notes

1. Compare and contrast the behavioristic and mentalistic views of instruction.

(Continued)

245

2. Are the examples in note 2 concerned with the effect of instructions on decreasing behavior, increasing behavior, or both?

3. In a sentence, what is often required to ensure the effectiveness of instruction? Give an example from note 2.

4. Describe four processes by which imitative behavior might be learned, and give an example of each.

5. What experimental psychologist has contributed greatly to our understanding of modeling?

6. Concerning the efforts of Foy et al. to teach a carpenter to respond more effectively to the demands of his boss:
  a) how did they use instructions?
  b) how did they use modeling?

7. Discuss how Lovaas et al. showed the importance of reinforcement in their program.

8. What is generalized imitation? Give an example.

9. What is implosive therapy? How does it differ from systematic desensitization (pp. 214–217)?

CHAPTER 16

ALTERNATIVE STRATEGIES
For Decreasing Behavior

In our experience, the majority of problems referred to behavior modifiers are phrased in terms of behavioral excesses. This is probably due largely to the habitual way in which the average person thinks about behavior problems. That is, people tend to focus more on what is "wrong" about what a person is doing rather than on what they would like that person to be doing instead. "Susie keeps running around the room during class" and "Johnny just sits staring into space" are common complaints that teachers make.

Other behavior modifiers have also noted this tendency. Greenspoon (1976, p. 176), for example, commented, "The specification of desired behaviors . . . is not an easy task. The difficulty is well illustrated by the parent who spent 30 minutes telling the psychologist all the behaviors that her son emitted that she did not like. When asked what she wanted the boy to do, she replied 'Well, I just want him to be a good boy.' When asked what behaviors constituted a 'good boy,' she conceded that she didn't know and would have to think about it."

When referrals are presented in this way, the skillful behavior modifier does not automatically think, "Aha! Here's a behavioral excess to be decreased." Rather, she asks the teacher or parent, "What

248

Some
Preliminary
Considerations
to Effective
Programming
Strategies

is the appropriate behavior to increase in this situation?" Through such examination, it may be found that the teacher, for example, is really concerned about Susie's and Johnny's "undesirable" behaviors only to the extent that they keep these children from engaging in more desirable behaviors (such as completing their classwork assignments). So the behavior modifier would reformulate the problem in terms of increasing a behavior that doesn't occur frequently enough rather than decreasing a behavior that occurs too frequently (see Goldiamond, 1975).

Although one should always think in terms of increasing desirable behavior, it is sometimes necessary to focus also on decreasing undesirable behavior. This does not mean, however, that the first thought that should come to mind is to use extinction or punishment. As explained in Chapters 3 and 12, these procedures have a number of drawbacks. They frequently produce undesirable side effects, and they frequently require many trials before the undesirable behavior decreases to zero (or at least to a tolerable level). Moreover, it is not always easy to apply them effectively. For example, time-out punishment may be impractical if a suitable time-out room is not available. Additionally, an individual receives attention while being placed in a time-out room, and this attention, being immediately contingent upon the undesirable behavior, may therefore serve to maintain it. The application of time-out may also be quite variable, depending upon the behavior modification skills of the individual using it. A teacher whose particular mood strongly influences his application of time-out might, when in a good mood, say, "Now, now, you're being naughty. You know you shouldn't do that. I'm going to have to put you in the time-out room. Come on, let's go." Then the teacher takes the student gently by the hand and leads him to the time-out room. On the other hand, imagine the same teacher on a day when he's in a bad mood. He yells, "No! Come on!" grabs the boy by the scruff of his neck, and "bounces" him off to the time-out room.

Due to the difficulties associated with extinction and punishment, it is important to explore alternative ways of managing undesirable behavior. Some of these alternatives might include a component of extinction, together with other principles. Others might involve partial rather than complete suppression of behavior. All of the alternatives to be discussed later in this chapter focus on increasing desirable behavior as a part of the strategy of decreasing undesirable behavior.

After pointing out some reasons for considering the causes of behavior, we will discuss some of these alternatives. At the end of the chapter, we list guidelines indicating the order in which we believe the methods described in this and the preceding chapters should generally be considered in selecting a method to decrease a particular undesirable behavior.

In Part II of this book, we gave many examples of how ignorance of the basic principles and procedures of behavior modification can lead to behavior problems. The knowledge thus generated about the causes of those problems can clearly be useful: it can help to prevent those problems. Ultimately, prevention may be the most important reason for considering the causes of behavior.

Even after a problem behavior has been detected, however, knowledge of the causes of that behavior can often help in deciding how to deal with it. For example, if the sources of reinforcement for the behavior can be identified, it may be possible to alter or eliminate them so that extinction may proceed. Sometimes, however, consideration of the causes will indicate that extinction is not the best strategy because the sources of reinforcement cannot be effectively changed—at least not in the situation in which the behavior is occurring. For example, the individual may be receiving reinforcement from his peers, and it may not be feasible to get them to stop reinforcing him.

Due consideration to the causes of behavior may also lead one to the appropriate conclusion that specialists more competent than oneself should deal with the problem. For example, if a person is troubled by thoughts of suicide, the novice behavior modifier should not attempt to extinguish that behavior on the reasoning that "he's just trying to get my sympathy; well, I'll withhold it and he'll stop talking that way." Obviously, such an approach could prove disastrous. It would be much more ethical to refer the person to an experienced behavior therapist, who is qualified to identify the sources controlling the behavior and to undertake appropriate measures to counteract those sources.

Likewise, the novice behavior modifier should not attempt to eliminate behaviors that may have medical causes. Sneezing, vomiting, and seizures are obvious examples of behaviors for which the application of extinction or punishment might be as ridiculous as this tongue-in-cheek advice from Lewis Carroll:

> Speak roughly to your little boy,
>   And beat him when he sneezes:
> He only does it to annoy,
>   Because he knows it teases.

It is true that cases of almost continuous sneezing for which there are no known medical causes have been reported. Vomitting controlled entirely by nondeliberate reinforcement is not uncommon in institutions for the retarded. We have also observed retarded children whose "seizures" are not true seizures at all, but rather very realistic fake seizures shaped by the attention they attract from attendants, nurses, and doctors. However, it would be unethical for any behavior modifier to attempt to treat such cases without first consulting the appropriate medical authorities.[1]

ALTERNATIVE STRATEGIES FOR DECREASING BEHAVIOR

Situational Inducement

In Chapter 15, we described four somewhat overlapping categories of situational inducement: rearranging the existing surroundings, changing the activity to a new location, relocating people, and changing the time of the activity. As was illustrated by many of the examples in that chapter, it is frequently possible to decrease behavior by identifying stimuli that already control desirable alternative behaviors, and using these stimuli according to one or more of the situational-inducement procedures (for example, recall the efforts of Goldiamond to decrease a man's screaming at his wife).

If an undesirable behavior occurs in response to particular stimuli in very specific situations, it is sometimes possible to eliminate the behavior simply by changing the stimulus and eliminating the opportunity to emit the behavior. Consider the case of Edward, an eight-year-old mildly retarded boy who was in a special-education class.* His teacher, Ms. Millan, reported to one of the authors that Edward consistently (three or four times a day) emitted undesirable, classroom-disturbing behaviors. After some discussion with Ms. Millan, it became clear that the disturbing behaviors that she was concerned about involved a loud approximation of "Tarzan" noises. It was also clear that Edward made the Tarzan noises whenever he was asked questions for which he did not know the answer. Rather than giving wrong answers, Edward would burst out with "Eeee-ah, eeee-ah." Needless to say, the Tarzan noises disrupted the class. (Ms. Millan reported that one of the other boys climbed on a desk and jumped up and down while scratching himself underneath the armpits and making noises like Cheetah the chimp.) The program Ms. Millan implemented was simply to eliminate the occasion for the undesirable behavior to occur. She stopped asking questions for which Edward did not know the answers, and took him aside for some individual sessions regarding the work to be done the next day. During these sessions, she quizzed Edward on his knowledge of the subject matter. Although he would occasionally make mistakes, he did not make Tarzan noises. Since only he and Ms. Millan were

*The details of this case were provided by a student in a behavior modification course for resource teachers taught by G. Martin at the Winnipeg School Division No. 1, Winnipeg, Manitoba, January–March, 1973.

present during these sessions, the behavior apparently was under the stimulus control of the presence of the other class members.

During class, over a two-week period, Ms. Millan asked Edward questions to which he knew the answers and gave him a great deal of approval for correct answers. Then, over the next two weeks, Ms. Millan began fading in slightly more difficult questions, each of which she prefaced with a strong prompt, such as, "Now Edward, here is a question that's a little difficult. But I'm sure you can answer it, and if you can't we will figure out the answer together, won't we class." Thus, if Edward eventually did give a wrong answer, he was immediately engaged with the teacher and the rest of the class in an attempt to figure out the answer. This gave Edward the opportunity to receive the attention of the class for desirable behavior, rather than for the undesirable Tarzan noises. That, coupled with his recent history of receiving reinforcement for giving correct answers, solved the problem. The project required approximately a month of careful attention from Ms. Millan. Thereafter, Edward required no special attention. In order to maintain his good behavior, however, Ms. Millan made sure that she periodically asked Edward questions to which he knew the answers.

Instruction, Modeling, and Role Playing

Toby, the son of one of the authors, was attending nursery school three mornings per week. His parents (Garry and Nickie) were somewhat dismayed when Toby frequently reported that he had been fighting in school with a boy named Karle. Because of their concern, Garry and Nickie approached the nursery-school teacher, Mona, and asked if they could come and watch Toby's activities. Sure enough, they observed that Toby frequently engaged in rough housing with a boy named Karle. They also observed that Toby was not the instigator. During certain activities Karle would grab Toby and Toby would retaliate. The two children would then begin wrestling and playfully rolling along the floor in a boisterous fashion.

The problem was handled at home by means of a few sessions of instruction, modeling, and role playing involving Toby, Garry, and Nickie. One evening, Garry instructed Toby as follows: "Toby, let's pretend that Nickie is Mona and that we're at nursery school. Okay? Let's pretend that you and I are the kids at nursery school. You pretend to be Karle and I'll pretend to be you. Now, let's pretend that we are making animal noises like Mona sometimes tells us to." At this point, Nickie, playing the role of Mona, gave the appropriate instructions for the children to get down on the floor and pretend that they were tigers and to make tiger noises. Garry then said, "Now, Toby, remember you're Karle. What does Karle do when you're mak-

252
Some
Preliminary
Considerations
to Effective
Programming
Strategies

ing animal noises?" "He usually comes and tries to pretend he's eating me up like a tiger," said Toby. Garry replied, "OK, Toby, you do that to me." Toby responded vigorously, as though he were Karle. At that point Garry said, "Now, Toby, here's what I want you to do when Karle does that to you." Garry (playing the role of Toby) immediately stood up and said, "No, Karle. My dad doesn't like me to fight in school. Right, Mona?" To this, Nickie (playing the role of Mona) immediately responded with, "Good for you, Toby. Yes, that's right."

After several repetitions of the role playing, the roles were reversed and Toby was instructed to pretend and act as though he were "Toby at school." Garry assumed the role of Karle, and Nickie continued to play Mona. Over several trials and several different "typical nursery school" activities, Garry played the role of an aggressive Karle and grabbed Toby in an attempt to start to wrestle. Toby was prompted to immediately stand up and say, "No, Karle. My dad doesn't want me to fight in school. Right, Mona?" After a number of trials, Toby's reaction became quite automatic. During a period of approximately a week, Toby's fighting with Karle in the classroom decreased to near zero. Toby began emitting more desirable classroom behaviors, and in turn received more reinforcement from Mona. Six weeks after this program, Toby's fighting in school was still under good control.

Eliminate the Early Component of a Chain

Sometimes, an undesirable behavior is part of a consistent behavioral chain. It is therefore sometimes possible to eliminate an undesirable behavior by elminating an earlier component of the chain that leads up to it.[2]

Such a case was described to one of the authors by a mother of a retarded child who was living at home. Frequently during the day, and always just when the mother was busy in the kitchen, the child would go to the mother's bedroom, take a piece of jewelry out of the jewelry box, carry it to the bathroom, and flush it down the toilet. She would then come and tell her mother what she had done. Since the sequence of behaviors appeared to be quite consistent, the strategy employed was that of dealing with an earlier component of the chain, so as to indirectly rather than directly eliminate the actual behavior of flushing the jewelry down the toilet. Specifically, the girl was given several prompted trials during which, when mother and daughter were both in the kitchen, the mother took the daughter by the hand, went into the bedroom, prompted the daughter to take a piece of jewelry out of the box, and guided the daughter to bring the jewelry into the kitchen and place it in a jar on the kitchen table. This behavior was highly reinforced.

After several guided trials, mother was able to initiate the sequence of behaviors by instructing the child while they were both in the kitchen. The guidance and instruction trials occurred over a two-day period during which the child was not given an opportunity to go into the bedroom on her own. On the start of the third day, the child was instructed that anytime she wanted to, when mom was in the kitchen, she could get some jewelry, place it in the jar in the kitchen, and receive a "treat" from mom. In addition, the mother took a polaroid photograph of the daughter putting the jewelry into the jar on the kitchen table and placed the picture beside the jewelry box in the bedroom. During the next three weeks, the daughter continued periodically to bring jewelry to the kitchen and to receive "treats" for doing so. Not once did she flush jewelry down the toilet. Eventually, the girl stopped playing with mother's jewelry altogether.

Stimulus Control and Partial Elimination

Lori was an attractive, severely retarded little girl with a very angelic face.* She was small for her age, slightly chubby, and had short blond hair and irresistible appeal. Perhaps in part because of these characteristics, she had gradually been shaped to be extremely persistent in her approach to the staff, so much so that she became a chronic pest. The following sequence was typical. While Bonnie, the nurse in charge of the ward, sat working in her office, Lori peeked in and said, "Hi." "Hi, Lori, I'm busy now but I'll talk to you later," said Bonnie. "You busy now?" said Lori. There was no response from Bonnie, who was trying to work and to ignore Lori's pestering. "You work hard?" asked Lori. (No response from Bonnie.) "Hi," said Lori. (No response from Bonnie.) "You don't love me?" said Lori with a sad look. "Of course I love you, Lori," said Bonnie, unable to resist any longer.

This type of interaction between Lori and the staff was very common. Although the staff attempted to ignore Lori's behavior, it was almost impossible to do so consistently unless one were exceptionally cold-hearted toward cute little girls. Many undesirable behaviors are developed simply because repetitions of the behavior will finally produce a consequence. Lori was so cute in her approach and so persistent in her pestering that she inevitably received intermittent reinforcement from the staff for her pestering behavior.

Since total extinction would have been extremely difficult (for the reasons mentioned above), the staff designed a procedure for eliminating the behavior only partially—that is eliminating it only when it was most disruptive. Each staff member received a two-by-four-inch card to be pinned to his shirt or dress. The card was red on one side and green on the other. In general, during certain intervals

*The following example is based on an unpublished case report at Cedar Cottage, The Manitoba School, Portage la Prairie, Manitoba, 1971.

254

Some
Preliminary
Considerations
to Effective
Programming
Strategies

throughout the day, all of the staff would turn their cards to the green side and Lori's pestering would be reinforced. At other times of the day, the staff would turn their cards to the red side and no pestering would be reinforced. On the first morning of the procedure, a staff member walked towards Lori very quickly, before she had a chance to begin pestering, and said very quickly, and firmly, "Hi, Lori. See my card (while pointing to the card)? I can't talk to you because the card is red. I'll see you later." The staff member then quickly turned and walked away, leaving Lori standing there in a state of stunned silence. Within just a few seconds, the staff member returned with the green side of the card showing. Smiling pleasantly, she said, "Hi, Lori. See my card? It's on the green side, so now I can talk to you." The staff member then proceeded to engage Lori in a brief conversation. When there was a pause in the conversation, the staff member suddenly assumed an appearance of sternness and a businesslike attitude. Turning the card to the red side, she said, "I can't talk to you now, Lori. My card will be red for a while. I'll see you later." The staff member then quickly walked away before Lori had a chance to respond. All of the staff repeated this type of interaction with Lori throughout the day. Moreover, when all of the staff had their cards turned to the red side, if Lori attempted to approach one of them, that person immediately pointed to his card and instructed Lori that no conversation was possible. The staff member then left the vicinity immediately. Any conversation on Lori's part was consistently extinguished in those situations.

During the first few days of the procedure, the green side was usually showing. Over several days, the staff introduced the red side for longer and longer periods of time. By the end of the first two weeks, the staff had started managing their red and green cards individually. Lori quickly learned to discriminate whether a nearby staff member was available for conversation, and she responded appropriately. Not only did the procedure effectively manage Lori's pestering, but it also introduced a new reinforcer for her desirable behavior. During times when cards were red, if Lori emitted some desirable behavior on the ward (such as helping with the cleaning or playing appropriately with another child) a staff member would often approach Lori, turn the card green, and begin interacting with her. The presentation of the green side of the card had become a conditioned reinforcer.

There are many other examples of high-frequency behaviors that are disruptive for teachers, parents, and others. A useful strategy in many of these situations is to develop stimulus control and partial elimination of behavior. Implementing such a program is not only much easier than attempting to totally extinguish the behavior, it is usually much more pleasant for all concerned and it may lead to the development of a desirable conditioned reinforcer, as it did in Lori's case.

Throughout this text, a number of different procedures for decreasing undesirable behaviors have been described. Prior to deciding upon a particular procedure for a particular undesirable behavior, one should consider two questions:

1. How can the problem be formulated in terms of increasing a desirable behavior?
2. What are the likely causes of the undesirable behavior?

Depending on the answers to these questions, one might next (if appropriate) consider the procedures listed below. In general, for optimum results they should be considered in the order listed.

1. *Shortcut tactics*
   a) Instruction
   b) Situational inducement
      (1) Relocate people.
      (2) Change time of activity.
      (3) Move activity to new location.
      (4) Rearrange surroundings.
   c) Instruction, modeling, and role playing
   d) Instruction and physical guidance[3]
2. *Indirect tactics*
   a) Eliminate early component of a chain.
   b) Establish new stimulus control and use partial elimination.
3. *Reinforcement schedules combined with extinction*
   a) Extinguish undesirable behavior while reinforcing desirable alternative behavior (Chapter 3)
   b) DRO (Chapter 6)
   c) DRL (Chapter 6)
4. *Punishment*
   a) Time-out (Chapter 12)
   b) Aversive stimulation (Chapter 12)

Study Questions

(for examination purposes)

1. What should be a behavior modifier's first question after being given a thorough description of an undesirable behavior to be decreased? Explain with an example.
2. Discuss why extinction and punishment should not be among the first procedures to be considered for reducing an undesirable behavior.

256

Some
Preliminary
Considerations
to Effective
Programming
Strategies

3. State three broad reasons why it is important to consider the causes of undesirable behavior.

4. Give two examples (at least one of which is not from the text) of the use of situational inducement to reduce an undesirable behavior.

5. Give an example of the use of instruction, modeling, and role playing to reduce an undesirable behavior.

6. Give an example of reducing an undesirable behavior by eliminating an early component of a chain. Draw a diagram like those in Chapter 10 to illustrate your example.

7. Give an example of the use of stimulus control to partially eliminate an undesirable behavior. Draw a diagram like those in Chapter 7 to illustrate your example.

8. Before deciding on a particular procedure for decreasing an undesirable behavior, what two things should you consider?

Study Exercises

(to be practiced by the reader)

1. Identify two undesirable behaviors of someone you know well (but do not identify that person). Try to construct plausible explanations for (i.e., causes of) those behaviors. State which of the behaviors you think would be especially difficult or inappropriate to eliminate by extinction or punishment, and say why.

2. Design a program or programs for eliminating one or both of the undesirable behaviors in study exercise 1. Incorporate one or more of the following procedures:
   a) situational inducement
   b) instruction, modeling, and role playing
   c) eliminating an early component of a chain
   d) stimulus control and partial elimination

Self-Modification Exercises

(to be practiced by the reader)

1. Do study exercise 1 for two of your own undesirable behaviors.
2. Do study exercise 2 for the undesirable behaviors you listed for yourself.

EXTENDED DISCUSSION AND NOTES

1. However, the existence of a medical cause need not mean that a behavioral treatment will be ineffective. Nor, for that matter, does the existence of a purely environmental cause necessarily mean that a medical treatment will be ineffective (see Stolz, Wienckowski, and Brown, 1975,

(Continued)

(Continued)

p. 1034). That the same problem may be effectively treated either behaviorally or physiologically, irrespective of its cause, is illustrated in a study by Ayllon, Layman, and Kandel (1975). These investigators showed that hyperactivity in three children was decreased about 60 percent by either the drug methylphenidate or by a behavior modification procedure in which academic performance was reinforced. But the behavior modification procedure also resulted in large increases in academic performance, whereas the drug did not. It seems, therefore, that in this case the use of behavior modification was definitely to be preferred over the use of drugs. The two modes of treatment are not, however, necessarily incompatible. There might be cases in which drugs and behavior modification combined would be more effective than either alone. One study, however, did not show this to be true for hyperactivity: Christensen (1975) found that the drug methylphenidate did not produce any significant improvement in the classroom behavior of hyperactive retarded children who were also being treated with behavior modification procedures.

2. For example, there is evidence that seizures can be modified in this way. Seizures are sometimes preceded by very clearly defined behaviors. Zlutnick, Mayville, and Moffat (1975) found that they could often prevent the onset of a child's seizure by shouting "No!" and shaking the child vigorously immediately upon the occurrence of a preseizure behavior (which in one case consisted of a fixed gaze at a flat surface, such as a table top or a wall). In some cases, the preseizure behavior also decreased, suggesting that the procedure may have been punishing.

3. One procedure that usually involves instruction and guidance is called *overcorrection*. Originally developed by Azrin and Foxx (1971) as a component of their program for toilet-training adult retarded individuals, *overcorrection* is a procedure to "(1) overcorrect the environmental effects of an inappropriate act, and (2) to require the disrupter intensively to practice overly-correct forms of relevant behavior" (Foxx and Azrin, 1973, p. 2). The first part of the procedure is *restitutional overcorrection*, which requires the person who emitted an undesirable behavior "to correct the consequences of his misbehavior by having him restore the situation to a state vastly improved from that which existed before the disruption" (Foxx and Azrin, 1973, p. 2). For example, someone who throws a piece of paper on the floor might be required not only to pick up that piece of paper and put it in the garbage can, but also any other pieces of paper that are on the floor nearby. The second part of the procedure is *positive-practice overcorrection* which requires the individual to practice correct behaviors (as an alternative to misbehavior). For example, the individual who threw the paper on the floor might be required to practice putting bits of paper into a garbage can. Overcorrection procedures have been used successfully to decrease such behaviors as aggression (Foxx and Azrin, 1972), stealing (Azrin and Wesolowski, 1974), self-injury (Harris and Romanczyk, 1976), classroom disturbances (Azrin and Powers, 1975), bed-wetting (Azrin, Sneed, and Foxx, 1974), ingesting fecal and other nonnutritive material (Foxx and Martin, 1975), truancy from special self-care classes (Foxx, 1976), self-stimulatory behavior (Foxx and Azrin, 1973), and stereotyped behaviors (Rollings, Baumeister, and Baumeister, 1977).

   Positive-practice overcorrection may be used with restitutional overcorrection or by itself (with behaviors that do not produce some

(Continued)

obvious environmental disturbance). Although overcorrection has been referred to as a "principle" (Azrin and Wesolowski, 1974), it seems more reasonable to talk about it as a procedure that involves a combination of some of the basic principles described in the earlier chapters of this text. The procedure probably involves punishing the undesirable behavior in various ways (such as by time-out from some reinforcing activity while the undesirable behavior is being overcorrected; withdrawal of positive reinforcement, as when, for example, an individual is required to return stolen items; and the aversiveness of being physically guided through the restitution and/or positive-practice overcorrections), the development of appropriate stimulus control (in that individuals are forced to emit correct behavior in the presence of appropriate cues), fading (in that the guidance and stimuli that control positive practice are gradually eliminated), and positive reinforcement (in that the behavior that has been positively practiced comes under the eventual control of the social contingencies maintaining it).

Study Questions on Notes

1. Is it true that problem behaviors with medical causes must receive medical treatment? Explain.
2. What has been found about hyperactivity, behavior modification, and methylphenidate?
3. Briefly describe some evidence that seizures function like a behavioral chain.
4. Distinguish between *restitution overcorrection* and *positive-practice overcorrection*. Describe an example of each.
5. Describe how several basic behavioral principles appear to be involved in the overcorrection procedure.

CHAPTER 17

More About the Gradual Change Procedures: FADING, SHAPING and CHAINING

Novice behavior modifiers frequently have difficulty distinguishing among cases requiring shaping, fading, and chaining. In many situations, all three of these gradual-change procedures might be used. In other situations, one of these three techniques might be used primarily by itself. Although there is frequently insufficient evidence to decide conclusively that one of the procedures rather than another should be used, there are a number of guidelines that should be considered in making such decisions. However, in order to follow these guidelines, it is necessary to use the terms shaping, fading, and chaining precisely, and in keeping with their usage derived from basic research. Before describing the guidelines for selecting the appropriate gradual-change procedure, we will briefly describe some of the confusion between the terms shaping and chaining.

SOME MISUSES OF THE TERMS SHAPING AND CHAINING

Shaping is the differential reinforcement of successive approximations to a final desired behavior. In original basic research, descriptions of procedures labeled "shaping" involved such things as the

260
Some
Preliminary
Considerations
to Effective
Programming
Strategies

differential reinforcement of successive approximations to the bar-pressing behavior of a rat and the key-pecking behavior of a pigeon. Early applications of shaping in applied settings included the reinforcement of successive approximations to speech in a mute psychotic (through steps such as subtle eye movements, head movements, mouth movements, sounds, and finally specific words); overcoming withdrawal behavior in a child by reinforcing successive approaches to other children; and improving attention span in a severely retarded child by reinforcing approximations to a final desired duration of eye contact. In other words, as a technique, shaping is characterized by a clearly specifiable situation or set of circumstances in which the specific steps from a beginning response to a target response can be identified, measured, and differentially reinforced. In the above examples, it is very easy to describe the details of the procedure and to identify it as shaping.

However, increasing applications of the procedure have been accompanied by increasing instances of vagueness in the use of the term. It is not uncommon to hear students of behavioral psychology, when talking about behavioral programs, say something like; "That teacher really shapes good reading skills in his students." Even some recognized authorities have written statements such as this: "Shaping is used to develop new behaviors that have never been performed by the individual, such as reading, feeding, and dressing." However, a careful analysis would reveal that the experiences that lead to reading, feeding, and dressing in no way resemble the systematic application of differential reinforcement for successive approximations, as described in the above laboratory examples and in subsequent extensions of the shaping principle. In our opinion, there is nothing to be gained from such casual uses of the term shaping, as in the examples cited, and such uses may be seriously misleading.

Such statements may suggest to the novice behavior modifier that complex repertoires such as hockey skills and cooking are target behaviors that can be developed by shaping, in the more precise technological sense of the term. In fact, such terminal repertoires comprise a highly complex set of behaviors that are developed individually, in a variety of sequences, under varied stimulus control, over an extended period of time, and involving most, if not all, of the principles and procedures described in Chapters 2–13 of this text. More seriously, such casual use of the term may lead to casual attempts to apply some sort of general shaping program to the development of a global target. Such programs usually fail, and frequently lead to statements of this sort: "I tried behavior shaping and it didn't work."

The term chaining also suffers from increasing instances of

vagueness in its use. In basic research, the term "behavioral chain" originally meant a fixed sequence of specific responses, with specific stimuli (S^Ds) signaling each response in the sequence. "Chaining" refers to a procedure used to develop such a sequence of responses, in which a specific stimulus signals the end of each response and the start of the next. Some applications of backward chaining, as in teaching bedmaking, shoe lacing, and specific dressing and grooming skills, are consistent with this precise usage. The terminology is misused, in our judgment, when people speak about a variety of general behavioral sequences as behavioral chains. We are referring to such sequences as mastering a musical instrument, getting in shape for an athletic competition, studying two or three years for an advanced degree, and writing a book. It is true that each of these activities involves some kind of sequencing, in the sense that different behaviors leading to some goal follow each other in some order. However, the behavioral sequence in no way approximates the specificity of the behavioral chain involved in making a bed, or the chain involved when a rat presses a lever, pulls a string, and then turns a circle, each of its responses occurring in a particular order to a particular stimulus and being followed by food at the end of the sequence. There is much more than "chaining" involved in the above so-called examples of chains. In the writing of a book, for example, subtle shaping may occur between two co-authors as they gradually refine the contents of a specific paragraph by going over it several times in an hour. In addition, pauses occur when they are asleep, taking holidays, having a few beers, and so on. In our opinion, it is of no value to refer to such a complex set of activities as a chain of responses. Moreover, we feel that referring to such a combination of activities in this way is misleading, in that it implies a behavioral analysis that obviously has not occurred. Also, as with the misuse of the term shaping, such vague uses of chaining are likely to add to the difficulty and confusion that a novice behavior modifier may feel when trying to decide whether backward chaining, shaping, or some combination of the two might be appropriate for developing a target behavior in a client.

As Baer, Risley, and Wolf (1968) emphasized, we will make the most progress in communicating our behavioral techniques to others when we use precise and consistent language to describe those procedures. Behavior modifiers should refer to terminal repertoires such as "hockey skills" as behavior that is gradually developed rather than behavior that is gradually shaped, and to "writing a book" as a behavioral sequence rather than a behavioral chain. The following discussion of the guidelines for choosing among shaping, chaining, and fading assumes a precise use of these terms.

WHEN IS FADING,
SHAPING,
OR CHAINING MOST APPROPRIATE?

As you know, fading is a technique of gradually changing the stimuli controlling a response, until that response eventually occurs to a new (or partially new) set of stimuli. Fading is appropriate in specific training situations in which a particular response will occur to a particular stimulus but not to the target stimulus. For example, fading is appropriate for teaching a child who can imitate the name of an item to identify a picture of the item. Through fading, imitative control of the appropriate vocal response is transferred to an appropriate question (such as "What's that?") and gestural prompt (such as pointing to the picture). However, it is often less obvious to the novice that fading may be appropriate in relatively uncontrolled settings, such as the home, the schoolyard, and other community locations. That is, when concerned with helping a client develop a particular desirable behavior (one that is not presently occurring) or to eliminate an undesirable behavior (when a desirable alternative can be identified), a beginning behavior modifier is likely to think about developing that particular behavior in that setting with a shaping or chaining procedure. However, it is often possible to take a shortcut by thoroughly exploring other areas of the individual's life, in which the desirable behavior might be occurring under different stimulus control, and using a fading program instead. For example, one might be concerned with helping a client learn to be on time, to be courteous, to keep from swearing and making hostile comments, to overcome bursts of laughter in serious situations, and so forth. The last two problems can be managed by increasing desirable alternative behaviors. Thus, our first guidelines should be these:

1. When faced with a behavioral handicap, identify the target in terms of specific, positive behaviors to be increased.
2. Search the client's current repertoire thoroughly to try to identify existing control of these behaviors.
3. If existing control can be determined, consider the potential for a fading program.

Once the target behavior has been identified, the behavior modifier might ask such questions as these: Are there certain buildings or events where the desirable behavior occurs? (for instance in church? at a hockey game?) Are there certain people in whose presence the behavior is likely to occur? (prestigious persons? friends? mother-in law? priest?) Do other individuals emit the desired behavior in response to the desired stimuli, such that the client could have an opportunity to model these individuals in the presence of those stimuli? Are there any room settings that are likely to evoke the desired behavior? (bedrooms? bathrooms? auditoriums? bars?) It is important to remember that fading can be programmed to occur along almost any dimension. Fading might be managed along dimensions presented by means of audio or visual media (slides, tapes, movies, etc.). If, for example, a depressed person tends to feel relatively happy in the presence of certain people, it might be possible to transfer that control to pictures of those people paired with the sound of their voice on a tape recorder. If so, it might then be possible to transfer that control through the use of appropriate fading procedures to almost any stimuli that can be presented by auditory or visual cues. To take another example, if a therapist can evoke some desirable behavior in a client during therapy, it might be possible to get that behavior under the control of specific cues that can be taken with the client wherever he goes (for instance, cue cards and auditory devices).

In Chapter 15, we described a variety of ways of inducing behavior by managing antecedent stimuli. In essence, what we are suggesting here is that these methods of capitalizing on an existing form of stimulus control, combined with subsequent fading programs, can be used to solve a great many problems and to develop a wide variety of behaviors that will occur in response to appropriate cues.

Let's suppose a new behavior must be taught. If the behavior does not appear to occur in response to any stimulus in any situation, a shortcut fading program is ruled out. This leaves either shaping or chaining. How does one decide whether to design a shaping or a chaining program? This question can be answered more easily if we first compare shaping and chaining along the dimensions shown in Table 17-1 (on the top of the next page).

On the basis of the comparisons in Table 17-1, the decision to use shaping or backward chaining should be made after considering the nature of the behavior, the degree of structure in the training situation, and whether or not it is possible to train in a "backwards" fashion. Examples of terminal behaviors that might best be developed through shaping are attention span, the force of a hockey shot, loudness of speech, accuracy of shooting foul shots in basketball, firmness of grip in a handshake, speed of answering questions, pronunciation of certain words, and the quality of a certain yoga exercise. Examples of terminal behaviors that might best be developed through chaining are making a bed, setting a table, hitting a golf ball, putting together a certain puzzle, putting on a bra, and tying shoelaces.

Table 17-1. *Some Differences Between Shaping and Chaining as They Are Typically Applied*

	SHAPING	CHAINING
Target	a. To change behavior along some physical dimension, such as force, form (topography), duration, or latency. b. The terminal behavior is usually simple. c. The successive approximations do not necessarily form part of the terminal behavior.	a. To develop a sequence of responses, with a "clear-cut" stimulus signaling the end of each response and the start of the next. b. The terminal behavior is usually more complex than in shaping. c. All of the chaining steps are retained as part of the terminal behavior.
Training Procedure	a. Often involves selectively reinforcing a student's behavior in an unstructured environment in which the student has the opportunity to emit a variety of behaviors. b. Proceeds in a forward fashion in terms of the "natural order" of behavior.	a. Typically involves linking together stimulus-response components in semistructured or structured teaching environments. b. Often proceeds in a backward fashion in terms of "the natural order" of behavior.
When Used in Combination with Other Procedures	a. Often involves instructional control; may involve some physical prompting at successive steps, but usually minimally. May also involve some fading at successive steps, but this is unusual. b. Involves successive application of reinforcement and extinction.	a. Frequently involves verbal and physical prompts, physical guidance, fading, and perhaps shaping at successive steps. b. Typically involves fewer extinction trials than in shaping, because of the strong stimulus control established by prompting and fading at successive steps.

Study Questions

(for examination purposes)

1. Describe three examples of behavioral changes for which the authors would consider it appropriate to use the term "shaping."
2. Describe three examples of behavioral changes for which the authors would consider it inappropriate to use the term "shaping."
3. What are two possible dangers that might occur from casual use of the term "shaping"?

4. What is the specific laboratory meaning of the term *behavioral chain?*

5. Why is it inappropriate to refer to a *behavioral sequence* such as "getting in shape for an athletic competition" as a *behavioral chain?*

6. If we do not refer to terminal repertoires such as "hockey skills" as behavior that is shaped, or to "writing a book" as a behavior chain, how should we describe such activities?

7. When faced with the problem of developing a behavior, which procedure should be considered first: fading, shaping, or chaining? Why?

8. When you want a client to develop a particular behavior in a certain situation, you should first try to determine if the behavior occurs in other situations. You might then use a fading program to develop the terminal behavior. List thirty possible dimensions along which fading might occur, and about which you might question the client.

9. What are the major categories of "shortcut tactics" described in Chapter 15?

10. What are the differences between shaping and backward chaining as they are typically applied?

11. List six terminal behaviors that might best be developed by means of shaping (three from this chapter and three from your own experience).

12. List six examples of terminal behaviors that might best be developed by means of chaining (three from this chapter and three from your own experience).

Study Exercise

(to be practiced by the reader)

Suppose that you are a behavior therapist and a "typical" second-year university student comes to you for help. The problem is that the client "lacks self-confidence." After some discussion, you identify expressing self-confidence as the target behavior to increase.

(a) Identify five specific behaviors that might be considered indications of self-confidence. The development of these will be your target.

(b) You are convinced that somewhere, in some situation, your client probably has shown self-confidence, as defined in (a). Consider six categories to examine—namely, instructions, modeling, and the four categories of situational inducement. For each of these categories, prepare three questions to ask your client in order to try to identify some stimuli that may control his or her self-confidence. (Your subsequent programs will then enable you to use those stimuli in a fading program to transfer the client's self-confidence to various university situations.)

Self-Modification Exercise

(to be practiced by the reader)

Imagine you are the client in the study exercise above. If you so desire, substitute a behavior deficit of your own for the "lack of self-confidence" in the imaginary student mentioned above.

PART IV

Dealing With Data

CHAPTER 18

BEHAVIORAL ASSESSMENT:
Initial Considerations

Throughout this book, numerous examples illustrate the effectiveness of behavior modification procedures. Many of these examples are accompanied by graphs showing the changes (increases or decreases) that occurred in behavior when particular procedures were applied. Some of the graphs also include follow-up observations indicating that the improvements were maintained after the programs had terminated. The graphs were not presented just to make it easier for you to understand the material. Precise records of behavior are an inseparable part of behavior modification procedures. Indeed, some people have gone so far as to say that the major contribution of behavior modification has been the insistence on accurately recording specific behaviors and making decisions on the basis of recorded data rather than merely on the basis of subjective impressions. Like Linus and his blanket in the popular Peanuts cartoons, the behavior modifier and the data sheet are inseparable.

A successful behavior modification program typically involves at least three components during which behavior is recorded: (1) a baseline, or preprogram behavioral-assessment phase; (2) a treatment phase; and (3) a follow-up phase. During the _baseline_ phase, the behavior modifier assesses the behavior in order to determine its level prior to the introduction of the program or treatment. Ideally, after making a precise baseline assessment a behavior modifier will design an effective _treatment_ program in order to bring about the desired behavior change. In educational settings, such a program is typically referred to as a training or teaching program. In community and clinical settings, the program is referred to more often as an intervention strategy or a therapy program. A distinguishing characteristic of many behavior modification programs is the insistence on continuous observation and monitoring of the behavior of the students and clients during training or treatment. In some cases, the difference between behavior modification and other approaches on this point is primarily a matter of degree. Traditional educational practices typically involve periodic assessment during the teaching program for the purpose of monitoring the performance of the students. Certain clinical _treatment_ programs involve periodic assessment of the clients at various intervals. Moreover, some programs that have been labeled behavior modification have consisted primarily of before and after measures and have lacked precise, ongoing recording during treatment. Nevertheless, the majority of behavior modification strategies have emphasized and practiced, to a degree not often found in other approaches, continuous monitoring of the behavior during the application of the specific treatment strategies.[1]

In addition to the requirements of initial assessment and an intervention strategy, behavior modification experts agree that programs should include a _follow-up_ phase in which the persistence of the desirable behavior changes following termination of the program are evaluated. In many cases, such as behavior programs involving one or two behaviors and a small number of individuals, it is both possible and desirable to gather reliable follow-up information. In some cases, this might consist of precise observation or assessment under natural circumstances in which the behavior is expected to occur. For example, in Chapter 3 we indicated desirable control of Valerie's self-slapping behavior in two follow-up observation periods, conducted five and fourteen months after the termination of the treatment program. These observations were collected under conditions very similar to those during the treatment program. In other projects, however, precise follow-up observations simply are not possible.

Consider a behavior modification program set up for an entire class-room and conducted for many months. At the end of the program, the children may go on to another class, graduate to another program, leave the school, or in some other way become unavailable for follow-up observation. Under these circumstances, it would simply be impossible to do anything other than conduct a test that would sample a few of the behaviors developed by the behavior modification program.

In early behavior modification studies, follow-up observations were not reported as frequently as most critics would have desired.[2] Whether or not behavior modifiers are now doing a better job of providing such information, it is clear that follow-up observations are of the utmost importance in evaluating the ultimate value of behavior modification programs.

DATA! DATA! DATA! WHY BOTHER?

There are a number of reasons for recording accurate data during the baseline and throughout a program. First, and most important, _accurate baseline data provide a means for clearly determining whether the program has produced, or is producing, the desired change in behavior._ Sometimes people claim that they do not need to record data to know whether a desirable change in behavior has occurred. No doubt this is often true. A mother obviously needs no data sheet or graphs to tell her that her child is completely toilet-trained: there is ample evidence (or, hopefully, lack of it) in the child's pants.

But, not all cases are so clear-cut—at least not immediately. Suppose that a child is acquiring toileting behavior very slowly. The parent may think that the program is not working and abandon it prematurely. With accurate data, this type of mistake can be avoided. This point is nicely illustrated by the following case.* Dr. Lynn Caldwell was consulted by a woman whose six-year-old son was, in her words, "driving me up a wall with his constant slamming of the kitchen door everytime he goes out of the kitchen." Dr. Caldwell requested the mother to obtain a baseline of the target behavior by tallying each instance of it on a sheet of paper attached to the refrigerator. Over a three-day period, the total number of door slams was 123. Dr. Caldwell then instructed the mother to provide approval each time the boy went through the door without slamming it. But she was to administer a brief time-out whenever he slammed the

*This case was described by Dr. Lynn Caldwell, Department of Rehabilitation Medicine, University of Washington, in a taped presentation to the First Manitoba Behavior Change Conference, Portage la Prairie, Manitoba, 1971.

door (he was to go back and remain for three minutes in whichever room he had just left, and the mother was to ignore him during that time), and then require him to proceed through the door without slamming it. After applying this procedure for three days, the mother brought the tally sheet to Dr. Caldwell. "This behavior modification stuff doesn't work," she complained, pointing to the large number of tally marks on the data sheet. "He's just as bad as he ever was." But when the tally marks were counted, there were only 87 of them over the three days of treatment, compared with the 123 that were entered over the three days of baseline. Encouraged by this observation, the mother continued the program, and the behavior quickly dropped to an acceptable level of about five per day (after which the satisfied mother did not make further contact with Dr. Caldwell).

Without accurate data, one might also make the opposite type of error. One might conclude that a procedure is working and continue it when in fact it is ineffective and should be abandoned or modified. For example, Harris, Wolf, and Baer (1964) described the case of a boy in a laboratory preschool who had the annoying habit of pinching adults. His teachers decided to use a behavior modification procedure to encourage him to pat rather than pinch. After the procedure had been in effect for some time, the teachers agreed that they had succeeded in reducing pinching by substituting patting. When they looked at the data recorded by an outside observer, however, they saw clearly that although patting was considerably above the level it had been during the baseline recordings, pinching had not decreased from its baseline level. Perhaps concentrating on the procedure and/or the patting so diverted the teachers that they failed to notice the pinching as much as they had before introducing the procedure. In any case, had it not been for the recorded data, the teachers probably would have wasted a great deal more time and effort than they did on an ineffective procedure.[3]

A second reason for carefully assessing and recording behavior is that *the initial assessment process often helps the behavior modifier to identify the best treatment strategy.* Discovering potential reinforcers for a behavior during the baseline phase is clearly useful for designing an effective intervention program. Precise baseline observation can also help greatly in deciding upon a particular procedure, as described in other chapters. In fact, an accurate baseline will sometimes indicate that what someone thought to be a problem is actually not a problem. For example, a teacher may say, "I don't know what to do with Johnny; he's always hitting the other kids." But after taking a baseline, the teacher may discover that the behavior actually occurs so rarely that it is not worth worrying about. Both of the authors have experienced this phenomenon more than once. Others have too, as illustrated by the following example from Greenspoon (1976, p. 177):

The reliance on casual observation led a woman to complain to a psychologist that her husband rarely talked to her during meal time. She said that his failure to talk to her was becoming an increasing source of annoyance to her and she wanted to do something about it. The psychologist suggested that she prepare a chart and record on the chart the number of times that he initiated a conversation or responded to the verbal behavior that she emitted. She agreed to the suggestions. At the end of a week, she called back to inform the psychologist that she was surprised and pleased to report that she had been in error. It turned out that her husband both initiated conversation and responded to her verbal emissions at a very high rate.

A third reason for accurately recording and graphing behavior is that *publicly posted results can be a powerful reinforcer for carrying out a program* (*see* Figure 18-1). Staff in institutions for the retarded, for example, often become more conscientious in applying procedures when up-to-date charts or graphs clearly showing the effects of the procedures are posted conspicuously on the wards. Parents and teachers alike may find that their efforts to modify children's behavior are reinforced by graphic representation of the improved behavior.

A fourth reason for recording and graphing behavior is that *the displayed data may lead to improvements apart from any further treatment program.*[4] Students who graph their own study behavior (for instance, by recording the daily number of paragraphs or pages studied, or the amount of time spent studying) may find increases in the graph to be reinforcing. Data that are appropriately presented can be reinforcing even to young children. For example, an occupational therapist at a school for handicapped children once consulted one of the authors concerning a seven-year-old girl who each morning took an excessive amount of time taking off her outside garments and hanging them up. It appeared that the teachers could not be persuaded to stop attending to the child when she was in the cloakroom. The author suggested that the therapist somehow attempt to reinforce the child with a graph of the amount of time she spent in the cloakroom each morning. The procedure that the therapist devised proved to be as effective as it was ingenious.* A large chart was hung on the wall. The chart was colored green so as to represent grass, and a carrot patch was depicted near the bottom of it. Days were indicated along the bottom of the chart and the amount of time in the cloakroom was indicated along the side. Each day, a circle was marked on the chart to indicate the amount of time spent in the cloakroom in the morning, and a small paper rabbit was attached to the most recent circle. Using simple language, the therapist explained the procedure to the child and concluded by saying, "Now let's see if you can

*We are grateful to Nancy Staisey for providing us with the details of this procedure.

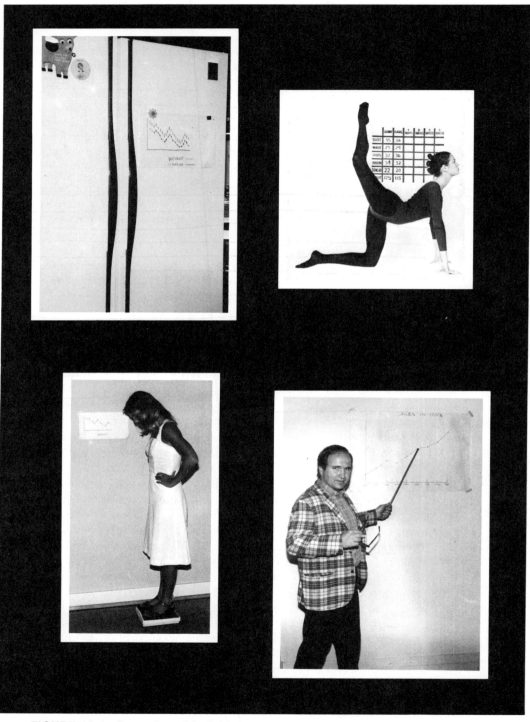

FIGURE 18-1. *Examples of individuals being reinforced by publicly posted data.*

get the bunny down to eat the carrots." When the rabbit was down to the level of the carrots, the child was encouraged to keep him there: "Remember, the longer the bunny stays in the carrot patch, the more he can eat." A follow-up showed that the improved behavior persisted over a period of one year.

Behavior modifiers were not the first to discover the usefulness of recording one's behavior to help modify that behavior. As with many other supposedly "new" psychological discoveries, the real credit should perhaps go to the writers of great literature. For example, in his autobiography, first published in 1883, Anthony Trollope stated:

> When I have commenced a new book, I have always prepared a diary, divided into weeks, and carried on for the period which I have allowed myself for the completion of the work. In this I have entered, day by day, the number of pages I have written, so that if at any time I have slipped into idleness for a day or two, the record of that idleness has been there, staring me in the face, and demanding of me increased labour, so that the deficiency might be supplied. According to the circumstances of the time,—whether my other business might then be heavy or light, or whether the book I was writing was or was not wanted with speed,—I have allotted myself so many pages a week. The average number has been about 40. It has been placed as low as 20, and has risen to 112. And as a page is an ambiguous term, my page has been made to contain 250 words; and as words, if not watched, will have a tendency to straggle, I have had every word counted as I went. . . . There has ever been the record before me, and a week passed with an insufficient number of pages has been a blister to my eye and a month so disgraced would have been a sorrow to my heart. (Trollope, 1946, p. 116)

Ernest Hemingway is another novelist who used self-recording to help maintain his literary output. One of his interviewers reported:

> He keeps track of his daily progress—"so as not to kid myself"—on a large chart made out of the side of a cardboard packing case and set up against the wall under the nose of a mounted gazelle head. The numbers on the chart showing the daily output of words differ from 450, 575, 462, 1250, back to 512, the higher figures on days Hemingway puts in extra work so he won't feel guilty spending the following day fishing on the gulf stream. (Plimpton, 1965, p. 219)

The well-known contemporary author Irving Wallace used self-recording even before he was aware that others had done the same. In a book touching on his writing methods, he commented:

I kept a work chart when I wrote my first book—which remains unpublished—at the age of nineteen. I maintained work charts while writing my first four published books. These charts showed the date I started each chapter, the date I finished it, and number of pages written in that period. With my fifth book, I started keeping a more detailed chart which also showed how many pages I had written by the end of every working day. I am not sure why I started keeping such records. I suspect that it was because, as a free-lance writer, entirely on my own, without employer or deadline, I wanted to create disciplines for myself, ones that were guilt-making when ignored. A chart on the wall served as such a discipline, its figures scolding me or encouraging me. (Wallace, 1971, pp. 65–66)

SOURCES OF INFORMATION FOR BASELINE ASSESSMENT

In the great majority of behavior modification programs, both during initial assessment and during the intervention phase, sources of information come from direct observation of the behavior to be modified.[5] In most of the case histories described in this book, the behavior of concern was directly observed and measured.

There are two major advantages to direct observation. First, it tends to influence the observer to be precise in describing behavior. When an observer attempts to record "aggression," or "sympathy," or "cooperation," she will experience tremendous difficulty in communicating the results of her observations and in having someone else repeat her observations unless she first specifies much more precisely just what behavioral components will be counted as "aggressive," "sympathetic," or "cooperative." Second, the emphasis on direct observation has helped to make the behavior modifier highly accountable for his programs. When one takes accurate observations prior to a program and during a program, it is more immediately obvious if a program is failing and/or producing undesirable side effects. This influences the behavior modifier to do a good job.

For some types of problems, direct observation may not be necessary or possible. Professional psychologists in private practice usually do not have the time, and/or their clients do not have the money, to make it possible for the psychologist to directly observe the behavior of the client outside the therapist's office. One alternative is to teach the client to observe and record his own behavior in a self-control program (discussed further in Chapters 25 and 26). In such cases, where the problem formulation is based on discussions with the client, it is sometimes desirable to use standardized questionnaires or inventories designed to help a behavior therapist collect information from a client that can be directly translated into suggestions for behavioral programming. Some examples of such inventories are the Behavioral Self-Rating Checklist (Upper, Cautela, and Brook, 1974); the Sundel-Lawrence Problem Behavior Checklist (Sundel, and Lawrence, 1974); the Fear Survey Schedule (Wolpe, 1969, Appendix 3; Wolpe and Lang, 1964); a measure of test taking anxiety (Suinn, 1969); and the Pre-Marital Counseling Inventory (Stuart and Stuart, 1973). Additional examples and discussion of behavioral assessment can be found in Hersen and Bellack (1976) and Mash and Terdal (1976).

Unreliable data

In some cases, information may be based on the subjective impressions and memories of others (parents, relatives, friends, employers, peers, and so forth). One would hope that this information would simply be supplemental to the development of a program and not be the major basis for a treatment strategy and its evaluation. Information that is to be obtained from interviews with individuals other than the student or client can generally be improved if questions are asked that relate to specific behaviors. For example, it's one thing to ask, "What do you think of the student's socializing ability?" It's quite another thing to ask, "Have you ever seen the student fight with anyone? Dance with anyone?" Some information may be of a medical or biological nature, indicating knowledge of the student's physical characteristics or medications that might be helpful in program design. *ask about speci. beh — not labels.*

SPECIFYING BEHAVIOR PRECISELY

Before collecting baseline information on specific problems, it is usually necessary to refine the definition of the behavior that will be observed. A standard rule is that a behavior should be defined precisely enough so that two observers can simultaneolusy but independently record a behavior of an individual and obtain agreement on their total count. The importance of this task can perhaps best be illustrated by some examples. The following hypothetical account is typical of many interactions the authors have had in teaching staff to precisely specify behavior for baselining purposes.

Just before lunch one day, Garry said to one of the attendants, "Mary, at lunchtime we should do some work with the feeding behavior of some of the severely retarded girls. Why don't you define a mealtime behavior, and then we'll record it. If our records compare closely, that would indicate that your definition is a good one. Now what should we record?" Mary replied, "Well, some of the girls slop a lot. I'll define slopping as the girls dropping food while they're eating. That should be easy to count." Ten minutes later, Garry and Mary were standing about ten feet apart from each other watching the slopping behavior of one of the residents. Each time that either observer judged that a slop occurred, they independently scored it on their data sheet. After recording slops for the duration of the meal (about twelve minutes of actual eating time), Garry and Mary compared their "slops." "Hey, what's this?" said Garry. "I've got forty-two slops and you only have twenty-one. How come I have twice as many slops?" "Well," said Mary, "whenever Sheryl dribbled some food from her mouth and it landed on her plate, I didn't count that as a slop. Did you count that?" "Yes, I counted everything that dropped from the spoon when Sheryl was transferring the food to her mouth. What about when she drooled her soup and it seemed like a steady stream running down her chin and dripping on her blouse? How did you count that?" asked Garry. "It seemed that that was one steady slop so I just counted that as one," replied Mary. "Oh, I counted that as a slop if it occurred once in every ten seconds, so that gave me about ten more slops than you right there." After some further discussion and prompts from Garry, Mary refined the definition so that it read as follows: "Slopping food: An instance of slopping is to be recorded whenever food drops and lands anywhere except in the person's mouth or back on the plate, as a result of (a) the student moving a utensil from her plate to her mouth, or vice versa; (b) the student loading her utensil with food or attempting to cut through it; (c) the student moving her plate or dish around; (d) the student dropping food from her mouth (i.e., slobbering). These occurrences are to be counted as one instance of slopping, regardless of the actual amount of food that may be dropped on any one trial or movement."

We have also encountered problems of response definition in testing whether or not a particular skill or task could be performed. For example, we asked the staff which of the severely retarded girls could put on a pair of slacks. A staff member indicated that Agnes could put on a pair of slacks by herself. One of the authors took a pair of slacks, placed them in front of Agnes, and asked, "Agnes, please put on the slacks." Agnes played with the slacks, turned them over, grabbed them at the bottom, but had not put them on appropriately within a three-minute period. At that point, the staff member offered, "When she puts on the slacks for me, I always unfold them first and place them in front of her with the front part of the slacks facing forward so that all she has to do is grab them at the top of the two sides and put them on." This example illustrates a second standard rule for specifying behavior precisely: a response definition must include all the instructions or stimulus conditions on the basis of which the response can be scored as correct. Numerous similar examples could be cited. The point here is that behaviors initially described merely as "aggressive," "cooperative," "dressing," and so forth, must be given more precise descriptions for observational and recording purposes.

Study Questions

(for examination purposes)

1. What do some people consider to be a major contribution of behavior modification (other than behavior principles and procedures)?
2. What are the minimal components of a behavior modification program?
3. What is the difference between a training program, a therapy program, and an intervention strategy?
4. What is one thing that makes behavior modification programs different from many traditional educational and clinical programs?
5. What are four reasons for collecting accurate data throughout a program?
6. What type of error is exemplified by the case of Dr. Caldwell and the door slammer's mother? Explain how accurately recorded data counteracted this error.
7. What type of error is exemplified by the case of the pinching patter? Explain how accurately recorded data counteracted this error.
8. Briefly describe the details of the clever graphing system devised for the child who got the rabbit to the carrot patch.
9. What are two advantages of direct observation of the behavior to be modified?
10. When interviewing someone about the behavior of concern, how should one ask the questions? Explain with reference to an example.
11. What two standard rules should be followed when describing behavior for observational purposes? Explain with reference to an example.
12. Describe how Trollope followed one of the two standard rules for defining behavior.

EXTENDED DISCUSSION AND NOTES

1. Willems (1974) suggests that behavior modifiers should become even more concerned with assessing the side effects and long-term effects of their behavioral programs. He suggests that a behavioral program or intervention strategy might have a variety of unintended effects that may occur in behaviors not managed directly by the behavior modifier. Such unintended effects might include the following: "(a) desirable, neutral, or undesirable behaviors may be affected; (b) the behaviors may increase or decrease; (c) the target subjects, other persons, or both may
(Continued)

be affected; (d) effects may occur in the setting where the manipulation occurred, other settings, or both; (e) effects may occur immediately, somewhat later, or much later." Thus, although it may seem to you that behavior modifiers are very "data-conscious," Willems suggests that we should be far more data-conscious than we have been in the past concerning the effects and side effects of behavioral procedures.

2. For example, Pawlicki (1970) reviewed behavior-therapy research with children that was published between 1965 and 1969. Of fifty-four studies reported, 44 percent had some sort of follow-up. Some of these follow-ups, however, were not based on direct observations of the children but rather on information gathered from telephone discussions with parents, the reliability of which is obviously questionable.

3. The two types of errors illustrated here are so common that they have been given special names: "Type I errors" and "Type II errors." A Type I error is that of concluding that a given procedure is effective when in fact it is not. A Type II error is that of concluding that a given procedure is not effective when in fact it is. From our experience, we would advise the novice to be especially wary of making Type II errors. It seems that beginning behavior modifiers tend to give up on a procedure if dramatic results are not obtained quickly. Even programs that are ultimately very effective may take some time to begin showing tangible results.

4. A convincing demonstration of this effect was made by Maletzky (1974). He presented data from case studies of five clients who wore wrist counters in an attempt to decrease repetitive, unwanted behaviors merely by counting them on the counters and recording them on graph paper daily. Three of the five cases were completely successful, even though Maletzky was careful not to introduce any treatment other than the counting and graphing of unwanted behaviors. The first case concerned repetitive scratching that resulted in unsightly lesions on the arms and legs of a fifty-two-year-old woman. The woman had been suffering with this problem for thirty years. The second case concerned a nine-year-old boy's repetitive hand raising in class. (Often, he didn't know the answer to the teacher's questions.) The third case involved the out-of-seat behavior, in class, of a hyperactive eleven-year-old girl. In all three cases, the behavior decreased over a six-week period as a result of the daily counting and graphing. When each of the clients stopped counting after six weeks, the behavior began to increase again. The counters and the daily graphing procedure were reintroduced, and over the next few weeks all three clients again showed dramatic decreases in the undesirable behaviors. All three cases had successful follow-up reports, varying from six to twelve months following the termination of the projects. In two additional cases reported by Maletzky, the recording and graphing led to initial decreases in the unwanted behavior, but it seemed necessary to continue the counting in order to keep the behavior at a low level.

In some cases, it might even be possible to count each thought, desire, or urge to emit the behavior before the behavior occurs. For example, McFall (1970) reported a study in which recording each urge to have a cigarette was sufficient to decrease not only the likelihood of subsequently taking a cigarette but also the number of urges.

5. In describing the dimensions of applied behavior analysis, Baer, Risley, and Wolf (1968, p. 93) suggested that a person's "verbal description of his own nonverbal behavior usually would not be accepted as a measure of his actual behavior unless it were independently substantiated. Hence, there is little applied value in demonstrating that an impotent man can be made to say that he is no longer impotent. The relevant question is not what he can say, but what he can do. Application has not been achieved until his question has been answered satisfactorily."

Study Questions on Notes

1. Willems described several potential unintended effects of a behavioral program. Speculate about a *potential* unintended effect of a case in this chapter such that the effect meets all five of the following categories: the effect might be (1) an undesirable behavior of (2) one individual, which (3) increases, (4) occurs in another setting, and (5) occurs somewhat later.
2. What were Pawlicki's findings with regard to the reporting of follow-up data by behavior modifiers?
3. What was the example of a Type I error given in this chapter?
4. What was the example of a Type II error given in this chapter?
5. Describe the importance of self-recording data, with reference to Maletzky's report.
6. How can one get observers to agree that a behavior occurred if the behavior is an "urge"? (Note: This is an open-ended question.)

Type 1 – given procedure is effective when its <u>not</u>

Type 11 – give procedure is said not to be effective when 1 + <u>is</u>

CHAPTER 19
BEHAVIORAL ASSESSMENT:
What to Record and How

Let's suppose you are convinced that you cannot be a behavior modifier unless you keep good records of what the client is doing. What do you record? You could record everything that an individual does from the time he gets up until the time he goes to bed, including a report of the time he sleeps and the number of times he turns over in his sleep. You could record the number of squares of toilet paper he uses per day, the number of times he burps, or his total sitting time. If you did attempt to record everything, two things would immediately become obvious: it would be an impossible task, and you would wind up with a lot of useless data that would be stored away and never looked at again. But suppose you have chosen a particular behavior to work on. How do you measure, assess, or evaluate that behavior? It seems that in measuring behavior, there are four general dimensions that could be examined.

CHARACTERISTICS OF BEHAVIOR TO BE RECORDED

Frequency

A measure that is often useful is the number of instances of the behavior that occur in a given period of time. If you are interested in teaching self-feeding to a child, for example, you might examine the frequency of slops and the frequency of eating with hands during mealtime. (Another word often used interchangeably with frequency, is rate). The first step would be to attempt to define slopping and eating with hands in such a way that you or anyone else could observe the child and decide when either of these responses occur. Let us suppose you define the responses in the following way:

1. Slopping food: An instance of slopping is to be recorded whenever food drops and lands anywhere except in the mouth or back on the plate, as a result of:
   a) the child moving a utensil from her plate to her mouth, or vice versa;
   b) the child loading her utensil with food or attempting to cut through it;
   c) the child moving her plate around;
   d) the child dropping food from her mouth.
   Each of these occurrences is to be counted as one instance of slopping, regardless of the actual amount of food that may be dropped on any one occasion.
2. Eating with hands: An instance of eating with hands will be recorded any time the student touches her food with her hand(s) while in the process of placing food in her mouth. If the student slops while using her hands, then we will record an instance of slopping as well as an instance of eating with hands.

Now you know what behaviors to look for. Your next step is to take a baseline of how many slops and how many instances of eating with hands occur during several meals. If you have a helper to observe your student during the meal, he might use a data sheet such as that shown in Figure 19-1.

In many situations, an individual simply doesn't have a helper or the time to take nice neat data with paper and pencil. Fortunately, there are other ways of measuring quantity that require minimal time. One such method is to use a counter, such as the relatively inexpensive (about $5.00) wrist-watch type used by golfers to record their score. With these counters you can count up to ninety-nine simply by pressing a button for each instance of the behavior.[1] Another easy recording technique is to transfer an item, such as a bead, from

	Instances	Total	Observation Time	Additional Comments
SLOPS	⊥⊥⊤ ⊥⊥⊤ //	12	20 min	Evening meal, three other students at the table. Meal: soup, mashed potatoes, hamburger, veg., jello, milk.
EATING WITH HANDS	///	3	20 min	

Date: _January 1_   OBSERVER: _John H._
STUDENT: _Corrine_

FIGURE 19-1. *A sample data sheet for recording slopping and eating with hands at mealtimes.*

one pocket to another. At the end of the session, or at the end of the day, depending on the particular behavior being recorded, the number of beads in the second pocket is counted and recorded. There is usually no excuse for not taking data. Individuals who argue that they don't have time usually are not showing much ingenuity. Adequate ways of measuring behavior that require little of the observer's time can almost always be found.

After the daily data have been tallied, they are transferred to a graph. Let us suppose that over ten meals, our observer recorded the following number of slops: 21, 27, 19, 18, 20, 24, 26, 16, 17, 23. Let us assume, further, that during the next ten meals the student was presented with a brief time-out (in which she and her chair were pulled back from the table and held there for ten seconds) following each slopping response. During this program of time-out, the slops per meal were as follows: 10, 8, 5, 3, 1, 3, 2, 5, 6, 4. As shown in Figure 19-2, these data might be graphed in either of two ways. Figure 19-2A is called a *cumulative record* since each of the responses cumulate, or are added to the previous response. For example, consider meal 1. During meal 1, 21 slops occurred; therefore, a dot is made up the side at 21 and across the bottom at meal 1 (see point A). At meal 2, 27 slops occurred. These 27 slops cumulate (i.e., are added) to the 21 slops at meal 1, making a total of 48 slops. Therefore, our second dot is placed so that it corresponds to 48 at the side and to meal 2 across the bottom (see point B). During Meal 3, 19 slops occurred, and these 19 are added to the cumulative total, 48, from the previous two meals. Thus, our third dot is placed at a spot corresponding to 67 on the vertical line and meal 3 on the horizontal line. In this way, the performance during any one meal is added to the total performance during previous meals in order to be graphed on the cumulative record.

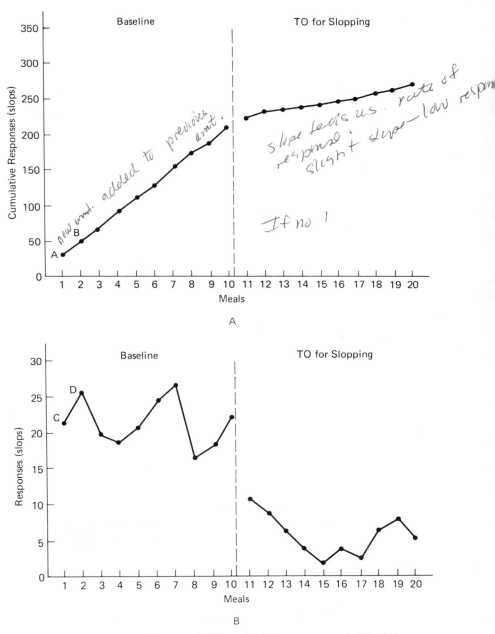

FIGURE 19-2. *A cumulative graph (A) and a frequency graph (B) of the same data.*

The first ten points of the graph describe the child's performance during the evening meal, when no attempt was made to influence slopping. An inspection of the performance on the first ten meals of the cumulative record shows a medium slope (not too steep and not too low) of the graph line. The slope of the line gives us an idea of how many responses occurred over a given period of time. In other words, it provides an indication of the rate of response. The rate of response is directly related to the slope of the graph line: a steep slope indicates a very high rate of response and a low slope indicates a low rate of response. In Figure 19-2A, the medium slope during our initial observations indicated a medium rate of responding. One feature of the cumulative record should be noted: the line can never decrease. If the child is not performing at all, in which case there are no responses cumulating to what is already there, then the line would be flat.

The next ten points of the graph describe the child's performance during the treatment program. During meals 11–20, each time the child slopped, her chair was pulled back from the table and held there for ten seconds. If the child was quiet at the end of ten seconds, she was allowed to move up to the table again and resume her meal. This brief time-out clearly served as a punishment for slopping, and decreased the slopping behavior.[2] This is represented on the cumulative record by a very low slope.

A second type of graph is shown in Figure 19-2B. We call it a *frequency graph.* The features of this graph will become obvious if we consider how each of the points is plotted. Since 21 slops occurred during meal 1, a point is made corresponding to 21 on the vertical line and meal 1 on the horizontal line (see point C). Since 27 slops occurred during the second meal, a point is made corresponding to 27 on the vertical axis and meal 2 on the horizontal axis. Thus, the line can decrease, increase, or stay flat, depending on the number of instances of the response during successive meals. The differences and similarities between a cumulative record and frequency graph can be seen by comparing Figure 19-2A with Figure 19-2B.[3]

It is sometimes possible to design a recording sheet that both records the raw data and serves as a final graph. Let us consider the fictitious case of a child, Jackie, who engaged in frequent biting attacks on other children. Let us suppose that a bite was defined as any instance of Jackie touching his teeth to the skin or clothes of another child, and that staff members were requested to watch Jackie as closely as possible during the day. Each time they observed an instance of biting, they were to go to the chart in the main office and place an X in the appropriate place. The chart is shown in Figure 19-3.

As you can see from Figure 19-3, the instances of biting were recorded up the side of the graph and the days of the program were recorded across the bottom of the graph. Each time an instance of biting occurred, the staff member would simply add an X for the appropriate day to the number of Xs that were already on the chart for that particular day. The graph shows clearly that the hypothetical treatment program of placing Jackie in a time-out room (a small, empty room) for three minutes following each instance of biting

Baseline   Time Out for Biting

Instances of Biting	1	2	3	4	5	6	7	8	9	10	11	12	13	14	15	16	17	18	19	20	21	22	23	24	25	26	27	28	29
18																													
17																													
16			X																										
15	X		X			X																							
14	X	X		X		X	X			X																			
13	X	X		X	X	X	X		X	X																			
12	X	X	X	X	X	X	X	X	X	X																			
11	X	X	X	X	X	X	X	X	X	X																			
10	X	X	X	X	X	X	X	X	X	X																			
9	X	X	X	X	X	X	X	X	X	X																			
8	X	X	X	X	X	X	X	X	X	X																			
7	X	X	X	X	X	X	X	X	X	X																			
6	X	X	X	X	X	X	X	X	X	X																			
5	X	X	X	X	X	X	X	X	X	X																			
4	X	X	X	X	X	X	X	X	X	X	X				X														
3	X	X	X	X	X	X	X	X	X	X	X				X														
2	X	X	X	X	X	X	X	X	X	X	X	X	X	X	X			X											
1	X	X	X	X	X	X	X	X	X	X	X	X	X	X	X	X	X	X	X			X			X				

Days

FIGURE 19-3. *Jackie's biting behavior. Each X represents one bite.*

worked quite well to decrease the biting attacks to zero. This type of graph is especially useful for those who do not have the time to re-chart their behavior tallies from their data sheet to a graph.*

Each instance of a behavior that is recorded in terms of frequency, such as slopping or biting as defined above, is a separate, individually distinct behavior that is easy to tally in a given period of time. Behavior modifiers have recorded the frequency of such behaviors as saying a particular word, swearing, throwing objects, completing arithmetic problems, mouthfuls of food, puffs on a cigarette, and nervous twitches. Each of these behaviors has characteristics such that successive occurrences of the given behavior are relatively discrete and the amount of time that it takes to perform the behavior is relatively similar from one occasion to the next.[4]

Quality

Many general evaluations of whether or not a person is good at something or poor at something relate to how many times they tend to emit some behavior in a given period of time. For example, the

*Another description of this type of graph is provided by Deibert and Harmon (1970).

[handwritten marginalia: greet frequenc — may be good at it — may have poor quality]

person who is a good student is most likely someone who shows a high frequency of studying and answering test questions correctly. An individual who is said to be a "cooperative child" is one who shows a high frequency of doing what she is told. In assessing the quality of eating performance, we might arbitrarily decide that any child who slops more than two times per meal shows a poor quality of eating behavior. This involves a measurement and graphing of the actual number of slops—in other words, a frequency graph as described in the previous section. A more refined variation of quality assessment would be to specify a particular behavior and then to identify different levels of the quality of that behavior. For example, consider the behavior of arm raising in terms of the steps shown in Table 19-1.

TABLE 19-1. *Levels of arm raising from poor quality to good quality.*

1. While sitting at a table and resting both arms on the table,	the student raises an arm so that the hand and forearm are two inches off the table.
2. While sitting at a table and resting both arms on the table,	the student raises an arm so that it is approximately at the student's chin level.
3. While sitting at a table and resting both arms on the table,	the student raises an arm so that it is approximately at the student's eye level.
4. While sitting at a table and resting both arms on the table,	the student raises an arm so that his hand is slightly above his head.
5. While sitting at a table and resting both arms on the table,	the student raises an arm so that it is pointing upward with his hand six inches above his head, but the elbow is still bent.
6. While sitting at a table and resting both arms on the table,	the student raises an arm so that it is pointing straight above his head.

In Table 19-1, arm raising is analyzed in terms of the steps that a severely handicapped child might go through in gradually acquiring an arm-raising response. A level-1 response is the poorest quality of arm raising, and a level-6 response is the finest quality of arm raising. One could keep track of the individual's performance over a number of trials simply by recording which of the various levels of response the child achieves. This would provide us with an indication of the quality of arm raising at any point in time on any given training trial.

In some cases, one might assess quality by utilizing instrumentation to make the appropriate judgments. An example of part of a system for improving the quality of a verbal imitative response is shown in Table 19-2. The decibel level (the loudness of the sound) is measured by a device called a voice meter.

TABLE 19-2. *Levels of quality of the verbal response "M."*

STEPS	TEACHER BEHAVIOR*	STUDENT BEHAVIORS
12	T says "M"	S says "M" within 2 tries at 60 decibels or more
11	T says "M"	S says "M" within 2 tries at 55 decibels or more
10	T says "M"	S says "M" within 2 tries at 50 decibels or more
9	T says "M"	S says "M" within 2 tries at 45 decibels or more
8	T says "M"	S says "M" within 2 tries at 40 decibels or more
7	T says "M"	S says "M" within 2 tries at 35 decibels or more
6	T says "M"	S says "M" within 2 tries at 30 decibels or more
5	T says "M"	S says "M" within 2 tries at 25 decibels or more
4	T says "M"	S says "M" within 2 tries at 20 decibels or more
3	T says "M"	S says "M" within 2 tries at 15 decibels or more
2	T says "M"	S says "M" within 2 tries at 10 decibels or more
1	T says "M"	S says "M" within 2 tries at 5 decibels or more

*When the teacher (T) asks the student (S) to say "M," the student initially responds with a very quiet "M." Over several trials, beginning at step 1, T shapes louder (better-quality) "M"'s. (Table from, Kaprowy, 1975)

Questionnaires have also been prepared that enable teachers to assess subjectively the quality of certain behaviors. An example is the *Adaptive Behavior Scale* (1974) which is designed for severely handicapped individuals.

Timing

Timing is of concern in two major ways. The first aspect of concern is the *duration* of the particular behavior. For example, in dealing with temper tantrums you may not be particularly concerned (at least initially) with their frequency (how often they occur) or with their quality (their severity) but you might be quite concerned with how long they last. Other examples of situations in which duration of responding is important are attention span, sitting in one's seat in a classroom, watching television, talking on the telephone, and taking coffee breaks.

If you are concerned with changing the duration of a behavior in sessions, then the type of data sheet shown in Figure 19-4 might be appropriate. However, if you are concerned simply with keeping track of the total duration of some activity over successive sessions, or days, then you might easily tabulate and present these data for ef-

Teacher: *Mary* Student: *Agnes* Date: *Jan 5/73*

Attention Span — Session Minutes

Attention Span	0			1			2			3			4			5	
1–2 secs.	///		/														
3–4 secs.		//	X	/	//												
5–6 secs.					/	/	/		/								
7–8 secs.							X	/	/	/			/	/			
9–10 secs.										/	/	X	X		//	/	

Procedure: While sitting in front of the student (S) (who has his hands on the table), hold a reinforcer (e.g., a candy) at eye level until S looks at it for the specified duration (beginning with 1–2 seconds), then give S a reinforcer other than the one attended to. After three consecutive reinforced trials at a given attention span, move down to the next level. If a 15-second interval passes without a reinforced trial, return to the previous attention span for one reinforced trial. Record the data in the appropriate column throughout a five-minute session.

FIGURE 19-4. *A data sheet and procedure used to increase the attention span of a severely retarded student.*

fective visual display on a combined data-sheet/graph. For example, an individual concerned with monitoring his TV watching might prepare a chart showing cumulative minutes of TV watching up the side, and days across the bottom.[5]

The second aspect of timing is the reaction time, or *latency*, of a particular response to a particular stimulus. Latency is the time that elapses between the initial presentation of a stimulus and the onset of a behavior. For example, a child in a classroom might work effectively once she gets started; the problem is that she shows a very long latency, in that after the teacher asks her to do something, she fools around "forever" before starting.

Ordinary stopwatches or clocks are usually used to record time.

Stimulus Control

Frequently, we wish to assess a behavior in terms of the conditions under which it might be observed to occur. As we pointed out in Chapter 7, the term *stimulus control* is used to indicate that certain behaviors occur in some situations and not in others. Martin, Murrell, Nicholson, and Tallman (1975) designed a detailed system called the MIMR Basic Behavior Test, which assesses the stimulus control of the basic skills of the severely and profoundly retarded. In this test, the student is instructed to perform a particular behavior—for example,

Dls
that prompt
the
beh -

"Please put on your socks." The student's behavior is then scored as follows:

The behavior was performed appropriately in all respects without further prompting or guidance of any kind. ....Score 4

The behavior was performed appropriately only after one additional verbal prompt (for example a verbal hint) was provided by the tester. ......Score 3

The behavior was performed appropriately only after one additional verbal prompt and one gestural prompt were provided by the tester. ....Score 2

The behavior was performed appropriately only after verbal prompts, gestural prompts, and minimal physical guidance were provided by the tester. ....Score 1

More than minimal physical guidance was necessary for the behavior to be performed appropriately. ....Score 0

Martin et al. identified specific behaviors that appear to be taught in most self-care training programs with the severely and profoundly retarded. Those target behaviors were then specified in the behavior test, instructions were prepared for the tester, and definitions of the different types of prompts were standardized so that the behaviors could all be assessed on the basis of the rating system just described. This testing system for identifying the conditions under which the behavior will occur is very useful as a prerequisite to training programs with severely deficient individuals, in that it identifies the specific level of guidance and prompting at which training should be initiated.

In many cases, behavior modification programs concerned with the development of preverbal and verbal skills are typically preceded by behavior assessments of the stimulus control of the student's verbal behavior. Tests are available that determine the conditions under which the students will emit appropriate imitative behavior, echoic behavior, or object identification (for example, see Kaprowy, 1975). For that matter, any test in which a student is given instructions, some paper, and a pencil and asked to answer the questions is a test of the stimulus control of behavior—are the correct answers under the control of the questions?

Does student
identify
the proper
S^D to
respond to?

In many training programs, the critical measure of behavior is whether or not the student correctly identifies some pictorial or printed stimulus. During sessions in which children are taught to identify pictures, the teacher might be concerned with the overall number of correct responses relative to errors, perhaps computed as a "percentage correct." Across a number of training sessions, the teacher is likely to be concerned also with the total number of new picture names learned. An example of such a program was reported by Martin (1975b); it involved individual daily sessions in which retarded children were taught to name a variety of pictures. The training program was standardized, and each new (unknown) picture was presented to a student in a series of prompt and question trials. Question trials on the new picture were interspersed with trials that required the student to name a known object (such as part of the student's anatomy or items of clothing). For example, a new picture, "horse," was taught in the following way:*

1. The teacher pointed to the picture of the horse and said, "What's that? That's a horse. What's that?" (a prompt trial)
2. Following a correct response to the prompt trial, the teacher pointed to the picture and asked, "What's that?" (a question trial)
3. Following a correct response to a question trial, the student was given a prompt trial, followed by a question trial, on a known object, each trial being accompanied by the teacher's pointing to the object to be named.
4. If there were no errors, the teacher then randomly presented six question trials on the new picture and the known object.
5. If an error occurred on any trial, the teacher turned away from the student for a few seconds and then repeated the entire series of prompt and question trials.
6. Following errorless performance on the series of trials, the teacher repeated the cycle with that picture and a second known object.
7. Following errorless performance on the series of trials with the second known object, the teacher again repeated the cycle, this time with a third known object.

When the new picture was correctly identified, following the alternations with three known objects, the new picture was scored as reaching criterion within a session, and trials were then initiated with another new picture. An example of the data sheet for individual sessions for such a program appears in Figure 19-5.

The results of such a procedure might be graphed in terms of the percentage-correct performance, the percentage-of-errors performance, and the words learned per training session, on either frequency or cumulative graphs.

CONTINUOUS RECORDING, INTERVAL RECORDING, AND TIME-SAMPLING RECORDING

For any given behavior, one could attempt to record that behavior continuously, day and night. In most cases, this method is far too ambitious for our time and resources. One alternative is to designate a specific segment of time, such as a one-hour training session, an afternoon, a mealtime, or a recess time, and attempt to record every instance of the specified behavior throughout that interval. Recording every instance of a behavior during a specified time segment is called *continuous recording.*

---

*This example was taken from Martin (1975b), and is closely paraphrased by permission of the publisher.

DATE _____

SESSION _____

EXPERIMENTER _____

SUBJECT _____

NEW WORD: Elephant

Column A		Column B		Column C	
k1 eye		k2 nose		k3 ear	
1	Pn		Pn		Pn
2	Qn		Qn		Qn
3	Pk		Pk		Pk
4	Qk		Qk		Qk
5	Qn	11	Qn	17	Qn
6	Qk	12	Qk	18	Qk
7	Qn	13	Qn	19	Qk
8	Qk	14	Qn	20	Qn
9	Qn	15	Qk	21	Qk
10	Qk	16	Qk	22	Qn

TOTAL ERRORS TO REACH CRITERION WITHIN A SESSION

N _____

K1 _____

K2 _____

K3 _____

FIGURE 19-5. *A sample data sheet for teaching picture names; "k" represents known object, "n" represents new (unknown) picture, "P" stands for prompt trial, and "Q" stands for question trial.*

An alternative strategy is *interval recording*. Here, a specific block of time is selected (such as a thirty-minute observation period). This time is then divided into equal intervals of relatively short duration (frequently, intervals of ten seconds). A specified behavior is then recorded a maximum of once per interval throughout the observation period, regardless of how many times the behavior might occur during each interval and regardless of the duration of the behavior. An observer might use a tape recorder that plays a prerecorded beep (or some such signal) every ten seconds. Let us suppose that the behavior of concern is an appropriately defined social-interaction response. If the response occurs once during a ten-second interval, a tally is made on the data sheet (for a sample data sheet, see p. 296). If several responses or continuous social interaction occurs during the ten-second interval, the observer still makes only one tally. As soon as the beep is heard, indicating the start of the next ten-second interval, the behavior is again recorded either 1 or 0 depending on its occurrence. Behavior recorded in this way is typically graphed in terms of the percentage of observation intervals in which it is observed.

Another behavior-observation technique frequently used is *time sampling.* In time-sampling procedure, a behavior is scored as occurring or not occurring during very brief observation intervals, each of which is separated from the others by some longer period of time. For example, a parent of a preschool child might be concerned about the frequency of the child's sitting and rocking back and forth (a self-stimulation behavior). It might be nice to have records of this behavior whenever it occurs and for as long as it occurs throughout the child's waking hours, but in general this is not realistic. An alternative is for the parent to seek out the child once every hour and make a note of whether or not the child shows any sitting and rocking behavior during a fifteen-second observation interval: each observation interval is separated from the next by approximately one hour. This type of observational technique enables one observer to observe one or more behaviors of one or more students, even though the observer has many other commitments during the day. An example of a data sheet for time sampling appears in Figure 19-6.

Frequently, interval recording is combined with time-sampling recording.[6] One reason for this is the possibility of missing observa-

DATE _____

Time	Behavior			Location			Comments
	Sitting	Standing	Rocking	Kitchen	Living Room	Bedroom	
8:00 AM							
9:00							
10:00							
11:00							
12:00 PM							
1:00							
2:00							
3:00							
4:00							
5:00							
6:00							
7:00							
8:00							
9:00 PM							

FIGURE 19-6. *A time-sampling data sheet for recording behavior of a child who frequently sits and rocks.*

tions while recording data according to a strict interval-recording system. For example, assume that an observer is attempting to record the occurrence or nonoccurrence of a behavior during ten-second intervals. The behavior might occur at the start of the next ten-second interval, while the observer is recording the results of the previous interval, and the observer might therefore miss the occurrence of the behavior. Thus, it is common for an observer to watch the student for a specified interval (say, ten seconds) and then to record the behavior during the next interval (the next ten seconds) over a given period of time (for instance, half an hour). Another reason for combining the two systems is that one observer may wish to record the behavior of several students. In such a case, the observer might watch one student for ten seconds and then record a behavior as occurring or not occurring, watch another student for ten seconds and record a behavior as occurring or not occurring, and so forth, until all of the students have been observed once. All of the students would then be observed a second time, a third time, and so forth, throughout the observation period.[7] Strictly speaking, such an observation system could also be described as time sampling with a very brief time between observation intervals.

① Beh may not be operationally defined.
② might be difficult to observe
③ observer may be poorly trained unmotivated or incompetent.

ASSESSING THE ACCURACY OF OBSERVATIONS

Hawkins and Dotson (1975) identified three sources of error that can affect the accuracy of observations. First the *response definition* might be vague, subjective, or incomplete, such that the observer has problems in taking accurate observations. Second, the behavior, even if it is precisely defined, might be difficult for an observer to detect, because of distractions in the *observational situation*, because of other obstructions to the observing process, or because the behavior is very subtle or very complex. Third, the *observer* might be poorly trained, unmotivated, or generally incompetent. To this, we might add that the observer might also be biased, and might therefore record data inaccurately, either consciously or unconsciously. We might also add a fourth possible source of error: poorly designed *data sheets* and cumbersome recording procedures. Because any one of these sources of error, or a combination of them, might be present in any behavior modification project, behavior modifiers frequently conduct what are referred to as interobserver-reliability (IOR) estimates. Two independent observers might record observations of the same behavior of the same student. They are careful not to influence or signal each other while they are recording, or to peek at each other's observations. The question is, given their best efforts while using the available behavior definitions and recording procedures, and considering their own training, how close will their scores compare? There are several ways of comparing their scores, but two are more common than the others.

Intraobserver - reliability estimates - 2 observers compare data they received thru observation

Let us return to our example of the observer who is recording the number of slops, as defined earlier in this chapter. On day 1 our observer recorded 21 slops. Let us suppose that on day 2 we bring in a second observer, who stands on the other side of the table and watches our student. The second observer is familiar with the definition of slopping and uses exactly the same data-recording sheet as our first observer. At the end of the meal, our first observer recorded 27 slops. Let us suppose that our second observer scored 29 slops. This can be converted to an estimate of our IOR by dividing the smaller number by the larger number and multiplying by 100: IOR = 27 divided by 29 times 100 equals 93%. Now it is important to ask what this IOR score means. It means that the two observers agreed quite closely (almost 100%) on the total *number* of slops. It does not mean that they agreed on 27 specific responses, with the second observer counting 2 extra to make 29. It is quite possible, for example, that one observer recorded a stop and the second observer missed it. The second observer could then have counted a slop that the first observer missed. This could have gone on throughout the meal, in which case the two observers would have disagreed completely. Nevertheless, their agreement on the total gives us more confidence in the actual total number of slops that were tallied, in spite of the possible disagreement on individual cases. This approach of counting two totals and then dividing the smaller by the larger and multiplying by 100 is quite common when two observers are counting the frequency of a particular response over a period of time.

The second IOR procedure is used with interval recordings. Recall that in interval-recording procedures, one and only one response can be recorded during each brief period of time (usually five or ten seconds) over an extended observation period. If we have two independent observers recording the same behavior, and each is using an interval-recording procedure, then the question is how do their successive intervals compare in terms of those that contain a response versus those that don't. Let us suppose that two observers are recording two types of social interaction for one child. The behaviors are defined as touching another child and vocalizing in the direction of the other child. Their interval scores are shown in the chart on the top of the following page.

As you can see, the first observer counted 18 instances of touching, as did the second observer. However, the two observers agreed on only 16 of these 18 instances. Each counted 2 instances that the other missed, yielding a total of four disagreements. Our IOR is obtained by dividing the number of intervals on which they agree that the behavior occurred, by the total number of intervals on which

Observer 1

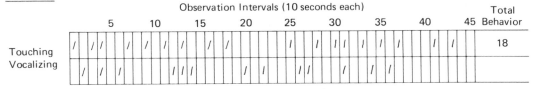

Observation Intervals (10 seconds each)

	5	10	15	20	25	30	35	40	45	Total Behavior
Touching										18
Vocalizing										

Observer 2

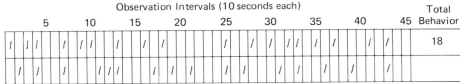

Observation Intervals (10 seconds each)

	5	10	15	20	25	30	35	40	45	Total Behavior
Touching										18
Vocalizing										

either recorded a behavior (agreements divided by agreements plus disagreements on the occurrence of a behavior), and multiplying by 100:

$$IOR = \frac{16}{16+4} \times 100 = \frac{16}{20} \times 100 = 80\%$$

What is considered an acceptable IOR in behavior modification studies? It has been suggested that, by convention IOR should be between 80 and 100% (Kazdin, 1975). However, potential variation in computational procedures renders the final IOR value potentially misleading when considered by itself.[8] We would suggest that readers of behavior modification literature consider the response definitions, observer-training procedures, recording system, method of calculating IOR, and the final IOR value as a total package when judging the reliability of reported data. Defects in any of these might make the results suspect.

SELECTING AN ASSESSMENT SYSTEM: DECISIONS! DECISIONS!

Let us suppose that you have selected a particular behavior for which you want to develop a treatment program. Now you must decide what to record and how to record it. Usually, there are several behavioral measures that might be taken, and several assessment systems that might be used. We offer the suggestions in Table 19-3 in order to help you select the strategy that will be most appropriate, accurate, and convenient.

TABLE 19-3. *Guidelines for selecting an assessment system.*

BEHAVIORAL CHARACTERISTICS	SOME CONSIDERATIONS	RECOMMENDED ASSESSMENT SYSTEM	SOME SAMPLE BEHAVIORS
Frequency	1. Responses are relatively discrete. 2. Successive responses are quite similar in duration. 3. Total number of responses is of concern. 4. An observer is available.	continuous frequency	cigarettes smoked pinches objects thrown saying "ain't" reprimands math problems completed self-slaps teacher attention to child going to the bathroom
Stimulus Control	Same as 1–4 above, plus: 5. Main concern is percentage of appropriate responses.	continuous frequency per opportunity	correct imitations pictures identified school attendance spelling errors compliance to requests (All of the above may be converted to percentage of total opportunities.)
Quantity (frequency or duration)	Same as 4 and 5 above, plus: 6. Instances of behavior can be of long duration. 7. Successive responses can be of variable duration. 8. Precise duration is not of major concern.	interval recording	smiling sitting lying down talking social behavior withdrawn behavior TV watching studying on-task behavior or off-task behavior (e.g., in a classroom)
Quantity (frequency or duration)	Same as 5–8 above, plus: 9. An observer is recording two or more behaviors of two or more students.	combination of interval recording and time-sampling recording	(same as those listed for interval recording)

TABLE 19-3. *(Continued)*

BEHAVIORAL CHARACTERISTICS	SOME CONSIDERATIONS	RECOMMENDED ASSESSMENT SYSTEM	SOME SAMPLE BEHAVIORS
Quantity (frequency or duration)	Same as 5–9 above, plus: 10. The behavior has a high frequency or duration throughout long periods (e.g., a morning or a day). 11. The observer has many other things to do and can devote only brief periods of time, which are separated from one another by long intervals.	time-sampling recording	sitting talking walking playing working rocking being in a particular location
Timing	12. Precise duration is of major concern. 13. An observer is available.	continuous duration recording	sitting social interaction time to run errands tantrums practicing piano task completion
Timing	Same as 12 above, plus: 14. Appropriate behavior occurs with some frequency. 15. Main concern is that the behavior occur at the time specified for it.	continuous latency recording	(same as those listed for Stimulus Control)

Study Questions

(for examination purposes)

1. Describe three ways of keeping track of the number of times a certain response occurs during a day. *counter beads, writing*

2. Prepare a cumulative graph of the following instances of self-slaps that were observed during successive sessions: 3, 7, 19, 0, 0, 0, 27, 12, 6.

3. Describe at least four ways in which a cumulative graph of a set of data differs from a frequency graph of the same data.

4. On a cumulative graph, what can you infer from the following?
   a) a steep slope   *↑ response rate*
   b) a low slope   *↓ response rate*
   c) a flat line   *no response*

5. Draw and briefly describe a data sheet that would also serve as a graph.

6. In what two major ways is timing important? Give examples of each.

7. What do we mean by the latency of a response? Give an example.

8. What behavioral characteristic does the MIMR Basic Behavior Test assess? Explain your answer. *assesses the SP/s of the basic skills — the severely + profoundly retarded.*

9. Describe with an example the continuous-recording system. *Recording every beh in the specific time segments — does beh occur or*

10. Describe with an example the interval-recording system. *Specific period of time selected + divided into intervals*

11. Describe with an example the time-sampling-recording system. *Record beh at spec. time + lge int of time B/w*

12. Describe with an example how interval recording might be combined with time-sampling recording.

13. When would one likely select an interval-recording system over a continuous-recording system? (Hint: See Table 19-3.)

14. Describe four sources of error in recording observations.

15. In a sentence or two, what do we mean by inter-observer reliability? (Describe it in words, and don't give the procedures for calculating IORs.) *2 observers observe — compare amt + quality of data*

16. Using the procedure described in the text for computing IORs with interval data, compute an IOR for the data of vocalizing, as recorded by observers 1 and 2 (p. 296). Show all your computations. *IOR = 16/16+4 × 100· IOR = 80 %*

17. According to convention, what is an acceptable IOR in a research program? What does "by convention" mean anyhow? *80-100%*

18. What are the considerations that would likely lead one to use a continuous-frequency assessment system? Give some sample behaviors (See Table 19-3.) *to assess SP/s*

19. What are the considerations that would likely lead one to use an interval-recording system combined with a time-sampling system? Give examples. (See Table 19-3.) *an observer recording err mar be for far more students*

20. What two considerations would likely lead one to use the time-sampling system rather than a system that combined interval recording and time-sampling? (See Table 19-3.)

Observer has other things to do + can only spend certain amt of time observing — or beh occurs for long duration at certain pt in day.

Study Exercise

(to be practiced by the reader)

Select a behavioral deficiency, excess, or inappropriateness that was successfully modified (for example, Peter's tantrums or Charles's pill swallowing), as described in one of the other chapters. For that behavior:
- a) design a plausible data sheet;
- b) prepare a summary of some representative data (real or hypothesized);
- c) graph your data in a frequency graph;
- d) graph your data in a cumulative graph.

Self-Modification Exercise

(to be practiced by the reader)

Select one of your behavioral excesses, deficiencies, or inappropriatenesses. For that behavior, answer questions a–d in the study exercise above.

EXTENDED DISCUSSION AND NOTES

1. A similar type of dial wrist counter for recording two behaviors up to 99 and 9 responses, respectively, or one behavior up to 999 responses, can be obtained for about $6.00 from: Behaviordelia/PO Box 1044–J7/Kalamazoo, Michigan 49005. This company also makes a bead wrist counter, consisting of a leather band with four rows of nine moveable beads, which sells for about $11.00. A much more inexpensive counter that has been used effectively by behavior modifiers is the Knit Talley counter, used in knitting. It costs about forty cents and is highly reliable, even after extensive use. For more information, see Sheehan and Casey (1974).

2. That brief time-outs presented immediately following slopping responses can effectively decrease such responses was demonstrated in a study by Martin, McDonald, and Omichinski (1971). They described a program in which undergraduate university students studied several undesirable mealtime behaviors of four severely retarded institutionalized girls. The administration of a fifteen-second time-out for each instance of slopping effectively decreased slopping behavior in three of the four students, and had a small but consistent effect on the fourth student. The authors also observed a desirable side effect: permanent decreases occurred in one or more other undesirable responses of two of the students. Another side effect was a temporary increase in one other undesirable response of three of the students, although the increase did not last long.

3. Simple frequency graphs are much more common than cumulative graphs in behavior modification studies. In some situations, however, a cumulative graph is more advantageous. For example, a cumulative

(Continued)

301

graph can give one a direct impression of rate of response much more easily than a frequency graph because in a cumulative graph the rate can be inferred from the slope of the line, as we pointed out in the text. A cumulative graph is also to be preferred when an experimenter is comparing two or more behaviors or conditions concurrently. For example, one of the authors conducted an experiment in which severely retarded and autistic children were taught to identify pictures of antonyms (wet versus dry, big versus small, etc.; Martin, 1975b). The children received two training sessions per day, one training session utilizing one set of antonyms and the other training session being used to teach a second set. The procedure in both cases was the same, except for one factor. With one set of antonyms, wrong responses were followed by a brief time-out (five to ten seconds) in which the teacher simply turned her head from the child and ignored him. With the second set of antonyms, wrong responses by the child resulted in a longer time-out (fifteen to twenty seconds). The question being asked was which of the two time-out durations would have a greater suppression effect on error responding. The results for one child, Roger, are plotted cumulatively in Figure 19-7.

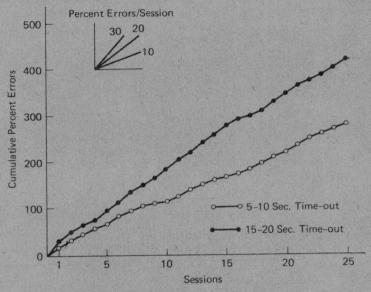

FIGURE 19-7. *Cumulative percentage of errors by Roger during a picture-naming task under two experimental conditions.*

It can be seen from Figure 19-7 that Roger consistently made fewer errors when errors were followed by the shorter time-out. Although the differences were small within any one session, the gradual spread of the cumulative graphs clearly showed the consistent effect. If these results were plotted as frequency graphs, the effect would be much more difficult to detect visually, because the two lines would be very close to each other across the graph and would frequently overlap.

4. In basic experimental research with lower organisms, response rate (frequency of a specific response over time) is a highly popular and

(Continued)

Shorter time outs are more desirable to reduce problem beh.

(Continued)

valuable behavioral measure. For the most part, the behavioral principles described in Chapters 2–13 refer to changes in the frequency of a response. It has been argued several times that the response rate is probably the best measure of behavior for behavior modifiers to examine in applied settings (see, for example, Bijou et al. 1969; Kazdin, 1973a). However, it has also been argued that rate may not be the best measure in applied settings (Wolf, 1973). We would encourage serious students of behavior modification to acquaint themselves with these arguments.

5. Timing the duration of a response can sometimes be managed automatically if one appropriately connects timers to critical features of the environment. For example, for about twenty dollars it would be possible to wire up a chair that would automatically record the amount of time a student sits in it, assuming that this might be a desirable behavior. For a more detailed discussion of such a device, see Wolff and Baugh (1974).

6. Behavior modifiers have not been completely consistent in the way they have described time-sampling recording procedures. Schaefer and Martin (1969) described time sampling as a procedure carried out by making observations at specified intervals over a given period of time. In their program, which took place in a mental hospital, observations were made every half-hour during the day. Behaviors were scored as occurring or not occurring during the few seconds that the patients were observed. However, Sundel and Sundel (1975), while explaining time-sampling recording, described an example in which an individual might be observed at the end of every fifteen-second interval throughout a twenty-minute observation period that occurs twice per day. Thus, the time between observations was extremely brief (fifteen seconds), in contrast with what seems to be the more usual half-hour or one-hour interval between observations. To carry the inconsistencies even further, Kazdin (1975) does not distinguish between interval recording and time-sampling recording, suggesting that interval recording is "sometimes referred to as time-sampling." To take a final example, Powell, Martindale, and Kulp (1975a) distinguished between whole-interval time sampling (equivalent to what we described as interval recording, with the stipulation that the behavior must occur throughout an interval in order to be counted), partial-interval time sampling (equivalent to what we described as interval recording), and momentary time sampling (equivalent to what we described as time sampling). We suspect that such terms will gradually acquire more precise and consistent usage as the field of behavior modification develops during the next few years. In the meantime, it is probably wise to carefully explain how you are using these terms when describing your procedures to others.

7. Powell, Martindale, and Kulp (1975) examined the extent to which various time-sampling arrangements compared with a continuous measure of the in-seat behavior of a secretary. As expected, the more frequently the sample measures were made, the closer the agreement between the sample and continuous measures was. In addition, different types of sampling rules produced different types of errors.

8. The procedure that we have suggested for computing IOR during interval recording is that of dividing the number of intervals on which observers agree that a behavior occurred, by the total number of intervals on which either recorded a behavior (agreements plus disagreements on a behavior), and multiplying by 100. Some researchers, however, in-

(Continued)

(Continued)

clude in their measure of agreements, agreements between two observers that no behavior occurred—in other words, agreements on blank intervals. However, when very few behaviors have been recorded, this can greatly inflate a reliability score. For example, consider the forty-five observation intervals given on p. 296. Let us suppose that observer 1 recorded an instance of touching during interval 5, and observer 2 recorded an instance of touching during interval 6. No other instances of touching were recorded. In such a case, the two observers would completely disagree on the occurrence of the behavior; the IOR would be zero if IOR is computed as suggested in the text. However, if agreements on blank intervals are included, their IOR equals 43 agreements divided by 43 agreements plus 2 disagreements times 100, equals 95.6%. Because of this distortion, many researchers follow the proposal that we have suggested in the text for computing IOR, and do *not* count agreements on blank intervals. In other words, intervals in which neither observer scores a behavior are ignored. An acceptable exception to this would be when one is concerned with decreasing behavior and having agreement that the behavior did not occur. These points and other comments on the complexity of computing IOR are discussed in more detail in Bijou et al. (1969); Hawkins and Dotson (1975); and Johnson and Bolstad (1973).

Study Questions on Notes

1. What were the two side effects observed by Martin, McDonald, and Omichinski (1971) in their study of brief time-outs presented following slopping responses by severely retarded girls?
2. What are two types of situations in which a cumulative graph might be more informative than a frequency graph in terms of the direct impression obtained from viewing the graph?
3. Briefly identify three responses whose durations might be timed automatically.
4. Why is it necessary to clearly explain how you are using the term "time-sampling recording"?
5. What terms in this book are equivalent in meaning to the terms "partial-inverval time-sampling" and "momentary time-sampling," as used by Powell et al.?
6. When is it especially misleading to include agreement on blank intervals in computing IOR?
7. For the data given on p. 296, compute the IOR but include agreements on blank intervals in your number of agreements. Now, compute IOR but include only agreements on intervals during which behavior occurred. How do your two measures compare?
8. When might it be acceptable to include agreement on blank intervals in your computation of IOR? Why would this be acceptable?

CHAPTER 20

Doing **RESEARCH**
In Behavior Modification

In Chapter 18, as in many of the other chapters in this text, we emphasize that a minimal behavior modification program should have at least three phases: a *baseline phase,* for determining the initial level of the behavior prior to the program; a *treatment phase,* in which the intervention strategy is initiated; and a *follow-up phase,* for evaluating the persistence of the desirable behavior changes following termination of the program. If a behavior modifier has done a good job of programming for generalization (described in Chapter 11), then the follow-up phase should show that the improved behavior is persisting. However, many publications concerning behavior modification go far beyond these three minimal phases and describe data that demonstrate convincingly that it was indeed the treatment that caused a particular change in behavior. It is this emphasis on scientific demonstration that a particular treatment was responsible for a specific behavioral change that has produced a continual refinement of behavior modification procedures to their present highly effective

Some programs add to minimal
component of program — showing
how they know it was the Tx
that improved beh. + not other
intervening variables.

level. The value of such demonstrations might best be illustrated with a hypothetical example.

Our example involves a second-grade student's frequency of successfully completing addition and subtraction problems in daily half-hour math classes. The student, Billie, was performing at a much lower level than any of the other students and was showing a great deal of disruptive behavior during the class. The teacher, Ms. Johnson, reasoned that an increase in Billie's performance of solving the assigned math problems might make it more pleasurable for Billie to work at the problems and might thereby decrease his disruptive interactions with those around him. During a one-week baseline, Ms. Johnson assigned a certain number of problems to the class and recorded the number that Billie completed successfully during each half-hour period. Billie averaged successful completion of seven math problems per half-hour. Ms. Johnson next introduced a reinforcement program. She told Billie that for each math problem he completed successfully he could add one extra minute of time to his physical education class on Friday afternoon, an activity that appeared to be highly pleasurable for him. Billie's performance improved during the first week of the program. During the second week, he averaged nineteen correct math problems per half-hour class.

Can the teacher attribute the improvement in Billie's performance to the treatment? Our initial tendency might be to say yes, in that performance is much better now than it was during the original baseline. However, it is plausible that the improvement was due to any of a number of other factors. For example, Billie may have had a bad cold during baseline and may have started to get over his illness during the first week of the program; his recovery could have resulted in the subsequent mathematical improvements. Or a new student who set a good example for Billie to model may have been seated near him during the treatment phase but not during the baseline. Or perhaps the problems assigned during the treatment phase were easier than those assigned during baseline. Or perhaps something that the teacher could not possibly have been aware of was responsible for his improved performance.

In any program in which a treatment phase is introduced for the purpose of modifying the behavior of some individual, it is quite possible for some uncontrolled or interfering variable or condition to occur concurrently with the treatment, such that the change in the behavior is due to the uncontrolled variable rather than the treatment itself. A behavior modification research project attempts to demonstrate convincingly that it was the treatment rather than some uncontrolled variable that was responsible for a change in the behavior of concern.[1]

Let us suppose that Ms. Johnson, being scientifically inclined, is aware of the above possibilities and would like to demonstrate convincingly that it was indeed her program that was responsible for Billie's improvement. (Besides satisfying her curiosity, there are several practical reasons why she might have wanted to demonstrate the success of her program. For example, such a demonstration would indicate whether she should try a similar procedure with another problem Billie might have, whether she should recommend similar procedures to Billie's other teachers, and whether she should try similar procedures with other students in her class.) Therefore, at the end of the second week of the reinforcement program, she eliminated the reinforcement and returned to the baseline condition. Let us suppose that the hypothetical results of this manipulation by the teacher are those shown in Figure 20-1.

By the end of the second week of our return to the baseline conditions (which is called a *reversal*), Billie was performing at a level approximately that of his original baseline. Ms. Johnson then reintroduced the treatment phase, just as it had been before, and, as can

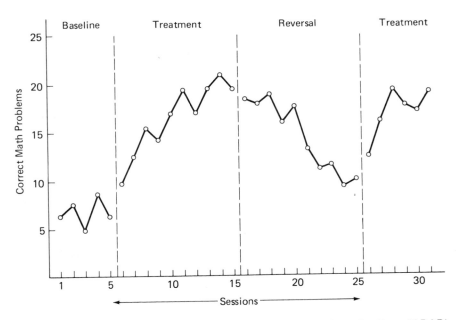

FIGURE 20-1. *Hypothetical data showing a reversal-replication (ABAB) design for Billie.*

be seen in Figure 20-1, Billie again improved his performance. Ms. Johnson had replicated both the original-baseline and the original-treatment effects. If some uncontrolled variable was operating, one must hypothesize that it was mysteriously occurring at exactly the same time the treatment program was operative, and was not occurring when the treatment program was removed. This becomes much less plausible with each successful replication of the effect. We now have much more confidence that it was indeed the teacher's procedure that produced the desired behavior change. Ms. Johnson demonstrated a cause-effect relationship between a particular behavior, sometimes referred to as a *dependent variable,* and her treatment program, sometimes referred to as the *independent variable.*[2]

The type of experimental strategy that Ms. Johnson employed is called a *reversal-replication* design. It is so named because it includes a reversal to baseline conditions followed by a replication of the treatment phase (and, hopefully, of the effect). The baseline condition is often abbreviated "A," and the treatment condition "B." Hence, this design is also called an *ABAB* design.[3]

The reversal-replication strategy is the most common type of behavior modification research design (Kazdin, 1975b). It has been used to demonstrate experimental control over such behaviors as slopping at mealtime (Martin, McDonald, and Omichinski, 1971), recruitment of members at a community club (Pierce and Risley, 1974), sentence acquisition in an autistic child (Stevens-Long and Rasmussen, 1974), littering in an underdeveloped canyon (Powers, Osborne, and Anderson, 1973), composition writing rate (Van Houten, Morrison, Jarvis, and McDonald, 1974), and a great many others (see issues of the *Journal of Applied Behavior Analysis*).

Although the reversal-replication design appears simple at first glance, beginning students doing behavior modification research very quickly encounter several questions that are not very easy to answer. Assuming that problems of response definition, observer accuracy, and data recording (discussed in Chapter 19) have been solved, the first question is this: How long should the baseline phase last? The difficulties of answering this question might best be appreciated by viewing Figure 20-2. Which of the baselines in Figure 20-2 do you consider to be the most adequate? If you selected baselines 4 and 5, we agree. Baseline 4 is acceptable because the pattern of behavior appears stable and predictable. Baseline 5 is acceptable because the trend observed is in a direction opposite to the effect caused by the independent variable. Ideally then, a baseline phase should continue until the pattern of performance is stable or until it shows a trend in the direction opposite to that predicted when the independent variable is introduced.

However, other considerations may lead one to shorten or lengthen a baseline in any applied research project. First, there are scientific considerations related to the newness of the behavior and

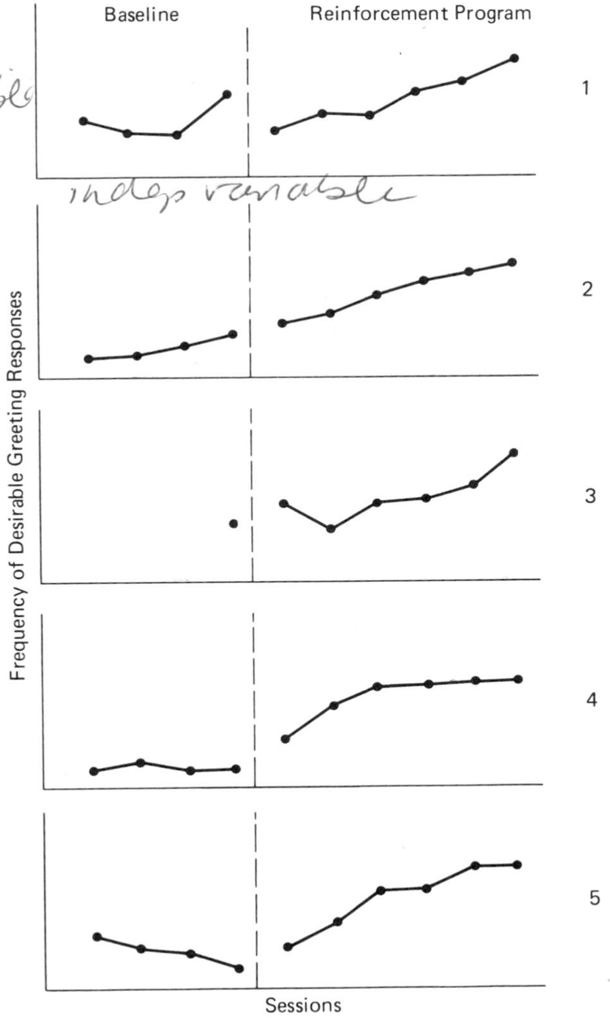

FIGURE 20-2. *Hypothetical data for five children.*

the independent variables being studied. The area of behavior analysis reported most frequently in the *Journal of Applied Behavior Analysis* is that of classroom behavior (Kazdin, 1975b). Consequently, one might be more comfortable conducting a shorter baseline in a new study of classroom behavior than in a study of a completely unexplored area, such as seat-belt wearing by car drivers. Second, practical considerations might limit the length of baseline observations. The available time of the experimenter, the availability of observers, restrictions on students for completing projects on time, and any of a number of other factors might lead one to limit or extend the baseline for completely nonscientific reasons. Finally, ethical considerations often affect baseline length. For example, if one is attempting to manage the self-abusive behavior of a retarded child, then an extended baseline phase is ethically unacceptable.

Another question that a beginning student in behavior modification research will encounter is this: How many reversals and replications are necessary? Again, there is no easy answer to this question. If one observes a very large effect when the independent variable is introduced, and if the area is one that has been explored before, then one replication may be sufficient. Other combinations of factors might lead the student to conduct several replications in order to convincingly demonstrate a cause-effect relationship.

Although a reversal-replication design is the most common behavior modification research strategy, it does have limitations that make it inappropriate in certain situations. First, it may be undesirable to reverse to baseline conditions following a treatment phase. For example, in the case of Valerie's self-abusiveness (described in Chapter 3), it was ethically unacceptable to reverse to baseline immediately following the successful treatment.

Second, it may be impossible to obtain a reversal. For example, "behavioral trapping" may prevent a reversal. In Chapter 11, (p. 165) we described how a shy child might be taught to interact with his peers; once the teacher's reinforcement produces the desirable interaction, the child's behavior might be "trapped" by his peers who maintain it after the withdrawal of the teacher's attention. Other behaviors may not reverse to baseline conditions because the behavior has become "self-reinforcing." Once a golf pro has taught a novice golfer to hit a golf ball over 200 yards, it is unlikely that the golfer will deliberately return to his original, unorthodox swing, which produced a 20-yard drive. Occasionally, it may be impossible to do a reversal because of changes in body structure. For example, it is impossible to use the reversal-replication design to investigate the effects of hysterectomies on the emotional behavior of females.

MULTIPLE-BASELINE DESIGNS

As we noted above, a major purpose of behavior modification research is to demonstrate the control imposed on behavior by a particular treatment. Multiple-baseline designs are used to accomplish this without reversing to baseline conditions.

A multiple baseline across behaviors

Let us suppose that Ms. Johnson was concerned with demonstrating the effects of her reinforcement procedure on Billie's academic performance, but did not want to do a reversal and risk losing the improvement shown by Billie. She might have accomplished her demonstration of treatment control over improved performance by constructing a multiple baseline across behaviors. Her first step would have been to baseline two or more behaviors concurrently. Specifically, she might have recorded Billie's performance in solving math problems during math class, his performance in spelling correctly during English class, and his sentence writing during creative-writing class. These baselines might have been those shown in Figure 20-3. The multiple-baseline design across behaviors calls for the introduction of the treatment sequentially across two or more behaviors. The extra minute of physical education class per correct problem might have been introduced in the math class while the baseline condition was continued during spelling and writing classes. If the results were those shown in Figure 20-3, the teacher might next have introduced the treatment for the second behavior—correct spelling.

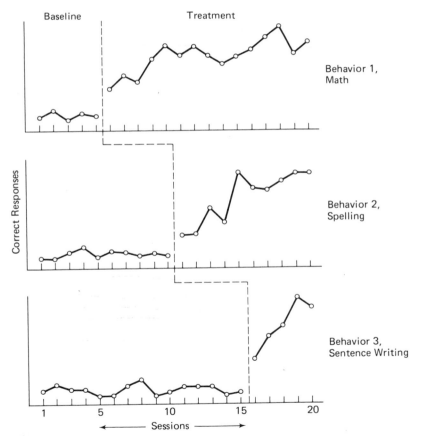

FIGURE 20-3. Hypothetical data illustrating a multiple-baseline-across-behaviors design for Billie.

Finally, the teacher might have introduced the treatment for the third behavior—sentence writing. If performance was as indicated in Figure 20-3, then it clearly indicated that the behavior changed only when the treatment was introduced. This provides a very clear demonstration of the control of the treatment over several behaviors.[4]

The application of this design assumes that the behaviors are relatively independent. If Ms. Johnson had applied the treatment program to one behavior while the other two behaviors were kept at baseline conditions, and if an improvement had been observed in all three behaviors, then she could not have confidently attributed the improvement to the treatment itself. An example of such generalization across behaviors was reported by Nordquist (1971).

Do mult basline across beh ⊂ independent beh's.

A multiple baseline across situations

Another variety of multiple-baseline design studies the effects of a treatment on a single behavior that occurs in several situations. For example, Corte, Wolf, and Locke (1971) were concerned with eliminating the self-abusive, face-hitting responses of a profoundly retarded adolescent in an institution. A number of procedures had been unsuccessful in eliminating this behavior. As a last resort, the authors designed a very carefully controlled program utilizing brief electric-shock punishment to decrease the self-abusive behavior. Because of the obvious practical value of scientifically researching a treatment for eliminating self-abuse, because the authors did not want other therapists to use electric-shock punishment unless there was strong evidence for its success (where other procedures had failed), and because a reversal design was unacceptable, the authors decided to use a multiple baseline across situations to evaluate the effects of the treatment. They recorded self-abusive behavior in two settings—a small session room and a general ward. Self-abusiveness occurred at a high rate in both settings. The shock procedure was then introduced in the session room; the other setting continued to be baselined. Following the successful reduction of the self-abusive behavior as a consequence of the treatment program in the session room, the shock was introduced in the general-ward setting. The treatment program led to a decrease in the second setting as well as the first, demonstrating that the successful treatment of the self-abusiveness was due to the shock contingency.[5]

A potential problem with a multiple baseline across settings is that when the treatment is applied to the behavior in the first setting, it may cause subsequent improvement in all settings. When this happens, the experimenter is not able to conclude that the improvement was necessarily due to the treatment.

Limit. — Improvement in all other settings. Generalize to all other settings?

A multiple baseline across people

Yet another multiple-baseline design demonstrates the effectiveness of a treatment by applying it sequentially to individuals. For example, Fawcett and Miller (1975) utilized a multiple-baseline-across-people method to demonstrate the effectiveness of a combination of procedures (called a treatment package) designed to improve public-speaking behaviors. Public-speaking skills of three individuals were recorded during initial public-speaking sessions. The first individual was then given the package while the others continued on baseline. Exposure to the treatment improved the public-speaking behaviors of the first individual. The package was introduced sequentially to the second person, and then to the third person, and each time it led to an improvement in public speaking behaviors. This demonstration of improvement in individuals who receive treatment sequentially across time is also a convincing demonstration of the effectiveness of a treatment program.[6] A potential problem with this design is that the individuals involved might deliberately communicate with or otherwise influence other individuals who are being baselined, and thereby cause these other individuals to show a change in behavior prior to the introduction of the treatment program (for example, see Kazdin, 1973).

The obvious advantage of these three multiple-baseline designs over a reversal-replication design is that they eliminate the need for reversing to baseline conditions. On the other hand, it is not always possible to find two or more behaviors, two or more settings, or two or more individuals that can be multiple-baselined such that there is complete independence between the multiple measures. Moreover, it often takes additional time and/or observers to gather the necessary data for multiple baselines.[7]

DATA ANALYSIS AND INTERPRETATION

Researchers who employ the behavior modification research designs described above typically analyze their data without the use of statistical techniques that are more common in other areas of psychology.[8] The evaluation of the effect of a particular treatment is typically made on the basis of two major sets of criteria, scientific and practical. Scientific criteria are used to evaluate whether or not there has been a convincing demonstration that the treatment was responsible for producing a reliable effect on the dependent variable. This judgment is commonly made by visually inspecting the graph of the results. Problems in deciding whether or not a treatment produced a reliable effect on a dependent variable might best be appreciated by examining

Figure 20-4. Most observers of the five graphs contained therein would probably agree that there is a clear, large effect in graph 1, a reliable though small effect in graph 2, and questionable effects in the remaining graphs.

Although there appear to be no consistently applied guidelines for inspecting one's data in order to judge whether or not a significant effect has occurred, there are a number of scientific considerations that should be kept in mind. One has greater confidence that an effect has been observed, the greater number of times that it is

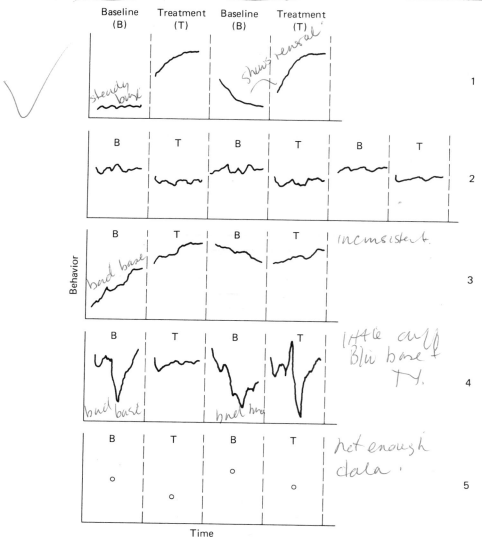

FIGURE 20-4. *Some hypothetical data.*

replicated; the fewer the overlapping points between baseline and treatment phases; the sooner the effect is observed following the introduction of the treatment; the larger the effect in comparison to baseline; the more precisely the treatment procedures and response measures are specified;[9] and the more consistent the findings with existing data and accepted behavioral theory.[10]

The practical considerations for evaluating the effects of a treatment are based on the importance of the behavior change to the client or other significant individuals in the client's life rather than the experimental reliability of the treatment's effect on behavior. That is, if graph 2 in Figure 20-4 were a graph of self-abusive behavior, the reliable cause-effect relationship demonstrated therein might be of little clinical significance. If the individual is still extremely self-abusive, as indicated by the performance during treatment phases, then the people responsible for caring for that child would not be satisfied. These practical considerations make the behavior modifier accountable to the client whom he or she is treating.[11]

Study Questions

(for examination purposes)

1. Briefly, what are the minimal components of a behavior modification program?
2. In two or three sentences, distinguish between a minimal behavior modification program and behavior modification research.
3. In two or three sentences, explain why we cannot necessarily claim that a change in behavior during a minimal behavior modification program was due to the treatment.
4. Briefly describe, with reference to an example, the four components of the reversal–replication design.
5. Ideally, how long should the baseline phase of the reversal research design continue?
6. In a sentence or two each, describe why baselines 1, 2, and 3 from Figure 20-2 are inadequate.
7. What scientific, practical, and ethical considerations might lead one to lengthen or shorten a baseline?
8. How many reversals and replications are necessary in a reversal–replication design?
9. Identify two limitations of the reversal-replication design, and give a brief example of each.

10. Briefly describe, with reference to an example, a multiple-baseline-across-behaviors design.

11. When is a multiple-baseline-across-behaviors design inappropriate? *when beh* *to the original behavior treated*

12. Briefly describe, with reference to an example, a multiple-baseline-across-situations design.

13. When is a multiple-baseline-across-situations design inappropriate? *when* *beh improved in I setting generalizes to all other setting*

14. Briefly describe, with reference to an example, a multiple-baseline-across-people design.

15. When is a multiple-baseline-across-people design inappropriate?

sci - inspect graphs 16. In a sentence or two each, what are the scientific and practical criteria for
prac - importance of evaluating the effects of a particular treatment?
beh change to ind

17. For each of graphs 3, 4, and 5 in Figure 20-4, describe why the effects of the treatment are questionable.

-lge diff after tx
-repeated over retrials 18. Let us suppose that you have conducted an ABAB design in order to
-diff Blw base + Tx analyze the effects of a treatment. You are now inspecting your data in
-person's beh is better order to judge whether or not a significant effect has occurred. Meeting
far then what six criteria would give you maximum confidence that the treatment
had produced a significant effect on the dependent variable?

19. How does one go about evaluating the clinical effectiveness of a treatment?

Study Exercise

(to be practiced by the reader)

Suppose that you are teaching some students about doing research that utilizes reversal and multiple-baseline designs. Your students must do a research project in which they select a dependent variable and then evaluate the effects of some treatment upon that dependent variable. Your task as teacher is to analyze the material in this chapter in order to prepare a guide that will help the students select the appropriate research design. Your guide should take the form of a series of questions that they might ask, the answers to which would lead to a particular design. For example, if (a) and (b), then choose a reversal design; but if (c), (d), and (e), then choose a multiple-baseline design; and so forth.

Self-Modification Exercise

(to be practiced by the reader)

As described in Chapter 18, self recording without any additional behavioral procedures sometimes leads to behavioral change. Let us suppose you have decided to describe a self-recording procedure and then to investigate that as a treatment in a self-modification program. Describe a plausible multiple-baseline design that would enable you to assess self recording as an effective self-control treatment.

EXTENDED DISCUSSION AND NOTES

1. Actually, there are a number of reasons for conducting behavior modification research. Most often, the research is probably conducted to demonstrate that a particular treatment was responsible for a specific behavioral change. In addition, however, research might be conducted to determine which components of the treatment may have been responsible for the behavioral change observed; to assess the relative benefits derived from a particular treatment in relationship to the costs (this type of research is called cost-benefit research); to help students complete Master's theses and Ph.D. dissertations in order to obtain advanced degrees; to enable researchers to obtain research grants; to enable one to publish, so as not to perish in one's professorial profession; and for a host of other reasons.

2. Potential interfering variables that might be mistaken for treatment effects are often discussed as factors that threaten "internal validity." An experiment is internally valid if the independent variable did in fact cause observed changes in the dependent variable. Campbell and Stanley (1963) listed several classes of variables that threaten internal validity. Slightly paraphrased, these are:

1. *History:* the specific events (such as a new student moving beside Billie, as described on p. 306) occurring between the baseline and treatment measures in addition to the treatment variable.
2. *Maturation:* processes within the student (such as Billie overcoming his cold, as described on p. 306) operating as a function of the passage of time, such as growing older, growing hungrier, or growing more tired.
3. *Testing:* the effects of being assessed upon one's performance in subsequent assessments (for example, Billie saying to himself, "Gee, Ms. Johnson is starting to keep my scores every math class. I guess I better shape up.").
4. *Instrumentation:* changes in the calibration of a measuring instrument or in the observer's criteria (for example, Ms. Johnson may have asked easier questions during treatment).
5. *Statistical regression:* a statistical law stating that a person who has been selected on the basis of his extreme scores will tend to score less deviantly upon further measurement.

3. In a reversal research design, the reversal phase frequently involves a return to baseline conditions, as we have described in the text. However, there are two other alternatives, either of which might be inappropriate for particular research problems. To illustrate the first alternative, consider Ms. Johnson's program for improving Billie's mathematics performance. Following the treatment phase, Ms. Johnson eliminated the reinforcement program. However, she might have simply have delivered the one-minute additions to the physical education program (the reinforcers) on a noncontingent basis. This delivery of reinforcers independent of behavior during the reversal is one alternative to completely eliminating the reinforcers, as described in the text, and is referred to as an ABCB design.

A second alternative is for the researcher to continue delivering the reinforcer during the reversal phase, but to deliver it for any behavior other than the behavior that was reinforced during treatment (such as *not* doing math problems, in Billie's case). (This type of reinforcement schedule, called "DRO," is discussed in Chapter 6.) A complete

(Continued)

reversal of the reinforcement rule during the reversal phase is likely to demonstrate very quickly whether or not the treatment was responsible for a behavior change, in that the reinforcer is now presented contingent on any behavior "other" than the behavior influenced during treatment. Examples of this variation during the reversal phase can be found in Bostow and Bailey (1969) and Kazdin (1973b). Leitenberg (1973) called this alternative a "true reversal design," and called the reversal-replication design described in the text "a withdrawal design."

4. Multiple baselines across behaviors have demonstrated control over such behaviors as articulation errors (Bailey, Timbers, Phillips, and Wolf, 1971), homework tasks (Hall, Cristler, Cranston and Tucker, 1970), academic skills of hyperactive children in the absence of reinforcement (Ayllon, Layman, and Kandel, 1975), and problem solving by a community board (Briscoe, Hoffman, and Bailey, 1975). Other examples can be found in such journals as the *Journal of Applied Behavior Analysis* and *Behavior Therapy.*

5. The Corte et al. (1971) study contains additional examples of multiple baselines across situations. Another example of this research design was described by Hayes, Johnson, and Cone (1975). They demonstrated the use of a marked-item technique to control littering by inmates at a youth correctional facility. The inmates were free to move around the campus-like grounds of an open, coeducational prison in Morgantown, West Virginia. They typically littered candy wrappers cigarette butts, and other trash in a wide variety of areas. When a reinforcement program was instituted involving money or special privileges for the collection of each piece of inconspicuously marked litter (planted by the experimenters), the inmates voluntarily collected trash. A multiple-baseline design across three areas demonstrated that this procedure significantly controlled litter collection. Other examples of multiple baselines across situations can be found in the *Journal of Applied Behavior Analysis* and *Behavior Therapy.*

6. Other examples of multiple baselines across people can be found in Copeland, Brown, and Hall (1974), who demonstrate the effects of principal-implemented techniques on the behavior of pupils; Jones and Eimers (1975), who demonstrate the effects of role playing in training elementary teachers to use a classroom-management "skill package"; and Gladstone and Sherman (1975), who are concerned with the development of generalized behavior modification skills in high school students working with retarded children.

7. Although the reversal and multiple-baseline designs are used in the majority of behavior modification research projects, other research designs are occasionally utilized. One such design is the *multi-element design*. With this design, two or more conditions or treatments are studied concurrently, typically with one session per condition on each experimental day. An example of such a design is described briefly in note 3 of Chapter 19. Martin (1975b) conducted two daily sessions with each child to teach antonyms. One session utilized a brief time-out (five to ten seconds) following errors; the second session utilized a longer time-out (fifteen to twenty seconds) following errors. In this way, the author could compare the relative effects of the two time-out durations by having each time-out in effect as one element of the multi-element design. Additional discussion of this design can be found in Ulman and Sulzer-Azaroff (1975).

(Continued)

(Continued)

Another type of design is the *changing-criteria design* (see Axelrod, Hall, Weis, and Rohrer, 1974). This design attempts to demonstrate stepwise changes in the dependent variable being studied corresponding to stepwise changes in the treatment. Axelrod et al. demonstrated control over cigarette smoking with this design by reducing the daily cigarettes allowed in a stepwise fashion. If more than the allowed number of cigarettes was smoked per day, the client was required to tear up a dollar bill for each cigarette smoked over the daily allowed amount. Additional discussion of this design can be found in Craighead, Kazdin, and Mahoney (1976). Another research design, one that is common in other areas of psychology, is the *control-group design*. This design typically involves at least two groups, one that receives the treatment and one that doesn't. The average performance of the two groups is then compared according to appropriate statistical procedures. Each of the other research designs described in this chapter focuses on the behavior of individuals. Control-group designs focus on the *average* performance of groups. For this and other reasons, control-group designs have not been popular in behavior modification research. For additional discussion of a variety of control-group designs suitable for applied research, see Campbell and Stanley (1963).

8. This is not meant to imply that statistical research designs are not utilized in behavior modification research. The "odd" statistical research design can be found in the *Journal of Applied Behavior Analysis* since its inception in 1968. Moreover, there has been a recent surge in suggestions of appropriate statistical techniques for research in applied behavior analysis (for example, see Hersen and Barlow, 1976). Michael (1974) noted that the experimental and applied analyses of behavior have developed increasingly sophisticated and reliable methods of behavioral control, and have done so largely without the use of statistical research designs that characterize other areas of psychology. He argued, further, that because of this, and because the value of statistical-inference procedures for behavior modification has not been empirically demonstrated, applied behavior analysis should continue utilizing research designs such as those described in this chapter, rather than adopting statistical-inference procedures that are concurrently being recommended by some researchers.

9. Baer, Wolf, and Risley (1968) have labeled this criterion of an applied study as *technological*. A study is technological when the procedures have been specified precisely enough so that a "typically trained reader could replicate the procedure well enough to produce the same results, given only a reading of the description."

10. A part of the tradition of behavior modification has been the exceptional emphasis on objectivity and data taking, as indicated in Chapters 18 and 19 and throughout this text. Accompanying this emphasis is a strong tendency to publish procedures and results of behavioral applications. Thus, although there appear to be no consistently applied guidelines for inspecting one's data in order to judge whether or not a treatment was responsible for a particular behavioral change, the tendency of behavior modifiers to publish, and consequently to replicate the findings of others, has imposed an automatic self-correcting mechanism that ensures consistency of judgments from one behavior modifier to the next. These behavior publications can be found in a wide variety of sources, varying from behavior modification journals to more local newsletters and publication outlets.

(Continued)

(Continued)
11. The therapeutic criterion of effectiveness is discussed in more detail by Baer, Wolf, and Risley (1968), and Risley (1969).

Study Questions on Notes

1. What do we mean by *internal validity*?
2. Briefly list and describe the five classes of variables cited by Campbell and Stanley that threaten internal validity.
3. What are some of the reasons why people do behavior modification research?
4. Describe the details of the ABAB research design that Ms. Johnson might have applied in which the second A phase would have been noncontingent reinforcement rather than a reversal. Can you say why this might have been an improvement over the design she used?
5. Describe the details of an ABAB research design that Ms. Johnson might have applied in which the second A phase would have involved reinforcement of any behavior other than that reinforced during the treatment phase, rather than a reversal. Can you say why this might have been an improvement over the design she used?
6. Besides the obvious differences in setting, dependent variables, etc., between the Corte et al. study and the Hayes et al. study, there is a very subtle difference. Can you identify that subtle difference between the two studies?
7. Briefly describe, with reference to an example, the multi-element design.
8. Briefly describe, with reference to an example, the changing-criterion design.
9. Briefly describe the control-group statistical research design.
10. Why did Michael argue against the use of the control-group statistical research designs in behavior modification research?
11. What is a *technological study*?
12. What is the correction factor that tends to keep behavior modifiers from utilizing invalid criteria in analyzing the effects of their treatments? (In other words, what keeps them honest?)

PART V

Putting
It All Together

CHAPTER 21
DESIGNING A PROGRAM
to Overcome
A Behavioral Handicap

In previous chapters, we described a variety of principles and procedures for overcoming behavioral handicaps (that is, behavioral deficiencies, excesses, or inappropriatenesses). It is probably obvious by now that most behavioral applications involve combinations of principles and basic procedures. We suspect that it is also obvious that one must make a number of decisions in designing and implementing a program that are not really a part of the scientific principles and procedures themselves. Some behavior modifiers are better than others at the "art" of program design and implementation. In the next five chapters, we will present a number of guidelines that will help you become proficient at designing *specific* types of behavior programs. This chapter provides *general* guidelines that should be followed when designing *any type* of behavioral program. The client might be a retarded child, a mental-hospital patient, a normal child at home, a normal child in a classroom setting, or perhaps a normal adult. The situation is one in which you, the behavior modifier, or a mediator (parent, teacher, or some other person) would be largely responsible for carrying out the program.

Behavioral handicaps have a variety of sources, exist in a variety of different forms, and differ widely in degree of complexity and severity. The fact that a problem has been referred is not always sufficient reason for proceeding with program design and implementation. In order to decide where to begin or, indeed, if one should begin at all, it is helpful to try to answer the following questions:

1. Was the problem referred primarily for the benefit of the client?
2. Can the problem and the goal be specified such that you are dealing with a specific behavior or set of behaviors that can be counted, timed, or measured in some other way?
3. Is the problem important to the client or to others?
4. Have you eliminated the possibility that there are medical or psychological complications involved in this problem that would necessitate referring the problem to another specialist? (In other words, are you the appropriate person to deal with this problem?)
5. Is the problem one that would appear to be easily manageable?
6. If the goal is reached, might it be easily generalized and maintained?
7. Can you identify significant individuals (such as relatives, friends, and teachers) in the client's natural environment who might help record observations and manage controlling stimuli and reinforcers?
8. If there are individuals who might hinder the program, can you identify ways of minimizing their potential?
9. On the basis of your tentative answers to these eight questions, does your daily schedule and available time seem adequate for you to participate in the program?

If you answered yes to all these questions, then you might proceed. But let's consider the questions in more detail. Regarding question 1, if the problem was referred by others, then you must determine if the accomplishment of the goal will be for the benefit of the client. If the accomplishment of the goal is for the benefit of others, it should *at least* be neutral for the client. One must be very careful about one's ethics, and some referrals might simply stop here.

Concerning question 2, many referrals are very vague, subjective, and general, such as, "Johnny is hyperactive"; "My child is driving me up a wall"; "I'm really an unorganized person"; "I don't want Teddy to be so darn stubborn." If the problem is initially vague (for example, if it is merely labeled "aggression"), you must specify a component behavior(s) (for example, kicking furniture) that can be measured or assessed behaviorally. However, in such cases it is extremely important then to ask whether dealing with the component(s) will solve the general problem in the eyes of the referring agent or agencies. If it is impossible to agree with the agent on the component behaviors that define the problem, then you should probably stop here. If you do achieve agreement, it should be specified in writing, because people are sometimes forgetful and may later feel that you did not deal with the problem that they referred to you.

Concerning question 3, there are several questions that one might ask in order to evaluate the importance of the problem. If the problem is an undesirable behavior, does it usually lead to much immediate aversiveness for the client or others? Will solving the problem lead to much more positive reinforcement for the client or others? Will solving the problem be likely to stimulate other desirable behaviors, either directly or indirectly? If the answers to the above questions are yes, then it is likely that the problem is important. If the answer is no to some of these questions, then you might reconsider your involvement with that particular problem.

Concerning question 4, it should be obvious that if there is any chance that the problem has serious medical complications (for instance, excessive weight gain or loss) or serious psychological complications (for instance, the danger of suicide), the appropriate type of specialist should be consulted. You should then proceed to treat the problem if at all, only in a manner that is consistent with the recommendation of that specialist.

Concerning question 5, you might consider the following: If the major problem is to decrease an undesirable behavior, has the behavior been occurring for a short time, under narrow stimulus control, and with few instances of intermittent reinforcement? A problem having these characteristics is likely to be much easier to solve than an undesirable behavior that has been occurring for a long time, under the control of many stimulus situations, and with a history of intermittent reinforcement. Moreover, you should be able to identify desirable behaviors that can replace the undesirable behavior. If the problem is to teach a new behavior, you should assess whether or not the client has the prerequisite skills.

Concerning question 6, you should consider the following: Can the problem and the improved behavior be managed in the natural environment? If not, can a special training setting be developed that can easily be faded into the natural environment? You should also consider whether there are natural contingencies that will likely maintain the behavioral objective after it has been achieved, whether you can change the people in the natural environment so that they help maintain the desired behavior, and whether it is possible for the client to learn a self-control program (discussed in Chapter 25) so that the improved behavior will persist.

Concerning question 7, you must consider who is available to help manage a program. For example, it makes little sense to accept a referral concerned with the development of a language-training program that will require approximately an hour of concentrated effort per day, if you have only about ten minutes per day to spend on the project, if the mother and father are separated, and if the mother works full-time during the day and has four other children who occupy her attention in the evening.

Concerning question 8, it makes little sense for you to design a program if people are going to be sabotaging it all the time. When a behavior modifier first enters a ward for the retarded, the home of a family with a problem child, or the classroom of a second-grade teacher, the behavioral problems and the number and complexity of potentially disruptive influences are often mind-boggling. For obvious reasons, it is better to start simply so as to succeed in a small way, rather than to attempt too much and risk failing gloriously. A careful evaluation of the initial referral in terms of the above questions and considerations can often contribute greatly to the initial success of the behavior program.

Concerning question 9, you should only accept those referrals for which you have adequate time to carry out an effective program.

SELECTING AND IMPLEMENTING
AN ASSESSMENT PROCEDURE

Let's suppose that you have decided to proceed with designing and implementing a behavioral program for a behavioral handicap referred to you. You might then proceed through the following steps:

1. Define the behavioral handicap in precise behavioral terms, for reliable baselining.
2. Select an appropriate baseline procedure (see Chapters 18 and 19).
3. Select appropriate baseline procedures for monitoring potential side effects of the program.
4. Design recording procedures that will enable you to log the amount of time devoted to the project by the professionals working on it (such as teachers and behavior modifiers). This will help you when you do a cost-benefit analysis.
5. Ensure that the observers have received appropriate training in identifying critical aspects of the behavior, applying the recording procedures, and graphing data.
6. Select a procedure for increasing and maintaining the strength of the record-keeping behavior of the data recorders.
7. Select a procedure for insuring the reliability of the baseline observations (see Chapter 19).
8. Ensure, if appropriate, that your baseline procedure will allow you to identify the current stimulus control and maintaining consequences of the problem behavior.
9. After beginning to collect baseline data, carefully analyze those data in order to select an appropriate intervention strategy and decide when to terminate the baseline phase and begin the intervention phase.

We reviewed the guidelines for defining, recording, and graphing behaviors in Chapters 18 and 19, and we will not repeat them here. However, there are some additional considerations that a behavior modifier should review before, and during, assessment procedures.

What are the daily times the mediator(s) can schedule for this project? If, for example, a teacher has about ten minutes per day just before lunchtime to devote to the project, it is senseless to design time-sampling data sheets that require her to assess behavior throughout the day. It is also senseless to gather data on a wide variety of behaviors that the teacher will never have time to examine. Many behavior modification projects are killed before they start when the behavior modifier designs complex data-collection systems that the teacher doesn't have a hope of using.

Will others in the situation help or hinder your data collection? There is no sense in designing a baseline procedure to record the duration of a child's tantruming in a home situation if a grandmother, an aunt, a brother, or other relatives are going to give the child a candy to stop tantrums because "they can't stand seeing the poor little boy upset." On the other hand, friends and relatives can often be extremely helpful, either by directly recording data or by reminding others to do so. If the help of others is to be utilized, posting data sheets and a summary of the recording procedures where everyone involved in the project can see them (such as in a conspicuous place in the kitchen) is usually a very desirable practice.

Will the physical environment help or hinder your assessment? Let's suppose that you wish to take a baseline on the frequency and timing of a child's urinating and defecating throughout the day. If the house has many rooms and the child wanders through them, it may be difficult to immediately detect instances of the "dirty deed." Or suppose that someone wishes to take a baseline of smoking behavior, but during the baseline spends some time in the house of a friend who doesn't smoke and doesn't have ashtrays around. Obviously, this is not ideal for assessment procedures. If you wish to assess the basic self-dressing skills of a severely retarded individual by presenting clothing items with appropriate instructions, and the child's favorite TV program is blaring in the background, then your assessment is not likely to be accurate.

What is the nature of the existing behavior? Is it a behavior that occurs frequently throughout the day in many situations, such as thumb-sucking, fingernail biting, whining, or pestering? Or is it one that occurs once every two or three weeks, such as occasional but severe tantrums, stealing, or running away from home? Is the behavior one that requires a quality assessment, such as dusting furniture or washing and drying dishes? In some cases, your answers to these questions might influence you to scrap the project. For example, a problem behavior that occurs very rarely is extremely difficult to treat if you have very limited time available for the project. Certainly, the nature of the behavior will dictate the type of recording procedure to be selected, as described in Chapter 19.

How rapidly should the behavior change? Does the behavior require immediate attention because of its inherent danger (as, for example, in the case of self-abuse)? Or, is the behavior one whose immediate change would be extremely convenient for those concerned (for instance, parents who want to toilet-train their child just before going on vacation)? If the behavior is one that has been occurring for many years, and if another few days or weeks more or less won't make much difference, then you might be much more diligent in the design of the detailed data-recording system in order to reliably assess baseline levels of performance. Examples of this latter type of behavior might include smoking, excessive TV watching, and poor housecleaning.

PRELIMINARY CONSIDERATIONS OF PROGRAM DESIGN

Let us suppose that you have completed your assessment of the current level of performance concerning the problem. Before writing out the details of your program, you should review a number of preliminary design considerations:

1. Review the target behavior and the desired stimulus control.
2. Identify individuals (relatives, friends, teachers, and others) who might help manage controlling stimuli and reinforcers. Also, identify individuals who might hinder the program.
3. Review alternative combinations of principles and procedures.
   a) If you are overcoming a behavioral deficit:
      (1) think of shortcut tactics first:
         (a) instruction (oral and/or written)
         (b) situational inducement (rearrange the surroundings, move the activity to a new location, relocate people, and/or change the time of the activity)
         (c) modeling
         (d) guidance
      (2) consider whether you want to increase the frequency of an existing behavior or establish a new behavior.
      (3) decide whether shaping or chaining is more appropriate.
   b) If you are decreasing a behavioral excess:
      (1) think of shortcut tactics first:
         (a) instructions
         (b) situational inducement (relocate people, change time of activity, move activity to a new location, and/or rearrange existing surroundings)
         (c) instructions and modeling
         (d) instructions and guidance

(2) Can you try an indirect or partial solution?
    (a) Eliminate early component of a chain.
    (b) For high-frequency behaviors, introduce new stimulus control and partial elimination.
(3) Decide whether DRL, DRO, extinction, or punishment should be used.
(4) In all cases, consider alternative desirable behavior to be increased.

c) If you are changing the stimulus control of an existing behavior:
    (1) Select the controlling S^{D}s such that they:
        (a) are different from other stimuli along more than one dimension;
        (b) are encountered mainly in situations in which the desired stimulus control should occur;
        (c) evoke attending behavior;
        (d) do not evoke undesirable behavior.
    (2) Determine the current stimulus control of the desired behavior.
    (3) Decide how the current stimulus control can be faded so as to achieve the target stimulus control. (Remember that fading can occur along any dimension: color, sound, room size, number of people, appearance of people, gestures, furniture arrangements, familiarity, and so on.)

4. Review the guidelines for the effective application of the selected principles at the end of Chapters 2–12.

Let us suppose that your problem is to overcome a behavioral deficit. The behavior that you wish to occur is not now occurring. You should then ask a number of questions designed to determine if one or more of the shortcut tactics cited above might be appropriate. Do any of the significant individuals in the client's life know of any instructions that might produce the desired behavior? Is there any significant individual whose modeling of the desired behavior the client might readily imitate? Is there any easily administered physical-guidance procedure that, combined with fading, would produce the desired end product? Would the desired behavior occur if the existing surroundings were rearranged? If the activity was moved to a new location or a new time? If significant people were made more obvious or less obvious? If anything from these shortcut tactics might be identified that will produce the desired behavior, then the problem might be phrased primarily in terms of item 3c above—changing the stimulus control of the existing behavior. That is, if there are some shortcut tactics that will produce the behavior, then it should be possible to identify some dimensions along which those controlling stimuli can be faded in order to achieve the desired stimulus control and behavioral objective. If so, then you should examine very carefully the surrounding individuals and the surrounding environment in relationship to the client in order to select controlling S^{D}s according to the guidelines cited above.

If your major concern is decreasing some undesirable behavior, there are also a number of preliminary considerations that should be reviewed. These inevitably amount to various strategies for increasing some desirable alternative behavior, as opposed to concentrating on the use of extinction or punishment to decrease the undesirable behavior. A thorough review of the problem behavior in terms of these considerations (see item 3b above, and Chapter 16) will frequently lead to effective and rapid decelerating procedures such that extinction and/or punishment are not the primary focus of attention.

After an appropriate combination of principles and procedures has been selected, the guidelines for their effective application should be reviewed prior to the explicit design and implementation of a program.

STRATEGIES OF PROGRAM DESIGN AND IMPLEMENTATION

Some behavior modifiers appear to be extremely skillfull at designing effective programs "off the top of their heads"—that is, identifying the program details critical to their success and designing programs that show quick, desirable results. There is probably no set of guidelines for you to follow that will immediately turn you into that kind of behavior modifier. Nor are there any rigid sets of guidelines that you should adhere to for every program you design. Many behaviors can be managed successfully with a very minor rearrangement of existing contingencies, while others require much creativity. The following guidelines, however, will help you to design an effective program.

1. Define the target behavior and identify its desired level of occurrence (i.e., frequency) and stimulus control. Then answer these questions:
   a) Is the description precise?
   b) On what grounds was the goal chosen, and how is that in the client's best interests?
   c) Has the client been given all possible information about the goal?
   d) What are potential side effects of accomplishing the goal, for both the client and others?
   e) Do the answers to these questions suggest that you should proceed? If so, then continue, keeping in mind the answers to considerations 2, 3, and 4 in the preceding section.
2. Specify the shortcut tactics and/or positive alternatives (if any) that will be tried (see Chapters 15 and 16 and considerations 3a and 3b in the preceding section).
3. Specify the details of the behavioral-programming steps by answering these questions:
   a) What reinforcers will be used?
   b) How will shaping, fading, chaining, token training, and schedules of reinforcement be used?
   c) What are the necessary precurrent behaviors, and how will they be developed?

    d) What problems might arise, and how can they be managed?

4. Specify the details of the data-recording and graphing procedures.

5. Specify the training setting. What environmental rearrangement will be necessary in order to maximize the desired behavior, minimize errors and competing behavior, and maximize proper recording and stimulus management by the mediators (those directly carrying out the program)?

6. Specify the reinforcer system by answering the following questions:

    a) How will reinforcers be selected? (See Chapter 2.)

    b) How will reinforcer effectiveness be continually monitored and by whom?

    c) How will reinforcers be stored and dispensed, and by whom?

    d) If a token system is used, what are the details of its implementation? (See Chapter 9.)

7. Describe how you will assure generalization (Chapter 11) by:

    a) making the training and natural-environment situations similar;

    b) preparing for possible maintaining contingencies in the natural environment:

        (1) Shifting to natural reinforcers?

        (2) Reeducating the people in the natural environment?

        (3) Using intermittent schedules in the natural environment?

        (4) Teaching the client to maintain by using self-control (as discussed later in Chapter 25)?

    c) using more than one training situation.

8. Collect the necessary materials (such as reinforcers, a reinforcer-storage system, data sheets and graphs, and curriculum materials).

9. Make check lists of rules and responsibilities for all participants in the program (staff, teachers, parents, peers, students, the client, and others).

10. Specify the dates for data and program reviews, and identify those who will attend.

11. Identify some contingencies that will reinforce the behavior modifier(s) and mediators (in addition to feedback related to the data and program reviews).

12. Review the potential cost of the program as designed (cost of materials, teacher time, professional consulting time, and so forth), and judge its merit against its cost. Reprogram as necessary or desired on the basis of this review.

13. Implement the program.

    If you have followed all of these guidelines, the program is ready to go. The implementation of your program also requires a great deal of consideration. This might be done in two parts. First, you must be certain that those responsible for carrying out the program, the mediators, are emitting appropriate behavior. This might involve a detailed discussion and review session with the mediators. It may also involve some modeling and demonstration on your part, perhaps some role playing on the part of the mediators (depending on the complexity of the programs), and finally some on-the-spot feedback when the program is actually implemented, so that parents and/or teachers and/or others are encouraged to follow the program and are reinforced for doing so (see Martin, 1972). The second aspect of program implementation is introducing it to the client. It is obviously very important that the initial contact of the client with the program be highly reinforcing, so that the probability of further contacts is increased. Presumably, a well-designed program will include a great deal of specific information for introducing the programming steps (as suggested in guideline 3) to the client.

PROGRAM MAINTENANCE AND EVALUATION

Is your program having a satisfactory effect? This is not always an easy question to answer. It is also not always easy to decide, by some criterion or other, what to do if the program is not having a satisfactory effect. We suggest reviewing the following guidelines in order to assess a program that has been implemented:

1. Monitor your data to determine whether the recorded behaviors are changing in the desired direction.
2. Consult the people who must deal with the behavioral handicap, and determine if they are satisfied with the progress.
3. Consult the behavioral journals, professional behavior modifiers, or others with experience in using similar procedures on similar problems to determine if your results are reasonable in terms of the amount of behavior change during the period the program has been in effect.
4. If on the basis of guidelines 1, 2, and 3 the results are satisfactory, proceed directly to guideline 8.
5. If on the basis of guidelines 1, 2, or 3 your results are unsatisfactory, answer the following questions and make the appropriate adjustment for any yes answer:
   a) Have the reinforcers that are being used lost their appeal?
   b) Are the procedures being applied incorrectly?
   c) Is there outside interference from others that is disrupting the program?
   d) Are there any subjective variables—staff attitudes, teacher enthusiasm, and so forth—that might be affecting the program?
6. If none of the answers to these four questions are yes, check to see if additional programming steps need to be added or removed. The data may show excessive error rates, which would suggest the need for additional programming steps. Or it may show excessive rates of correct responses, which would indicate that the program is too easy and that a certain amount of boredom is occurring. Add, remove, or modify steps as necessary.
7. If the results are now satisfactory, proceed to guideline 8; otherwise, redesign the entire program.
8. Identify the schedule that will enable you to provide appropriate program maintenance until the behavioral objective is reached.
9. Following attainment of the behavioral goal, outline an appropriate arrangement for assessing performance during follow-up observations.

10. After successful follow-up observations have been obtained, do a cost-benefit analysis on the basis of all the information available.
11. Where possible and appropriate, analyze your data and communicate your specific procedures and results to other behavior modifiers and interested individuals.

Study Questions

(for examination purposes)

1. What is the purpose of this chapter, and how does this chapter relate to the other chapters in the book?

Evaluating the Referral

2. Assume that you are a professional behavior modifier. List at least four possible conditions under which you would *not* treat a behavior problem that has been referred to you. *① of med or psych origin ② If beh isn't clearly spec ③ if no one in env will help.*
3. What does a behavior modifier do when given a vague problem (such as "aggression") to work on? *Define the exact behaviors. how disruptive to clients lives, other lives*
4. How does a behavior modifier evaluate the importance of a problem?
5. How does a behavior modifier evaluate the ease with which a problem might be solved? *Narrow reinf? Intermittent reinf? Been occun for long time*
6. How does a behavior modifier evaluate the ease with which the desired behavior change might be generalized to, and maintained in, the natural environment? *Are there natural contingencies? Con person self-maintain? → Sig. others giving reinf?*

Preliminary Considerations of Program Design

7. If you are thinking of overcoming a behavioral deficit, state four shortcut tactics that you might consider. *Instruction, modelling, sit. inducem + guidance.*
8. If you are thinking of decreasing a behavioral excess, describe two indirect or partial solutions you might consider. *- change SP - stim control - eliminate early comp of chain*
9. If you are thinking of changing the stimulus control of an existing behavior, what three steps should you consider—and in what order? (Do not list the substeps.) *What is present control SP? Select a new controlling SP. Decide how existing SP can be faded + how SP faded in*

Strategies of Program Design and Implementation

10. You are now about to design a treatment program. However, after defining the target behavior and identifying its desired level of occurrence and stimulus control, what four questions should you answer before proceeding to the design? *Is the description concise? On what grounds was the goal chosen? has client been given all info about the goal? what are potential*
11. In designing a behavioral program, for what three reasons might you decide to rearrange the training environment (guideline 5). Give an example of each.

① to minimize errors + competing beh. ② to maximize proper recording + stim. management by the mediators

12. What factors should you consider in programming for generalization?

13. How can you increase the likelihood that the client's initial contact with the program will be favorable?

[handwritten: explain to him]

[handwritten left margin: (1) making the training + natural env. situations similar (2) prepare for possible maintained contingencies in the nat. env.]

Program Maintenance and Evaluation

[handwritten: if its changing in right direction]

14. After a program has been implemented, what three things should be done to determine whether it is producing satisfactory results? (guidelines 1, 2, and 3)

[handwritten left margin: (1) monitor data – see if there are satisfied (2) consult sig. others (3) bring results to pro]

15. If a program is producing satisfactory results, what two things should be done prior to successfully terminating the program? (guidelines 8 and 9)

[handwritten left margin: (1) put on sched of (2) cont. to monitor (3) outline follow up observations.]

16. Describe in detail the steps that should be followed if a program is not producing satisfactory results. (guidelines 5, 6, and 7)

[handwritten: (1) have reinf lost their appeal – is program being applied properly? Are there outside interferences of subjective interferences? (2) Do programming steps need to be added or removed? (3) may need to redesign program]

Study Exercise

(to be practiced by the reader)

Suppose that you are a behavior modifier. The mother of a "normal" four-year-old child asks for your help in designing a program to overcome the child's extreme disobedience. Construct realistic but hypothetical details of the behavior problem and take it through *all* the steps in each of the following stages of programming:

    a) deciding whether you should design a program to treat the problem
    b) selecting and implementing an assessment procedure
    c) preliminary considerations of program design
    d) strategies of program design and implementation
    e) program maintenance and evaluation

(*Note:* The problem will have to be fairly complex in order for you to take it through *all* of the steps in each of these stages.)

Self-Modification Exercise

(to be practiced by the reader)

Suppose that you are a behavior therapist and a client asks for your help in overcoming problems of extreme jealousy concerning his (or her) girlfriend (or boyfriend). Construct realistic but hypothetical details of the problem, and take it through *all* the steps in each of the following stages of programming:

    a) deciding whether you should design a program to treat the problem
    b) selecting and implementing an assessment procedure
    c) preliminary considerations of program design
    d) strategies of program design and implementation
    e) program maintenance and evaluation

(*Note:* The problem will have to be fairly complex in order for you to take it through *all* of the steps in each of these stages.)

CHAPTER 22

TOKEN ECONOMIES:
Factors to Consider When Designing One

Conditioned reinforcement was first defined and discussed in Chapter 9. In that chapter, a conditioned reinforcer was defined as a stimulus that is not originally reinforcing, but that acquires reinforcing power from being paired appropriately with other reinforcers. Some conditioned reinforcers, such as praise, are quite brief. The stimulus is gone almost as soon as it is presented. Other conditioned reinforcers, such as money, endure until they are exchanged for back-up reinforcers, such as food. Conditioned reinforcers of the latter type are called tokens.[1]

A program employing tokens with a group of individuals is called a *token economy*. The types of groups with whom token economies are used include psychotic patients in institutions and halfway houses; retarded individuals and multiple disabled individuals in institutions, day-care centers, and sheltered workshops; juvenile delinquents and "predelinquents" in correctional institutions and group homes; criminal offenders in prisons; slow learners and emotionally disturbed children in private schools and special-education classes; armed forces personnel; welfare recipients; nursery school children, normal school children and adolescents in all grades; and college students. Clearly, the ability to design and manage a token economy in a wide variety of settings is a useful skill for behavior modifiers. The purpose of this and the next two chapters is to describe the considerations involved in designing and setting up an extensive token economy for a group of individuals. Considerations for designing a more limited token system for a single individual would be similar, although less detailed.

ADVANTAGES OF A TOKEN ECONOMY

In deciding whether or not to use tokens, one has to weigh the advantages and disadvantages of doing so in specific training situations. Tokens are usually cumbersome to deal with and the time and effort spent in handling them may distract both the client and the behavior modifier from important aspects of the learning task. In addition, most natural environments do not provide tokens for desirable behavior. One of the few exceptions is working at a job, which is repaid with money. Therefore, transfer to the natural environment usually requires weaning the individual from tokens, which is not the case (at least not to the same extent) when conditioned reinforcers such as praise are the only type used.

On the other hand, there are a number of advantages to using tokens. First, tokens help to make reinforcement more effective for several reasons: (a) The most important reason is that they can be given immediately after a desirable behavior occurs, and can be cashed in at a later time. In this way, they can be used to "bridge" very long delays between the response and the back-up reinforcer. This is especially important when it is impractical or impossible to deliver the back-up reinforcer immediately after a desirable response. (b) With tokens, the amount of any given instance of reinforcement is immediately obvious and can be easily increased or decreased depending on important aspects (such as quality, effort involved, and probability) of the desired behavior. True, the magnitude of conditioned reinforcers such as praise can also be adjusted. One can whisper "good" or one can shout "GOOD." One can vary the magnitude of praise by using adjectives to form expressions such as "pretty good" and "very good." One can use different terms of approval, such as "not bad" and "excellent." One can even repeat "good, good, good, . . ." until an appropriate number have been delivered, although this could become tiring to both the praiser and the "praisee" if the desirable behavior is highly praiseworthy. Finally, one could combine all of these methods—for instance, "Good! Wow, that was really good! Great! Good for you!" But it must be conceded that the variation is not very precise, and its range is limited. Tokens, on the other hand, are precisely quantifiable (there is no question that two tokens, for example, are twice as many as one), and a large number can be quickly delivered. If the numbers to be delivered become unwieldly, denominations can be formed like those in our money system, where one dollar, for example, is worth one hundred pennies. (c) Tokens permit an individual to see his progress in a tangible form. If the program is well designed, the number of tokens an individual collects will correlate with the improvement in his behavior. To the extent that this improvement is reinforcing to the client, it will add to the reinforcing power of the tokens and thus help increase the rate of improvement. (d) The type of praise delivered can vary greatly, depending on the mood of the praiser. If the praiser is in a "bad mood," the praise delivered may not be too reinforcing, especially if the "bad mood" is reflected in a tone of voice that lacks enthusiasm. However, a token is always a token, and its value does not vary with the mood of the person delivering it.

Second, tokens provide stimuli that control the teacher's behavior more effectively. Other conditioned reinforcers, such as praise, do not provide this same stimulus control. (a) Tokens in the hands of the behavior modifier serve as an additional S^D to remind her to reinforce the student's appropriate behavior. If the behavior modifier carries a lot of tokens, their sheer weight will probably provide an S^D and perhaps even a reinforcer in the form of a lighter load for handing them out. (b) Token delivery can act as an S^D for delivering other conditioned reinforcers, such as praise. As we noted above, tokens are more likely to be given out than praise. It follows, therefore, that praise will probably be awarded more often when tokens are used than when tokens are not used (see, for example, Breyer and Allen, 1975). Staff should, of course, be instructed to praise when they award tokens, and should be reinforced for doing so. (c) Token delivery can act as an S^D for another important staff behavior: keeping data on student behavior. When the tokens are stars on a chart or marks on a piece of paper, awarding tokens and recording desirable behavior are equivalent.

Third, besides being an effective motivating device, tokens are also a teaching tool. (a) Their use can help to teach simple arithmetic and some of the behaviors involved in working for and dealing with money. In cases where these behaviors are deficient, this could be a factor that leads to a quicker transfer to the natural environment. (b) Students can learn important self-management skills if they are taught to deliver their own tokens, as described in Chapter 9.

These advantages become more important when one is dealing with groups rather than single individuals. As the number of clients per staff member increases, it becomes more difficult to administer consistent and effective programs for all clients. Tokens provide a concrete basis for managing such programs. In addition, they might make possible greater efficiency through increased specialization: different staff members can be assigned different jobs having to do with dispensing tokens for specific behaviors and awarding back-up reinforcers. Some routine jobs can even be automated, thereby freeing the staff for more complex training functions. For example, by using tokens that will operate automatic equipment, such as timing devices on TV sets, vending machines for candy, cigarettes, and other reinforcing items, and turnstiles giving access to areas where movies, dances, parties, and other reinforcing activities are available, the staff may be freed from the job of having to dispense these reinforcers.

Chapter 21 discussed the considerations involved in designing procedures for dealing with specific behavioral handicaps. The very same considerations are appropriate for designing token economies, because a token economy is a set of procedures—more complex than, but fundamentally the same as, those described in the previous chapters—for dealing with specific behavioral handicaps. The main difference is that a token economy deals simultaneously with a number of target behaviors of a number of different individuals. To avoid excessive repetition, we will not stress these considerations. Instead, we will emphasize considerations specific to designing token economies.

CONSIDERATIONS IN DESIGNING A TOKEN ECONOMY

Deciding what you need to know

Although some people have started a token economy with little background knowledge other than that provided by their own good judgment and common sense, we would not generally endorse this approach. Instead, we would recommend that the designer of a token economy first master, as a bare minimum, all of the material covered in Chapters 1–24 of this text. In addition, the designer should read some current literature describing token economies that have been used with the specific types of individuals with whom she is concerned. Since new findings are being made constantly, and old ones confirmed, expanded upon, and sometimes even found to be faulty, we strongly recommend that token-economy designers, managers, and directors never neglect the most recent issues of the behavior modification journals.

Deciding on your target behaviors

The target behaviors will be determined largely by the type of individuals with whom you are working; by the short-range and long-range objectives you wish to accomplish with those individuals; and by specific behavior problems you are encountering that interfere with the realization of those objectives. For example, if you are the classroom teacher of a bunch of rowdy first graders, your objectives will likely include teaching printing, counting, addition, subtraction, and constructive social interaction. Your target behaviors would include behaviors that are involved in these skills or prerequisite to them. Thus, at least one of your target behaviors might be "sitting quietly when the teacher gives out instructions." A more advanced target behavior might be "correctly completing problems in a workbook." If you are a college instructor, your objectives would not be substantially different. Instead of a workbook, however, you might use a list of study questions and exercises—such as those in this text—that cover all of the concepts and skills you wish to teach. Target behaviors would be acceptable responses with respect to the study questions and exercises. If you are a psychologist or psychiatrist in charge of a psychiatric ward, your objectives will probably include establishing normal types of behavior, such as self-care skills, meaningful social interaction, appropriate verbal behavior, and productive work. In our view, a behavior modifier should always strive to ensure that the behaviors he establishes in his clients will eventually prove useful to those individuals in the natural environment.

The more homogeneous the group with whom you are dealing, the easier it is to standardize the rules concerning which specific responses will be reinforced with what specific number of tokens. From this perspective, at least, it is fortunate that many groups for whom token economies are appropriate are composed of individuals who are at roughly the same behavioral level (for example, severely retarded individuals, or college students enrolled in introductory physics). However, even with very homogeneous groups, it will probably be necessary to have some specific reinforcement rules for certain individuals, according to their respective behavioral needs. This necessity for individualizing programs adds to the complexity of administering a token economy, but the resulting difficulties are not serious if a staff member is not required to handle too many radically different individual programs at once. Assigning special cases to special-treatment groups may be one efficient way in which to solve the problem of individualization in certain types of settings.

Taking baselines

Just as one does before initiating other procedures, one should obtain baseline data on the specific target behaviors before initiating a token economy. It may be that your clients are already performing at a satisfactory level and that the potential benefits to be gained from setting up a token economy do not justify the time, effort, and cost involved in doing so.

Selecting back-up reinforcers

The methods for selecting back-up reinforcers are essentially the same as the methods for selecting reinforcers (described in Chapter 2). Keep in mind, however, that a token system will generally increase the variety of practical reinforcers that you can use. Take into account the kinds of things that are generally effective reinforcers for the type of individuals (children, adults, or whomever), with whom you are working. Use the Premack Principle (see p. 22), including noting what individuals buy with their tokens after the token economy is initiated, and obtain verbal information from the clients concerning their reinforcers. For some groups of individuals, verbal information may be difficult to obtain. Ayllon and Azrin (1968b) increased the amount of this information by reinforcing spontaneous requests of mental patients (such as "Gee, I'd sure like some scrambled eggs for breakfast for a change!") as quickly as possible with the requested items. In addition, "on a regular schedule, an attendant was assigned to ask each patient on the ward whether there was anything she would like to have. This formal procedure was designed to obtain more requests than would have resulted had only the spontaneous request been made" (Ayllon and Azrin, 1968b, p. 69). Catalogues were made available to patients as a means of helping them specify items that would be reinforcing to them.

Back-up reinforcers may, of course, be as expensive as your operating budget will allow, but it is encouraging to note that many highly effective reinforcers need not be expensive at all. Before rushing out to purchase items, you should first consider using reinforcers that are already available in your system and that involve little or no added cost. Free time, the opportunity to play with toys or read books, field trips, early recess, recess itself, refreshments, and even the opportunity to help the teacher are all examples of reinforcers that are freely available in many classrooms. Access to the dining hall, eating in an attractive setting (for instance, at a table with a tablecloth, comfortable chairs, good silverware, and candles), sleeping on a comfortable bed rather than a cot, and attending picnics, parties, dances, and the movies have been used as back-up reinforcers for mental patients. The opportunity to watch television and access to the game room have been used as reinforcers for juvenile delinquents. High grades, being allowed to miss classes, and completing coursework before the end of the normal academic term appear to be effective back-up reinforcers for most college students.

In considering reinforcers that are normally available, however, one should take extreme caution to avoid the serious ethical problems that can arise. For example, several states have passed legislation affirming the rights of mental patients to have access to meals, comfortable beds, T.V., etc. Furthermore, a number of court decisions have upheld these civil rights of patients. One should, therefore, *never* plan a program which might involve depriving an individual of something that already legally and morally belongs to him.[2]

Although back-up reinforcers are available at no cost in many settings, it is generally desirable or necessary to also use back-up reinforcers that must be bought commercially. It is usually important to have as wide a variety of back-up reinforcers as possible (especially in the early stages of the program), and it is also usually important to have some, such as candies, that can be delivered and consumed very quickly. Most purchases, however, can be relatively inexpensive ones. More work can be required for more expensive items, so that they are not used up more rapidly than your budget can afford. In addition, more expensive items—for example, a bicycle—can be rented, rather than sold, for tokens. In this way, they can be reused many times as back-up reinforcers.

Although there is a great deal of flexibility in the cost of running a token program, having some extra funds is often highly desirable. Additional funds might be obtained from administrators of institutions and/or appropriate government agencies at various levels—for example, city school boards, or state, provincial, or federal departments of education or health. Inquiries to such agencies might reveal that there are special boards set up to grant funds to innovative projects in the category of your proposal. A well-thought-out, well-written proposal showing exactly how much money is needed, exactly how it is to be spent on a daily or weekly basis, exactly how the program will work (including solutions to anticipated problems) and the short-range and long-range benefits expected from the program (preferably in terms of future overall savings of money to the institution as well as increased benefits to its clients) must usually be presented to those who provide this support. Such a proposal will also prove invaluable in guiding the designer of a token economy when it is put into effect.

Donations from the general public, private organizations, civic organizations, and community-action groups are other possible sources of funds. For example, in conducting a token economy with welfare recipients, Miller and Miller (1970) were able to obtain contributions (not only of money, but also of used appliances otherwise destined for attics, basements, garages, and junkyards) from people of liberal political persuasions.

After having established what your back-up reinforcers are going to be and how you are going to obtain them, you should next consider the general method of dispensing them. A store or commissary is an essential feature of most token economies. In a small token economy, such as a classroom, the store can be quite simple—say, a box located on the teacher's desk, or another table in the room. In a larger token economy, such as a mental institution, the store would typically be much larger perhaps occupying one or more rooms. Regardless of the size of the store, a definite method of keeping records of purchases must be devised so that an adequate inventory (especially of items in high demand) can be maintained at all times, within the limit of your budget.

Selecting the type of tokens to use

Tokens can take on any of the forms that money has assumed (including clamshells, if nothing better is available). Poker chips are often used, but personal "checks," entries in a "bankbook," marks on a chart on the wall or in notebooks carried by clients, stars or stamps to be pasted in booklets—all these and numerous other possibilities may suit the needs of your particular token economy.

The main considerations in selecting the type of token are the type of clients with whom you are dealing and the setting. For very small children and severely retarded individuals in a classroom, the

FIGURE 22-1. *"Tokens should not be easily counterfeited."*

pegboard system described in Chapter 9 seems ideal. The number of tokens earned is always clearly in full view in front of the child, and the tokens are held firmly in place by the pegboard so that they are not dropped or played with excessively. Chain tokens—tokens that can be linked together—can be used for kindergarten children. For high school and college students, marks entered on some sort of record sheet are generally adequate. Even the more abstract types of tokens should be easily available for inspection by the client whenever she wishes to review the number she has earned.

In general, tokens should be attractive, lightweight, portable, durable, easy to handle, and, of course, not easily counterfeited. If automatic dispensers of back-up reinforcement are used, you should insure that your tokens will operate those devices. You should also insure that you have an adequate number of tokens for your clients. Stainback et al. (1973) suggest that one should have on hand about 100 tokens per child when starting a token economy in the classroom.

One should acquire the necessary accessories for handling and storing tokens. For example, schoolchildren may need boxes, bags, or purses in which to store the tokens they have earned. A teacher should have an apron with large pockets, a money pouch, or whatever he needs in order to always have enough to be able to dispense immediate reinforcement. The cost of tokens and token accessories should be included in the budget submitted with the proposal mentioned above.

Identifying available help

Help from other individuals may not be essential in a small token economy, such as a classroom, but it is certainly to be desired—especially in the initial stages of the program. In a large token economy, such as a large ward in a mental institution, such help is essential.

The first source of help to consider is people already assigned to work with the clients. Teacher's aides and teaching assistants are often assigned, in apprenticeship roles, to schoolteachers and college instructors, respectively. Nurse's aides are assigned to help with ward routines in institutions for mental patients, retarded people, etc. If a teacher's aide helps to teach, through helping to manage a token economy, then he is doing his job. If a nurse's aide successfully uses tokens to reinforce self-dressing behavior by the patients for whom she is responsible, then she is doing that part of her job that involves helping the patients to dress.[3]

No special educational background other than that normally required by one's present duties appears to be necessary for employees whose help in managing a token economy is to be enlisted. For example, no special criteria were used in selecting the nurse's aides who helped manage Ayllon and Azrin's (1968) token economy with mental patients. None of those workers had ever attended college, and some of them did not have high school diplomas.

Volunteers constitute another source of potential help. Civic organizations and community-action groups in your area may be able to provide such individuals. Also, by checking with friends and acquaintances you might be able to locate homemakers, retired couples, or senior citizens who are able and willing to become involved in an interesting and worthwhile project. Departments of psychology, education, social work, physiotherapy, occupational therapy, and nursing at nearby colleges and universities might also be contacted with fruitful results. Many professors would look favorably upon involving their students in the valuable learning experiences provided by helping to manage a token economy.

Behaviorally advanced individuals within the institution itself constitute yet another source of potential help. For example, conscientious fifth graders might be enlisted for part of one day per week to help manage a token economy for first graders. The small amount of time they spend outside of their classes to participate in the first graders' token economy can easily be justified on the basis of the important social skills they thereby learn—including individual initiative, responsibility, and helping to teach those who are less knowledgeable than themselves. With similar justification, college students in more advanced courses might help manage token economies for students in less advanced courses. Reasoning that teaching a particular subject matter is an excellent way to master it, a number of university departments offer courses for which a student may obtain academic credit by acting as an assistant in a lower-level course that he has previously taken and passed with a high grade. A university department that does not have such a course probably has courses (such as independent study courses) whose catalogue descriptions are broad enough to allow them to be used for this purpose.

Another important source of help, and certainly the most available, is from members of the token economy itself. After the token economy begins to function smoothly, more and more of its members will gradually become able to assume more and more responsibility in helping to achieve its goals. For example, at Achievement Place, a group home for predelinquent boys, some of the youths supervised others in carrying out routine household tasks. The supervisor, or "manager," as he was called, had the authority both to administer and remove tokens for his peers' performances. Of the several methods that were studied for selecting managers, democratic elections proved to be best in terms of the performances of the youths and their effectiveness in accomplishing their tasks (Phillips, Phillips, Wolf, and Fixsen, 1973). In another experiment at Achievement Place, some youths served with remarkable effectiveness, despite having very little adult supervision and no specific training, as therapists for others who had speech problems (Bailey, Timbers, Phillips, and Wolf, 1971). In token economies in college and university classrooms students who are among the first to master an assignment have served to evaluate the performance of other students on that assignment, and to give them immediate feedback concerning their performance. Another method used in college and university classes is to give the students a test near the beginning of the term on the first several sections of the course material. Those students who demonstrate on this test that they can readily master the course material are each put in charge of a small group of students, whom they help tutor and supervise throughout the remainder of the course.

In deciding how you are going to obtain workers who will help manage your token economy, you will need to consider how their helping behavior is to be reinforced. Ideally, your client's improvement will be a strong reinforcer for your workers. Your approval is, of course, a potential reinforcer that should be used generously. Permission to continue working in the token economy and to work at desired jobs are additional reinforcers at your disposal. For volunteers, few or no potential reinforcers other than those just listed are available. This is one reason why volunteers do not, as a rule, make the best helpers. (However, reinforcers such as coffee, lunches, and parties could be programmed for volunteers.) But for paid employees, additional potential reinforcers include wages, salary increases, preferred work shifts, extra time off the job, and preferred holiday and vacation times. For students working in your token economy in partial fulfillment of a course requirement, credit towards grades is a good potential reinforcer. For clients who help in the running of their own token economy, the most obvious reinforcers are, of course, tokens. Paying tokens for the help of your clients is usually more than justified by the many useful behaviors (independence, initiative, responsibility, helpfulness, social maturity, and so forth) that are thereby strengthened in them.

Location and Apparatus

In designing their token economy in a mental institution, Ayllon and Azrin (1968b) initially assumed that a completely closed ward would be necessary for effective control of the reinforcers that were received by the patients, for accurate recording of responses, and for adequate supervision of patients and staff. But they soon realized that many desired responses and many effective reinforcements could occur only outside of the ward. "The solution was to allow availability of all those reinforcers and responses by creating an open system in which access was regulated but never prevented" (Ayllon and Azrin, 1968b, p. 194).

For similar reasons, similar freedom of movement seems desirable in classroom token economies. Open-area classrooms are ideal, but not essential. College instructors using token economies often arrange to have their courses scheduled in lecture halls or very large classrooms originally designed for at least twice as many students as the number anticipated to attend class at any given time. Movable desks are generally preferred over stationary ones because they enable students to work easily in small groups. Classrooms with token economies are often very noisy places and give the initial impression of mass confusion to a casual observer. Surprising as it may seem, however, almost all students soon adjust quite well to the noise, so that it does not prevent them from working with great efficiency.

No special apparatus is necessary for the functioning of a token economy. Ayllon and Azrin had continuous-surveillance devices (one-way windows, TV cameras, and microphones) installed on their mental hospital ward, only to find that such devices were not only unnecessary but also impractical to utilize. Automatic devices for dispensing reinforcement, which we mentioned earlier in this chapter, were found to be somewhat useful, however. Teaching machines that automatically dispense reinforcement (including tokens) for correct responses can be purchased from commercial firms. These and other types of teaching aides can be especially useful in token economies. If you wish to use special equipment in your token economy, be sure to itemize it in the budget that you present with your proposal to the administrator of your institution and to various governmental and granting agencies.

A SUMMARY OF CONSIDERATIONS IN DESIGNING A TOKEN ECONOMY

1. Review some appropriate literature.
2. Identify your target behaviors.
   a) List some short-range and long-range objectives.
   b) Arrange your objectives in order of priority.
   c) Select those objectives that are most important for the clients and that are prerequisites to later objectives.
   d) Identify several of the above-mentioned priority objectives on which to start, emphasizing those that can be accomplished quickly.
   e) Pinpoint a number of target behaviors for each of the starting objectives.
3. Take a baseline on your target behaviors.
4. Select your back-up reinforcers.
   a) Use reinforcers that are usually effective with the population of interest.

b) Use the Premack Principle.

c) Collect verbal information from the clients concerning their reinforcers.

d) Give the clients catalogues that will help them identify reinforcers.

e) Identify a variety of "free-time" reinforcers.

f) Identify natural reinforcers that might be programmed.

g) If necessary, talk to administrators, government agencies, private organizations, civic organizations, community-action groups, and the general public in regard to funding your program.

h) Consider the ethics and legalities regarding the reinforcers on your list.

i) Design an appropriate store to keep, display, and dispense your back-up reinforcers.

5. Select the most appropriate type of token for your clients. (They should be attractive, lightweight, portable, durable, easy to handle, and not easy to counterfeit.)

6. Identify those who are available to help manage the program.

a) existing staff

b) volunteers

c) university students

d) residents of the institution

e) the members of the token economy themselves (plan to reinforce the helpers)

7. Obtain an appropriate location and necessary equipment.

a) Accept the location with the greater space.

b) Equipment and furnishings should be easily movable.

c) Rearrange the setting so that behaviors of the clients can be detected most easily and reinforced immediately.

Study Questions

(for examination purposes)

1. What is a *token economy*?

2. In what four ways do tokens help make reinforcement more effective?

3. In what three ways do tokens provide stimuli that help control the behavior of the behavior modifier?

4. In what two ways are tokens an effective teaching tool?

5. List the seven major categories of considerations in designing a token economy.

6. What do we mean by the phrase "serious ethical problem"? Relate this concept to the design of token economies.

7. What are two solutions to the problem of managing very expensive back-up reinforcers?

8. What are the sources of funds that you might explore before designing a token economy?

9. What is the store of a token economy? Give examples.

10. Suppose that you are designing tokens for individuals who can read. Design a paper token with all the necessary information on it such that the token could also be used as a source of data when collected in the store. (Hint: amount? behavior? date? time? etc.) *light, easy to carry,*

11. What six characteristics should a token have? *impossible to counterfeit, attractive, durable,*

12. How many tokens should you have for each student in the group? *uprox 100 token / child*

13. What are the three problems of token storage that must be considered? (Hint: teacher, student, store) Briefly discuss solutions to the problems.

14. People who help manage a token economy must have a Ph.D. Right? Explain. *N requires no extra knowledge*

15. Briefly identify three sources of potential volunteer help in managing a token economy. Briefly identify three sources of help from within the setting of the token economy.

16. What are the advantages in having the members of the token economy themselves function as the main source of help?

17. Briefly describe three considerations in selecting the best location for a token economy. (Hint: space? regulation? supervision?)

Study Exercises

(to be practiced by the reader)

1. For a group of individuals of your choosing (for instance, in an elementary school classroom, a university class, or a ward in an institution for the retarded), identify five plausible goals for a token economy.

2. Precisely define the target behaviors related to each of the five goals listed in the previous question.

3. Describe a number of things you might do to identify back-up reinforcers for the group of individuals you chose in study question 1.

EXTENDED DISCUSSION AND NOTES

1. Much of the material in this and the next two chapters is covered in greater detail in the following major works on token economies: Ayllon and Azrin (1968b), which deals with token economies in mental hospitals; Stainback, Payne, Stainback, and Payne (1973), which deals with token economies in elementary school classrooms; Welch and Gist (1974), which deals primarily with token economies in sheltered workshops; and Kazdin (1977), which presents a comprehensive review of token-economy research.

For more information on the use of token-economy procedures in college and high school courses, in which systems incorporating these

(Continued)

(Continued)

procedures are sometimes called Personalized System of Instruction, or the Keller Plan (after F. S. Keller, 1968), see Johnston (1975), Keller and Sherman (1974), Kulik, Kulik, and Carmichael (1974), Ryan (1974), and Sherman (1974).

2. However, Martin (1975, pp. 84–85) pointed out that legal restraints on reinforcer use need not prevent the development of a token economy. Individuals must receive nutritional meals and (in some institutions) access to common rooms equipped with a television set, but it may be possible to use such things as special desserts, being first in line for lunch, and personal television sets in bedrooms (for example, see Cohen and Filipczak, 1971) as reinforcers. Thus, with some creative arrangement, basic items can still serve as reinforcers.

3. However, check this out with your workers' union, if they have one. Quite understandably, the workers may not view the matter in this way. Moreover, their job description may very well bear them out.

Study Questions on Notes

1. What source texts might you recommend for someone interested in developing a token economy in a mental hospital? In an elementary school classroom? In a sheltered workshop?

2. Considering that laws in many areas require that individuals be given such basic items as their meals and access to recreation, how might it be possible to work such items into a token economy?

CHAPTER 23

Engineering
A **TOKEN ECONOMY**

Chapter 22 discussed the materials, tools, equipment, facilities, and personnel necessary for setting up a token economy, and how to go about obtaining them. The present chapter deals with the engineering—that is, the designing and managing—of a smoothly functioning, effective token economy.

MORE ABOUT MANAGING THE REINFORCERS

We cannot overemphasize the importance of attending closely to the contingencies related to tokens, token delivery, and token exchange for back-up reinforcers. In this section we comment further on these areas.

Making Tokens Reinforcing

A token economy exists only if its tokens are reinforcing to its members. For very sophisticated clients, simply telling them what the tokens can purchase is usually sufficient. For example, simply telling college students that 500 points earned throughout the course term may be exchanged for an A, 450 points for a B, and so on, appears (from our experience) to render a point a very strong reinforcer for most students.

Frequently, however, clients require some initial token training. Thus, in the early stages of many token economies, a client will immediately be given a back-up reinforcer in exchange for one token that he has just earned. For example, a mental patient may be denied entry to a party because he lacks the one-token entrance fee. But at the same time he will be given an immediate opportunity to acquire the necessary token by performing a simple task. For example, he may be asked to perform the simple social task of conversing for a moment with a specific staff member, who in return will immediately give him the required token.

For completely unsophisticated clients, such as very small children and severely retarded individuals, training procedures involving prompting, fading, and chaining will be necessary for establishing tokens as reinforcers and teaching the clients how to use them. Such training procedures were illustrated in Chapter 9 by the token-training method that Nickie used.

Delivering Token Reinforcement

Tokens should be delivered in a positive and conspicuous manner immediately following a desired response. Friendly smiling approval should be administered at the same time the token is given, and the client should be told (at least in the initial stages) why she is receiving the token.

The Reinforcing Agent

It is generally agreed that the role of administering reinforcement should gradually be shifted from outside help to the clients themselves. The ultimate extension of this principle would seem to be that each client would become his own reinforcing agent, his own controller of his behavior. (Methods for developing self-control are discussed in Chapter 25.) In the meantime, other agents must be given the task of administering reinforcers. Ayllon and Azrin recommend that in situations where several managers dispense tokens to several clients (such as on a hospital ward), only one person should be assigned to reinforce a particular response at a particular time. Otherwise, "no one individual can be held responsible for failure to administer the reinforcement procedure properly, since any deviation, omission, or modification is easily attributed to the behavior of some other employee'' (Ayllon and Azrin, 1968b, p. 136).

Amount of Tokens to Pay

Tokens should be paid frequently in the early stages of the token economy. Stainback et al. (1973) recommend that twenty-five to seventy-five tokens per child is not excessive on the first day of a token economy in a classroom. They recommend further that the number be gradually decreased to fifteen to thirty per day.

Ayllon and Azrin (1968) recommend that the amount of tokens paid to mental patients for performing a specific job should be based on the desirability of that job rather than on any subjective judgment of how difficult or how important it is. One of their highest paid jobs was that of giving tours to visitors to the institution, because relatively few patients were willing to sign up for this job. Another consideration is the therapeutic value of the behavior: a particular job may pay more than others if the behaviors to be strengthened by performing the job are of particular value to the clients. Yet another consideration is the amount of pay that would be given were the job to be performed by a regular employee. Recent court decisions have indicated that mental patients are not to be exploited as a cheap source of labor. It appears from these decisions, and from the ethical judgments on which they are based, that clients should be remunerated at the same rate that regular employees would be for performing the same duties.[1]

Managing the Store

The time at which back-up reinforcers may be purchased—"store time"—should be scheduled frequently at first and less frequently later on. For schoolchildren, Stainback et al. (1973) recommend that store time be held once or twice per day for the first three or four days, and then gradually decreased in frequency until it is held only once per week (Friday afternoon) by the third week of the token economy. At least initially, there should be many low-cost items that can be readily consumed (such as candy bars), so that every member of the token economy can frequently obtain immediate back-up reinforcement regardless of the number of tokens she has earned. To reduce the mass confusion in the early stages of the token economy, Stainback et al. also suggest that at first only one or two children at a time be permitted at the store. All members should, however, be able to observe other members receiving back-up reinforcement. To optimize the effectiveness of available back-up reinforcers, one should never schedule competing back-up reinforcers concurently. For example, a movie should never be held at the same time as store time.

In general, the price of each back-up reinforcer should be directly related to its cost in money. Stainback et al. give a simple method for calculating the monetary worth of a token. First, one needs to know the amount of money available (M), the number of days the token economy is to be in effect (D), the number of children in the token economy (C), and the number of tokens each child is expected to earn per day (T). Then, the amount of money each token should be worth (W) is given by this equation:

$$W = \frac{M}{D \times C \times T}$$

Besides their monetary cost, two other factors should be considered in assigning token values to back-up reinforcers. One is supply and demand. That is, charge more for items whose demand exceeds the supply, and less for items whose supply exceeds the demand. This will help to maintain an adequate supply of effective reinforcers and promote optimal utilization of the reinforcing power of each back-up reinforcer. The other factor to consider is the therapeutic value of the back-up reinforcer. A client should be charged very little for a back-up reinforcer that is beneficial to him. This will help induce him to partake of the reinforcer. For example, a client may be charged only a few tokens for admission to a party because of the important social skills that participating in this event may help to develop.

POSSIBLE PUNISHMENT CONTINGENCIES

The use of tokens provides the possibility of using fines as punishment for inappropriate behavior. This type of punishment may be preferable, from an ethical point of view, to physical punishment and time-out. As with all forms of punishment, it should be used sparingly and only for clearly defined behaviors. An appropriate goal to strive for is one in which the clients themselves manage their own punishment contingencies. One suggested approach to this goal is the issuing of tickets (similar to traffic tickets) for infractions of rules. The client receiving a ticket may then challenge the appropriateness of the fine by appealing it to the managers of the economy. As the token economy progresses, this "jury" would consist of more and more of the clients themselves. At a highly advanced stage of the economy, the members themselves would participate in formulating the rules of the economy and the fines to be imposed for infractions of the rules.

If fines are used in a token economy, it may be necessary to add training contingencies that teach clients how to accept fines in a relatively nonemotional, nonaggressive manner. Such contingencies were described by Phillips, Phillips, Fixsen, and Wolf (1973) for their token economy with predelinquent youths. In that economy, the contingencies related to fines probably taught the youths an important social skill: how to accept reprimands from law enforcers in society.

RECORDS

Up-to-date record keeping is an essential aspect of a token economy. It should therefore be built into the procedure of the economy. Records should be kept on the following:

1. *Target behaviors:* The target behaviors of each client, and the conditions under which they occur, should be objectively defined and recorded so that the effectiveness of the procedures for each client can be objectively assessed and modified if they are not producing satisfactory results.
2. *Token reinforcements:* The tokens received by each client, the behavior that was reinforced, the time and location of each reinforcement, and the name of the individual administering each reinforcement should all be recorded. These data will permit an assessment of whether each client is receiving adequate reinforcement.
3. *Back-up reinforcement:* Each item bought, the number of tokens paid for it, and the name of the client who purchased it should be recorded. The data will provide a basis for assessing whether each client is receiving adequate back-up reinforcement and for evaluating the effectiveness of different back-up reinforcers for different clients. Also, such data will indicate the extent of the demand for each back-up reinforcer, so that an adequate supply can be maintained.

SUPERVISION OF STAFF

The managers of a token economy, no less than the clients, are subject to the laws of behavior. They must receive frequent reinforcement for appropriate behavior and their inappropriate behavior must be corrected if the token economy is to function effectively. Their duties must therefore be specified clearly and they must be supervised in the performance of those duties.

Continuous supervision is generally impractical. Therefore, time sampling should be used. The director of the economy should start with frequent supervision and then gradually reduce its frequency. A desirable schedule of staff supervision and reinforcement might be a VI/LH to maintain a high, steady rate of appropriate staff performance (see Ayllon and Azrin, 1968b, p. 151).

Records of reinforcement transactions (see the previous section) are another means of ensuring that the staff members are employing appropriate reinforcement procedures. These records should therefore be evaluated frequently, and staff members should be given frequent feedback on the basis of these evaluations.

PREPARING A MANUAL

The final stage to complete before implementing the token economy is to prepare a manual or written set of rules describing exactly how the economy is to be run. This manual should explain in detail what behaviors are to be reinforced, how they are to be reinforced with tokens and back-up reinforcers, the times at which reinforcement is to be available, what data are to be recorded, how and when they are to be recorded, and the responsibilities and duties of every staff member. Each rule should be logically justified by the goals of the token economy. This ensures that the rule will be reasonable and acceptable to clients and staff. Every staff member should be given a copy of the manual, or a clear and accurate version of those portions of it pertaining to his specific duties and responsibilities. If feasible, each client should be given a clear and accurate version of those portions of the manual pertaining to him. If the client is not able to read fluently, but can understand the spoken language, he should be given a clear explanation of those portions of the manual that are relevant to him.

The manual should include definite procedures for evaluating whether the rules are being adequately followed, and procedures for ensuring that they are. Methods for arbitrating disputes concerning the rules should be included in the manual, and the participation of clients in the arbitration procedures should be provided for to the greatest extent that is practical and consistent with the goals of the token economy. Effecting such client participation is a step toward developing the behaviors involved in individual initiative, self-government, and other skills that are so highly prized in the natural environment. Toward this end, it is desirable at some stage in the token economy to have the clients themselves participate in constructively revising old rules and designing new rules for running the economy. The rules should also be capable of modification when there is evidence that a change is desirable. However, sudden and drastic changes can generate undesirable emotional behavior in clients. Moreover, clients may become disinclined to follow the rules when they are changed frequently or arbitrarily. So that rule modifications may occur in the smoothest manner possible, it seems advisable to have the manual itself specify the basis on which it will be revised. Advance notification of impending rule changes should be given to all concerned, and revisions and additions to the manual should be appropriately explained, discussed, justified, put in writing, and disseminated prior to being put into effect.

Study Questions

(for examination purposes)

[handwritten: prompting fading / chaining]

1. Describe three different types of token-training procedures for three different functioning levels of students—severely retarded individuals, a normal kindergarten class, and university students.

2. How should tokens be delivered? *[handwritten: immed., w social reinf. + explaination of why / verbal explain.]*

3. What are some of the advantages and disadvantages of assigning only one person to reinforce a particular response at a particular time in a token economy on an institutional ward? *[handwritten: Person may not always be around. / But knew who is/isn't giving tokens]*

4. Suppose that a teacher initiates a token economy and initially arranges for each child to earn up to five tokens per day. Is that likely to be a good token economy? Why or why not (based on your knowledge of behavior modification principles)? *[handwritten: No — not enough induction — need alot at first]*

5. List three considerations that might influence a designer of a token economy in deciding how many tokens to pay for a particular behavior. *[handwritten: demand / Therapeutic value]*

6. According to Stainback et al., how often should store time be held during the first few days of a token economy? How does this recommendation of Stainback et al. compare with the store-time frequency utilized by Nickie in her token economy? (See Chapter 9.) *[handwritten: often 1-2x day]*

7. Why do we recommend that all members participating in the token economy be able to observe other members receiving back-up reinforcement? *[handwritten: modeling]*

8. Let's suppose that a teacher has initiated a token economy in a classroom and has managed to get along for the first three or four weeks. But because we are in hard times, the principal has allowed a total of five dollars for purchasing back-up reinforcers during the next month (twenty school days). There are twenty-two pupils in the class, and the teacher expects each of them to earn an average of fifteen tokens per day. According to the Stainback et al. formula, how much should each token be worth?

9. Besides the monetary cost of the reinforcers, we mentioned two other factors that might be considered in assigning token values to back-up reinforcers. However, these factors might be somewhat contradictory in certain instances. Describe an example in which this would be true.

10. Considering the disadvantages of punishment discussed in Chapter 12, what are two possible bad side effects of introducing a punishment contingency of token loss (or fines) in a token economy?

11. For a token economy on a ward in an institution (for the retarded, mental patients, or juvenile delinquents), describe a plausible VI/LH schedule of staff supervision.

[handwritten margin notes, left side:]

$$W = \frac{M}{C \times D \times T}$$? supply

desireability of the x/b
therapeutic value of it "
...that would be ... to an employee.

$$W = \frac{5 \text{ dollars}}{22 \times 20 \times 15}$$

$$W = .076 \text{ cents}$$

supply + demand
therapeutic value
of the beh

may extinguish beh — make it less common

12. Why would a VI/LH schedule be preferred to an FI/LH schedule for staff supervision?

13. What should be included in a manual describing how the token economy is to be run?

EXTENDED DISCUSSION AND NOTES

1. Stolz, Wienckowski, and Brown (1975 p. 1042), state:

> Usually when patients work on hospital jobs, they are compensated at a level far below the prevailing wage or even below the minimum legal wage. This practice of employing institutionalized persons to perform productive labor associated with the maintenance of the institution without normal compensation has been called "institutionalized peonage" (Bartlett, 1964). The *Wyatt* decision [503 F. 2d 1305 (5 Cir., 1974)] specified jobs that may be performed by mentally handicapped patients and held that the patients must be compensated for that work at the prevailing minimum wage. Another recent case, *Souder v. Brennan* [367 F. Supp. 808 (D.D.C. 1973)], extended the principle of the minimum wage compensation to all institutionalized persons in nonfederal facilities for the mentally ill and mentally retarded. Although the minimum wage requirement might seem reasonable on the face of it, it could be a problem for many mental institutions and institutions for the retarded that cannot afford even the minimum wage. Under *Wyatt*, apparently the only types of work exempt from minimum wage coverage are therapeutic work unrelated to hospital functioning and tasks of a personal housekeeping nature (Wexler, 1973).

The question is certainly a difficult one from an ethical point of view, in that one may have to weigh a patient's right to a minimum wage against his right to a treatment that could facilitate his recovery. Which right should take precedence? One point that is perhaps relevant to this issue is that in society at large, wages must normally cover such basic necessities as food and housing. The question thus arises as to whether mental patients and retarded people should not also be expected to pay for these things if their earnings are at or above the level of the minimum wage. Of course, it should also be recognized that workers in society at large generally have some choice about where they live and what they eat. These and other considerations indicate that the problem of ensuring the rights of institutionalized people, including their right to effective behavioral programs, will not have an easy solution.

Study Question on Notes

Do you agree or disagree with recent court decisions concerning the amount of money mental patients should be paid for working on hospital jobs? Considering the major arguments and counterarguments, logically defend your position.

CHAPTER 24

You've Started
Your **TOKEN ECONOMY:**
Now What?

This chapter describes some problems commonly encountered in running a token economy, the problem of transferring control to the natural environment, and some additional ethical considerations.

TYPICAL PROBLEMS AND SOLUTIONS

In the design of a token economy, as with any new, complex procedure, it is wise to plan for potential problems. Let's consider some of the problems that are commonly encountered, and some suggested solutions.

Confusion

During the first few days after their initiation, most token economies probably resemble mass confusion. We do not know of any way to completely avoid this problem. All we can suggest is that adequate planning, including a clear, adequately explained, and workable set of rules, will limit the amount and duration of this confusion. Within a few days, clients and staff should have adjusted fairly well to the routine of the token economy. If they have not, it may be necessary to redesign the system.

Shortage of Staff

It may be that there are not enough staff members available to manage an extensive token economy, and that it is not feasible to utilize the clients themselves as managers. For example, in an elementary school classroom with one teacher and no available help, it simply may not be feasible for that teacher to perform all the duties a token economy necessitates — such as counting specific behaviors and handing out tokens — and at the same time continuing his other teaching duties. Stainback et al. (1973) suggest that if it is not feasible to distribute at least twenty-five tokens per day to each child, then it is best not to attempt a token economy. However, if a teacher does not have the necessary time to follow Steinback et al.'s suggestion, she might consider a partial token economy, which deals only with a manageable number of behaviors in a manageable number of clients. If desirable, such a token economy could then be gradually extended to more clients and more behaviors.

Attempts to Beat the System

Initially, a number of clients will attempt to beat the system by demanding tokens they have not earned or by demanding back-up reinforcers for which they do not have enough tokens. After ensuring that the clients understand the rules of the token economy, the managers should then extinguish undesirable requests by ignoring them. If the extinction procedure is applied consistently, the behavior will, hopefully, soon subside.

Unauthorized Acquisition of Tokens

In many token systems, it is possible that clients will obtain tokens without earning them. For example, tokens may be obtained from other clients by stealing, gambling, borrowing, selling goods, or favors. One solution to this problem is to individualize the tokens that each client is awarded, so that the tokens cannot be spent by anyone else. Tokens with different colors or other markings (including the client's name) may be used for this purpose.

Token individualization adds extra work and inconvenience to managing a token economy. It is often wise, therefore, to wait until inappropriate token acquisition has proved to be a problem that cannot be handled adequately and more conveniently in other ways. Stealing may quickly drop to a negligible level: many clients, after having lost a number of tokens, will learn to protect them. Or it may be sufficient simply to confiscate unauthorized tokens so that there is no advantage to be gained from them. The number of unauthorized tokens a client has acquired can be determined by comparing the record of the number of tokens he has earned with the record of the number he attempts to spend.

Playing with Tokens

Initially, children will play with their tokens and this will seem undesirable because of the distraction it produces. According to Stainback et al., this behavior usually disappears soon. It should be tolerated in the early stages of the program because it helps (presumably) to firmly establish the tokens as reinforcers (on the reasoning that the more physical stimulation a conditioned reinforcer provides, the more effectively it mediates the time—or "bridges the gap"—between the reinforced behavior and the back-up reinforcer). Should the behavior continue in strength beyond the initial stages, however, it may be a good idea to eliminate it by introducing an appropriate token-storage system.

Job-Selection Problems

When a client can sign up for various jobs that earn tokens, she may select a job at which there is little chance that she will work conscientiously. If the job is an important one that requires more than the normal amount of responsibility, and if it is difficult to get a substitute, this problem could be of some concern. Ayllon and Azrin (1968b) solved the problem (or at least reduced its magnitude) by charging tokens for the opportunity to work at such jobs. This ensured that patients had to have already demonstrated some degree of responsibility (by earning tokens in other ways) prior to working at a job requiring more responsible behavior.

Sometimes the demand to perform a particular job is greater than the number of positions available for that job. Again, one solution to this problem is to charge tokens for the opportunity to perform that job. A fixed price may be set for the job, but it is also possible to hold an auction in which the job is given to the highest bidder. Of course, the pay scale for jobs can also be adjusted according to supply and demand, as we pointed out above.

Failure to Purchase Back-up Reinforcers

A particular back-up reinforcer may never be bought because the clients are unable to save enough tokens for its purchase. The law of supply and demand would seem to suggest that the price of such a reinforcer be reduced. The director of the economy may not, however, be inclined to do this if the item's cash value is quite high. A satisfactory alternative might be to sell the item in pieces, which would be assembled as they are bought. Stainback et al. gave the example of a bicycle whose parts were bought piecemeal and assembled in a classroom over a lengthy period of time. By being able to save enough tokens for the parts but not for the whole bicycle, the student who did this provided an interesting example of "the sum of the parts being greater (in reinforcement value) than the whole." It is likely that she also learned a number of useful mechanical skills in the process. Another problem is that particular back-up reinforcers may not be purchased even though clients have ample tokens to buy them. One solution to this problem is reinforcer sampling (see Chapter 4, note 1).

Tendencies to Reinforce Nontherapeutic Activities

A great hazard of powerful contingencies of reinforcement—such as those that exist in effective token economies—is that they may be used to generate and maintain behaviors that are not beneficial to the clients subjected to such contingencies.[1] For example, Stainback et al. pointed out the tendency of teachers to assign "busy-work"—nonproductive exercises whose sole purpose appears to be to keep pupils engaged at some sort of academic task—after the students in a token economy have thoroughly learned the material normally assigned to their age group. Because students in a token economy often learn their lessons so well and so quickly, it is frequently difficult to keep them productively occupied with academic work. Part of the solution to this problem, as Stainback et al. see it, is for teachers to recognize that nonacademic activities are also acceptable. Students who have satisfactorily learned their coursework should be permitted to engage in other activities, such as playing or reading for their own pleasure.

Similarly, Ayllon and Azrin noted the tendency of staff members to want to keep mental patients working at jobs long after the jobs ceased to benefit the patients. Here, the tendency stemmed not from a desire to keep the patients busy, but rather from the fact that the patients were genuinely helping the staff members perform their duties. To offset this problem, Ayllon and Azrin instituted a job rotation rule: "A patient should not be allowed to hold the same job without interruption for more than a week at a time." In this way, patients could learn a number of different skills and participate with a greater variety of social interactions. The staff readily accepted this rule when its rationale was clearly explained to them beforehand.

Moreover, although having to train new help each week was somewhat inconvenient to the staff at first, they ultimately benefited by
the large pool of skilled helpers thereby generated.

TRANSFERRING BEHAVIOR TO THE
NATURAL ENVIRONMENT

Token economies are sometimes regarded as ways to manage problem behavior in institutional settings. They do serve this function,
but it would be unfortunate if this observation led us to neglect their
more important function of helping clients adjust to the natural environment beyond the institution. Because social reinforcement, not tokens, prevails in the natural environment, a token economy should
be designed such that social reinforcement gradually replaces token
reinforcement.[2] There appear to be two general ways of fading tokens. One is to gradually eliminate them. The second is to gradually
decrease their value. The first alternative can be accomplished by
gradually making the schedule of token delivery more and more intermittent, by gradually decreasing the number of behaviors that earn
tokens, or by gradually increasing the delay between the target behavior and token delivery. The second alternative can be accomplished by gradually decreasing the amount of back-up reinforcement
that a given number of tokens can purchase, or by gradually increasing the delay between token acquisition and the purchase of back-up
reinforcers. At present, we cannot say which method or combination
of methods produces the best results. In addition, all of the considerations involved in programming generalization (discussed in Chapter 11) should be reviewed.

Gradually transferring control to the clients themselves so that
they plan and administer their own reinforcements is another step in
preparing clients for the natural environment. An individual who can
evaluate his own behavior, rationally decide what changes need to be
made in it, and effectively program for these changes is clearly in a
good position to cope with almost any environment in which he
finds himself. Methods for establishing these skills are discussed in
Chapter 25.

ETHICAL CONSIDERATIONS

Token economies involve the systematic application of behavior
modification techniques on a relatively large scale. The possibilities
of abusing the techniques, even unintentionally, are thereby magni-
fied. Precautions should be taken to avoid such abuse. One such precaution is to make the system completely open to public scrutiny.

Visits by outsiders, including newspaper reporters and other repre-sentatives of the media, should be encouraged. Visitors should be al-lowed free access to the manual of rules governing the token econ-omy. Their questions and criticisms should be answered satisfactorily by the administrators of the economy. Visitors should be also per-mitted to talk to the clients of the economy and obtain their impres-sions of it. Ayllon and Azrin even adopted the commendable policy of giving visitors tours conducted by the clients themselves. An open-door policy of this sort will help not only to ensure high ethical standards, but also to allay the fears and suspicions about behavior modification that too often exist in the minds of the public in general and the relatives of the clients in particular.

Another precaution is to clearly inform the clients of their legal and moral rights. Furthermore, clients and managers should be in-structed to report any infringements of those rights. Such reports, as well as other complaints and criticisms, should be listened to and quickly acted upon in a morally responsible fashion.

The ends of a token economy and the suitability to those ends of the means for obtaining them constitute the "acid test" of the eth-ics of the token economy. Thus, the ethics of a token economy will ultimately be judged on the basis of how effectively and humanely the transfer to the natural environment is carried out. (For additional discussion of ethical issues concerned with behavior modification, see Chapter 29.)

Study Questions

(for examination purposes)

1. The problem of confusion during the first few days of a token economy might be viewed as a behavior modification problem. Outline the steps that you might take (in a general sense) to solve this problem.
2. Discuss how shortage of staff to manage a token economy can be han-dled.
3. Suppose that the attempts to beat the system by one particular student in a token economy do not seem to extinguish. Suppose that you have de-cided that this is a behavioral problem that must be solved. Briefly out-line the "shortcut" strategies that you might follow to eliminate this be-havior (see Chapter 16).
4. How did Nickie handle the problem of children playing with the tokens? (See Chapter 9, p. 135) What do Stainback et al. recommend concerning this, and why?

5. Allowing clients to select jobs at which they would like to work, or perhaps requiring them to pay some of their hard-earned tokens for the opportunity to perform certain jobs (and hence earn even more tokens) is a plausible approach for highly verbal patients. True or False? Discuss.

6. What is a possible solution for the management of very expensive items for which the clients seem unable to save enough tokens to purchase? Give an example.

7. Ayllon and Azrin instituted a job-rotation procedure to ensure that mental patients would not be kept at jobs long after the jobs ceased to benefit the patients. Outline a rule, or set of rules, that teachers might follow to ensure that students are not kept doing "busywork" or classroom exercises long after the exercises have benefited the students.

8. What are the two general methods of fading tokens when transferring behavior to the natural environment? Explain the different ways these methods can be carried out.

9. If one decides to gradually decrease the number of behaviors that earn tokens, what general guidelines might be followed in deciding which behaviors no longer require token reinforcement? That is, where do you start, and which behaviors do you start on?

10. What precautions should you take to help ensure high ethical standards for your token economy?

EXTENDED DISCUSSION AND NOTES

1. Holland (1974, p. 201) expressed this concern as follows:

> The token economy in ... many ... instances follows an elitist system, and, at least as a secondary effect, seems to legitimize that form. Moreover, while I know those conducting such token economies on hospital wards and in prisons, etc. will take issue with me, the decisions as to what behaviors should be reinforced very often seem to depend upon the creation of the kind of ward behavior pleasing to hospital personnel—to "Big Nurse" for those fans of Kesey's novel, *One Flew Over the Cuckoo's Nest*. I will admit here some of my own ambiguity and uncertainty. Well-made beds, well-groomed patients, patients sweeping the floor and keeping neat may be valuable behaviors to the patients themselves, but it is clear they reflect most definitely what Big Nurse desires. It is questionable whether nurses who walk around handing out tokens do much to establish personal self-esteem in the patient.

Speaking in a similar vein, Krasner (1976, p. 635) stated:

> My own experience with token economies continued by developing a program involving systematic economic planning in a state hospital (Winkler & Krasner, 1971). One observation that Winkler and I made was that to the extent that we were successful in developing a token economy program on a hospital ward, we were helping maintain a social institution, the mental hospital, that in its current form, was no longer desirable in our society. We decided that based on our own value system, we would not develop further token economy programs in mental hospitals.

2. Levine and Fasnacht (1974) argued that the use of tokens to reinforce a behavior may impede the generalization of that behavior to the

(Continued)

natural environment. Their argument is based mainly on the results of experiments purporting to show that "extrinsic" reward for performing a task tends to undermine "intrinsic" interest in the task. In these experiments, college students or children were given money or prizes for solving puzzles, drawing, or playing a game. A control group of comparable individuals was instructed to engage in the same activities, but was not rewarded for doing so. Following this, when both groups were given the opportunity to engage in the specified activities without being rewarded, it was found that on the average those individuals who had previously been rewarded spent less time engaging in the activities (and also ranked them as being less enjoyable) than those individuals who had not previously been rewarded.

These experiments, however, do not seem to be very relevant to the way in which competent behavior modifiers use tokens. For one thing, as two critics of Levine and Fasnacht's article (Bornstein and Hamilton, 1975) pointed out, behavior modifiers do not typically make tokens contingent upon desirable behaviors that already occur at a high rate. Moreover, as two other critics (Reiss and Sushinsky, 1975) pointed out, the results can very likely be explained in terms of behavioral processes that should not be a serious obstacle in programming generalization from a token economy to the natural environment. Specifically, it is known that if a period of high reinforcement precedes a period of low reinforcement, responding during the period of low reinforcement will tend to be less than it would have been if the period of high reinforcement had not occurred. However, this effect—which appears to be related to the behavioral-contrast effect described in note 1 of Chapter 12—is quite temporary. As the period of low reinforcement continues, responding soon returns to the level it would have been at if the period of high reinforcement had not occurred. Thus, if a token economy is designed appropriately, such that social reinforcement gradually replaces token reinforcement, the social reinforcement should then be at least as effective as it would have been if tokens had not been used.

A third consideration is that there is inconsistent evidence concerning intrinsic and extrinsic reinforcement (see the discussion of the Feingold and Mahoney study in note 4 of Chapter 3).

Study Questions on Notes

1. Briefly discuss why it might not be ethical to establish token economies in mental hospitals. Briefly discuss possible ways in which these ethical problems might be solved.

2. Discuss whether using tokens to reinforce behavior can impede the generalization of that behavior to the natural environment.

CHAPTER 25

Helping an Individual to Acquire
SELF CONTROL

"If you had more will power, you could get rid of that bad habit." "If you had more will power you could improve yourself and get some better habits." If you are like most people, you have probably heard such advice many times. It is also likely that you have seldom appreciated it. And for good reason: it is usually not very helpful advice because the person offering it almost always neglects to tell you how you can get more of this so-called will power.

Behavior, as this book has constantly emphasized, is controlled by the environment—not by inner forces such as "will power." So your bad habits exist, not because you lack will power, but because they are supported by "bad" contingencies of reinforcement in your environment. Likewise, your good habits are not as strong as you would like because they are not controlled strongly enough by "good" contingencies of reinforcement.

What others might call will power is referred to by behavior modifiers as techniques of *self-control* (or *self-management*).[1] These techniques do not differ in principle from behavior modification procedures described in previous chapters. They involve defining a problem in behavioral terms, taking data on the problem, introducing a treatment program based on behavior principles, evaluating the effectiveness of the program, and appropriately changing the program if the data show that it is not producing satisfactory results. Self-control procedures differ from other procedures, however, in that the client assumes the major responsibility for carrying out the program, including arranging his own contingencies of reinforcement. This presents certain difficulties that are unique to self-control programs. The most troublesome of these difficulties is called *short-circuiting of contingencies.* This process can be easily seen in two simple examples:

1. Suppose you want to study more efficiently because this behavior will eventually bring you a great deal of reinforcement—such as getting the kind of job you want, being able to talk intelligently with other people, and understanding events in the world around you. But this reinforcement is far in the future. It is therefore very difficult for it to compete with the weaker but more immediate reinforcement of even a moderately entertaining TV program. It might seem logical to use your TV watching to reinforce your studying behavior. On the other hand, studying does not turn on the TV; flicking the switch on the TV set does. There is a good chance, therefore, that the reinforcement contingency will be short-circuited, in the sense that the reinforcer will be consumed without the desired behavior having occurred, as illustrated in Figure 25–3, pg. 377.

2. Suppose that you want to decrease your food intake because you know overeating can cause health problems and make you less attractive physically to other people. But these punishers are long delayed. Therefore, they have a hard time competing with the reinforcement residing in that piece of pie sitting in front of you. You might decide to bring some more immediate punishment to bear on the problem by pinching yourself each time you take a bite of pie. But, the pain that you feel punishes the skin squeezing (pinching) as much as it punishes pie eating. There is a good chance, therefore, that the punishment contingency will be short-circuited, in the sense that the undesirable behavior will occur and the punisher will not follow it. The pinching disappears while you, feeling perhaps only a little guilty, continue to enjoy the pie.

Despite the problem of short–circuiting, research indicates that self-control can be developed. This is fortunate for people with very severe behavioral handicaps, because it means that many of them can progressively assume greater responsibility for their own behavior, and thereby lead more normal lives. It is also fortunate for those who are already behaviorally well developed (such as the "average" person), because they can learn to manage their own behavior problems without having to depend on others to do it for them.

The difficulties and advantages of self-control procedures relative to procedures considered previously in this book can be clarified if we discuss them under five general headings: *identifying the prob-*

lem, baselining the problem, designing a self-modification program, con-
tracting to ensure the management of the program, and *circumventing the*
therapist.

IDENTIFYING THE PROBLEM

Unlike most of the cases considered previously in this book, the can-
didate for a self-control program realizes that he has a problem and
has probably attempted to solve it himself. Failing in that effort, he
has, let us assume, come to a behavior modifier or behavior therapist
for help. The therapist does not attempt to solve the problem directly,
but acts more as a consultant, providing the client with the procedures he must undertake in order to solve his problem.[2] At each
step in the treatment, the therapist should not just give advice; she
should also clearly explain to the client the reasons for that advice,
and should proceed only with the client's informed consent. This is
desirable (1) because of the consultant-client nature of their relationship, (2) because the client might carry out the procedures more accurately if he understands and accepts their rational, and (3) because
this approach should help the client learn how to solve other behavior problems he may encounter.

The therapist helps the client to define the problem in behavioral terms, shows him how to take data on the problem, recom-
mends a treatment program, and helps the client evaluate the outcome of the program. In this section, we will concentrate on defining
the problem and data collection.

The first step is to define the problem behaviorally. This may
require one or more very intensive interviews. The client himself
may not have a clear idea of what the problem is. Or he may be
ashamed to acknowledge the problem and start out by describing a
trivial or nonexistent problem. The therapist must therefore take
pains to assure the client that he is not judging him. All behavior is
lawful. Therefore, if the client has an undesirable behavior pattern, it
is only because he—like everyone else—is following natural laws.
These laws cannot be changed, but the client can use them to change
his own behavior. Quite often, it is useful to help the client fill out a
factual-information sheet. This approach helps the client relax and
provides information that may be useful in program design. A
sample of such a sheet is shown in Figure 25-1.

Gradually, the client will begin to talk more and more about
what is really bothering him. Specification of the problem can then
begin. This is usually not too difficult if the problem involves a behavior that is easily observed and measured, such as excessive smoking. On the other hand, it may be very difficult to pinpoint the exact
behaviors involved in a problem such as depression or anxiety. An

FIGURE 25-1. *A factual-information sheet (containing questions for a therapist to ask of a client).**

Client's name _____   Married or single _____
Address _____   Date of last medical exam _____
Telephone (home) _____ (work) _____   Physical handicaps? _____
Age _____

Did someone refer you to me? _____
If yes, (a) Who? _____
       (b) Why did they refer me and not someone else? _____

If no, why me and not someone else? _____

Children _____ Male _____ Female _____ Ages _____
Do they live at home? _____
Occupation of client _____
Occupation of spouse _____
How long have you been in current location? _____
     and before here? _____
Any relatives here? _____
     elsewhere? _____
Hobbies or involvement other than work? _____
     How often? _____
Is anyone else in the family interested in your well-being? _____
Are any friends interested in your well-being? _____
What are your favorite pastimes? _____

What is the best time of the day for you, and why? _____

What is the worst time of the day for you, and why? _____

In your own words, why are you here? _____
_____
_____
_____
_____

*This information sheet was described in an unpublished paper by Lyle Wray and Larry Williams, University of Manitoba, 1975.

approach used by Schwartz and Goldiamond (1975) is to tell the client to imagine that Martians have landed on earth and are doing an observational study of its inhabitants. One of these Martians has been assigned to observe the client. Now these Martians, of course, know nothing about human feelings. They can observe only behavior. The client, having imagined this, is then asked, What will your Martian observe now, when you are still suffering from your problem, and what will he observe later, when the problem has been solved? By this or some similar means, the client is induced to specify both the problem and the treatment goal in behavioral terms. For example, a depressed person might say that his Martian would see him sitting alone in his room staring at the walls a great deal before treatment, and spending more time reading novels and interacting with other people after treatment. If it is difficult for you to encourage the client to clearly identify the problem, you might prepare a specific set of questions designed to identify the problem and its controlling variables. For example, the questions in Figure 25-2 are designed to help identify the details when the problem is to get rid of an undesirable behavior that is currently occurring.

FIGURE 25-2. *Some questions to ask a client in order to help identify a problem and its controlling variables*

SPECIFYING THE PROBLEM

1. In your own words, could you describe what your problem seems to be?
2. Could you write out at least three examples of everyday situations in which this behavior occurs or does not occur.
3. Are there other behaviors that you engage in that seem to be related to the problem behavior? E.g., if your problem is extreme nervousness when asking for dates, do you bite your nails and stammer at the same time?
4. Do you have any emotional reactions when your problem behavior is occurring? E.g., does you heart beat faster? Do you feel weak? Angry? Frustrated? Try to state any emotional reactions in terms of the behaviors involved. E.g., if you feel angry, you may feel your palms sweating and your heart beating faster.
5. Can you state the problem in positive terms? E.g., if the problem behavior is nail biting when studying then rather than saying "I want to stop nail biting when I study," you could say "I want to keep my hands clasped on the desk or at my sides when I am studying."
6. Now that your behavior is positively stated ("I want to engage in a particular behavior in a particular situation"), could you specify a chain of events that could possibly lead to the accomplishment of that behavior? E.g., "I go to the study area. I sit at my desk. I get all my material ready (open books, take out pen, etc.). I clasp my hands on the desk and separate them only to turn pages or to write."
7. Now that you have had time to think about your problem behavior, could you be more precise in specifying your problem in terms of the actual behaviors that are occurring? E.g., feeling sorry for yourself might be broken down into thinking about a girl who turned you down for a date, talking to a specific friend about how "broke" you are, and looking in store windows at all the things you would like but can't afford.
8. How often does the problem behavior occur?

WHEN DOES THE BEHAVIOR OCCUR?

1. When does your problem behavior typically occur? E.g., what time of day? What day of the week? What time of the month?
2. What other activities are you typically engaging in when your problem behavior does or does not occur? Can you be exact?
3. Can you specify at least three recent situations when your problem behavior typically would have occurred but did not? What behavior were you engaging in at this time?

FIGURE 25-2 (continued)

WHERE DOES THE BEHAVIOR OCCUR?

1. Where does your problem behavior occur? Try to specify at least five typical situations. E.g., at home? (Any particular room?) At work (At your desk? In someone else's office?) In your car? At social events?
2. Do you engage in the behavior by yourself? With one person? In groups? If others are present, what type of people are they? Family? Friends? Acquaintances? Enemies? etc.
3. In which situations does your problem behavior not occur? E.g., what are the physical surroundings? What people are present?
4. Why do you think you do not engage in the behavior in the situations you mentioned in Question 3? That is, what alternative behavior are you engaging in that is preventing you from engaging in your problem behavior?

WHAT ARE THE TYPICAL CONSEQUENCES OF THE BEHAVIOR?

1. Does the behavior change the environment? In what way?
2. Is there another behavior you always emit just before or after the problem behavior?
3. Is what happens after the behavior due *only* to the behavior?
4. Do you emit the behavior to cause something you like?
5. Do you emit the behavior to prevent something you don't like?
6. Is the consequence a physiological event—that is a sense or a feeling?
7. Is the consequence a social event—that is, other people's behavior?
8. Does someone else you know emit this behavior?
9. Do people "hassle" you for emitting this behavior?
10. Do people encourage or condone your behavior?

The client may have more than one problem. Or what he perceives as one problem may be easier to deal with if it is subdivided into several smaller problems. In such cases, the therapist should treat only one of these problems or at most a few of them. Priority should, of course, be given to problems that appear to be truly urgent. Otherwise, the easier problems should be dealt with as soon as possible because the quick resolution of one or two problems will reinforce the client's efforts to control his own behavior.

BASELINING THE PROBLEM

Having reached a tentative decision on the problem behavior, the therapist will encourage the client to take data on the occurrence of the problem—for instance, when, where, and how often it occurs. There are a number of techniques that the therapist might recommend for increasing the strength of record keeping. For example, if the problem behavior is smoking, the client should be instructed to record each cigarette before it is smoked, so that the behavior will reinforce recording it. The client might set up external reinforcers that are controlled by other people. For example, he may give control of his spending money to someone (for example, his spouse) who can monitor his behavior continuously for extended periods of time and who could return his money contingent upon his consistent data taking. The client might also get other people to reinforce his recording behavior by (1) telling his friends about his self-modification project; (2) keeping his recording chart or graph in an obvious place in order to increase the likelihood of feedback from friends; and (3) keeping his friends informed on how the project and results are progressing. Contingencies mediated by other people are an important safeguard against the short-circuiting processes described at the beginning of this chapter.

The client should also streamline the recording system so that the behavior counted is as simple as possible and the data sheets are portable and appropriate to all situations in which the behavior occurs. Additionally, the recording chart or graph should be designed so that behavior improvements will be conspicuous. If the client is using graph paper and wants to plot the number of cigarettes smoked per day, he should have a scale that will use all of the vertical axis rather than just half of it. Finally, the client should be encouraged to provide S^Ds for recording. For example, if he is to record his weight each morning, he might post his weight chart on the mirror he uses for shaving.

The therapist meets with the client periodically (for instance, one hour per week) and goes over the data with him. Before the treatment procedure is initiated, the data provide a baseline indicating the magnitude of the problem and its controlling conditions. Both types of information help to define the problem further and indicate whether it is really serious enough to merit treatment. (Sometimes, simply recording the behavior results in its improvement. See pp. 273–6.) If the problem does not require treatment, the therapist should so advise the client. The preliminary data also help indicate what treatment procedure, if any, should be used. After treatment begins, the client continues to take data for the purpose of evaluating the effectiveness of the treatment (the reasons for taking data discussed in Chapter 18 apply equally well to the area of self-control).

Usually, during the problem-defining and baseline stages the therapist determines whether other people besides the client are significantly involved in the problem (these people are referred to as *significant others*). For example, frequent arguing within a family indirectly involves more than one person contributing to and suffering from the problem. Even a problem that seems at first glance to have only one victim probably involves other people directly. For example, a wife may wish to help her husband give up smoking because she is concerned about his health and because she is concerned about the effect the smoke is having on the health of the rest of the family. It is usually desirable to involve significant others in a client's treatment if—but *only if*—they are willing to be involved. If they are not willing to cooperate in the treatment, the therapist treats the problem as being the client's. This makes good ethical sense, because if the significant others have not chosen to be the therapist's clients, she has no business trying to treat them. It also makes good practical sense because of the danger inherent in basing a program on cooperation that is not likely to be available.

However, during the treatment a client's changed behavior may indirectly change the behavior of significant others, even though they themselves have not contracted for treatment. Consider the following hypothetical case. A woman comes to a behavior modifier for treatment of what she calls "depression." The initial interview and baseline data indicate that the depression stems from (or is perhaps a label for) overwork and insufficient reinforcement. Her two adult sons, both living at home, refuse to do any household chores. Instead, they expect her to do all of the work, including cleaning up after them. Moreover, they will not consider participating in a treatment program. Analysis of the preliminary data indicates that the problem is due, at least in part, to the client being unable to refuse excessive demands on her time and labor. If the client agrees with this assessment, a self-control program might then be initiated whereby the client learns to be more assertive when her sons make demands. This might lead, indirectly, to her withholding reinforcement for excessive demands and reinforcing more desirable forms of behavior by her sons. If the program is successful, it might result in a desirable change in their behavior, even though they are not directly involved in the program.

During the baseline, the client should be taught to take a close look at the situations that exist just before the undesirable behavior occurs, as well as the consequences of undesirable behavior. From this simple exercise generally comes suggestions for successful programming strategies. For example, a problem frequently reported by the university students is that they get tired fairly quickly when they are studying at home.* Such students usually report a typical pattern. The student sits down wherever she studies and begins reading or working at the material. After a certain period of time, she begins to feel drowsy and decides to take a break. The break usually consists of making a cup of coffee and something to eat, watching a few minutes of TV, or phoning a friend. After the break (which is sometimes very extended), the student returns to work. But after a relatively short period of time, she again becomes drowsy and the pattern repeats itself. Now let's examine the situation. What are the immediate positive

*This discussion is based on a paper by Martin (1975ª) and is closely paraphrased by permission of the publisher.

consequences of the initial desirable behavior of working in an alert fashion? None. Rather, the individual simply continues working until she starts to feel drowsy. On the other hand, what are the consequences of the individual feeling drowsy? Obviously, a very reinforcing break period. In other words, the student is following the worst possible course of action. Feeling drowsy in a study situation is being highly reinforced by taking a break, whereas working effectively does not lead to immediate reinforcing consequences. Once realized, an effective strategy for the individual is to take a break earlier than usual. If a student can study normally for fifteen minutes without feeling drowsy, then at about the thirteen-minute mark, *while still working effectively,* she should take a brief break. Over a period of time, the duration of the effective studying (rather than feeling drowsy) is increased in the presence of the cues appropriate to proper study behavior. In general, then, while taking a baseline the individual should be on the alert for immediate consequences that might be maintaining the undesirable behavior to be eliminated, as well as the immediate consequences (or lack of them) of the behavior that the individual wishes to develop.

DESIGNING THE SELF-MODIFICATION PROGRAM

The therapist next helps the client to design the self-control program. Sometimes a program will consist of a simple rearrangement of particular consequences of specific behaviors, as in the example of managing fatigue and increasing alertness while studying. Another example of rearranging consequences was reported by a Canadian "Mountie," whom we'll call George, who wanted to quit smoking. His girlfriend, Sally, while taking a course from one of the authors, had noted that in addition to the smoke itself other reinforcers were usually associated with smoking. For example, George smoked while having coffee, while drinking beer in the pub, while talking to friends, and while talking on the phone. Following some strong prompts from Sally, George decided that his initial attempt to control smoking would be to simply rearrange the consequences of smoking. Previously, he had tried unsuccessfully to quit "cold turkey." He had been unable to control his cigarette urges in such situations as described above. Therefore, to help avoid the problem of short-circuiting, George and Sally agreed that he could smoke whenever he felt like it (rather than trying to quit outright or gradually cut down), but he had to do so by himself in the bathroom. Thus, if he was in the house and wanted a cigarette he could have one, but he had to go to the bathroom and couldn't come out until he had finished smoking. If he was driving in a car and wanted a cigarette, he had to stop at a service station and go into the bathroom for a smoke. Within two weeks, smoking became quite disinteresting for George. Sitting on the "throne" and having a cigarette just isn't that much of a "thrill." By the end of the second week, his cigarette smoking had dropped to a very low level (from a baseline of approximately a package a day). Even the few that he smoked usually involved only a few puffs each, since after a couple of puffs in the bathroom he would simply throw the cigarette in the toilet and leave. By the end of the first month, George had ceased smoking, his urges were few and far between, and the urges he did experience were controlled. A follow-up one year later indicated that George was still not smoking.

If simply rearranging existing reinforcers is not adequate, it may be possible to solve the problem by introducing some new reinforcers for desirable behavior. Consider a recent self-modification program initiated by one of the authors. During the winter, he began an exercise program that involved running two miles three times per week at the underground track at the University of Manitoba. A two-mile run on the track is fourteen laps. The author found that after nine or ten laps, he began to think a lot of fatigue thoughts and would frequently talk himself out of doing the last few laps, saying things such as "Oh well, I've done pretty good by running eleven laps," or "Gee, my legs are tired; I guess I'm not in good shape yet." He decided that as a behavioral psychologist, he should be able to cure the problem. He therefore planned that during each of the tenth through the fourteen laps he would think some antifatigue thoughts and then allow himself some reinforcement. The particular antifatigue thought that he chose was about a TV physical fitness commercial claiming that the "average sixty-year-old Swede is in the same physical condition as the average thirty-year-old Canadian." (We have since learned that the claim is false, but this is not important to our illustration.) Thus, he would think this thought and imagine the commerical showing the extremely healthy sixty-year-old Swede jogging along through the bushes and looking trim and full of vim and vigor. The author picked a particular spot at one end of the track, and each time he got to that spot he would force himself to think the particular antifatigue thought about the very healthy Swede jogging merrily along. When he reached the next corner of the track, he would then think a highly reinforcing thought, which varied somewhat from day to day and included such things as making love with his wife (or perhaps fantasizing about someone else) and watching his son play hockey. He allowed himself to think the reinforcing thought across the end of the track, and then would simply not think either the Swede thought or the reinforcing thought down the other side of the track. In this way, he was able to engage in a private behavior that counteracted the fatigue thoughts and was also able to reinforce that behavior. After practicing this determinedly for about two weeks, he was able to put the fatigue thoughts completely "out of mind."[3]

Many everyday activities that people take for granted are potential reinforcers in a self-management project. Activities that have been used as reinforcers include closing drawers, rising and sitting at a desk, entering buildings, answering a telephone, sipping coffee, puffing on a cigar or cigarette, sitting in a favorite chair, turning on a faucet, and urinating.[4] Watson and Tharp (1972) provide detailed methods and examples of using such reinforcing events in self-management projects.

So far, we have considered only very simple examples of self-management. Some problems, however, require a step-by-step self-modification project that may last several months or more. Such cases may involve a therapist providing instructions, some modeling, and an opportunity for behavioral rehearsal and role playing by the client. Recall the example in Chapter 15 in which the therapist utilized instructions, modeling, shaping, and role playing to help a college student learn how to ask for a date over the telephone. In other cases, a therapist might interact extensively with a client in order to help him develop self-control over his self-verbalizations regarding his behavior and its causes. Cognitive psychologists generally describe this approach (which we discuss in more detail in Chapter 27) as helping an individual to change his behavior by helping him to change his beliefs or thoughts about his behavior. In some cases, therapists helping clients in complex self-control programs might go through all the steps in the guidelines in Chapter 21, especially those cited in the section entitled "Strategies of Program Design and Implementation."

CONTRACTING: A WAY TO ENSURE MANAGEMENT OF THE PROBLEM

As mentioned earlier, contingencies mediated by other people help to counteract short-circuiting. It is largely for this reason that, before the initiation of a self-control program, the therapist may encourage the client to prepare a behavioral contract. Such a contract is simply a very clear statement of what behaviors of what individuals will produce what reinforcers, and who will deliver those reinforcers. Some authors have described behavioral contracting as scheduling the exchange of reinforcers between two or more individuals (DeRisi and Butz, 1975; Sundel and Sundel, 1975). The majority of published work on contracting involves two or more individuals and has been concerned primarily with family interactions, such as between parents and children, and between husbands and wives. However, a contract need not necessarily involve others: an individual might prepare a "self-contract" (see Watson and Tharp, 1972).

When helping a client to develop self-control, the therapist would likely encourage her to prepare a contract of the proposed program that would include:

1. a clear statement of the target behaviors;
2. the method of data collection;
3. reinforcers to be used, their schedule of delivery, and who will deliver them;
4. potential problems and their resolution;
5. bonus and/or penalty clauses;
6. a schedule of review for progress;
7. signatures of all involved, and the dates of the agreement.

The contract serves at least four important S^D functions:

1. It ensures that all parties involved agree to the goals and procedures, and that they do not lose sight of them during the course of the treatment.
2. Because the goals are specified behaviorally, the contract also ensures that throughout the program all parties will agree on how close they are to reaching the goals.
3. The contract provides the client with a realistic estimate of the cost of the program to him in time, effort, and money.
4. The signatures on the contract help ensure that all parties will faithfully follow the specified procedures, because in our society signing a document is a strong S^D indicating a commitment.

FIGURE 25-3. *An example of short-circuiting.*

As we have stressed in previous chapters, behavior modification procedures should be revised in appropriate ways when the data indicate that they are not producing satisfactory results. Thus, the contract should be open to renegotiation at any time. If, for example, a signatory finds that she simply cannot meet some commitment specified in the contract, she should so inform the other signatories at the next meeting with the therapist. The difficulty would then be discussed, and, if it seemed desirable, a new contract replacing the previous one would be negotiated, drafted, and signed.

The following contract was prepared by a student in a course on behavior modification and self-control taught by one of the authors. This student worked in a mental-retardation institution, where she had experienced considerable difficulty because of her tendency to become upset with other staff members. After preparing a baseline of the problem behaviors, the student prepared and followed the program described in this contract.

SAMPLE CONTRACT

A. Problem and Goal

Achieving a frequency of zero instances per day of anger in response to hearing someone lying or being dishonest or in response to remembering an instance of someone lying or being dishonest.

Definitions:

Beh clearly defined in behaviorial terms

Anger: muscle tension, particularly in the hands and face, in response to hearing someone lie.

One instance: an uninterrupted episode of anger—that is, an episode not interrupted by thinking about something else that did not cause anger.

Lying: any verbal statement, verbal omission. or shake or nod of the head that I consider to be a lie. Note: Whether or not the other person is lying is based on my own feeling that it is a lie.

B. Data Collection

Each instance of anger is recorded as one count on a wrist counter (golf scorer) that I am to wear. These instances will be graphed each evening before I go to bed.

C. Reinforcers and Their Delivery

1. *Daily:* if the target for that day, as described in the shaping steps below, is reached, I permit myself to have my pillow when I go to sleep. If

it is not reached, I must place my pillow in the kitchen cupboard and sleep without it.

2. *Weekly:* I have given $400, which I saved up to buy a stereo, to Sally. As I meet the weekly criterion for each step, I will receive portions of the money back, as specified below:

Reaching criterion for Step 1:	$10
Reaching criterion for Step 2:	$10
Reaching criterion for Step 3:	$10
Reaching criterion for Step 4:	$10
Reaching criterion for Step 5:	$20
Reaching criterion for Step 6:	$20
Reaching criterion for Step 7:	$40
Reaching criterion for Step 8:	$60
Reaching criterion for Step 9:	$80
Reaching criterion for Step 10:	$140

Steps:

Step 1:	6 instances or less per day for one week.
Step 2:	5 instances or less per day for one week.
Step 3:	4 instances or less per day for one week.
Step 4:	3 instances or less per day for one week.
Step 5:	2 instances or less per day for one week.
Step 6:	1 instance or less per day for one week.
Step 7:	0 instances per day for one week.
Step 8:	0 instances per day for the second consecutive week.
Step 9:	0 instances per day for the third consecutive week.
Step 10:	0 instances per day for the fourth consecutive week.

D. Potential Problems and their Resolutions

1. I have guarded against the feeling of being strongly punished by the fact that if I do not meet my criterion for that week, I do not lose the money; I am simply delayed in buying the stereo.

2. I will minimize the two problems of short-circuiting as follows: (1) I will control taking my pillow when I have not earned it by putting the pillow in the kitchen cupboard at the far end of my apartment so that I have to walk a fair distance to get it. (2) I will control buying the stereo before the program is complete by reminding myself that if I bought the stereo prematurely I would not be able to get as good a quality stereo, because I would not have all the money returned to me. Also, I will inform several of my friends about my project and my progress, in order to avoid doing this.

3. I have encountered a problem in deciding on which day I should begin my week. My baseline shows Wednesday to be a "high day." That is, counts are typically higher on Wednesday than any other day. My week, therefore, will begin on Thursday and run until Wednesday afternoon. This will be an incentive not to "blow a week's work in the last day of the week."

E. Bonus or Penalty Clauses

None, other than specified above.

F. Schedule for Review of Progress

Every Wednesday evening with Sally.

G. Signatures of all Involved, and the Dates of the Agreement

Client __Suzy_____   Date ___January 30th_____
Others Involved __Sally_____   Date ___January 30th_____
_____   Date_____
Therapist_____   Date_____

Sometimes a therapist and a client may design a program and prepare a contract that produces completely successful and satisfactory results. Often, however, the initial contract may have to be revised before success is likely to be achieved. If problems arise in the following of the contract and the implementation of the program contained therein, a number of relevant factors might be discussed at the review meetings. DeRisi and Butz (1975) have suggested that the client and therapist might examine the following "trouble-shooting guide" when satisfactory progress is not being made.

Troubleshooting Guide*

The following questions may help you to spot the problems in your contracting system.

The Contract

1. Was the target behavior clearly specified?
2. Did the contract provide for immediate reinforcement?
3. Did it ask for small approximations to the desired behavior?
4. Was reinforcement frequent and in small amounts?
5. Did the contract call for and reward accomplishment rather than obedience?
6. Was the performance rewarded after its occurrence?
7. Was the contract fair?
8. Were the terms of the contract clear?
9. Was the contract honest?
10. Was the contract positive?
11. Was contracting as a method being used systematically?
12. Was the contract mutually negotiated?
13. Was the penalty clause too punitive?

*Adapted from William J. DeRisi and George Butz, *Writing Behavioral Contracts: A Case Simulation Practice Manual* (Champaign, Ill.: Research Press, 1975) pp. 58–60.

The Client

1. Did he understand the contract?
2. Is he getting the reinforcer from some other source?
3. Do the reinforcers have to be reevaluated.
4. Has a new problem behavior developed that is drawing the mediator's attention away from the target behavior?

The Mediator

1. Did the mediator understand the contract?
2. Did she dispense the kind and amount of reinforcement specified in the contract?
3. Did she dispense it according to instructions, at the rate specified, and with consistency?
4. Did punishment accidentally accompany the performance being reinforced?
5. Did she stop mediating?
6. Do you need a new mediator?

Measurement

1. Has the data been verified as accurate?
2. Did your data collector understand what he was supposed to count?
3. Did you rehearse the counting task with him?
4. Did you reinforce him for his behavior?
5. Is the data-collection task too complex or too difficult?
6. Should you try to get another data collector?

CIRCUMVENTING THE THERAPIST

It should be clear from the preceding four sections that many people who have mastered some behavior modification principles can use them to control their own behavior without having to see a therapist. For example, the student who has mastered this and previous chapters should have little difficulty in handling a simple behavior problem that has been bothering her (although we would still recommend seeing a therapist about serious problems). Perhaps the student would like to decrease her smoking, nail biting, swearing, or abusive remarks to others. Or perhaps she would like to enhance her studying, exercising, personal tidiness, consideration of others, or public speaking. She probably does not really need a therapist to help her accomplish these goals.

A person who has read this book already knows how to take data; he does not need a therapist to help him do that. He knows also how to plan a program and evaluate its effectiveness. He knows a large number of behavior modification principles and techniques and how to apply them; hence, it is likely that he can apply an appropriate combination of them to his own case. Moreover, the present chapter has made him aware of short–circuiting, a major difficulty in self-control programs, and has illustrated how contracting can minimize this difficulty. A behavioral contract can be negotiated with any person who is close to you and wants to help you change your behavior. In short, many people can be their own behavior therapist.[5]

Study Questions

(for examination purposes)

1. Is it true that behavior modifiers believe that "will power" is some mysterious power within you? If not, what do they think it is?

2. How do self-control procedures differ from other behavior modification procedures?

3. What are the two types of "short-circuiting"? Give an example of each.

4. Why should a therapist who is helping a client develop self-control clearly explain the reason for his advice to the client?

5. After reviewing the questions in Figure 25-2, describe two plausible problems that clients might express in nonbehavioral terms, and redescribe those problems in behavioral terms.

6. If the laws of behavior can't be changed, how is it that you can use them to change your behavior? (This is a "think" question.)

7. The questions asked of the client in Figure 25-2 can best be summarized by the question "What, when, where, and why?" Explain.

8. What suggestions does this chapter make for strengthening record keeping by a client?

9. What do we mean by "significant others" in problems of self-control?

10. Describe how a simple rearrangement of consequences might help a student whose problem is getting tired while reading.

11. Explain how George's program to quit smoking included reinforcement, extinction, and stimulus control.

12. Briefly describe a self-reinforcement program for reinforcing "antifatigue" thoughts.

13. What is a behavioral contract? Describe its essential features.

14. What important stimulus-control functions does a behavioral contract serve?

15. How did the behavioral contract for controlling the student's anger attempt to alleviate potential problems of short-circuiting?

16. Is it plausible to suggest that many individuals can become their own behavior therapists? Justify your answer.

Self-Modification Exercises

(to be practiced by the reader)

1. Utilizing the information in this and the preceding chapters, outline a complete self-modification program for overcoming one of your behavioral deficiencies, excesses, or inappropriatenesses.
2. Carry out your program and report its results.

EXTENDED DISCUSSION AND NOTES

1. Watson and Tharp (1972, pp. 241–249) described several everyday uses of the term "will power." They state, for example, that willpower "often means self-restraint: 'I had the willpower not to eat too much!' Sometimes willpower means a force that enables one to pass up some immediate gratification in favor of a long-range goal or in favor of personal values. Sometimes willpower is used to explain doing something one expects to be unpleasant. At other times the word is used to explain doing something that is very difficult or that requires a long wait for positive reinforcement" (p. 248). Watson and Tharp point out, further, that at the onset of a self-modification program, the amount of "will" necessary to accomplish the end result may seem excessive. For a smoker, for example, the amount of "will power" necessary to quit "cold turkey" may seem beyond the individual's control. However, with the application of each step in a behavior modification program, the required amount of "will power" seems to decrease. For example, in the case of the Canadian Mountie who wanted to quit smoking (see p. 374), the amount of "will power" necessary to take a baseline intuitively seemed relatively little. The amount of "will power" necessary to agree to the rule, "Whenever I feel like a cigarette, I will go to a bathroom and smoke," seemed to be minimal. The amount of "will power" necessary to go to the bathroom to have a cigarette the first time that the smoking urge was experienced during the program was relatively minimal. In other words, Watson and Tharp argue, the greater the degree of specification of self-control procedures, and the smaller the step at any one time, the less it is necessary to consider "will power" as a factor in the achievement of the final goal. Whether or not "will power" can be eliminated completely is unclear. It is clear that it is not useful to talk about the amount of "will power" needed to achieve a particular goal. However, an individual who expresses a strong desire to achieve a particular goal is more apt to achieve that goal than one who does not.

2. You might be asking, "If the client is receiving some help from a consultant, in what sense is the project one of self-control?" In answering, we would like to point out that behavioral programming might be viewed as a continuum varying from complete self-control to complete therapist control. Some procedures have been described such that the "average" person can read about them and then develop a self-management program completely on his own (see, for example, Foster, 1974; Miller and Muñoz, 1976; Watson and Tharp, 1972; Williams and

(Continued)

Long, 1975). Other procedures (such as aversion therapy, described in Chapter 14) require constant therapist supervision. The approach adopted in this chapter is close to the self-control end of the continuum, in that we describe a therapist making suggestions similar to those found in self-control books, and the procedures are designed and carried out by the client.

3. Catania (1975, 1976) and Goldiamond (1976) have argued that it is inappropriate to call this type of procedure "self-reinforcement." Because of the short-circuiting processes described at the beginning of this chapter, it appears that it may be logically impossible for people to directly reinforce or punish their own behavior. (No one questions the fact that people may do so indirectly—for example, by asking another person to apply a reinforcement or punishment contingency to one of their behaviors.) Catania and Goldiamond would argue, therefore, that the jogging author could not really have been reinforcing his anti-fatigue thoughts. This does not mean, however, that they would necessarily deny the effectiveness of the author's procedure. Rather, they would argue that its effectiveness must have been due to some process other than self-reinforcement. For example, the author's procedure may simply have made anti-fatigue thoughts, which were already reinforcing, more discriminable—hence enhancing their reinforcing effectiveness.

4. As we mentioned in Chapter 2, using a behavior that occurs often to reinforce a behavior that seldom occurs is a principle formulated by David Premack, and is therefore generally called the Premack Principle. In Premack's words, "the most probable response of a set of responses will reinforce all members of a set; the least probable will reinforce no members of the set" (1965, p. 132). In an interesting extension of this principle, Homme (1965) described ways in which the Premack Principle might be applied to manage one's private behaviors (such as thoughts, images). Homme coined the phrase "coverant" (meaning "covert operant response") to refer to private behaviors that could be influenced by their consequences. Thus, the example described in the text in which the author used highly probable (i.e., high-frequency) thoughts to strengthen an improbable (i.e., low-frequency) antifatigue thought is an example of both coverant control and the Premack Principle. A number of authors have described self-control procedures in which individuals successfully modified their behaviors by utilizing Homme's coverant control. However, in two review articles, Danaher (1974) and Knapp (1976) were highly critical of the available data in support of both the Premack Principle applied to observable behaviors and its extension to self-control involving coverants. Danaher and Knapp didn't seem to doubt the reports of behavior change by individuals claiming to use either the Premack Principle or Homme's coverant extension. What they questioned is the empirical evidence that the behavior change was due only to the Premack Principle. They cite problems of directly and independently measuring both the high-probability and low-probability responses, of obtaining adequate baselines prior to application of the Premack Principle, and of control of extraneous factors that might also have influenced the improved performance.

5. This view was aptly expressed in the title and contents of a book by Mahoney and Thoresen (1974), *Self-Control: Power to the Person.*

Study Questions on Notes

1. How do behavior modifiers manipulate "will power"?
2. What is the logical conclusion of the Watson and Tharp position regarding will power?
3. What is the Premack Principle?
4. What did Homme mean by "coverant"? *(covert operant responses.)*
5. From the information in this chapter, briefly describe how you might utilize Homme's coverant control to manage one of your private attitudes.
6. Is self-reinforcement possible? Defend your answer.

CHAPTER 26

SYSTEMATIC SELF-DESENSITIZATION

In Chapter 14, we explained that systematic desensitization is a procedure in which a client gradually progresses through a hierarchy of *imagined* anxiety-producing situations, arranged from those that elicit the least anxiety to those that elicit the most anxiety, while maintaining a completely relaxed state in order to counteract the anxiety. Systematic *self*-desensitization is essentially the same procedure, except that the client progresses through the various desensitization stages by himself. In other words, it is a self-modification procedure that is much like the self-modification procedures discussed in Chapter 25, except that it focuses strictly on problematic fears. We will therefore explain the procedure by assuming that you have an undesirable fear that you would like to eliminate (for example, a fear of flying).

A basic behavioral assumption is that fear and anxiety are learned behaviors, and that by following appropriate procedures a person can unlearn these behaviors. The steps we have outlined below are generally consistent with the recommendations of other behavioral psychologists in this area. Your systematic self-desensitization program will take you through the following phases: (1) constructing a fear hierarchy; (2) learning deep muscle relaxation; and (3) carrying out the actual therapy steps of the self-desensitization process.

CONSTRUCTING THE FEAR HIERARCHY

To construct a fear hierarchy, first list from ten to thirty fear-producing situations related to your undesirable fear. Then arrange these situations in order, starting with the situation that causes the least fear and ending with the situation that causes the most fear. To accomplish this task, get a stack of three-by-five-inch index cards and proceed as follows.

A. Take one of the index cards, and on the front write a brief phrase about the fear-eliciting situation that makes you only slightly nervous. For example, if your fear is that of flying, the phrase might be "sitting at home and phoning the airline to make a reservation." Now turn the index card over, and on the back list several stimuli that will help prompt you to realistically imagine yourself actually experiencing the phone call. The prompts might include such things as the color of your phone and the sound of a voice saying, "Airline reservations desk—may I help you?" A sample index card is shown in Figure 26-1.

B. Take another index card, and list a situation that elicits a slightly larger amount of fear. Again, on the back of that card provide yourself with some verbal prompts that will help you clearly imagine experiencing that situation. Continue in this manner until all of the fear-producing situations are listed on note cards arranged so that each situation produces a little more anxiety than the preceding one. You now have a fear hierarchy. An example of a fear hierarchy for an individual who was afraid of flying is shown in Table 26-1.

Note that each item in Table 26-1 refers to a specific, concrete situation that can be imagined in vivid detail, rather than a vague general idea. For example, item 10 is to be preferred to "waiting for the plane," for it is more likely to prompt specific images of sitting in the lobby, listening to the announcements of flight numbers, and so forth.

C. Your next step is to validate your fear hierarchy by making sure that your cards have been arranged in the proper order (they should start with the situation that produces the least anxiety and end with the situation that generates the most anxiety), and that the steps between them are sufficiently small (no "jump" in anxiety level from one item to the next should be too large). This should be done as follows:

1. Rate each item in your hierarchy on a scale from 0 to 100, where 100 means that the situation elicits the maximum conceivable amount of anxiety (extreme panic and absolute terror) when encountered in the natural environment, and 0 means that the situation produces absolutely no emotion when encountered in real life. This value is referred to as the number of *subjective units of discomfort* (suds) elicited by the situation.[1]

2. Check whether your original order of items in the hierarchy and your suds ratings are consistent (each item in the hierarchy should have a higher suds ranking than the item below it and a lower ranking than the item above it). If they are not consistent, redo both the hierarchy and the suds ratings until they are completely consistent.

3. Use your suds ratings to ensure that the distances between items in the hierarchy are sufficiently small and approximately equal (rule of thumb: distances between items should be no greater than five to ten suds[2]).

Talking to the travel agent, making reservations

Front side

1. Phoning the travel agent — dial number, call answered.

2. Giving particulars of destination, dates of trip.

3. Writing down flight numbers and times.

4. Marking calendar with dates, flight times, and flight numbers.

Back side

FIGURE 26-1. *A sample index card for a fear-producing situation.*

Construct new items and insert them between any items that are greater than ten suds apart.

4. Number each of the cards in order, starting with the card causing the least anxiety as number 1.

5. If you cannot make suds ratings without apparent inconsistencies between the ratings and your hierarchy, or within the ratings themselves, cease your attempt at self-desensitization and seek professional clinical desensitization (since it would appear that several major anxieties are present and interacting—a condition that may be too complex to be dealt with by the nonprofessional).

If a strong anxiety has occurred while you are constructing the hierarchy or developing your suds ratings, you might adopt one of two strategies: either discontinue your program and seek professional clinical desensitization, or continue your program but eliminate the five most anxiety-producing situations. After completing your desensitization program minus the five most anxiety-producing situations, you should then be able to develop a program for those items, since they will likely cause much less anxiety if you have successfully completed the earlier items.

TABLE 26-1. *An example of a fear-of-flying hierarchy.**

1. The plane has landed and stopped at the terminal. I get off the plane and enter the terminal, where I am met by friends.

2. A trip has been planned, and I have examined the possible methods of travel and decided "out loud" to travel by plane.

3. I have called the travel agent and told him of my plans. He gives me the times and flight numbers.

4. It is the day before the trip, and I pack my suitcase, close it, and lock it.

5. It is ten days before the trip, and I receive the tickets in the mail. I note the return address, open the envelope, and check the tickets for the correct dates, times, and flight numbers.

6. It is the day of the flight. I am leaving home. I lock the house, put the bags in the car, and make sure that I have the tickets and money.

7. I am driving to the airport for my flight. I am aware of every plane I see. As I get close to the airport, I see several planes—some taking off, some landing, and some just sitting on the ground by the terminal.

8. I am entering the terminal. I am carrying my bags and tickets.

9. I proceed to the airline desk, wait in line, and have the agent check my tickets and then weigh and check my bags.

10. I am in the lounge with many other people, some with bags also waiting for flights. I hear the announcements over the intercom and listen for my flight number to be called.

11. I hear my flight number announced, and I proceed to the security check-point with my hand luggage.

12. I approach the air-line desk beyond the security check-point, and the agent asks me to choose a seat from the "map" of the plane.

13. I walk down the ramp leading to the plane and enter the door of the plane.

14. I am now inside the plane. I look at the interior of the plane and walk down the aisle, looking for my seat number. I then move in from the aisle and sit down in my assigned seat.

15. The plane is in flight, and I decide to leave my seat and walk to the washroom at the back of the plane.

16. I notice the seat-belt signs light up, so I fasten my seat belt and I notice the sound of the motors starting.

17. Everyone is seated with their seat belts fastened, and the plane slowly moves away from the terminal.

18. I notice the seat-belt signs are again lighted, and the pilot announces that we are preparing to land.

19. I am looking out the window and suddenly the plane enters clouds and I cannot see out the window.

20. The plane has stopped at the end of the runway and is sitting, waiting for instructions to take off.

21. The plane is descending to the runway for a landing. I feel the speed and see the ground getting closer.

22. The plane has taken off from the airport and banks as it changes direction. I am aware of the "tilt."

23. The plane starts down the runway, and the motors get louder as the plane increases speed and suddenly lifts off.

*This hierarchy was prepared by a client who initiated a self-desensitization project after reading a preliminary draft of this chapter. (Her case is described in more detail by Roscoe, Martin, and Pear, 1977).

LEARNING DEEP MUSCLE RELAXATION

After you have constructed your hierarchy, you should next learn to completely relax all your muscles and to recognize when they are relaxed.[3] Do this by alternately tensing and relaxing your muscles while attending closely to the internal activities and sensations you are feeling at the time.[4] Instructions for achieving deep muscle relaxation are presented in Table 26-2.

TABLE 26-2. *Instructions to be recorded on tape and played to achieve deep muscle relaxation. Each "(p)" represents a pause of five seconds. (The numerals should not be read aloud.)*

1. Listen closely to these instructions. They will help you increase your ability to relax. Each time I pause, continue doing what you were doing before the pause. Now, close your eyes and take three deep breaths. (p) (p)

2. Make a tight fist with your left hand. Squeeze it tight. Note how it feels. (p) Now relax. (p)

3. Once again, squeeze your left hand tightly and study the tension that you feel. (p) And once again, just relax and think of the tension disappearing from your fingers. (p) (p)

4. Make a tight fist with your right hand. Squeeze it as tight as you can, and note the tension in your fingers and your hand, and your forearm. (p) Now relax. (p)

5. Once again, squeeze your right fist tightly. (p) And again, just relax. (p) (p)

6. Make a tight fist with your left hand, and bend your arm to make your left biceps hard. Hold it tense. (p) Now relax totally. Feel the warmth escape down your biceps, through your forearm, and out of your fingers. (p) (p)

7. Now make a tight fist with the other hand, and raise your hand to make your right biceps hard. Hold it tight, and feel the tension. (p) Now relax. Concentrate on the feelings flowing through your arm. (p) (p)

8. Now, squeeze both fists at once and bend both arms to make them totally tense throughout. Hold it, and think about the tension you feel. (p) Now relax, and feel the total warmth and relaxation flowing through your muscles. All of the tension is flowing out of your fingertips. (p) (p)

9. Now, wrinkle your forehead and squint your eyes very tight and hard.* Squeeze them tight and hard. Feel the tension across your forehead and through your eyes. Now relax. Note the sensations running through your eyes. Just relax. (p) (p)

10. Okay, squeeze your jaws tight together and raise your chin to make your neck muscles hard. Hold it, bite down hard, tense your neck, and squeeze your lips really tight. (p) Now relax. (p) (p)

11. Now, all together, wrinkle up your forehead and squeeze your eyes tight, bite down hard with your jaws, raise your chin and tighten up your neck, and make your lips tight. Hold them all, and feel the tension throughout your forehead, and eyes, and jaw, and neck, and lips. Hold it. Now relax. Just totally relax and enjoy the tingling sensations. (p) (p) (p)

12. Now, squeeze both your shoulders forward as hard as you can until you feel your muscles pulling tightly right across your back, especially in the area between your shoulder blades. Squeeze them. Hold them tight. Now relax. (p) (p)

13. Now, squeeze your shoulders forward again, and at the same time, suck your stomach in as far as you can and tense your stomach muscles. Feel the tension throughout your stomach. Hold it. (p) Now relax. (p) (p)

14. Now, one more time, squeeze your shoulder blades forward again, suck in your stomach as far as you can, tense your stomach muscles, and feel the tension throughout your upper body. Now relax. (p) (p)

15. Now, we are going to review all of the muscle systems that we have covered so far. First, take three deep breaths. Ready? Tighten up both fists and bend both of your arms to squeeze your biceps tight. Wrinkle your forehead and squeeze your eyes tight. Bite down hard with your jaws, raise your chin, and hold your lips tight. Squeeze your shoulders forward and suck in your stomach and push your stomach muscles

against it. Hold them all. Feel the tremendous tension throughout. Now relax. Take a deep breath. Just feel the tension disappearing. Think about the total relaxation throughout all of your muscles—in your arms, in your head, in your shoulders, in your stomach. Just relax. (p) (p)

16. Now, let's go to your legs. Bring your left heel in tight towards your chair, push it down hard, and raise your toes so that your calf and your thigh are extremely tense. Squeeze your toes up, and push your heel down hard. (p) Now relax. (p) (p)

17. One more time, bring your left heel in tight towards your chair, push it down hard, and raise your toes so that your calf and your thigh are extremely tense. Push down on the heel and raise your toes. Now relax. (p) (p)

18. Now, bring your right heel in tight towards your chair and push it down and raise your toes so that your calf and your thigh are extremely tense. Push your heel down, squeeze your toes up, and squeeze your leg in tight. (p) Now relax. (p) (p)

19. Now, let's do both legs together. Squeeze your heels in tight towards your chair, push down on your heels, and raise your toes as high and as tight as you can. Hold it. (p) Now relax. (p) (p)

20. Now, take three deep breaths. (p) Now, tense all of the muscles as they are named, exactly as you have practiced: left fist and biceps, right fist and biceps, forehead, eyes, jaw, neck, lips, shoulders, stomach, left leg, right leg. Hold it. (p) Now relax. (p) (p) Breathe in deeply three times and then repeat the total tensing and then the total relaxing, and while you are breathing in deeply and then tensing and then relaxing, notice how relaxed all of your muscles feel. Now tense (p) and relax (p). Now, breathe normally and enjoy the completely tension-free state of your body and muscles. (p) (p) (p) (p) (p) (p) Now turn the tape off.

---

*Persons who wear contact lenses should remove them before doing this exercise.

It would be maximally effective for you if a friend with a low, even, soothing voice could record these relaxation instructions on tape. That way, you can listen to them rather than having to read them.[5] While your friend is reading the instructions, he or she should pause five seconds for each "(p)" that appears in them.

Let us assume that the instructions have been recorded on tape. You should now find a quiet, dimly lit, private setting with as few distracting stimuli as possible; a comfortable couch, bed, or reclining chair; and a time when you will not be interrupted for twenty to thirty minutes. Lie or sit on the couch, bed, or chair, which should support you with minimal use of your own muscles. Now turn on the tape recorder and follow the instructions.

After you have practiced the relaxation method on several different occasions, you will find that you are able to skip some of the steps and achieve the same deeply relaxed state in a shorter period of time. Eventually, you should be able to go directly to step 20 and achieve a completely relaxed state within a matter of minutes. We recommend that you gradually eliminate steps according to the following pattern:

1. Practice the entire twenty steps in Table 26-2 on at least three occasions spread over a minimum of two days.
2. Make a new tape recording consisting of steps 1, 8, 15, and 20. Use this new tape on at least three occasions spread over a minimum of two days.
3. Make a new tape consisting of steps 1 and 20. Use this new tape on at least two occasions spread over a minimum of one day.

After completing this program, which takes approximately one week, you should be able to totally relax in a matter of minutes. When you accomplish that goal, you are ready to begin the next phase of your self-desensitization program. You should *not* attempt to apply relaxation procedures in the actual fear-producing settings until you have completed the above training. Even then, it would be best to wait until your self-desensitization program is progressing smoothly before making any unnecessary contacts with the actual fear-producing stimuli.

IMPLEMENTING THE SELF-DESENSITIZATION PROGRAM

Now that you have constructed your fear hierarchy and are able to relax completely within minutes,[6] you are ready to start your program. This is done according to the following steps.

1. Find a quiet, private place that is free from distractions (preferably, the same place in which your relaxation practice sessions were conducted).
2. Place your stack of cards containing the fear items within easy reach. The cards should be in order, with the least fear-producing card on top and the most fear-producing card on the bottom.
3. Take several minutes and relax completely, as you have been practicing prior to this session.
4. When you are in a state of complete relaxation, take the card on top of the deck and look at the brief phrase that characterizes the situation that would normally cause some slight anxiety. Now turn the card over and look at the prompts that are to help you visualize the first situation clearly and vividly. After looking at the prompts, close your eyes and try to imagine that you are actually in that situation, as prompted by your card. After about ten seconds, place the card in a separate pile and totally relax. Relax for about thirty seconds, and during this time completely forget about the scene that you have just imagined. Think only of your muscles and how completely relaxed you feel while breathing deeply.
5. Now pick up the same card again, and then close your eyes and imagine that situation for at least ten seconds. Put the card down in a separate place, and completely relax for another thirty seconds. During this time do not think of the scene that you were just imagining while in a relaxed state. After the thirty seconds are up, consider the amount of anxiety you felt while imagining this scene the second time. If you were able to imagine the scene with approximately five or fewer suds, then you are ready to proceed to card two. If you felt more than five suds of anxiety, you should repeat the above routine once or twice more. If you felt less

than five suds of anxiety, then relax for two minutes and repeat the procedure with the second card.

6. If you have great difficulty in imagining a scene, or in relaxing while imagining it, or if you feel more than ten suds of anxiety, immediately stop imagining and induce deep muscle relaxation for a minute or two. Then repeat the item for only three to five seconds rather than a full ten seconds.

7. If step 6 doesn't work, go back to the previous item and imagine that item for twenty seconds on two successive presentations of the item. Then, again try the item that caused the difficulty.

8. If you still have problems with a particular item, try to construct three new items with smaller steps between them in order to correct the difficulty encountered with that item. Proceed through the new items exactly as described above.

9. In general, you should be able to proceed through one to four items per session. However, it is all right to go as slow as one item per session, if necessary. On the other hand, if you do not feel anxiety, you should not hesitate to go through as many as four items per session, or perhaps more.

10. Each session should begin with an item that was completed successfully in the previous session.

11. Sessions should not last more than about twenty minutes. Sessions might be conducted as frequently as twice per day and no less frequently than twice per week.

12. If you experience difficulties that do not yield to the corrective procedures in steps 6–8, cease self-desensitization attempts and seek professional clinical desensitization.

It is important to keep track of your progress. Thus, at the end of each session, you should record on a separate sheet of paper the name and number of the particular items you imagined successfully, the number of exposures to each item successfully imagined, the suds ratings of the items completed in that session, and the date of the session. We also recommend that you graph your data in a way that is meaningful to you. To better understand your progress, you should also indicate the suds rating of the item when you first prepared your anxiety hierarchy and the final suds rating, which ideally, will be less than five. In addition, if in real life you experience the actual situation represented by a successfully completed item, assess your suds rating in the real situation and compare it with your rating when imagining the situation. This will give you some indication of the success of your generalization to the natural environment. Self-desensitization data taken by the client who prepared the hierarchy shown in Table 26-1 is presented in Table 26-3.

CONDITIONS UNDER WHICH PROFESSIONAL ASSISTANCE SHOULD BE SOUGHT

Watson and Tharp (1972, p. 189) suggest that professional assistance be sought if any of the following occur:

TABLE 26-3. *Data recorded by the client whose fear-of-flying hierarchy is shown in Table 26-1. (For the descriptions of the items listed in the table, see the corresponding item numbers in Table 26-1.)*

SESSION (AND DATE)	TASK	ORIGINAL SUDS RANKING*	SUDS RANKING OF ITEMS IMMEDIATELY AFTER DESENSITIZATION OF THOSE ITEMS	SUDS RANKING OF ITEMS WHEN ENCOUNTERED IN THE NATURAL ENVIRONMENT 1ST CONTACT (OUTBOUND FLIGHT: AUG. 26)	2ND CONTACT (RETURN FLIGHT: SEPT. 6)
1 (Aug. 11)	Prepare hierarchy and do suds ranking on all items				
2 (Aug. 13)	Prepare cards				
3 (Aug. 14)					
4 (Aug. 15)	Learn deep muscle relaxation				
5 (Aug. 16)					
6 (Aug. 17)					
7 (Aug. 18)	Item 1	0	0	0	0
	2	5	0	5**	−†
	3	6	0	6**	−†
	4	10	0	0	0
	5	13	0	0	−†
8 (Aug. 19)	6	17	0	0	0
	7	23	0	1	0
	8	27	0	0	0
	9	29	0	0	0
	10	30	0	0	0
	11	35	0	1	0
9 (Aug. 20)	12	38	0	0	0
	13	43	0	0	0
	14	46	0	0	0
10 (Aug. 21)	15	50	0	0	0
	16	60	0	0	0
	17	70	0	0	0
11 (Aug. 22)	18	75	0	0	0
	19	80	0	−†	−†
	20	90	0	1	0
12 (Aug. 23)	21	97	3	3	0
	22	99	9	9	10
	23	100	6	(25) 5‡	0

*The original suds ranking was done during session 1.

**These items were encountered in the natural environment prior to desensitization training.

†These items were not encountered in the natural environment.

‡When the plane suddenly moved from the end of the runway after having been stopped, the client was unprepared and a suds ranking of 25 resulted. However, she was able to recover her composure during the actual situation and reduce her anxiety to a suds ranking of 5.

1. Uncomfortable anxiety during the creation of the hierarchy.
2. Overlapping hierarchies, indicated by contradictory or paradoxical suds ratings of the items.
3. Inability to produce vivid imagery.
4. Inability to control the beginning or ending of an image.
5. The inability to desensitize high enough up on the hierarchy to meet your goals.

Wenrich, General, and Dawley (1976) have also outlined several potential problems in systematic self-desensitization. Nevertheless, as indicated by Wenrich et al., there is evidence in support of the general recommendations of this chapter. It appears that individuals can learn to overcome their own fears by following the specific procedures of self-desensitization.[7]

Study Questions

(for examination purposes)

1. Briefly explain the difference between systematic desensitization and systematic self-desensitization. *Self – go through by self*
2. List the three main phases of a systematic self-desensitization project. Describe each in a paragraph or less. *Make heirarchy Implement. learn to Relax*
3. What is a fear hierarchy (in two or three sentences)?
4. What is a suds rating? How are suds ratings used?
5. At the beginning of the section entitled "Learning Deep Muscle Relaxation," there are several suggestions that amount to using situational inducement. Briefly describe three such suggestions.
6. When carrying out a self-desensitization program, what should an individual do if the anxiety felt while imagining a particular scene is greater than ten suds?
7. How fast should one go through the hierarchy in a self-desensitization program?
8. What are the conditions under which self-desensitization should be discontinued and professional advice sought?

[handwritten margin notes: fear producing items & stimuli that describe fear. in order from least frightening to most frightening. dim room quiet room private setting. repeat them twice. 3–4 /session 20 min session]

Self-Modification Exercise

(to be practiced by the reader)

Choose a particular undesirable fear or phobia that you have, and attempt a self-desensitization program by following the procedures described in this chapter. Prepare a written report of your procedures and results.

EXTENDED DISCUSSION AND NOTES

1. This rating scale was first recommended by Wolpe and Lazarus (1966). They assumed that attaching numerical values to subjective evaluations of one's discomfort may help an individual to more consistently identify items in a hierarchy that are approximately the same distance apart in terms of the amount of anxiety they produce. However, one's skill at developing a suds rating will probably depend upon the extent to which she has learned to label those private behaviors accurately. Although Skinner (1957) has provided a plausible theoretical account of how we learn to label private behaviors, research in this area is sadly lacking.

2. Although others have also recommended that the distance between items be approximately five to ten suds (such as Wenrich et al., 1976, p. 28), this figure seems to be based on informal clinical observations rather than on rigorous empirical data.

3. Since Jacobson (1938) first described his relaxation method, a number of individuals have described different variations on the method (see, for example, Goldfried and Davison, 1976; Rimm and Masters, 1974; Watson and Tharp, 1972; Wenrich et al., 1976). The present description of the tension-relaxation induction approach was influenced by our reading of these sources.

4. In introductory courses in psychology, students are often told that behaviorists deal only with measurable behavior and do not consider such "mental events" as sensations, feelings, and images. Although some behaviorists might be that way, those who ascribe to the analysis of behavior offered by B. F. Skinner clearly are not. As Skinner has argued repeatedly, a small part of the universe is "private." It is possible to offer an interpretive explanation of the control of private behaviors. The reader who is interested in more detailed discussion of a behavioral approach to private events should consult Skinner (1953, pp. 227–294; 1969, pp. 221–297) and Day (1969). This approach is called "radical behaviorism" because it assumes that private behaviors (i.e., so-called "mental events") are no different, in principle, from public behavior or any other aspect of the physical universe.

5. On the basis of clinical observations, Goldfried and Davison (1976) suggested that having clients practice relaxation exercises at home without accompanying tapes as guides seldom does little good and may often be harmful.

6. Goldfried and Davison (1976) have described a number of potential therapeutic applications of relaxation, in addition to the role it plays in systematic desensitization.

7. Another variation on desensitization procedures is referred to as "*in vivo* desensitization." This is a procedure in which the individual desensitizes a fear in "real life" (i.e., *in vivo*) rather than desensitizing the fear in her imagination, as described in this chapter. The steps for *in vivo* desensitization are very similar to those described in this chapter, except that rather than progressing through a hierarchy of imagined fear situations the individual actually approaches the fear-producing stimuli.

(Continued)

(Continued)

In vivo desensitization has been used to overcome fears of darkness, birds, animals, and a variety of other situations for which it is relatively easy to arrange for real-life hierarchies. For a more extended discussion of *in vivo* desensitization, see Watson and Tharp (1972).

Study Questions on Notes

1. Why did Wolpe and Lazarus recommend using the suds scale?
2. How firm is the evidence that the starting distance between self-desensitization items should be five to ten suds?
3. Who first described procedures of deep muscle relaxation?
4. What is *in vivo* desensitization? Give an example.
5. Briefly, what is radical behaviorism?

CHAPTER 27

COGNITIVE BEHAVIOR MODIFICATION

Although behavior modifiers have generally tended to reject other psychological approaches (such as Freudian psychoanalysis), some blending is taking place between behavior modification and certain types of treatment collectively called *cognitive therapy*. The word *cognition* means "belief," "thought," "perception." Accordingly, cognitive therapists regard their approach to be primarily that of helping a client overcome his difficulties by getting rid of unproductive, debilitating thoughts or beliefs and adopting more constructive ones. Some behavior modifiers have noted certain similarities between the goals and procedures of cognitive therapists and their own. Cognitive therapists, in turn, have adopted some behavior modification methods. Out of this mutual appreciation has grown an area that has come to be known as *cognitive behavior modification* (see Mahoney, 1974; Meichenbaum, 1974). The purpose of this chapter is to briefly describe some of the procedures that are often considered to fall within this area. But first, a word about words.

Behavior modifiers generally believe that they can best discover and apply effective procedures if the terms they use to talk about behavior are clear and precise. This is why they have developed a special language consisting of well-defined terms (such as reinforcer, S^D, S^Δ, and contingency of reinforcement). They have also tended to avoid certain everyday words, such as "thinking" and "believing," that are used quite freely by other social scientists.

Of course, it is not necessarily incorrect to say that someone "thinks that . . ." or "believes that . . ." such and such is the case. Obviously, such words serve well in everyday conversation. It's just that there are usually more precise ways of talking about behavior and behavioral procedures. Although every example presented in this book could have been stated in terms of someone "thinking" or "believing" something about the reinforcement contingencies controlling her behavior, we generally did not do this. Mixing vague, everyday conversational terms with the more precise technical language would only have confused the issue by making the technical descriptions less clear and precise (see Skinner's comments in note 1 of Chapter 2).

When talking about public (i.e., overt or observable) behavior, most behavior modifiers are quite consistent and precise. However, as some behavior modifiers have taken more of an interest in private behavior, the language seems to be getting more variable and less precise. Throughout this text, we have stated or implied repeatedly that behavior modifiers have concentrated on public behavior largely because of its amenability to direct observation and reliability checks, and because most behavioral problems are, in fact, public. However, contrary to the impression given in many introductory psychology courses, no reputable behavior modification expert has ever denied the existence and importance of private behavior. When solving a problem or puzzle, for example, a person may "talk silently to himself" and these private self-statements may be part of a behavioral chain (or sequence) that leads him to the correct solution. He may also imagine (that is, engage in private "seeing behavior") certain aspects of the problem, and these images may also be part of the behavioral chain leading to the solution. A number of behavior modifiers have tended to equate private behaviors such as these with words such as "thinking" and "believing."[1]

The problem with the everyday terms "thinking" and "believing" is that they do not refer precisely to the actual behavior of interest (whether it is private or public) and the variables controlling that behavior. Moreover, to use special words such as "believing" and "thinking" to refer to private behavior implies that the principles and procedures applicable to private behavior are fundamentally different from those that apply to public behavior. Although private behavior is more difficult to "get at," we may assume that in other respects it is the same as public behavior. Although this assumption is currently unproved, it does appear to be scientifically and practically useful. For example, in Chapter 25 we described how George instructed himself to go to the washroom every time he felt like having a cigarette. Although he probably gave himself this instruction silently rather than out loud, its effect was the same in either case. He followed his self-instruction, and his smoking decreased. In Chapter 25, we also described how one of the authors, while jogging, increased his antifatigue thoughts by following them with thoughts of a highly reinforcing activity. Although the effect was probably not as strong as it would have been had his jogging been immediately reinforced with the actual experiences that he merely imagined, the principle was still the same. (But see note 3 of Chapter 25.) In Chapter 26, we described how a client self-desensitized her fear of flying by imagining the fear-producing situations while in a relaxed state. Presumably, the private "seeing behavior" (imagining) was so similar to actually seeing the fear-producing situations that the relaxation response generalized to those situations.

In each of these cases, as well as in a number of other examples presented in this book, private behavior was modified in order to bring about desired changes in public behavior. In no case, however, was it necessary to assume that private behavior is fundamentally different from public behavior. In no case was it necessary to use vague terms such as "believing" and "thinking" to distinguish private behavior from public behavior. On the contrary, the treatments used were based on the assumption that the same general principles and procedures are applicable to both public and private behavior.

From this point of view of public and private behavior, we will now discuss some methods that others have called "cognitive" procedures.

SOME COGNITIVE PROCEDURES

Cognitive therapists and cognitive behavior modifiers speak of achieving desirable changes in a client's behavior (including emotional behavior) by altering thought patterns, beliefs, attitudes, and opinions. Their methods, however, deal mainly with the client's private verbal behavior and images relating to himself and the world around him. Much of the evidence supporting the effectiveness of these techniques comes from case studies rather than from well-controlled experiments.

Rational-Emotive Therapy

Cognitive behavior modification has received strong impetus from the well-known cognitive therapist Albert Ellis (see, for example, Ellis, 1962; Ellis and Harper, 1975). A psychotherapist originally trained in Freudian psychoanalytic methods, Ellis became very disillusioned with those methods. He found that although his clients perhaps gained some insight into their problems by remembering and talking about their childhood experiences, this insight was of little value in solving their problems. Ellis became convinced that the solutions were to be found in the situations in which the problems are encountered, not in the client's distant past. In shifting the focus of treatment to the client's present environment, Ellis developed what he called rational-emotive therapy.

As its name suggests, rational-emotive therapy is based on the premise that there is a very close connection between what we say to ourselves and how we feel. According to Ellis, most everyday emotional problems (and related behaviors) stem from irrational statements people make to themselves when events in their lives are not the way they would like them to be. People tend to "catastrophize": they tell themselves that things are so horrible they can't possibly "stand it." Basically, Ellis's approach is to teach his clients to counteract such "irrational" self-statements with more positive and realistic statements. For example, they may tell themselves that although their situation may be annoying or inconvenient, it is not catastrophic, and, moreover, there are usually things that they can do to improve it.[2] (For example see Figure 27-1).

An important component of rational-emotive therapy involves *in vivo* "homework" assignments in which clients learn how to overcome their behavioral deficits as well as verbally counteract their negative self-statements. Bandura (1977, p. 190) has suggested that the corrective homework assignments may be more important than attempts to change the client's self-verbalizations, since there is little evidence that the latter approach produces large or consistent improvements in the behavior. Nevertheless, on the basis of his clinical experience, Ellis reports that rational-emotive therapy has been used successfully with a wide variety of problems, such as depression due to a broken love affair (the client may be telling himself that he simply cannot live without the love of a particular person); extreme fears, such as speech anxiety (the client may be telling herself that it would be absolutely horrible if some members of the audience thought poorly of her speaking skills); impotence (the client may be "sabotaging" his sexual arousal and enjoyment by telling himself that he must perform well in order to prove that he is a "true" man); homosexual-

Figure 27-1. An extreme example of rational-emotive therapy.

ity (the client may be telling himself that it is better to make love with another man than to risk the "terrible fate" of being rejected by a woman); and lack of self-confidence and subsequent failures (the client may be telling herself that she will inevitably fail at whatever she attempts, and that such failure will only prove once again what a rotten person she is). An interesting question that has yet to be tested scientifically is the extent to which people really do tell themselves such things.

Self-Instructional Methods

Donald Meichenbaum (1974), one of the leading cognitive behavior modifiers, has strongly emphasized the role of self-instruction (that is, telling oneself what to do in various situations) in bringing about desired behavior changes. Like Ellis, he teaches clients to recognize their negative self-statements and to counteract them with

emphasis is
on coping
not eliminating
making person
comfortable
tolerate

stressful stimuli
treat g to feel
are S^D's for
self
instruction

more realistic, positive statements (see Meichenbaum, 1975). In addition, he uses the relaxation method (described in Chapter 26) and other behavior modification techniques. In general, his approach centers on teaching the client to instruct himself to engage in appropriate "coping" behavior in situations that cause anxiety or stress. The emphasis is more on coping with the negative emotions than on completely eliminating them. For example, following treatment, one phobic client said, "It (self-instructing) makes me able to be in the situation, not to be comfortable, but to tolerate it. I don't talk myself out of being afraid, just out of appearing afraid. . . . You immediately react to the thing you're afraid of and then start to reason with yourself. I talk myself out of panic." (Meichenbaum, 1975, p. 371)

The client is taught to respond to certain stimuli produced by the stressful situation, and by his own behavior in that situation, as S^Ds for engaging in appropriate self-instruction. The coping behavior generally includes counteracting negative self-statements and inducing relaxation in the presence of the stressful situation. Sometimes it also involves reinterpreting one's emotions—that is, saying things to oneself that presumably make the negative emotions less aversive. For example, the client may be instructed to say to himself, "The reason my heart beats fast and my legs feel wobbly when I'm with a woman I like is because I'm sexually aroused, not because I'm terribly afraid"; or, "The fact that I'm anxious before giving a speech doesn't mean I'm going to blow it—my anxiety is just a way of preparing me to be alert and do a good job." The client is also instructed to make reinforcing self-statements immediately after he has successfully coped with the stressful situation (for example, "I did it!" and "Wait until I tell my therapist about this!").

To help the client develop coping skills before he deals with stressful situations in the natural environment, the therapist may give him "stress inoculations." These are stressful stimuli, such as unpredictable electric shocks or gruesome films, to which the client is exposed in the therapy setting. During these stressful situations, the client practices appropriate coping skills. Another tactic is for the client to recall stressful situations (for example, visits to the dentist) with which he has previously coped, and to generalize these coping techniques to the stressful situations with which he is presently unable to cope.

Besides working with adults, Meichenbaum has also used self-instructional techniques in helping hyperactive and withdrawn children to manage their behavior (see Meichenbaum, 1977).

Problem Solving

Teaching people how to proceed through logical reasoning to satisfactory solutions to personal problems is another approach that is sometimes considered to fall within the area of cognitive behavior modification. D'Zurilla and Goldfried (1971) outline the following five general steps in personal problem solving.

1. *General orientation:* The client is encouraged to recognize problems and to realize that it is possible to deal with them by acting systematically rather than impulsively. The client may be taught to recognize problems by being presented with common examples of them and/or by being asked to describe such situations that she has encountered in her own life.

2. *Problem definition:* When asked to specify the problem, most clients reply in very vague terms—for example, "I've been very upset lately." By clearly specifying the history of the problem and the variables that seem to be controlling it, it is generally possible to define the problem more precisely. For example, a close analysis might indicate that what is upsetting the client is that she shares an apartment with a very untidy roommate, and she can't stand the "mess" she feels forced to live in.

3. *Generation of alternatives:* After precisely defining the problem, the client is instructed to "brainstorm" possible solutions—that is, to "let her mind run free" and to think of as many solutions as she can, no matter how far-fetched. For example, possible solutions that she might come up with are (a) to move, (b) to self-desensitize to messiness, (c) to speak assertively to her roommate about keeping the place neat, (d) to try to shape neat behavior in her roommate, (e) to negotiate a behavioral contract with her roommate, (f) to throw her roommate's things out the window, and (g) to throw her roommate out the window.

4. *Decision making:* The next step is to carefully examine the alternatives, eliminating those that are obviously unacceptable, such as (f) and (g). She should then try to estimate the likely effectiveness and the likely short-range and long-range consequences of the remaining alternatives. On the basis of these considerations, she should select the alternative that seems most likely to provide the optimum solution, and (with the help of the therapist) devise a plan for carrying it out.

5. *Verification:* When the plan is put into effect, does it solve the problem? That is, is the client satisfied? If not, the problem-solving sequence must be started again and another solution attempted.

Thought-Stopping

Thought-stopping (Wolpe, 1958) is used in cases in which a person engages in persistent, obsessive private verbal behavior that he cannot seem to control. (If you've ever had a tune that just kept going through your head no matter what you did to try to get rid of it, you probably have some idea of the nature of this problem.) The procedure involves, first, instructing the client to think the obsessive thought. The therapist then suddenly yells "Stop!" Immediately, according to anecdotal clinical reports, the undesirable private verbal behavior ceases. After a few such trials demonstrate the effectiveness of the procedure, the client himself is instructed to yell "Stop!" while he is engaging in the undesirable private behavior. Again, the behavior ceases. Over trials, the self-instruction "Stop!" is faded to the private level so that eventually the client can "turn off" the undesirable private behavior simply by "yelling" "Stop!" silently to himself.

An interesting variation of this procedure was reported by Rimm and Masters (1974, p. 434). They described the case of a young man who was obsessed with self-statements concerning "having a nervous breakdown" or "going crazy." Instead of interrupting the negative thoughts by covertly shouting "Stop!" the client, with the help of the therapist, worked out a slightly different procedure. Whenever he was disturbed by his negative self-statements about going crazy, the client said to himself, "Screw it! I'm perfectly normal."

Although thought stopping has been generally used to manage obsessive private verbal behavior, Cautela and Wisocki (1977, p. 259) claim that it "may also be employed with feelings and images as well as several overtly observable behaviors." They also acknowledge that empirical support for the effectiveness of the procedure is weak.

Other Cognitive Techniques

It appears that all of the principles and procedures discussed in this book can be applied covertly (i.e., privately), although it is by no means clear that it is effective to do so. Since we don't wish to rewrite this book strictly from a private-behavior point of view, let us simply close this section with the following observation by Craighead, Kazdin, and Mahoney (1976, p. 151):

> Recently, a number of covert techniques have been derived from operant conditioning principles. For example, one technique referred to as *covert reinforcement* requires an individual to imagine engaging in some response he or she wishes to increase, such as speaking up in groups. After the response is imagined, the individual imagines some reinforcing event taking place, such as skiing down a mountain. The procedure is designed to increase the probability that the client will engage in the imagined target behaviors. There are additional covert techniques such as *covert extinction, covert punishment,* and *covert modeling,* which are conducted entirely in imagination. With each technique the imagery of the client is guided by instructions from the therapist.

CONCLUDING COMMENTS

Although the behavioral applications we have briefly described in this chapter are usually called "cognitive," and although they are often said to be directed towards modifying thoughts, beliefs, and attitudes, their distinguishing characteristic seems to be that they deal with private verbal behavior and images, as well as public behavior.[3] They do not appear to involve any behavior principles besides those discussed in the previous chapters of this book. All behavior practitioners should be open to innovative procedures for helping people change their behavior. At the same time, there are advantages to examining such procedures from a consistent behavioral viewpoint.

As some behavior modifiers become more involved with the realm of private behavior, we can anticipate many exciting developments. Nevertheless, covert behavior modification is still very much in its exploratory stages. It is not yet possible to make definitive statements about the effectiveness of its procedures.

Study Questions

(for examination purposes)

1. Cognitive behavior modification is a blend of what two types of treatment? *Cognitive Therapy + behavioral modification*
2. What does the word "cognition" mean? *"belief, thought"*
3. Why have behavior modifiers tended to avoid certain everyday language words, such as "thinking" and "believing"? *don't refer exactly to beh. occuring. Too vague*
4. Do reputable behavior modifiers deny the existence and importance of private behaviors? Discuss.
5. Describe several examples cited in this chapter and Chapter 25 in which individuals' private behaviors influenced their public behaviors.
6. What basic assumption do the authors of this text make about public and private behavior?
7. What do cognitive therapists, and cognitive behavior modifiers mainly deal with? (See p. 401.) *try to change beh. by altering thought patterns, beliefs, attitude + opinion.*
8. What is rational-emotive therapy? Who developed it?
9. According to Ellis, rational-emotive therapy has been used successfully to improve what types of problems? Explain briefly. *Catastrophizing. Counteract ive statement → realistic + ve statements.*
10. How does Meichenbaum's self-instructional approach differ from Ellis's rational-emotive therapy? *Uses relaxation technique as well. Uses stressful environment stimuli + own beh. as SD to do self-instruct*
11. What are "stress inoculations"? *Endured stressor to allow practicing of coping beh.*
12. In two or three sentences each, outline the five steps of problem solving described by D'Zurilla and Goldfried?
13. Briefly outline the procedure of thought-stopping.
14. Why is covert reinforcement considered a cognitive technique? *is imagined in head*
15. In half a page or less, outline the authors' view of cognitive techniques, as described in this chapter.

16. Choose a hypothetical problem and describe how you think it might be modified through the use of covert reinforcement.

17. Choose a hypothetical problem and describe how you think it might be modified through the use of covert extinction.

18. Choose a hypothetical problem and describe how you think it might be modified through the use of covert punishment.

19. Choose a hypothetical problem and describe how you think it might be modified through the use of covert modeling.

EXTENDED DISCUSSION AND NOTES

1. In the last chapter of his book *Verbal Behavior*, Skinner (1957) closely examines what the words "thinking" and "thought" seem to mean in everyday language (that is, what sorts of activities seem to evoke phrases such as "I was thinking . . ." and "I thought that . . ."). He considers several possibilities. One view is that thinking is simply covert verbal behavior. For example, people often talk silently to themselves when solving problems, and this silent self-talk is often called "thinking." However, essentially the same kind of self-talk may also be emitted overtly, rather than covertly, as when people "think out loud." Although most people usually talk to themselves silently rather than aloud, this is merely because silent talk requires less effort, and (perhaps more important) because talking to oneself aloud is frequently punished (it distracts other people, and it reveals things that may displease them). There is nothing special about *silent* self-talk, as opposed to *overt* self-talk, that causes it to merit the special label "thinking." Skinner therefore rejects the view that thinking is merely covert verbal behavior.

Skinner also rejects the view that thinking is simply self-talk since he sees no essential differences between verbal behavior directed toward the self and verbal behavior directed toward others.

Another view is that thinking is simply verbal behavior. Skinner rejects this view also. People often imagine things to themselves (that is, they often engage in private seeing, hearing, smelling, and other behavior), and this is often called "thinking." Yet it is not verbal behavior.

Finally, Skinner (1957, pp. 449–552) concludes that thinking is nothing more or less than behaving:

> The simplest and most satisfactory view is that thought is simply *behavior*—verbal or nonverbal, covert or overt. It is not some mysterious process responsible for behavior but the very behavior itself in all the complexity of its controlling relations, with respect to both man the behaver and the environment in which he lives. . . . When we study human thought, we study behavior. In the broadest possible sense, the thought of Julius Caesar [for example] was simply the sum total of his responses to the complex world in which he lived. . . . When we say that he "thought Brutus could be trusted," we do not necessarily mean that he ever said as much. He behaved, verbally and otherwise, as if Brutus could be trusted. The rest of his behavior, his plans and achievements, are also part of his thought in this sense.

(Continued)

(Continued)

2. According to Ellis and Harper (1975), our culture fosters a number of irrational beliefs or ideas that account for most of the common forms of emotional distress (and related behavioral difficulties) that people experience. The ten most common of these ideas are:

A. "the idea that you must—yes, must—have love and approval from all the people you find significant" (p. 88);

B. "the idea that you must prove thoroughly competent, adequate, and achieving," or, "that you must at least have competence or talent in some important area" (p. 102);

C. "the idea that when people act obnoxiously and unfairly you should blame and damn them, and see them as bad, wicked, or rotten individuals" (p. 113);

D. "the idea that you have to view things as awful, terrible, horrible, and catastrophic when you get seriously frustrated, treated unfairly, or rejected" (p. 124);

E. "the idea that emotional misery comes from external pressures and that you have little ability to control or change your feelings" (p. 138);

F. "the idea that if something seems dangerous or fearsome, you must preoccupy yourself with and make yourself anxious about it" (p. 145);

G. "the idea that you can more easily avoid facing many life difficulties and self-responsibilities than undertake more rewarding forms of self-discipline" (p. 158);

H. "the idea that your past remains all-important and that because something once strongly influenced your life, it has to keep determining your feelings and behavior today" (p. 168);

I. "the idea that people and things should turn out better than they do and that you must view it as awful and horrible if you do not find good solutions to life's grim realities" (p. 177);

J. "the idea that you can achieve maximum human happiness by inertia and inaction or by passively and uncommitedly enjoying yourself." (p. 186).

Ellis and Harper sometimes speak as though these ideas exist independent of behavior, and are causes of it. This naturally leads one to ask where they exist, what they are and how they can act as causes of behavior. These questions appear to be unanswerable. Skinner's position (see note 1, above) avoids such linguistic difficulties. To say, for example, that someone believes it is horrible for him to be rejected is to say simply that he behaves as though this were true (in other words, when someone rejects him, he reacts as others might under conditions of a major catastrophy). It does not mean that there is something called an "idea," "belief," or "thought" that causes him to behave in this way. Moreover, contrary to what Ellis and Harper imply, it does not necessarily even mean that he tells himself that things are horrible when someone rejects him (although, of course, he may). This is more than an abstract philosophical point. It may have practical implications, as the following comment by Goldfried and Davison (1976, p. 169) suggests: "There are times when a client may insist that he is not telling himself anything while in an anxiety-provoking situation. Even if a client has difficulty acknowledging the existence of any irrational self-statements, he may be willing to accept the interpretation that, in light of his emotional overreaction to a particular situation, it is *as if* he did believe something catastrophic might occur." [italics in original]

3. In addition, cognitive behavior modifiers deal largely with what Skinner (1969) calls "rule-governed behavior." Rules are verbal stimuli that describe specific contingencies of reinforcement. Because rules

(Continued)

(Continued)

can function as S^Ds, a highly verbal person may not require many exposures to a particular contingency in order to respond appropriately to it. She may, for example, construct a rule describing the contingency and then respond to the rule rather than directly to the contingency itself. Or, she may respond appropriately to someone else's description without herself having had any direct exposure at all to the contingency. Thus, for example, presenting a person with statistics showing that air travel is much safer than traveling by car may help to counteract that person's fear of flying—provided that the person has previously been successful in obtaining reinforcement or avoiding punishment by responding to similar descriptions of empirical data.

Study Questions on Notes

1. Why does Skinner reject the view that thinking is simply covert verbal behavior?
2. Why, according to Skinner, do we usually talk to ourselves silently?
3. Why does Skinner reject the view that thinking is simply verbal behavior?
4. What does Skinner think about thinking?
5. Choose one of the common irrational beliefs cited by Ellis and Harper that you have held at one time or another. Describe some of the particular details of that belief. Indicate why you now believe that it was irrational.
6. What is a linguistic difficulty that Ellis and Harper sometimes appear to encounter?
7. According to Skinner, what does it mean when someone has a particular belief (such as that person believing that it is harmful for him to be rejected)?
8. From this chapter, give three examples of how cognitive behavior modifiers rely on the presence of rule-governed behavior in the repertoires of their clients.

PART VI

Behavior Modification: A Rapidly Growing Concern

CHAPTER 28

Giving It All
Some Perspective:
A BRIEF HISTORY

What is behavior modification? A reader attempting to answer this question from the information presented in this book might suggest that behavior modification:

concentrates on behavior, especially observable behavior;

emphasizes collecting and graphing objective data, and making treatment decisions primarily on the basis of those data;

is based on principles and techniques that have been researched in laboratory and applied studies;

is used to bring about specific behavioral improvements in individualized programs;

can be applied almost anywhere people are behaving.

This chapter traces some of the highlights of the remarkable and very recent growth of the field of behavior modification. The chapter should be read with the following qualifications in mind:

1. Although we will describe behavior modification as developing primarily through two major and separate lines of influence, there are obvious cross-influences, blends, and offshoots, and it might be possible to make a case for somewhat different histories.

414

Behavior
Modification:
A Rapidly
Growing
Concern

2. We will identify what we consider to be major highlights of the recent development of behavior modification; we will not attempt a complete historical account.

3. Behavior modification as we know it today is primarily a product of the 1960s and 1970s. Very few historical highlights prior to the 1950s will be discussed.[1]

4. This chapter will describe mainly North American historical highlights.[2]

THE TWO MAJOR LINES OF DEVELOPMENT

The operant-conditioning orientation.

In 1938, B. F. Skinner published his book *The Behavior of Organisms,* in which he described the results of experiments on the lever-pressing behavior of rats for food or water reinforcement and, on the basis of his findings, outlined the basic principles of operant behavior.[3] This pioneering work gradually influenced other experimental psychologists to begin studying the effects of contingencies of reinforcement on the behavior of rats and other animals.

In 1950, Keller and Schoenfeld wrote an introductory psychology text, *Principles of Psychology,* that was unlike any other text of its kind. Keller and Skinner had been graduate students together at Harvard University, and the Keller and Schoenfeld text was inspired largely by the work and writings of Skinner. *Principles of Psychology* contributed significantly to the development of the field of behavior analysis. Although less well known outside Skinnerian-operant circles, this influential introductory text had a tremendous impact within the operant tradition.[4]

In 1953, Skinner published his book *Science and Human Behavior.* In this book, he offered his interpretation of how the basic behavioral principles (which had been researched on lower organisms, and which are described in Part II of this text) influence the behavior of people in all kinds of everyday situations. Although there was very little supporting data for Skinner's generalizations to humans, his interpretations influenced others to begin examining the effects of reinforcement variables on human behavior in a number of experimental and applied settings. The results of these efforts led to much of what has been described in this text as behavior modification. The highlights of this development are presented in Table 28-1.

Many of the reports in the 1950s were either demonstrations that positive reinforcement and extinction affect human behavior in predictable ways, and/or case demonstrations that an application of a behavioral program could effect a desired behavior change. For example, Fuller (1949) reported that an institutional, bedridden, profoundly retarded adult could be taught to raise his right arm to a vertical position when arm movements were appropriately shaped and a warm sugar-milk solution was used as the reinforcer. Greenspoon (1955) demonstrated that a simple social consequence (saying "mmm-hmm") could influence college students to say certain types of words (see Chapter 2, note 5). Azrin and Lindsley (1956), two of Skinner's graduate students, demonstrated that jellybean reinforcement could influence pairs of young children to cooperate in playing a simple game. Each of these experiments demonstrated that consequences influence human behavior in predictable ways. None of the above experiments, however, were primarily practically oriented. One of the first published reports of the 1950's that concerned practical, applied problems, was that of Ayllon and Michael (1959). With Michael as his Ph.D.-dissertation advisor, Ayllon conducted a number of behavioral demonstrations at the Saskatchewan Hospital, a psychiatric institution in Weyburn, Saskatchewan. These demonstrations showed how staff could use procedures such as reinforcement, extinction, and escape and avoidance conditioning to modify behaviors such as delusional talk, refusals to eat, and various disruptive behaviors.

Although it is difficult to determine the full impact of Ayllon and Michael's article, as well as several subsequent papers published by Ayllon and his colleagues from their work at Weyburn, similar demonstrations of behavioral control began to appear with some frequency in the early 1960s (see Table 28-1). This early work was characterized by two features: (1) much of it was done with very resistant populations (such as the mentally retarded, autistic children, and severely regressed psychotics) that had not received a great deal of successful input from traditional psychology; (2) many of the applications took place in institutional or highly controlled settings. A notable exception to this early work is Bijou and Baer's (1961) interpretation of child development from a strictly behavioral perspective.

In 1965, Ullmann and Krasner published their very influential collection of readings, *Case Studies in Behavior Modification* (see the "gray area" in Table 28-1). This appears to be the first book with "behavior modification" in its title. In addition to collecting a number of case histories and research reports by other authors, Ullmann and Krasner compared behavior modification and the behavioral model with more traditional psychotherapeutic strategies and the medical model. Although their book is not just in the operant tradition, since they also included many studies and discussions in the Pavlovian-Hullian tradition (to be discussed in the next section of this chapter), it undoubtedly had a significant impact on furthering behavior modification and providing, in one source, information on much of the preliminary work in this area.

In the late 1960s, the operant-conditioning orientation began to boom throughout North America. Several university training centers were developed, many universities initiated at least one or two courses in behavior modification at both the graduate and under-

TABLE 28-1. *Some historical highlights of behavior modification and behavior therapy*

	PRE-1950s	1950s	EARLY AND MIDDLE 1960s
OPERANT-CONDITIONING (SKINNERIAN) ORIENTATION	Some basic research and theory (Skinner, 1938)	Two major texts (Keller and Schoenfeld, 1950; Skinner, 1953) Some human studies and applications: e.g.,Profoundly Retarded (Fuller, 1949) schizophrenics (Lindsley, 1954) Psychotics (Ayllon and Michael, 1959) Verbal Conditioning (Greenspoon, 1955) Stuttering (Flanagan, Goldiamond, and Azrin, 1958) A basic operant research journal, with some applications (*Journal of the Experimental Analysis of Behavior,* 1958–)	Some major university training centers Several books of readings (e.g., Ulrich, Stachnik, and Mabry, 1966) More applications, many to "resistant" populations: e.g.,retardation (Birnbrauer, Bijou, Wolf, and Kidder, 1965; Girardeau and Spradlin, 1964), autism (Ferster and DeMyer, 1961; Lovaas, 1966; Wolf, Risley, and Mees, 1963), hyperactivity, (Patterson, 1965) delinquency (Schwitzgebel, 1964) psychotics (Isaacs, Thomas, and Goldiamond, 1960; Haughton and Ayllon, 1965) child development (Bijou and Baer, 1961)
			Premack Principle (Premack, 1965) Coverant control (Homme, 1965), Precision teaching (Lindsley, 1966).
OFFSHOOTS AND MIXTURES			Modeling (Bandura and Walters, 1963) A major book of readings (Ullmann and Krasner, 1965), An applied journal (*Behaviour Research and Therapy,* 1963–)
			Covert sensitization (Cautela, 1966)
RESPONDENT-CONDITIONING (AND HULLIAN AND WOLPEAN) ORIENTATION	Some basic research and theory (Pavlov, 1927; Watson and Rayner, 1920) An early application of fear desensitization (Jones, 1924) An early application of assertive training (Salter, 1949)	Two major texts (Dollard and Miller, 1950; Wolpe, 1958) Applications of systematic desensitization, assertive training, and aversion therapy to a variety of phobias and behavioral excesses. Comparisons of behavior therapy and psychotherapy (Eysenck, 1959)	Some major university training centers Several books of readings (e.g., Eysenck, 1960; Franks, 1964) More applications of systematic desensitization, assertive training, and aversion therapy to a variety of classic neurotic behaviors and sexual disorders.

5,6,7 Please see respective *Extended Discussion and Notes* at the end of this chapter.

LATE 1960s

Additional major university training centers
Isolated undergraduate and graduate courses in many universities
Additional books describing applied research and procedures applicable to a variety of areas:
    e.g., education (Skinner, 1968)
    parenting (Patterson and Gullion, 1968)
    community work (Tharp and Wetzel, 1969)
    mental hospitals (Schaefer and Martin, 1969)
Additional applications to a variety of areas, including self-control, delinquency, university teaching, marriage counseling, sexual behaviors, and academic skills
An applied journal (*Journal of Applied Behavior Analysis,* 1968 —)

1970s

Many "how-to-do it" books in a variety of areas[5]
Behavior modification procedures described for many "traditional" areas of psychology (e.g., social, developmental, personality, abnormal, and clinical)
Many other "helping professions" adopting behavior modification procedures (e.g., medicine, social work, nursing, and education[6]
Wide variety of individual, institutional, and community applications and research

Token economies (Ayllon and Azrin, 1968)
Contingency contracting (Homme *et al.,* 1969)

Numerous behavior modification–behavior therapy conferences and workshops

Concern for behavior modification–behavior therapy as a profession, and for controls against mis-applications[7]

Mixed paraprofessional and professional organizations (e.g., Midwestern Association of Behavior Analysis, 1974 —).

Two major books (Bandura, 1969; Franks, 1969)

Professional organizations (Association for the Advancement of Behavior Therapy, 1970 — ; Behavior Research and Therapy Society, 1970 — ; European Association of Behavior Therapy, 1971 —)

Five more journals (*Behavior Therapy,* 1970–; *Journal Behavior Therapy and Experimental Psychiatry,* 1970–; *Behaviorism,* 1972 — *Behavior Modification,* 1977 — ; *Advances in Behaviour Research and Therapy,* 1977 —)

Implosive therapy (Stampfl and Levis, 1967)

Several major university training centers
Additional books (e.g., Wolpe, 1969)
More applications to phobias, anger, asthmatic attacks, frigidity, homosexuality, insomnia, speech disorders, exhibitionism, and other behaviors

Many additional books, publications and training workshops; much additional research.

418

Behavior
Modification:
A Rapidly
Growing
Concern

graduate levels, and applications spread to normal school settings, to university teaching, to homes, and to other populations and settings.

By the 1970s, the operant orientation had grown tremendously. Applications now occur in almost all walks of life.

The respondent-conditioning (and Hullian and Wolpean) orientation

Pavlov conducted respondent-conditioning experiments in which he conditioned dogs to salivate at the sound of a tone (see Chapter 14, note 1). This work became available in English in the early 1900s. In 1913, John B. Watson published a very influential paper in which he argued that most human activities could be explained as learned habits.[8] After becoming familiar with the work of Pavlov (and another Russian physiologist, I. Bechterev), Watson adopted the conditioned reflex as the unit of habit and argued that most complex activities were due to respondent conditioning (this, of course, was before Skinner distinguished between operant and respondent conditioning). At that time, some of his extreme and unsupported generalizations shook the foundations of much of the traditional psychology. Watson followed his 1913 paper with a classic experiment in which he demonstrated that human emotional reactions could be conditioned in an experimental setting (Watson and Rayner, 1920). The experiment concerned conditioning a fear response in an eleven-month-old infant, "Little Albert." During preliminary observations, it was demonstrated that Little Albert was not afraid of a variety of things that were placed in his vicinity when he was happily playing on a rug on the floor. Following these observations, Watson introduced a white rat (of which Albert had shown no fear) and, when Albert was attending closely to the rat, banged a steel bar with a hammer just behind Albert's head. The loud noise caused crying and other emotional behavior in Albert. After a total of six pairings of the loud noises with the sight of the rat, over two separate sessions approximately one week apart, Albert showed a very strong fear reaction to the rat. Moreover, generalization occurred in that a rabbit, a dog, a sealskin coat, and a piece of cotton also elicited the fear. Unfortunately, Little Albert's parents moved away before Watson and Rayner had a chance to decondition the fear. However, subsequent experiments by Mary Cover Jones (1924) followed up some of Watson's suggestions and clearly demonstrated the elimination of fear reactions in infants through the use of respondent-conditioning procedures.

During the next twenty years, a number of somewhat isolated reports of the application of respondent-conditioning procedures to various behaviors appeared in the literature (for a list of many of these, see Yates, 1970). None of these applications, however, appear to have had any sustained impact on the development of behavior modification as we know it today.

Another influence that seems related to the respondent-conditioning orientation was the work of the American learning theorist Clark Hull (1943, 1952). Hull, an early contemporary of Skinner, developed a "learning theory" that tended to capitalize on both operant conditioning as described by Skinner and respondent conditioning as described by Pavlov, meshed together in Hull's particular brand of theorizing. Hull, however, did not attempt to interpret a wide variety of human behaviors to the extent that Skinner did (compare Hull, 1952 with Skinner, 1953). However, two other psychologists, Dollard and Miller (1950), translated a variety of Freudian psychodynamic concepts (which, despite their lack of empirical support, were extremely popular in those days) into the language of Hull's learning theory.

Within this Pavlovian-Hullian tradition, two significant developments occurred in the 1950s, both no doubt influenced to some extent by Dollard and Miller's book. One development occurred in South Africa, where Joseph Wolpe began some research and theorizing that drew heavily on Pavlovian conditioning, Hullian theory, and the earlier work of Watson, Mary Cover Jones, and the British physiologist Sir Charles Sherrington. Sherrington (1947) had noted that if one group of muscles is stimulated, an antagonistic muscle group will be inhibited—and vice versa. He called this *reciprocal inhibition,* and postulated it to be a general process acting throughout the nervous system. Wolpe extended the principle of reciprocal inhibition to state that if a response that is incompatible with fear or anxiety can be made to occur to a stimulus that normally produces fear or anxiety, then that stimulus will cease to elicit the fear reaction. In 1958, Wolpe published his first book on reciprocal inhibition. It was to provide a major force in the launching of the modern era of the respondent tradition of behavior therapy. Wolpe used relaxation responses, sexual responses, and assertion responses to reciprocally inhibit fear or anxiety. (When relaxation is used, the treatment procedure is typically called systematic desensitization; see the discussion of assertion training and systematic desensitization in Chapter 14.)

Also during the 1950s, Hans Eysenck in England was instrumental in criticizing traditional Freudian psychoanalytic-treatment procedures and advocating learning-theory procedures as alternatives. There appears to be little doubt of cross-influences between Wolpe and Eysenck in the late 1950s. In 1960, Eysenck published a book of readings, *Behaviour Therapy and the Neuroses,* in which he pre-

420
Behavior
Modification:
A Rapidly
Growing
Concern

sented a number of case histories in which variations of reciprocal-inhibition and respondent-conditioning procedures were used in clinical therapy. The respondent-conditioning orientation of behavior therapy has occasionally been referred to as the "Wolpe-Eysenck" school.

In the early 1960s, Wolpe moved to the United States. He began a program at Temple University in which he trained therapists in his particular version of behavior therapy. In 1963, Eysenck founded the journal *Behaviour Research and Therapy,* which publishes operant-oriented studies as well as studies with a Pavlovian flavor. As indicated in Table 28-1, behavior therapy within the respondent orientation grew quite rapidly in the 1960s and 1970s and developed applications to a variety of phobic and neurotic disorders.

Mixtures and offshoots of the two orientations

There seems to be little doubt that much of behavior modification and behavior therapy clearly falls within either the operant orientation or the Pavlovian-Hullian-Wolpean orientation. Other developments tend to be offshoots of one or the other of these traditions, and fall in a gray area somewhere in between them. One such development of significance is the work of Bandura and his colleagues on *modeling* procedures (see Chapter 15). During the late 1950s and early 1960s, people within the operant orientation were heavily emphasizing control by consequences (that is, reinforcement). Bandura complemented these developments by emphasizing control of behavior with stimulus management (namely, the presentation of models) while, however, somewhat de-emphasizing the importance of controlling consequences. Bandura's early work culminated in the publication in 1969 of his book on behavior modification, a major source book (for the early 1970s) that integrated a great deal of the work in the two major orientations.

Another important development is that of *precision teaching,* formulated in the mid 1960s by Ogden Lindsley. Lindsley pioneered the development of the Standard Behavior Chart, which he maintains has certain advantages over ordinary graph paper. (For discussion of standard charting, see Kunzelmann, 1970). Precision teaching involves a relatively simple set of guidelines designed to enable teachers to precisely manage the behavior of students. These guidelines encourage teachers to (1) pinpoint a behavior; (2) chart the behavior on a Standard Behavior Chart; (3) try something to change the behavior; and (4) if the results are unsuccessful, try something else. Precision teaching has promoted an emphasis on manipulating stimuli, curricula, and variables other than consequences in influencing behavior change. Precision-teaching workshops have spread through-out North America, and are having a significant influence in certain areas within education and special education (see, for example, Kun-zelmann, 1970; *Teaching Exceptional Children,* 1971).

Additional developments in the 1960s that fall in the gray area of offshoots include Homme's coverant control (see Chapter 25, note 3), covert sensitization (see Chapter 14), contingency contracting (see Chapter 25), implosive therapy (see Chapter 15, note 8), and the Pre-mack Principle (see Chapter 25, note 3), and token economies (see Chapters 22, 23, and 24).

BEHAVIOR THERAPY AND BEHAVIOR MODIFICATION COMPARED

Although many writers use the terms behavior modification and be-havior therapy interchangeably, there are some differences in their historical derivations. It appears that Lindsley, Skinner, and Solomon (1953) were the first to use the term "behavior therapy." They did so in a report describing some research in which psychotic patients in a mental hospital were reinforced with candy or cigarettes for pulling a plunger. However, those within the operant orientation sub-sequently made little use of the term (at least, until the 1970s). The term "behavior therapy" became popular among those within the re-spondent-Hullian-Wolpean orientation after Eysenck (1959) used it to describe procedures published by Wolpe.[9] The first use of the term "behavior modification" appears to be in an article by R. I. Watson (1962). Since that time, many writers have distinguished between be-havior modification with its roots in operant conditioning and be-havior therapy with its roots in Pavlovian conditioning and Hullian theory. Others, however, have not made that distinction consistently. Ullmann and Krasner (1965), for example, frequently used "behavior modification" and "behavior therapy" interchangeably. Also, critics tended to lump operant psychology with other learning theories (Chomsky, 1959), and behavior modification with Pavlovian condi-tioning, behavior therapy, conditioning therapy, and learning-based therapies (see, for example, Breger and McGaugh, 1965). It has been argued that critiques and historical accounts of behavior modification-behavior therapy that do not clarify the particular orientation being discussed (such as Mash, 1974) are often misleading (Martin, 1974). The distinctions that have tended to characterize the uses of the two terms are presented in Table 28-2. In spite of these historical distinctions, for which there is a fair amount of agreement, the terms appear to be blending more and more.

TABLE 28-2. *A comparison of the uses of the terms "behavior therapy" and "behavior modification."*

BEHAVIOR THERAPY	BEHAVIOR MODIFICATION
1. The term is used most often by followers of the Pavlovian-Hul-lian-Wolpean orientation.	The term is used most often by followers of the operant orientation.
2. The term tends to be used by behavioral psychologists and psychiatrists who are concerned primarily with treatment in traditional clinical settings.	The term tends to be used by behavior specialists in schools, homes, and other settings that are not primarily the domain of the clinical psychologist and psychiatrist.
3. The term tends to be used to refer to behavioral treatments conducted in the therapist's office by means of verbal interaction ("talk therapy") between therapist and client.	The term tends to be used for behavioral treatments carried out in the natural environment as well as in special training settings.
4. The term is associated with an experimental foundation that is based primarily on human studies in clinical settings.	The term tends to be associated with an experimental foundation in basic operant research with animals and humans, in addition to experimental studies in applied settings.
5. The term tends to be favored in European countries.	The term tends to be favored in the Americas.

THE FUTURE OF BEHAVIOR MODIFICATION AND BEHAVIOR THERAPY

As you can see in Table 28-1, in the 1970s behavior modification has been applied to nearly all conceivable kinds of individual and social problems. Issues of the *Journal of Applied Behavior Analysis* describe programs concerning such targets as littering in public parks and campgrounds, residential electrical-energy and fuel-oil consumption, management of cash shortages in small businesses, and recreation in urban recreation centers. If the 1960s were the era of treatment, then the 1970s have clearly involved more and more prevention and social engineering. Where all this will lead is difficult to determine. However, it is interesting to speculate that in the foreseeable future, behavioral techniques will be taught to children in elementary school along with good hygiene and physical fitness. Perhaps these children will grow up to see a world in which good applications of behavioral principles will be second nature to everyone, and will result in a happy, informed, skillful, productive culture without war, poverty, prejudice, or pollution.

Study Questions

(for examination purposes)

1. Cite five general statements that might answer the question, "What is behavior modification?"
2. How did Skinner's early work influence the initial development of behavior modification?
3. Discuss Keller's contribution to the development of behavior modification (see text and note 4).
4. Many of the early reports in the operant tradition in the 1950s were straightforward experiments that demonstrated that consequences influence human behavior. Briefly describe two such experiments.
5. Briefly describe one of the first published reports (a very influential one) that concerned practical applications within the operant tradition.
6. What is the *Journal of the Experimental Analysis of Behavior?*
7. The publications of the early 1960s within the operant orientation seem to have been characterized by two features. What were they?
8. Was the very influential book *Case Studies in Behavior Modification* strictly within the operant orientation? Why or why not?
9. What did Ullmann and Krasner do?
10. Briefly describe Watson and Rayner's experiment concerning a conditioned human reaction.
11. What behavior-therapy procedure do we credit to Joseph Wolpe?
12. What role did Hans Eysenck play in the development of behavior therapy in the 1950s?
13. What are the names of six behavior modification-behavior therapy journals?
14. Studies within the early operant orientation emphasized control of behavior by controlling its consequences. Briefly, how did Bandura's modeling studies complement this emphasis?
15. Briefly, what is precision teaching, and who is its founder?
16. Describe five differences in the usage of the terms "behavior therapy" and "behavior modification." (see Table 28-2).
17. If someone suggested, "Behavior modification is okay for some limited types of problems," what would you say?
18. Of the two major orientations in applied behavioral psychology, which do you think has influenced Martin and Pear more strongly? (Hint: They're the authors of this book.) Cite evidence to justify your answer.

1. For some discussion of the history of behavior modification from the early 1900s to the 1960s, see MacMillan (1973). More detailed discussion of the Pavlovian influences on the development of behavior therapy can be found in Franks (1969) and Yates (1970).

2. We believe that most of the major developments in the field of behavior modification and behavior therapy from the 1950s to the present have taken place in North America. This is not to imply that there were no significant developments in other countries. See, for example, Franks (1969), for discussion of Pavlovian developments in the USSR; selected papers in Bijou and Ribez-Inesta (1972), for discussion of behavior modification in Mexico and some other Latin American countries; Yates (1970), for discussion of the development of behavior therapy in England; and papers in Thompson and Dockens (1975), for discussion of behavior modification in Australia, Brazil, Canada, England, Holland, Japan, and Sweden.

3. For a complementary discussion of the development of Skinnerian-oriented behavior modification in the United States, see Goodall (1972). Of special interest in Goodall's report is his tracing of the movement of prominent behavior modifiers in American universities from 1930 through 1970. Another source of behavior modification reports is Britt (1975), who also lists the top fifty publishing authors, according to his criteria.

4. Keller journeyed to Brazil in 1961. He pioneered the first operant-conditioning course in that country and contributed immeasurably to the development of behavior modification there. Also while there, he and his Brazilian colleagues pioneered PSI (Personalized System of Instruction), a behavior modification approach to university teaching that is revolutionizing college instruction (see Keller, 1963, 1968; Ryan, 1974; Johnston, 1975). At the second annual meeting of the Midwestern Association of Behavior Analysis (Chicago, 1976), tribute was paid to Skinner and Keller together. They were referred to as the mother and father of behavior modification, with Skinner the master experimenter and theoretician, and Keller the master teacher.

5. These "how-to-do-it" books cover areas such as toilet-training children (Azrin and Foxx, 1974), developing self-control (Watson and Tharp, 1972), and teaching social behavior to young children (Sheppard, 1973).

6. Areas outside psychology in which behavior modification texts are available include medicine (Katz and Zlutnick, 1975), social work (Schwartz and Goldiamond, 1975), nursing (LeBow, 1973), education (Sulzer and Mayer, 1972; Johnston, 1975), psychiatry (*Task Force Report 5*, 1973), and rehabilitation medicine (Ince, 1976).

7. Wood (1975) edited the proceedings of the Drake Conference on Professional Issues and Behavior Analysis, which was concerned with a variety of issues—among them, the growth of behavior modification, behavior modification as a profession, ethics and behavior modification, and contingencies for controlling the controllers. This text is an excellent source for individuals interested in developments in these areas.

(Continued)

(continued)

8. The general philosophical underpinnings of early behaviorism were given their initial formulation by Watson in two influential papers (1913, 1916). At a time when American psychology was strongly influenced by instinct psychology and was soon to be influenced by Freudian psychology, Watson emphasized the value of an approach that concerned itself strictly with measurable behavior and its control by the environment. Watson called this position "behaviorism" and has earned the title of "Father of Behaviorism" in the history of psychology. For a brief discussion of Watson's contributions to behavioristic psychology, see Marx and Hillix (1963). For more discussion of Watson's system, see Watson (1924).

9. Yates (1970) credits Arnold Lazarus, an early colleague of Wolpe, with introducing the term in 1958. Moreover, Lazarus (1977, p. 551) states: "The terms *behavior therapy* and *behavior therapist* first appeared in print in the *South African Medical Journal* when I applied them to Wolpe's 'reciprocal inhibition' framework (Lazarus, 1958)."

CHAPTER 29

ETHICAL ISSUES

INTRODUCTION

Throughout this book we have emphasized the ethical or moral concerns that one should always bear in mind when applying behavior modification. It would be a great tragedy if this promising new scientific technology were somehow to be used in ways that harmed rather than helped humanity. Because this is a real danger, it is fitting that we devote the final chapter of this book to a more detailed discussion of ethical concerns. Although the ethical views advocated here are personal ones (ethics is, after all, a rather subjective topic), we believe (and hope) that they approximate those held by most other behavior modifiers.[1]

The history of civilization is a continuous story of the abuse of power. Throughout the ages, various groups have used the reinforcers and punishers at their disposal to control the behavior of less powerful groups (groups who had fewer reinforcers and punishers to deliver, or who lacked the means to deliver them contingent on selected target behaviors). The effect of this tradition has generally been to increase the reinforcements occurring to the more powerful at the expense of those occurring to the less powerful. From time to time, as the proportion of total reinforcement allotted to them steadily dwindled, groups subjected to this abuse of power have successfully revolted against their oppressors and have modified existing social structures, or established new ones, in order to check or eliminate the possibility of future abuses. Constitutions, bills of rights, and related political documents of modern states can be viewed as formal specifications of contingencies designed to control the behavior of those who control the behavior of others. (In Western democracies, for example, we have moved from the era of the divine right of kings to one of "government by laws, not men." Moreover, with the introduction of periodic popular elections, the people who are controlled by those who make the laws can exert a certain measure of reciprocal control: they can vote them out of office. In socialistic and communistic countries, on the other hand, the revolutionary process has concentrated on eradicating the abuses that stem from the disproportionate accumulation of personal wealth.) Nevertheless, the new social designs and practices that have emerged thus far have invariably fallen short of their objective; power continues to be abused throughout the world.

Because of this cultural history, and because of people's personal experiences with others who have abused their power (that is, used it for their own benefit and to the disadvantage of those over whom they exerted control), people have learned to react negatively to all overt attempts to control behavior. This negative reaction is so strong that those who would control our behavior usually find that their efforts are more successful when they disguise their aims (as when advertisers, for example, use the "soft sell" rather than "hard sell," or when people who want to change our opinion on an issue contrive to make it appear that we arrived at the new opinion essentially by ourselves). It should not be surprising, therefore, that the emergence of behavior modification has evoked many negative reactions, ranging from suspicion to outright hostility. Behavior modification is the technology based on the science that studies the factors that control behavior. This being the case, it is no secret that behavior modification is based on two propositions: (1) behavior can be controlled, and (2) it is desirable to do so in order to achieve certain objectives. Never before have such far-reaching techniques of behavior control been expressed so explicitly and advocated so strongly.

Some behavior modifiers, noting that terms such as "control" often evoke violently negative reactions to behavior modification, would prefer to use terms that have less of an emotional impact. They suggest, for example, substituting "influence" for "control," because they feel that the former term will help make behavior modification more acceptable to the vast majority of people. However, the weaker term may have the opposite disadvantage: it may lead people

428
Behavior
Modification:
A Rapidly
Growing
Concern

to underestimate the real power of behavior modification, and hence the dangers associated with its development, widespread use, and potential abuse.

Extreme wariness is a healthy reaction to any new, far-reaching advance in science or technology. Perhaps civilization would be in less danger if more precautions had been taken early in the development of, say, atomic energy. The solution to the present problems stemming from scientific and technological advances, however, does not lie in attempting to turn the clock back to a seemingly more secure, prescientific era. Science and technology are not the problem. They are merely highly sophisticated means that people have developed for solving problems. The real problem is that people frequently misuse these tools. This is, of course, a behavioral problem. It would seem, therefore, as Skinner argued in his book *Beyond Freedom and Dignity* (1971), that the science of behavior is the logical key to the solution of that problem. Like other powerful sciences and technologies, however, behavior modification can be misused. It therefore appears that it will be necessary to use behavior modification to control itself.

The above line of reasoning leads us to a rather ironic conclusion: the fear of behavior modification may be a major impediment to the control of behavior modification. Either because of this fear, or simply as a result of misunderstanding, behavior modification has frequently been subjected to invalid ethical criticisms. In order to put behavior modification in its proper ethical perspective, we will first discuss some of the most frequently heard criticisms and attempt to explain why we believe they are invalid. Then we will turn to what we feel is the most constructive ethical approach to behavior modification: how safeguards can be imposed on behavior modification in order to ensure that it will always be used in the best interests of humanity.

CRITICISMS OF BEHAVIOR MODIFICATION

The doctrine of free will

Whatever its logical merits, the doctrine of free will provides a certain amount of comfort to many who fear behavioral control. Basically, the doctrine states that a person can act independently of the environmental and genetic factors that influence his behavior. The doctrine is generally presented more as a criticism of the science of behavior than as a criticism of the technology based on that science. However, it is also directed against behavior modification, in the sense that if behavior is not completely determined, then it cannot be completely controlled; hence (the implication seems to be), it is pointless to attempt to discover laws of behavior, let alone to attempt to use those laws to control behavior.

Besides tending to be comforting, the doctrine of free will has the added advantage that it can never be proved false. Even if behavior is completely determined, it is improbable that all of the laws determining it will be discovered or that they will ever be used to obtain complete control over behavior. Perfect prediction and control seem not to be achievable in physics, so it is unlikely that they will be achievable in the behavioral sciences.

Whether or not behavior is *completely* determined by environmental and genetic factors (everyone agrees that it is at least partially determined by these factors) makes for interesting philosophical discussions. From a practical point of view, however, it may make little difference one way or the other. The important point seems to be that the amount of potential control over behavior is steadily increasing, as a result of new discoveries in behavioral science and refinements in behavioral technology. Therefore, denying that complete control is possible (if used as an argument against behavior modification) constitutes somewhat of a "head-in-the-sand" attitude towards the fact that behavior modification is already a powerful technology and is expanding rapidly.

Arguments against deliberately controlling behavior

It is frequently argued that all attempts to control behavior are unethical.[2] A moment's reflection, however, shows that the goal of any social-help profession (such as education, psychology, and psychiatry) can be achieved only to the extent that the practitioners of that profession exert control over behavior. The goal of education, for example, is to change behavior so that students will respond differently to their environment than they would had they not been educated. To teach a person to read, for example, is to change her behavior in such a way that she responds to signs, newspapers, books, and so forth, in a manner that is different from the way she responded prior to being able to read. The goals of counseling, psychological treatment, and psychiatry likewise involve changing people's behavior so that they can function more effectively then they did prior to receiving professional help.

Many members of social-help professions do not like to think that they are controlling behavior. They prefer to see themselves as merely helping their clients achieve control over their own behavior. Establishing self-control, however, is also a form of behavior control. One simply teaches an individual to emit behavior that controls other behavior in some desired fashion. In order to do that, however, it is necessary to control the behavior involved in self-control. In other words, it is necessary to control the behavior that controls other be-

430
Behavior
Modification:
A Rapidly
Growing
Concern

havior. The social-help practitioner may object that this is nevertheless not control on his part because he withdraws his influence over the client's behavior as soon as he is sure that the client is able to manage his behavior by himself. In actuality, as we have emphasized repeatedly throughout this book, the practitioner has simply shifted the control to the natural environment. One may speak of this as "withdrawing control," but the control still continues, even though its form has changed. If the practitioner has been successful in achieving the behavioral objectives, the desired behavior will be maintained, and in that sense the practitioner's control over the behavior will persist.

Some people will grant that social-help practitioners necessarily engage in the control of behavior, but will nevertheless argue that it is wrong to deliberately plan to control behavior. They regard planning to be "cold" and "mechanical," and feel that it interferes with warm, loving, "spontaneous" relationships that should exist between persons. It is difficult to determine where this objection to planning comes from, since we know of no logical or empirical evidence that supports it. On the contrary, many behavior modification programs that we know of are characterized by very friendly, warm interactions between the individuals involved. Good behavior modifiers are genuinely interested in their clients as persons, and seem to find the time to interact with them on a personal level, just as other social-help practitioners do. There is no doubt that some people show behavior that appears to be "cold" and "mechanical." However, it is our impression that such people are no more common among behavior modifiers than they are among any subgroup of those in the "helping professions" with other orientations.

A lack of planning, on the other hand, can be disastrous. For illustrations of this, refer back to Part II of this book, where we gave numerous examples of how behavioral principles and processes can work to the disadvantage of those who are ignorant of them or who do not plan for them. If a behavior practitioner does not skillfully construct programs for developing desirable behavior, she is very apt to unwittingly introduce contingencies that develop undesirable behavior.

Arguments against the methods of behavior modification

There are those who agree that behavior is determined, accept the idea that planning for behavior change is desirable, but nevertheless object to certain methods of behavior modification. Often, this view stems from the mistaken belief that behavior modifiers must confine themselves to a very small number of methods that are appropriate only to very simple behavior problems. On the contrary, behavior modification consists of a wide variety of methods that scientific research has indicated are effective in changing behavior. This is a very large set of methods (as the contents of this book demonstrate), and the behavior modifier is therefore in a good position to select the method that is likely to do the most good and the least harm in the treatment of any given problem.

Nevertheless, behavior modifiers often encounter objections to methods that they have judiciously selected. The objection is sometimes purely emotional, as when, for example, the use of reinforcement is said to constitute "bribery." The problem with this objection is that it is not based on a valid argument. It is merely name calling—attaching a negative label to something one wishes to discredit (see also Chapter 3, note 4). In order to be valid, the argument must show that the use of the procedure is likely to have an undesirable result. For example, one might argue that a child who has become accustomed to receiving tokens for doing her schoolwork will thereby be hindered in learning to do her schoolwork without receiving tangible reinforcement. Of course, much evidence that we now have fails to support this argument. Even if the opposite were the case, however, the argument would not refute behavior modification. It would merely cause a particular procedure to be questioned. One would then have to decide whether the advantages of using the procedure outweigh its disadvantages relative to the advantages and disadvantages of some other procedure. By comparing different procedures in this way, one eventually selects the procedure that seems best suited to the problem at hand.

ETHICAL SAFEGUARDS

As we indicated at the beginning of this chapter, behavior modification can be of great value but it also has the potential to be harmful. To promote the former and prevent the latter, we must build safeguards into the practice of behavior modification.

At present, society is in the process of imposing contingencies on behavior modification. For example, recent court decisions in the United States have affirmed certain basic rights of mental patients, such as the right to their meals whether or not they have earned tokens on ward programs.[3] Behavior modifiers have therefore had to modify the types of back-up reinforcers that they use with these patients, in order to ensure that these reinforcers are not items that already rightfully belong to them.

It is immediately obvious, therefore, that one obligation of behavior modifiers is to make sure that their practices are within the law. Another obligation is, of course, to make sure that their practices

432
Behavior
Modification:
A Rapidly
Growing
Concern

are consistent with sound ethical judgment. Where law and ethics seem to conflict, behavior modifiers should attempt to change the law.

Behavior modifiers (preferably acting through their professional organizations) should seek to have their practices controlled in reasonable ways. Being students of the control of behavior, they are in a position to contribute valuable information to legislators and judges concerning the most appropriate types of control that should be applied to the practice of behavior modification. Some reasonable recommendations would include the following: All persons practicing behavior modification should clearly demonstrate that they are professionally competent, that they use empirically validated methods, that they use the most effective methods with the least discomfort and harmful side effects, and that their goals and methods are always in the best interests of their clients.

The establishment of impartial ethical-review committees that formally ensure the accountability of behavior modifiers for their programs is also an important safeguard (see Krapfl, 1975). Such committees might function most effectively if they are appointed by, and report to, a public organization that is concerned with the welfare of the clients.

An important responsibility of all behavior modifiers is to help educate the general public with respect to behavior modification so that they can deal with it more effectively. An informed public is probably the best safeguard against possible abuses of behavior modification.[4] All behavior modification programs should be open to public scrutiny. In this regard, it is rather ironic that some of the aspects of behavior modification that have been most responsible for public alarm over behavior modification are those that provide the surest safeguards against its misuse. Behavior modification necessarily implies the specification of target behaviors and the methods to be used in establishing those behaviors. This makes it relatively easy to examine the goals and methods of any program and to question and criticize them.

An important check on potential abuses of behavioral control has been advocated by Skinner. Called *countercontrol,* it is the reciprocal control exerted by an individual or group whose behavior is being controlled. Behavior modification programs should incorporate countercontrol to whatever degree is feasible. The optimal balance of control between the behavior modifiers and clients will, of course, differ from one situation to another. It is therefore impossible to make any firm, all-embracing rules concerning this safeguard. One strong indication of insufficient countercontrol is rebellion (which can be described as a form of "spontaneous" countercontrol). However, it is most unadvisable to wait for this indicator to occur before taking corrective action by increasing the amount of countercontrol in the program.

There are several basic ways to incorporate countercontrol into a behavior modification program. These would include frequent opportunities for clients to discuss and negotiate aspects of the program with the behavior modifiers, and allowing clients or their representatives to participate in programming decisions. Perhaps the best way for behavior modifiers to develop effective countercontrol throughout society is to spread their skills as widely as possible. It should be rather difficult to use behavior modification to the disadvantage of any group whose members are well versed in the principles and tactics of behavior modification.

Study Questions

(for examination purposes)

1. Describe in behavioral terms how the history of civilization is a story of the continuous abuse of power. From your knowledge of history or current events, give an example of this abuse.
2. From your knowledge of history or current events, give an example of what often happens when the reinforcements occurring to one group in a society fall below a certain critical level relative to the reinforcements occurring to another group in that society.
3. From a behavioral point of view, how might we account for constitutions, bills of rights, and related political documents of modern states?
4. Explain why we tend to react negatively to all overt attempts to control our behavior.
5. Why and how do people who would control our behavior disguise their aims? Give an example of this that is not in the text.
6. State two propositions on which behavior modification is based.
7. Discuss whether behavior modifiers should tone down their language so as not to use terms (such as "control") that frighten many people.
8. Why is extreme wariness a healthy reaction to any new, far-reaching development in science or technology? Cite and discuss an example of this.
9. Why is the doctrine of free will not a valid criticism of attempts to develop a technology of behavior?
10. Explain why all social-help professions are involved in the control of behavior, whether or not their practitioners realize it. Give an example.
11. Discuss the relative merits of planning versus not planning for behavior change.
12. Discuss three ethical arguments against the methods of behavior modification, and the validity of these arguments.
13. Why are behavior modifiers ethically obligated to help educate the general public with respect to behavior modification?

434
Behavior
Modification:
A Rapidly
Growing
Concern

14. Briefly explain why some of the best safeguards against the abuse of behavior modification have been mostly responsible for public alarm over behavior modification.

15. Discuss countercontrol and ways in which it might be incorporated into behavior modification programs.

16. Briefly explain why it should be rather difficult to use behavior modification to the detriment of any group whose members are well versed in the principles and tactics of behavior modification.

Study Exercise

Make a fairly detailed list of ethical guidelines that behavior modifiers should follow.

EXTENDED DISCUSSION AND NOTES

1. For discussions of ethical issues in behavior modification, see, for example Begelman (1975), Krasner (1976), Holland (1974), Skinner (1971), Braun (1975), and R. Martin (1975).

2. Skinner (1971) argued that we can trace this attitude, at least in part, to the influence of eighteenth-century revolutionaries and social reformers. To counteract the aversive control utilized by tyrants, these activists developed the concept of "freedom." It was, said Skinner, a very worthwhile concept in its time, for it helped spur people to break away from aversive forms of control. Now, however, we have moved into an era in which positive reinforcement is a more predominant means of control (and will perhaps become increasingly so with the growth of behavior modification). The concept of "freedom" has therefore outlived its social usefulness. Indeed, it is harmful, in that it tends to prevent us from seeing how our behavior is controlled by positive reinforcement. It also tends to impede the development of a behavioral technology that can help us to solve many of civilization's current problems. Moreover, it encourages the view that some people deserve more "dignity" than others because of their achievements, whereas in actuality one's achievements (or failures to achieve) are due to one's conditioning history and genetic predispositions. Hence, the title of Skinner's book *Beyond Freedom and Dignity* (1971).

3. However, regardless of the seemingly straightforward court decision, the issue is perhaps not simply that of denying or granting an individual his basic rights. It is a question of whether the right not to be deprived of a particular item takes precedence over the right to be given effective behavioral treatment, assuming that this treatment requires deprivation. Concerning this, R. Martin (1975) writes:

> An interesting philosophical question is raised. Can using such extreme measures [i.e., severe deprivation of basic reinforcers] be justified in speeding an inmate toward his freedom, and is this preferable to kindly

(continued)

(continued)

custodial care that leaves him unchanged and thus confined? But this question no longer belongs in the theoretical realm—it is being answered by the courts and legislatures. (p. 84)

Martin sees the courts as being justified in this particular action. He goes on to state;

The law will no longer tolerate manipulation of basic needs because, in the past, such programs have always sunk to the lowest allowable level and attempted to motivate everyone in that way. The therapist who can show a Human Rights Committee or a court a specific individual who has not responded to any less restrictive alternatives can probably win a chance to restrict meals for a few days. But if it does not produce some results within a very short time, such as forty-eight hours, then it will certainly be discontinued. (p. 85)

4. G. L. Martin (1975c; p. 85) has suggested that grass-roots behavior modification associations are one way to ensure that at least some of the general public will be knowledgeable about behavior modification and aware of the behavior modification projects being conducted in their communities. As an example of such an organization, he cites the Manitoba Behavior Modification Association, which "is concerned with providing information about behavior modification and its possible application to any interested person in the province. Membership is open to anyone who ascribes to the goals of promoting behavior modification, abides by the ethical statement in the bylaws, and pays a nominal membership fee. Members include parents, psychiatric nurses, psychologists, social workers, high school students, etc."

Study Questions on Notes

1. Critically discuss Skinner's view that we must go "beyond freedom and dignity" if civilization is to solve some of its most difficult problems.
2. Discuss the philosophical question raised by recent court decisions on behavior modification.
3. Discuss how grass-roots behavior modification associations can help provide ethical controls on behavior modification.

References

Adaptive Behavior Scale. Washington, D.C.: American Association on Mental Deficiency, 1974.

ALLEN, K. E., TURNER, K. D., AND EVERETT, P. M. A behavior modification classroom for Head Start children with problem behaviors. *Exceptional Children,* 1970, *37,* 119–127.

AXELROD, S., HALL, R. V., WEIS, L., AND ROHRER, S. Use of self-imposed contingencies to reduce the frequency of smoking behavior. In M. J. Mahoney and C. E. Thoresen (eds.), *Self-Control: Power to the person.* Monterey, Calif.: Brooks/Cole, 1974, pp. 77–85.

AYLLON, T., AND AZRIN, N. H. Reinforcer sampling: A technique for increasing the behavior of mental patients. *Journal of Applied Behavior Analysis,* 1968, *1,* 13–20. (a)

——. *The token economy: A motivational system for therapy and rehabilitation.* New York: Appleton-Century-Crofts, 1968. (b)

AYLLON, T., LAYMAN, D., AND KANDEL, H. J. A behavioral-educational alternative to drug control of hyperactive children. *Journal of Applied Behavior Analysis,* 1975, *8,* 137–146.

AYLLON, T., AND MICHAEL, J. The psychiatric nurse as a behavioral engineer. *Journal of the Experimental Analysis of Behavior,* 1959,

2, 323–334. Reprinted in C. M. Franks (ed.), *Conditioning techniques in clinical practice and research.* New York: Springer, 1964, pp. 275–289.

AZRIN, N. H. Pain and aggression. *Psychology Today,* 1967, *1* (1), 27-33.

AZRIN, N. H., AND FOXX, R. M. A rapid method of toilet training the institutionalized retarded. *Journal of Applied Behavior* Analysis, 1971, *4,* 89–99.

AZRIN, N. H., AND FOXX, R. M. *Toilet training in less than a day.* Champaign, Ill.: Research Press, 1974.

AZRIN, N. H., AND HOLZ, W. C. Punishment. In W. K. Honig (ed.), *Operant behavior: Areas of research and application.* New York: Appleton-Century-Crofts, 1966, pp. 380–447.

AZRIN, N. H., AND LINDSLEY, O. R. The reinforcement of cooperation between children. *Journal of Abnormal and Social Psychology,* 1956, *52,* 100–102.

AZRIN, N. H., AND POWERS, M. A. Eliminating classroom disturbances of emotionally disturbed children by positive practice procedures. *Behavior Theraphy,* 1975, *6,* 525–534.

AZRIN, N. H., SNEED, T. J., AND FOXX, R. M. Dry-bed training: Rapid elimination of childhood enuresis. *Behaviour Research and Therapy,* 1974, *12,* 147–156.

AZRIN, N. H., AND WESOLOWSKI, M. D. Theft reversal: An overcorrection procedure for eliminating stealing by retarded persons. *Journal of Applied Behavior Analysis,* 1974, *7,* 577–581.

BAER, D. M., PETERSON, R. F., AND SHERMAN, J. A. The development of imitation by reinforcing behavioral similarity to a model. *Journal of the Experimental Analysis of Behavior,* 1967, *10,* 405–416.

BAER, D. M. AND WOLF, M. M. The entry into natural communities of reinforcement. In R. Ulrich, T. Stachnik, and J. Mabry (eds.), *Control of human behavior.* Vol. 2. Glenview, Ill.: Scott, Foresman, 1970, pp. 319–324.

BAER, D. M., WOLF, M. M., AND RISLEY, T. R. Some current dimensions of applied behavior analysis. *Journal of Applied Behavior Analysis,* 1968, *1,* 91–97. Reprinted in R. Ulrich, T. Stachnik, and J. Mabry (eds). *Control of human behavior,* Vol. 2. Scott, Foresman, 1970, pp. 9–15.

BAILEY, J. S., TIMBERS, G. D., PHILLIPS, E. L., AND WOLF, M. M. Modification of articulation errors of pre-delinquents by their peers. *Journal of Applied Behavior Analysis,* 1971, *4,* 265–281.

BAILEY, J. S., WOLF, M. M., AND PHILLIPS, E. L. Home-based reinforcement and the modification of pre-delinquents' classroom behavior. *Journal of Applied Behavior Analysis,* 1970, *3,* 223–233.

BANDURA, A. Influence of models' reinforcement contingencies on the acquisition of imitative responses. *Journal of Personality and Social Psychology,* 1965, *1,* 589–595.

————. *Principles of behavior modification.* New York: Holt, Rinehart & Winston, 1969.

————. Psychotherapy based upon modeling principles. In A. E. Bergin and S. L. Garfield (eds.), *Handbook of psychotherapy and behavior change: An empirical analysis.* New York: John Wiley, 1971, pp. 653–708.

————. *Social learning theory.* Englewood Cliffs, N.J.: Prentice Hall, 1977.

BANDURA, A., AND WALTERS R. H. *Social learning and personality development.* New York: Holt, Rinehart & Winston, 1963.

BARTLETT, F. L. Institutional peonage: Our exploitation of mental patients. *Atlantic Monthly,* 1964, *214(1),* 116–119.

BEGELMAN, D. A. Ethical and legal issues of behavior modification. In M. Hersen, R. M. Eisler, and P. M. Miller (eds.), *Progress in behavior modification,* Vol. 1. New York: Academic Press, 1975, pp. 159–189.

Bijou, S. W., and B a e r, D. M. *Child development: A systematic and empirical theory,* Vol. 1. New York: Appleton-Century-Crofts, 1961.

BIJOU, S. W., PETERSON, R. F., HARRIS, F. R., ALLEN, K. E., AND JOHNSON, M. S. Methodology for experimental studies of young children in natural settings. *The Psychological Record,* 1969, *19,* 177–210.

BIJOU, S. W., AND RIBES-INESTA, E. *Behavior modification: Issues and extension.* New York: Academic Press, 1972.

BIRNBRAUER, J. S., BIJOU, S. W., WOLF, M. M., AND KIDDER, J. D. Programmed instruction in the classroom. In L. P. Ullmann and L. Krasner (eds.), *Case studies in behavior modification.* New York: Holt, Rinehart, & Winston, 1965, pp. 358–363.

BLACKMAN, D. *Operant conditioning.* London: Methuen, 1974.

BORNSTEIN, P. H., AND HAMILTON, S. B. Token rewards and straw men. *American Psychologist,* 1975, *30,* 780–781.

BOSTOW, D. E., AND BAILEY, J. B. Modification of severe disruptive and aggressive behavior using brief timeout and reinforcement procedures. *Journal of Applied Behavior Analysis,* 1969, *2,* 31–37.

BRAGINSKY, D. D., AND BRAGINSKY, B. M. *Hansels and Gretels: Studies of children in institutions for the mentally retarded.* New York: Holt, Rinehart & Winston, 1971.

BRAUN, S. H. Ethical issues in behavior modification. *Behavior Therapy,* 1975, *6,* 51–62.

BREGER, L., AND McGAUGH, J. L. Critique and reformulation of "learning theory" approaches to psychotherapy and neurosis. *Psychological Bulletin,* 1965, *63,* 338–358.

BRETHOWER, D. M., AND REYNOLDS, G. S. A facilitative effect of punishment on unpunished behavior. *Journal of the Experimental Analysis of Behavior,* 1962, *5,* 191–199.

BRYER, N. L., AND ALLEN, G. J. Effects of implementing a token economy on teacher attending behavior. *Journal of Applied Behavior Analysis,* 1975, *8,* 373–380.

BRISCOE, R. V., HOFFMAN, D. B., AND BAILEY, J. S. Behavioral community psychology: Training a community board to problem solve. *Journal of Applied Behavior Analysis,* 1975, *8,* 157–167.

BRITT, M. *Bibliography of behavior modification: 1924–1975.* Privately printed by Dr. Morris Britt, 3000 Erwin Road, Durham, North Carolina, 27705.

BURGESS, R. L., CLARK R. N., AND HENDEE, J. C. An experimental analysis of anti-litter procedures. *Journal of Applied Behavior Analysis,* 1971, *4,* 71–75.

BUTTERFIELD, W. H. Electric shock—safety factors when used for the aversive conditioning of humans. *Behavior Therapy,* 1975, *6,* 98–110.

CAMPBELL, D. T., AND STANLEY, J. C. Experimental and quasi-experimental designs for research and teaching. In N. L. Gage, (ed.), *Handbook of research on teaching.* Chicago: Rand McNally, 1963, pp. 171–246.

CATANIA, A. C. The myth of self-reinforcement. *Behaviorism,* 1975, *3,* 192–199.

——. Self-reinforcement revisited. *Behaviorism,* 1976, *4,* 157–162.

CAUTELA, J. R. Treatment of compulsive behavior by covert sensitization. *The Psychological Record,* 1966, *16,* 33–41.

CAUTELA, J. R. AND WISOCKI, P. A. The thought stopping procedure: Description, application, and learning theory interpretations. *The Psychological Record,* 1977, *2,* 255–264.

CHOMSKY, N. A review of B. F. Skinner's *Verbal Behavior. Language,* 1959, *35,* 26–58.

CHRISTENSEN, D. E. Effects of combining methylphenidate and a classroom token system in modifying hyperactive behavior. *American Journal of Mental Deficiency,* 1975, *80,* 226–276.

COHEN, H. L., AND FILIPCZAK, J. *A new learning environment.* San Francisco: Jossey Bass, 1971.

CONRAD, R. D., DELK, J. L., AND WILLIAMS, C. Use of stimulus fading procedures in the treatment of situation specific mutism: A case study. *Journal of Behavior Therapy and Experimental Psychiatry,* 1974, *5,* 99–100.

COPELAND, R. E., BROWN, R. E., AND HALL, R. V. The effects of principal-implemented techniques on the behavior of pupils. *Journal of Applied Behavior Analysis,* 1974, *7,* 77–86.

CORTE, H. E., WOLF, M. M., AND LOCKE, B. J. A comparison of procedures for eliminating self-injurious behavior of retarded adolescents. *Journal of Applied Behavior Analysis,* 1971, *4,* 201–213.

CRAIGHEAD, W. E., KAZDIN, A. E., AND MAHONEY, M. J. *Behavior modification: Principles, issues, and applications.* Boston: Houghton Mifflin, 1976.

DANAHER, B. G. The theoretical foundations and clinical applications of the Premack Principle: A review and critique. *Behavior Therapy,* 1974, *5,* 307–324.

DAY, W. F. Radical behaviorism in reconciliation with phenomenology. *Journal of the Experimental Analysis of Behavior,* 1969, *12,* 315–328.

DEIBERT, A. N., AND HARMON, A. J. *New tools for changing behavior.* Champaign, Ill.: Research Press, 1970.

DeRISI, W. J., AND BUTZ, G. *Writing behavioral contracts: A case simulation practice manual.* Champaign, Ill.: Research Press, 1975.

DIETZ, S. M., AND REPP. A. C. Decreasing classroom misbehavior through the use of DRL schedules of reinforcement. *Journal of Applied Behavior Analysis,* 1973, *6,* 457–463.

DOLLARD, J., AND MILLER, N. E. *Personality and psychotherapy.* New York: McGraw-Hill, 1950.

DULANY, D. E. Awareness, rules, and propositional control: A confrontation with S–R behavior theory. In T. R. Dixon and D. L. Horton (eds.), *Verbal behavior and general behavior theory.* Englewood Cliffs, N.J. Prentice-Hall, 1968, pp. 340–387.

D'ZURILLA, T. J., AND GOLDFRIED, M. R. Problem solving and behavior modification. *Journal of Abnormal Psychology,* 1971, *78,* 107–126.

ELLIS, A. *Reason and emotion in psychotherapy.* New York: Lyle-Stuart, 1962.

ELLIS, A., AND HARPER, R. A. *A new guide to rational living.* Englewood Cliffs, N.J.: Prentice-Hall, 1975.

ELLIS, N. R., BARNETT, C. D., AND PRYER, M. W. Operant behavior in mental defectives: Exploratory studies. *Journal of the Experimental Analysis of Behavior,* 1960, *3,* 63–69.

EYSENCK, H. J. Learning theory and behaviour therapy. *Journal of Mental Science,* 1959, *105,* 61–75.

EYSENCK, H. J. (ed.) *Behaviour therapy and the neuroses.* London: Pergamon Press, 1960.

FAWCETT, S. B., AND MILLER, L. K. Training public–speaking behavior: An experimental analysis and social validation. *Journal of Applied Behavior Analysis,* 1975, *8,* 125–135.

FEINGOLD, B. D., AND MAHONEY, M. J. Reinforcement effects on intrinsic interest: Undermining the overjustification hypothesis. *Behavior Therapy,* 1975, *6,* 367–377.

FELDMAN, M. P., AND MacCULLOCH, M. J. The application of anticipatory avoidance learning to the treatment of homosexuality. I. Theory, technique and preliminary results. *Behaviour Research and Therapy,* 1965, *2,* 165–183.

FERSTER, C. B. Arbitrary and natural reinforcement. *The Psychological Record,* 1967, *17,* 341–347.

FERSTER, C. B., CULBERTSON, S., AND BOREN, M. C. P. *Behavior principles,* 2nd ed. Englewood Cliffs, N.J.: Prentice-Hall, 1975, 246–262.

FERSTER, C. B., AND DeMYER, M. K. A method for the experimental analysis of the behavior of autistic children. *The American Journal of Orthopsychiatry,* 1962, *32,* 89–98. Reprinted in L. P. Ullmann and L. Krasner (eds.), *Case studies in behavior modification.* New York: Holt, Rinehart & Winston, 1965, pp. 121–129.

Ferster, C. B., Nurnberger, J. L., and Levitt, E. G. The control of eating. *Journal of Mathetics*, 1962, *1*, 97–109.

Ferster, C. B., and Skinner, B. F., *Schedules of reinforcement*. New York: Appleton-Century-Crofts, 1957.

Flanagan, B., Goldiamond, I., and Azrin, N. Operant stuttering: The control of stuttering behavior through response-contingent consequences. *Journal of the Experimental Analysis of Behavior*, 1958, *1*, 173–177.

Foster, C. *Developing self control*. Kalamazoo, Mich.: Behaviordelia, 1974.

Fox, L. Effecting the use of efficient study habits. *Journal of Mathetics*, 1962, *1*, 75–86. Reprinted in R. Ulrich, T. Stachnik, and J. Mabry (eds.), *Control of human behavior*. Vol. 1. Glenview, Ill.: Scott, Foresman, 1966, pp. 85–90.

Foxx, R. M. Increasing a mildly retarded woman's attendance at self-help classes by overcorrection and instruction. *Behavior Therapy*, 1976, *7*, 390–396.

Foxx, R. M., and Azrin, N. H. Restitution: A method of eliminating aggressive-disruptive behavior of retarded and brain damaged patients. *Behaviour Research and Therapy*, 1972, *10*, 15–27.

———. The elimination of autistic self-stimulatory behavior by overcorrection. *Journal of Applied Behavior Analysis*, 1973, *6*, 1–14.

Foxx, R. M., and Martin, E. D. Treatment of scavenging behavior (coprophagy and pica) by overcorrection. *Behaviour Research and Therapy*, 1975, *13*, 153–162.

Foy, D. W., Eisler, R. M., and Pinkston, S. Modeled assertion of explosive rages. *Journal of Behavior Therapy and Experimental Psychiatry*, 1975, *6*, 135–137.

Franks, C. M. (ed.). *Behavior therapy: Appraisal and status*. New York: McGraw-Hill, 1969.

———. *Conditioning techniques in clinical practice and research*. New York: Springer, 1964.

Franzini, L. R., and Tilker, H. A. On the terminological confusion between behavior therapy and behavior modification. *Behavior Therapy*, 1972, *3*, 279–282.

Fuller, P. R. Operant conditioning of a vegetative human organism. *American Journal of Psychology*, 1949, *62*, 587–590. Reprinted in L. P. Ullmann and L. Krasner (eds.), *Case studies in behavior modification*. New York: Holt, Rinehart & Winston, 1965, pp. 337–339.

Gibson, F. W., Jr., Lawrence, P. S., and Nelson, R. O. Comparison of three training procedures for teaching social responses to developmentally disabled adults. *American Journal of Mental Deficiency*, 1977, *81*, 379–387.

Girardeau, F. L., and Spradlin, J. E. Token rewards on a cottage program. *Mental Retardation*, 1964, *2*, 345–351.

Gladstone, B. W., and Sherman, J. A. Developing generalized

behavior-modification skills in high-school students working with retarded children. *Journal of Applied Behavior Analysis*, 1975, *8*, 169–180.

GLYNN, E. L., AND THOMAS, J. D. Effect of cueing on self-control of classroom behavior. *Journal of Applied Behavior Analysis*, 1974, *7*, 299–306.

GOLDFRIED, M. R., AND DAVISON, G. C. *Clinical behavior therapy*. New York: Holt, Rinehart & Winston, 1976.

GOLDIAMOND, I. A constructional approach to self-control. In A. Schwartz and I. Goldiamond, *Social casework: A behavioral approach*. New York: Columbia University Press, 1975, pp. 67–138.

——. Self-control procedures in personal behavior problems. *Psychological Reports*, 1965, *17*, 851–868. Reprinted in R. Ulrich, T. Stachnik, and J. Mabry (eds.), *Control of human behavior*. Vol. 1. Glenview, Ill.: Scott, Foresman, 1966, pp. 115–127.

——. Self-reinforcement. *Journal of Applied Behavior Analysis*, 1976, *9*, 509–514.

GOODALL, K. Shapers at work. *Psychology Today*, 1972, 6 (6), 53–63 and 132–138.

GREENSPOON, J. The effect of verbal and nonverbal stimuli on the frequency of members of two verbal response classes. Unpublished Ph.D. dissertation, Indiana University, 1951.

——. The reinforcing effect of two spoken sounds on the frequency of two responses. *American Journal of Psychology*, 1955, *68*, 409–416.

——. *The sources of behavior: Abnormal and normal*. Monterey, Calif: Brooks/Cole, 1976.

HALL, R. V., AND BRODEN, M. Behavior changes in brain-injured children through social reinforcement. *Journal of Experimental Child Psychology*, 1967, *5*, 463–479.

HALL, R. V., CRISTLER, C., CRANSTON, S. S., AND TUCKER, B. Teachers and parents as researchers using multiple baseline designs. *Journal of Applied Behavior Analysis*, 1970, *3*, 247–255. Reprinted in O. I. Lovaas and B. D. Bucher (eds.), *Perspectives in behavior modification with deviant children*. Englewood Cliffs, N.J.: Prentice-Hall, 1974, pp. 282–297.

HALL, R. V., LUND, D., AND JACKSON, D. Effects of teacher attention on study behavior. *Journal of Applied Behavior Analysis*, 1968, *1*, 1–12.

HARRIS, F. R., WOLF, M. M., AND BAER, D. M. Effects of adult social reinforcement on child behavior. *Young Children*, 1964, *20*, 8–17. Reprinted in R. Ulrich, T. Stachnik, and J. Mabry (eds.), *Control of human behavior*, Vol. 1. Glenview, Ill.: Scott, Foresman, 1966, pp. 130–137.

HARRIS, S. L., AND ROMANCZYK, R. G. Treating self-injurious behavior of a retarded child by overcorrection. *Behavior Therapy,* 1976, *7,* 235–239.

HAUGHTON, E., AND AYLLON, T. Production and elimination of symptomatic behavior. In L. P. Ullmann and L. Krasner (eds.), *Case studies in behavior modification.* New York: Holt, Rinehart & Winston, 1965, p. 94–98.

HAWKINS, R. P., AND DOTSON, V. A. Reliability scores that delude: An Alice in Wonderland trip through the misleading characteristics of interobserver agreement scores in interval recording. In E. Ramp and G. Semp (eds.), *Behavior analysis: Areas of research and application.* Englewood Cliffs, N.J.: Prentice-Hall, 1975, pp. 359–376.

HAYES, S. C., JOHNSON, V. S., AND CONE, J. D. The marked item technique: A practical procedure for litter control. *Journal of Applied Behavior Analysis,* 1975, *8,* 381–386.

HEFFERLINE, R. F., KEENAN, B., AND HARFORD, R. A. Escape and avoidance conditioning in human subjects without their observation of the response. *Science,* 1959, *130,* 1338–1339. Reprinted in T. Verhave (ed.), *The experimental analysis of behavior.* New York: Appleton-Century-Crofts, 1966, pp. 264–267.

HERRNSTEIN, R. J. Method and theory in the study of avoidance. *Psychological Review,* 1969, *76,* 49–69.

HERSEN, M., AND BARLOW, D. H. *Single-case experimental designs.* New York: Pergamon Press, 1976.

HERSEN, M., AND BELLACK, A. S. *Behavioral assessment: A practical handbook.* New York: Pergamon Press, 1976.

HILGARD, E. R., AND MARQUIS, D. G. *Conditioning and learning.* New York: Appleton-Century-Crofts, 1940.

HOLLAND, J. G. Are behavioral principles for revolutionaries? In F. S. Keller and E. Ribes-Inesta (eds.), *Behavior modification: Applications to education.* New York: Academic Press, 1974, pp. 195–208.

HOMME, L. E. Perspectives in psychology: XXIV. Control of coverants, the operants of the mind. *Psychological Record,* 1965, *15,* 501–511.

HOMME, L. E., CSANYI, A. P., GONZALES, M. A., AND RECHS, J. R. *How to use contingency contracting in the classroom.* Champaign, Ill.: Research Press, 1969.

HULL, C. L. *A behavior system.* New Haven: Yale University Press, 1952.

———. *Principles of behavior.* New York: Appleton-Century-Crofts, 1943.

HUTCHINSON, R. R., AZRIN, N. H., AND HUNT, G. M. Attack produced by intermittent reinforcement of a concurrent operant response. *Journal of the Experimental Analysis of Behavior,* 1968, *11,* 489–495.

INCE, L. P. *Behavior modification in rehabilitation medicine.* Springfield, Ill.: Charles C Thomas, 1976.

IREY, P. A. Covert sensitization of cigarette smokers with high and low extraversion scores. Unpublished Master's thesis, Southern Illinois University, 1972.

ISAACS, W., THOMAS, J., AND GOLDIAMOND, I. Application of operant conditioning to reinstate verbal behavior in psychotics. *Journal of Speech and Hearing Disorders,* 1960, *25,* 8–12. Reprinted in R. Ulrich, T. Stachnik, and J. Mabry (eds.), *Control of human behavior,* Vol. 1. Glenview, Ill.: Scott, Foresman, 1966, pp. 199–202.

JACKSON, D. A., AND WALLACE, R. F. The modification and generalization of voice loudness in a fifteen-year-old retarded girl. *Journal of Applied Behavior Analysis,* 1974, *7,* 461–471.

JACOBSON, E. *Progressive relaxation.* Chicago: University of Chicago Press, 1938.

JOHNSON, S. M., AND BOLSTAD, O. D. Methodological issues in naturalistic observation: Some problems and solutions for field research. In L. A. Hamerlynck, L. C. Handy, and E. J. Mash (eds.), *Behavior change: Methodology, concepts, and practice.* Champaign, Ill.: Research Press, 1973, pp. 7–67.

JOHNSTON, J. M. Punishment of human behavior. *American Psychologist,* 1972, *27,* 1033–1054.

JOHNSTON, J. M. (ed.), *Behavior research and technology in higher education.* Springfield, Ill.: Charles C Thomas, 1975.

JONES, E. *The life and work of Sigmund Freud,* Vol. 1. New York: Basic Books, 1953.

JONES, F. H., AND EIMERS, R. C. Role-playing to train elementary teachers to use a classroom management "skill package." *Journal of Applied Behavior Analysis,* 1975, *8,* 421–433.

JONES, M. C. The elimination of children's fears. *Journal of Experimental Psychology,* 1924, *7,* 383–390.

KAHN, J. P. The emotional concomitants of the brain-damaged child. *Journal of Learning Disabilities,* 1969, *2,* 34–41.

KALE, R. J., KAYE, J. H., WHELAN, P. A., AND HOPKINS, B. L. The effects of reinforcement on the modification, maintenance, and generalization of social responses of mental patients. *Journal of Applied Behavior Analysis,* 1968, *1,* 307–314.

KAPROWY, E. A. Primary reinforcement, a token system, and attention criteria and feedback procedures with profound retardates in a verbal training classroom. Unpublished Ph.D. dissertation, University of Manitoba, 1975.

KATZ, R., AND ZLUTNICK, S. (eds.), *Behavior therapy and health care: Principles and applications.* New York: Pergamon Press, 1975.

KAZDIN, A. E. *Behavior modification in applied settings.* Homewood, Ill.: Dorsey Press, 1975. (a)

———. Characteristics and trends in applied behavior analysis. *Journal of Applied Behavior Analysis,* 1975, *8,* 332. (b)

———. Methodological and assessment considerations in evaluating reinforcement programs in applied settings. *Journal of Applied Behavior Analysis*, 1973, *6*, 517–531. (a)

———. Recent advances in token economy research. In M. Hersen, R. M. Eisler, and P. M. Miller (eds.), *Progress in behavior modification*. New York: Academic Press, 1975. (c)

———. The effect of vicarious reinforcement on attentive behavior in the classroom. *Journal of Applied Behavior Analysis*, 1973, *6*, 71–78. (b)

———. *The token economy: A review and evaluation*. New York: Plenum, 1977.

KAZDIN, A. E., AND BOOTZIN, R. R. The token economy: An evaluative review. *Journal of Applied Behavior Analysis*, 1972, *5*, 343–372.

KAZDIN, A. E., AND ERICKSON, L. M. Developing responsiveness to instructions in severely and profoundly retarded residents. *Journal of Behavior Therapy and Experimental Psychiatry*, 1975, *6*, 17–21.

KAZDIN, A. E., AND POLSTER, R. Intermittent token reinforcement and response maintenance in extinction. *Behavior Therapy*, 1973, *4*, 386–391.

KAZDIN, A. E., AND WILCOXON, L. A. Systematic desensitization and nonspecific treatment effects: A methodological evaluation. *Psychological Bulletin*, 1976, *83*, 729–758.

KEELEY, S. M., SHEMBURG, K. M., AND CARBONELL, J. Operant clinical intervention: Behavior management or beyond? Where are the data? *Behavior Therapy*, 1976, *7*, 292–305.

KELLEHER, R. T. Chaining and conditioned reinforcement. In W. K. Honig (ed.), *Operant behavior: Areas of research and application*. New York: Appleton-Century-Crofts, 1966, pp. 160–212.

KELLEHER, R. T., AND GOLLUB, L. R. A review of positive conditioned reinforcement. *Journal of the Experimental Analysis of Behavior*, 1962, *5*, 543–597.

KELLER, F. S. A personal course in psychology. Paper read at American Psychological Association, Philadelphia, August, 1963. Reprinted in R. Ulrich, T. Stachnik, and J. Mabry (eds.), *Control of human behavior*, Vol. 1. Glenview, Ill.: Scott, Foresman, 1966.

———. "Good-bye, teacher . . ." *Journal of Applied Behavior Analysis*, 1968, *1*, 79–89.

KELLER, F. S., AND SCHOENFELD, W. N. *Principles of psychology*. New York: Appleton-Century-Crofts, 1950.

KELLER, F. S. AND SHERMAN, J. G. *The Keller plan handbook*. Menlo Park, Calif.: W. A. Benjamin, 1974.

KENT, L. R. *Language acquisition program for the severely retarded*. Champaign, Ill.: Research Press, 1974.

KESEY, K. *One flew over the cuckoo's nest*. New York: Viking, 1962.

KIMBLE, G. A. *Hilgard and Marquis' conditioning and learning*. New York: Appleton-Century-Crofts, 1961.

KIRCHER, A. S., PEAR, J. J., AND MARTIN, G. L. Shock as punishment in a picture-naming task with retarded children. *Journal of Applied Behavior Analysis,* 1971, *4,* 227–233.

KNAPP, T. J. The Premack Principle in human experimental and applied settings. *Behaviour Research and Therapy,* 1976, *14,* 133–147.

KRAPFL, J. E. Accountability for behavioral engineers. In W. S. Wood (ed.), *Issues in evaluating behavior modification.* Champaign, Ill.: Research Press, 1975, 219–236.

KRASNER, L. Behavior modification: Ethical issues and future trends. In H. Leitenberg (ed.), *Handbook of behavior modification and behavior therapy.* Englewood Cliffs, N.J.: Prentice-Hall, 1976, 627–649.

KULIK, J. A., KULIK, C., AND CARMICHAEL, K. The Keller plan in science teaching. *Science,* 1974, *183,* 379–383.

KUNZELMANN, H. P. (ed.), *Precision teaching: An initial training sequence.* Seattle: Special Child Publications, 1970.

LANGE, A. J., AND JAKUBOWSKI, P. *Responsible assertive behavior.* Champaign, Ill.: Research Press, 1976.

LAZARUS, A. A. Has behavior therapy outlived its usefulness? *American Psychologist,* 1977, *32,* 550–554.

——— . New methods in psychotherapy: A case study. *South African Medical Journal,* 1958, *32,* 660–664.

LeBow, M. D. *Behavior modification: A significant method in nursing practice.* Englewood Cliffs, N.J.: Prentice-Hall, 1973.

LEITENBERG, H. The use of single-case methodology in psychotherapy research. *Journal of Abnormal Psychology,* 1973, *82,* 87–101.

LEMERE, F., AND VOEGTLIN, W. An evaluation of the aversion treatment of alcoholism. *Quarterly Journal of Studies on Alcohol,* 1950, *11,* 199–204.

LESSER, E. Behavior therapy with a narcotics user: A case report. *Behaviour Research and Therapy,* 1967, *5,* 251–252.

LEVINE, F. M., AND FASNACHT, G. Token rewards may lead to token learning. *American Psychologist,* 1974, *29,* 816–820.

LINDSLEY, O. R. An experiment with parents handling behavior at home. *Johnstone Bulletin,* 1966, *9,* 27–36.

LINDSLEY, O. R., SKINNER, B. F., AND SOLOMON, H. C. *Studies in behavior therapy: Status report I.* Waltham, Mass.: Metropolitan State Hospital, 1953.

LOGAN, D. L. A "paper money" token system as a recording aid in institutional settings. *Journal of Applied Behavior Analysis,* 1970, *3,* 183–184.

LONG, E. R., HAMMOCK, J. T., MAY, F., AND CAMPBELL, B. J. Intermittent reinforcement of operant behavior in children. *Journal of the Experimental Analysis of Behavior,* 1958, *1,* 315–339.

LOVAAS, O. I. A program for the establishment of speech in psychotic children. In J. K. Wing (ed.), *Early childhood autism.* New York: Pergamon Press, 1966.

LOVAAS, O. I., BERBERICH, J. P., PERLOFF, B. F., AND SCHAEFFER, B. Acquisition of imitative speech in schizophrenic children. *Science,* 1966, *151,* 705–707. Reprinted in O. I. Lovaas and B. D. Bucher (eds.), *Perspectives in behavior modification with deviant children.* Englewood Cliffs, N.J.: Prentice-Hall, 1974, pp. 143–149.

LOVAAS, O. I., SCHAEFFER, B., AND SIMMONS, J. Q. Building social behavior in autistic children by use of electric shock. *Journal of Experimental Research in Personality,* 1965, *1,* 99–109. Reprinted in O. I. Lovaas and B. D. Bucher (eds.), *Perspectives in behavior modification with deviant children.* Englewood Cliffs, N.J.: Prentice-Hall, 1974, pp. 107–122.

LOVAAS, O. I., AND SIMMONS, J. Q. Manipulation of self-destruction in three retarded children. *Journal of Applied Behavior Analysis,* 1969, *2,* 143–157. Reprinted in O. I. Lovaas and B. D. Bucher (eds.), *Perspectives in behavior modification with deviant children.* Englewood Cliffs, N. J.: Prentice-Hall, 1974, pp. 465–487.

LOWTHER, R., MARTIN, G., AND NICHOLSON, C. Generalization of improved posture with profoundly retarded girls. Unpublished manuscript, The Manitoba School, 1977.

LUBETKIN, B. The use of a planetarium in the desensitization of a case of bronto- and astra-phobia. *Behavior Therapy,* 1975, *6,* 276–277.

MACDONOUGH, T. S., AND FOREHAND, R. Response-contingent time-out: Important parameters in behavior modification with children. *Journal of Behavior Therapy and Experimental Psychiatry,* 1973, *4,* 231–236.

MACMILLAN, D. L. *Behavior modification in education.* New York: Macmillan, 1973.

MADSEN, C. H., BECKER, W. C., THOMAS, D. R., KOSER, L., AND PLAGER, E. An analysis of the reinforcing function of "sit down" commands. In R. K. Parker (ed.), *Readings in educational psychology.* Boston: Allon & Bacon, 1970.

MADSEN, C. H., JR., AND MADSEN, C. R. *Teaching discipline: Behavior principles towards a positive approach.* Boston: Allyn & Bacon, 1974.

MAHONEY, K., VANWAGENEN, R. K., AND MEYERSON, L. Toilet training of normal and retarded children. *Journal of Applied Behavior Analysis,* 1971, *4,* 173–181.

MAHONEY, M. J. *Cognition and behavior modification.* Cambridge, Mass.: Ballinger, 1974.

——. Fat fiction. *Behavior Therapy,* 1975, *6,* 416–418.

MAHONEY, M. J. AND THORESEN, C. E. *Self-control: Power to the person.* Belmont, Calif.: Brooks/Cole, 1974.

MALETZKY, B. M. Behavior recording as treatment: A brief note. *Behavior Therapy,* 1974, *5,* 107–111.

MARTIN, G. L. Behavior modification to develop self control. *The Canadian Journal of Psychiatric Nursing,* 1975, *6,* 8–10. (a)

——. Brief time-outs as consequences for errors during training programs with autistic and retarded children: A questionable procedure. *The Psychological Record,* 1975, *25,* 71–89. (b)

——. Response [to Todd R. Risley]. In W. S. Wood (ed.), *Issues in evaluating behavior modification: Proceedings of the First Drake Conference on Professional Issues in Behavior Analysis.* Champaign, Ill.: Research Press, 1975, pp. 182–186. (c)

——. Teaching operant technology to psychiatric nurses, aides, and attendants. In F. W. Clark, D. R. Evans, and L. A. Hamerlynck (eds.), *Implementing behavioral programs for schools and clinics.* Champaign, Ill.: Research Press, 1972, pp. 63–87.

——. Varieties of behaviour modification: A comment. *The Canadian Psychologist,* 1974, *15,* 378–381.

MARTIN, G. L., ENGLAND, G., AND ENGLAND, K. The use of backward chaining to teach bed-making to severely retarded girls: A demonstration. *Psychological Aspects of Disability,* 1971, *18,* 35–40.

MARTIN, G. L., ENGLAND, G., KAPROWY, E., KILGOUR, K., AND PILEK, V. Operant conditioning of kindergarten-class behavior in autistic children. *Behaviour Research and Therapy,* 1968, *6,* 281–294.

MARTIN, G. L., KEHOE, B., BIRD, E., JENSEN, V., AND DARBYSHIRE. Operant conditioning in dressing behavior of severely retarded girls. *Mental Retardation,* 1971, 9(3), 27–31.

MARTIN, G. L., McDONALD, S., AND OMICHINSKI, M. An operant analysis of response interactions during meals with severely retarded girls. *American Journal of Mental Deficiency,* 1971, *76,* 68–85.

MARTIN, G. L., MURRELL, M., NICHOLSON, C., AND TALLMAN, B. *Teaching basic skills to the severely and profoundly retarded: The MIMR basic behavior test, curriculum guide and programming strategy.* Portage la Prairie, Manitoba: Manitoba Institute on Mental Retardation, 1975.

MARTIN, G. L., AND OSBORNE, J. G. *Helping in the community: Behavioral applications.* In preparation.

MARTIN, G. L., AND POWERS, R. B. Attention span: An operant conditioning analysis. *Exceptional Children,* 1967, *33,* 565–570.

MARTIN, G. L., AND TREFFRY, D. Treating self-destruction and developing self-care with a severely retarded girl: A case study. *Psychological Aspects of Disability,* 1970, *17,* 125–131.

MARTIN, R. *Legal challenges to behavior modification: Trends in schools, corrections and mental health.* Champaign, Ill.: Research Press, 1975.

MARX, M. H., AND HILLIX, W. A. *Systems and theories in psychology.* New York: McGraw-Hill, 1963.

MASH, E. J. Has behaviour modification lost its identity? *Canadian Psychologist,* 1974, *15,* 271–280.

MASH, E. J. AND TERDAL, L. G. (eds.) *Behavior-therapy assessment: Diagnosis, design and evaluation.* New York: Springer, 1976.

MASTERS, J. C., AND DRISCOLL, S. A. Children's "imitation" as a function of the presence or absence of a model and the description of his instrumental behaviors. *Child Development,* 1971, *42,* 161–170.

McDONALD, S., MARTIN, G. L., WILLIAMS, L., AND HARDY, L. Errorless vs. traditional training on a simultaneous name discrimination task with severely retarded girls. Paper presented at the 81st Annual Convention of the American Psychological Association, Montreal, Quebec, August, 1973.

McFALL, R. M. The effects of self-monitoring on normal smoking behavior. *Journal of Consulting and Clinical Psychology*, 1970, *35*, 135–142.

McINNIS, T. Training and maintaining staff behaviors in residential treatment programs. In R. L. Patterson (ed.), *Maintaining effective token economies*. Springfield, Ill.: Charles C. Thomas, 1976, pp. 32–68.

MEICHENBAUM, D. H. *Cognitive behavior modification*. Morristown, N.J.: General Learning Press, 1974.

MEICHENBAUM, D. H. *Cognitive-behavior modification: An integrative approach*. New York: Plenum, 1977.

MEICHENBAUM, D. Self–instructional methods. In F. H. Kanfer and A. P. Goldstein (eds.), *Helping people change*. New York: Pergamon Press, 1975.

MEYERSON, L., AND MICHAEL, J. Hearing by operant conditioning procedures. *Proceedings of the International Congress on Education of the Deaf*, 1964, 238–242.

MICHAEL, J. Positive and negative reinforcement, a distinction that is no longer necessary; or, a better way to talk about bad things. *Behaviorism*, 1975, *3*, 33–44. Reprinted in E. Ramp & G. Semb (eds.), *Behavior analysis: Areas of research and application*. Englewood Cliffs, N.J.: Prentice-Hall, 1975, pp. 31–44.

——. Statistical inference: Mixed blessing or curse? *Journal of Applied Behavior Analysis*, 1974, *7*, 647–653.

MILLER, L. K. AND MILLER, O. L. Reinforcing self-help group activities of welfare recipients. *Journal of Applied Behavior Analysis*, 1970, *3*, 57–64.

MILLER, W. R. AND MUNOZ, R. F. *How to control your drinking*. Englewood Cliffs, N.J.: Prentice-Hall, 1976.

MORGANSTERN, K. P. Implosive therapy and flooding procedures: A critical review. *Psychological Bulletin*, 1973, *79*, 318–334.

——. Issues in implosive therapy: Reply to Levis. *Psychological Bulletin*, 1974, *81*, 380–382.

MORSE, W. H. Intermittent reinforcement. In W. K. Honig (ed.), *Operant behavior: Areas of research and application*. New York: Appleton-Century-Crofts, 1966, pp. 52–108.

MOWRER, O. H. Apparatus for the study and treatment of enuresis. *American Journal of Psychology*, 1938, *51*, 163–166.

——. *Learning theory and behavior*. New York: John Wiley, 1960.

MURRELL, M., HARDY, M. A., AND MARTIN, G. L. Danny learns to match digits with the number of objects. *Special Education in Canada*, 1974, *49*, 20–23.

MYKLEBUST, H. R. Learning disabilities: Definition and overview. In

H. R. Myklebust (ed.), *Progress in learning disabilities*, Vol. 1. New York: Grune & Straton, 1968.

NATHAN, P. E. Alcoholism. In H. Leitenberg (Ed.), *Handbook of behavior modification and behavior theraphy*. Englewood Cliffs: Prentice-Hall, 1976.

NORDQUIST, V. M. The modification of a child's enuresis: Some response-response relationships. *Journal of Applied Behavior Analysis*, 1971, *4*, 241–247.

O'CONNOR, R. Modification of social withdrawal through symbolic modeling. *Journal of Applied Behavior Analysis*, 1969, *2*, 15–22.

O'DELL, S. Training parents in behavior modification: A review. *Psychological Bulletin*, 1974, *81*, 418–433.

O'LEARY, K. D., BECKER, W. C., EVANS, M. B., AND SAUDARGAS, R. A. A token reinforcement program in a public school: A replication and systematic analysis. *Journal of Applied Behavior Analysis*, 1969, *2*, 3–13.

ORLANDO, R., AND BIJOU, S. W. Single and multiple schedules of reinforcement in developmentally retarded children. *Journal of the Experimental Analysis of Behavior*, 1960, *3*, 339–348.

PATTERSON, G. R. An application of conditioning techniques to the control of a hyperactive child. In L. P. Ullmann and L. Krasner (eds.), *Case studies in behavior modification*. New York: Holt, Rinehart & Winston, 1965, pp. 370–375.

PATTERSON, G. R., AND GULLION, M. E. *Living with children: New methods for parents and teachers*. Champaign, Ill.: Research Press, 1968.

PATTERSON, G. R., McNEAL, S., HAWKINS, N., AND PHELPS, R. Reprogramming the social environment. *Journal of Child Psychology and Psychiatry*, 1967, *8*, 181–195.

PATTERSON, R. L. (ed.), *Maintaining effective token economies*. Springfield, Ill.: Charles C Thomas, 1976.

PAUL, G. L. Outcome of systematic desensitization. I: Background procedures and uncontrolled reports of individual treatment. In C. M. Franks, (ed.), *Behavior therapy: Appraisal and status*. New York: McGraw-Hill, 1969, pp. 63–104.(a)

——. Outcome of systematic desensitization. II: Controlled investigations of individual treatment, technique variations, and current status. In C. M. Franks (ed.), *Behavior therapy: Appraisal and status*. New York: McGraw-Hill, 1969, pp. 105–159.(b)

PAVLOV, I. P. *Conditioned reflexes: An investigation of the physiological activity of the cerebral cortex*, Trans. G. V. Anrep. London: Oxford University Press, 1927.

PAWLICKI, R. Behaviour-therapy research with children: A critical review. *Canadian Journal of Behavioural Science*, 1970, *2*, 163–173.

PENDERGRASS, V. E. Timeout from positive reinforcement following persistent, high rate behavior in retardates. *Journal of Applied Behavior Analysis*, 1972, *5*, 85–91.

PHILLIPS, E. L. Achievement Place: Token reinforcement procedures in a home-style rehabilitation setting for "pre-delinquent" boys. *Journal of Applied Behavior Analysis,* 1968, *1,* 213–223. Reprinted in O. I. Lovaas and B. D. Bucher (eds.), *Perspectives in behavior modification with deviant children.* Englewood Cliffs, N.J.: Prentice-Hall, 1974, pp. 352–368.

PHILLIPS, E. L., PHILLIPS, E. A., FIXSEN, D. L., AND WOLF M. M. Behavior shaping works for delinquents. *Psychology Today,* 1973. 7(1), 75–79.

PHILLIPS, E. L., PHILLIPS, E. A., WOLF, M. M., AND FIXSEN, D. L. Achievement place: Development of the elected manager system. *Journal of Applied Behavior Analysis,* 1973, *6,* 541–546.

PIERCE, C. H., AND RISLEY, T. R. Recreation as a reinforcer: Increasing membership and decreasing disruption in an urban recreation center. *Journal of Applied Behavior Analysis,* 1974, *7,* 403–411.

PLIMPTON, G. Ernest Hemingway. In G. Plimpton (ed.), *Writers at work: The* Paris Review *interviews.* Second series. New York: Viking, 1965.

POOLE, A. D., AND YATES, A. J. The modification of excessive frequency of urination: A case study. *Behavior Therapy,* 1975, *6,* 78–86.

POWELL, J., MARTINDALE, A., AND KULP, S. An evaluation of time-sample measures of behavior. *Journal of Applied Behavior Analysis,* 1975, *8,* 463–469.

POWERS, R. B., AND OSBORNE, J. G. *Fundamentals of behavior.* St. Paul: West, 1976.

POWERS, R. B., OSBORNE, J. G., AND ANDERSON, E. G. Positive reinforcement of litter removal in the natural environment. *Journal of Applied Behavior Analysis,* 1973, *6,* 579–586.

PREMACK, D. Reinforcement theory. In D. Levin (ed.), *Nebraska symposium on motivation: 1965.* Lincoln, Nebr.: University of Nebraska, 1965, pp. 123–180.

———. Toward empirical behavioral laws: I. Positive reinforcement. *Psychological Review,* 1959, *66,* 219–233.

QUARTI, C., AND RENAUD, J. A new treatment of constipation by conditioning: A preliminary report. In C. M. Franks (ed.), *Conditioning techniques in clinical practice and research.* New York: Springer, 1964, pp. 219–227. Reprinted in R. Ulrich, T. Stachnik, and J. Mabry (eds.), *Control of human behavior.* Vol. 1. Glenview, Ill.: Scott, Foresman, 1966, pp. 138–143.

RACHLIN, H. *Behavior and learning.* San Franscisco: W. H. Freeman, 1976.

RACHMAN, S. Clinical applications of observational learning, imitation, and modeling. *Behavior Therapy,* 1972, *3,* 379–397.

REDD, W. H., AND BIRNBRAUER, J. S. Adults as discriminative stimuli for different reinforcement contingencies with retarded children. *Journal of Experimental Child Psychology,* 1969, *7,* 440–447.

REISS, S., AND SUSHINSKY, L. W. Undermining *extrinsic* interest. *American Psychologist,* 1975, *30,* 782–783.

REPP, A. C., DEITZ, S. M., AND DEITZ, D. E. Reducing inappropriate behaviors in classrooms and individual sessions through DRO schedules of reinforcement. *Mental Retardation,* 1976, *14,* 11–15.

REYNOLDS, G. S. *A primer of operant conditioning,* rev. ed. Glenview, Ill.: Scott, Foresman, 1975.

——. Behavioral contrast. *Journal of the Experimental Analysis of Behavior,* 1961, *4,* 57–71.

RILLING, M. Stimulus control and inhibitory processes. In W. K. Honig, and J. E. R. Staddon (eds.), *Handbook of operant behavior.* Englewood Cliffs, N.J.: Prentice-Hall, 1977, pp. 432–480.

RIMM, D. C., AND MASTERS, J. C. *Behavior therapy: Techniques and empirical findings.* New York: Academic Press, 1974.

RISLEY, T. R. Behavior modification: An experimental-therapeutic endeavor. In L. A. Hamerlynck, P. O. Davidson, and L. E. Acker (eds.), *Behavior modification and ideal mental health services.* Calgary, Alberta: University of Calgary Press, 1969, pp. 103–127.

——. The effects and side effects of punishing the autistic behaviors of a deviant child. *Journal of Applied Behavior Analysis,* 1968, *1,* 21–34.

ROLLINGS, J. P., BAUMEISTER, A. A., AND BAUMEISTER, A. A. The use of overcorrection procedures to eliminate the stereotyped behaviors of retarded individuals: An analysis of collateral behaviors and generalization of suppressive effects. *Behavior Modification,* 1977, *1,* 29–46.

ROSCOE, B., MARTIN, G. L., AND PEAR, J. J. Systematic self–desensitization of fear of flying: A case study. Paper presented at the Third Annual Conference of the Manitoba Behavior Modification Association, Winnipeg, Manitoba, March 4–5, 1977.

RYAN, B. A. *Keller's personalized system of instruction: An appraisal.* Washington, D.C.: American Psychological Association, 1974.

SAJWAJ, T., LIBET, J., AND AGRAS, S. Lemon-juice therapy: The control of life-threatening rumination in a six-month-old infant. *Journal of Applied Behavior Analysis,* 1974, *7,* 557–563.

SALTER, A. *Conditioned reflex therapy.* New York: Creative Age Press, 1949.

SCHAEFER, H. H., AND MARTIN, P. L. *Behavioral therapy.* New York: McGraw-Hill, 1969.

SCHWARTZ, A., AND GOLDIAMOND, I. *Social casework: A behavioral approach.* New York: Columbia University Press, 1975.

SCHWITZGEBEL, R. L. *Streetcorner research: An experimental approach to juvenile delinquency.* Cambridge, Mass.: Harvard University Press, 1964.

SCOTT, R. W., PETERS, D., GILLESPIE, W. J., BLANCHARD, E. B., EDMUNSON, E. D., AND YOUNG, L. D. The use of shaping and reinforcement in the operant acceleration and deceleration of heart rate. *Behaviour Research and Therapy,* 1973, *11,* 179–185.

SEMB, G., AND SEMB, S. A comparison of fixed-page and fixed-time reading assignments in elementary school children. In E. Ramp and G. Semb (eds.), *Behavior analysis: Areas of research and application.* Englewood Cliffs, N.J.: Prentice-Hall, 1975, pp. 233–243.

SHEEHAN, D. J., AND CASEY, B. Brief communication. *Journal of Applied Behavior Analysis,* 1974, *7,* 446.

SHEPPARD, W. C. *Teaching social behavior to young children.* Champaign, Ill.: Research Press, 1973.

SHERMAN, J. G. (ed.), *Personalized system of instruction: 41 germinal papers.* Menlo Park, Calif.: W. A. Benjamin, 1974.

SHERRINGTON, C. S. *The integrative action of the central nervous system.* Cambridge: Cambridge University Press, 1947.

SIDMAN, M. *Tactics of scientific research: Evaluating experimental data in psychology.* New York: Basic Books, 1960.

SKINNER, B. F. A case history in scientific method. *American Psychologist,* 1956, *11,* 221–233. Reprinted in B. F. Skinner (ed.), *Cumulative Record: A Selection of Papers,* 3rd. ed. New York: Appleton-Century-Crofts, 1972, pp. 101–124.

――. *About behaviorism.* New York: Knopf, 1974.

――. *Beyond freedom and dignity.* New York: Knopf, 1971.

――. *Contingencies of reinforcement: A theoretical analysis.* New York Appleton-Century-Crofts, 1969.

――. *Science and human behavior.* New York: Macmillan, 1953.

――. *The behavior of organisms.* New York: Appleton-Century-Crofts, 1938.

――. *The technology of teaching.* New York: Appleton-Century-Crofts, 1968.

――. Two types of conditioned reflex and a pseudotype. *Journal of General Psychology,* 1935, *12,* 66–77.

――. *Verbal behavior.* New York: Appleton-Century-Crofts, 1957.

STAATS, A. W. *Social behaviorism.* Homewood, Ill.: Dorsey Press, 1975.

STAINBACK, W. C., PAYNE, J. S., STAINBACK, S. B., AND PAYNE, R. A. *Establishing a token economy in the classroom.* Columbus, Ohio: Charles E. Merrill, 1973.

STAMPFL, T. G., AND LEVIS, D. J. Essentials of implosive therapy: A learning-theory-based psychodynamic behavioral therapy. *Journal of Abnormal Psychology,* 1967, *72,* 496–503.

STEPHENS, C. E., PEAR, J. J., WRAY, L. D., AND JACKSON, G. C. Some effects of reinforcement schedules in teaching picture names to retarded children. *Journal of Applied Behavior Analysis,* 1975, *8,* 435–447.

STEVENS-LONG, J., AND RASMUSSEN, M. The acquisition of simple and compound sentence structure in an autistic child. *Journal of Applied Behavior Analysis,* 1974, *7,* 473–479.

STEVENSON, J. G., AND CLAYTON, F. L. A response duration schedule: Effects of training, extinction, and deprivation. *Journal of the Experimental Analysis of Behavior,* 1970, *13,* 359–367.

STOKES, T. F., BAER, D. M., AND JACKSON, R. L. Programming the generalization of a greeting response in four retarded children. *Journal of Applied Behavior Analysis*, 1974, 7, 599–610.

STOKES, T. F. AND BAER, D. M. An implicit technology of generalization. *Journal of Applied Behavior Analysis*, 1977, 10, 349–367.

STOLZ, S. B., WIENCKOWSKI, L. A., AND BROWN, B. S. Behavior Modification: A perspective on critical issues. *American Psychologist*, 1975, 30, 1027–1048.

STUART, R. B. Assessment and change of the communication patterns of juvenile delinquents and their parents. In R. D. Rubin, H. Fensterheim, A. A. Lazarus, and C. M. Franks (eds.), *Advances in behavior therapy*. New York: Academic Press, 1971, pp. 183–196.

STUART, R. B., AND DAVIS, B. *Slim chance in a fat world: Behavioral control of obesity*. Champaign, Ill.: Research Press, 1972.

STUART, R. B., AND STUART, F. *Marital precounselling inventory*. Champaign, Ill.: Research Press, 1973.

SUINN, R. M. The STABS, a measure of test anxiety for behavior therapy: Normative data. *Behaviour Research and Therapy*, 1969, 7, 335–339.

SULZER, B., AND MAYER, G. R. *Behavior modification procedures for school personnel*. Hinsdale, Ill.: Dryden Press, 1972.

SUNDEL, M., AND LAWRENCE, H. Behavioral group treatment with adults in a family service agency. In P. Glasser, R. Sarri, and R. Vinter (eds.), *Individual change through small groups*. New York: Free Press, 1974, pp. 325–347.

SUNDEL, M., AND SUNDEL, S. S. *Behavior modification in the human services: A systematic introduction to concepts and applications*. New York: John Wiley, 1975.

TARNAPOL, L. Introduction to children with learning disabilities. In L. Tarnapol (ed.), *Learning disabilities—Introduction to educational and medical management*. Springfield, Ill.: Charles C. Thomas, 1969.

Task force report 5: Behavior therapy in psychiatry. Washington, D.C.: American Psychiatric Association, 1973.

Teaching exceptional children, 1971, 3, 106–160.

TERRACE, H. S. Discrimination learning with and without errors. *Journal of the Experimental Analysis of Behavior*, 1963, 6, 1–27.

THARP, R. G., AND WETZEL, R. J. *Behavior modification in the natural environment*. New York: Academic Press, 1969.

THOMPSON, T., AND DOCKINS, W. S. *Applications of behavior modification*. New York: Academic Press, 1975.

THORNDIKE, E. L. Animal intelligence: An experimental study of the associative processes in animals. *Psychological Review Monograph Supplements*, 1898, 2, No. 8.

——. *Animal intelligence: Experimental studies*. New York: Macmillan, 1911.

TROLLOPE, A. *An autobiography*. London: Williams & Norgate, 1946.

UHL, C. N., AND GARCIA, E. E. Comparison of omission with extinction in response elimination in rats. *Journal of Comparative and Physiological Psychology,* 1969, *69,* 554–562.

ULLMANN, L. P., AND KRASNER, L. (eds.), *Case studies in behavior modification.* New York: Holt, Rinehart & Winston, 1965.

ULMAN, J. D., AND SULZER-AZAROFF, B. Multielement baseline design in educational research. In E. Ramp and G. Semb (eds.), *Behavior analysis: Areas of research and application.* Englewood Cliffs, N.J.: Prentice-Hall, 1975, pp. 377–391.

ULRICH, R., STACHNIK, T., AND MABRY, J. (eds.), *Control of human behavior,* Vol. 1. Glenview Ill.: Scott, Foresman, 1966.

ULRICH, R., WOLFE, M., AND BLUHM, M. Operant conditioning in the public schools. In R. Ulrich, T. Stachnik, and J. Mabry (eds.), *Control of human behavior,* Vol. 2. Glenview, Ill.: Scott, Foresman, 1970, pp. 334–343.

UPPER, D., CAUTELA, J. R., AND BROOK, J. M. Behavioral self-rating checklist. Described in J. R. Cautela and D. Upper, The process of individual behavior therapy. In M. Hersen, R. M. Eisler, and P. M. Miller (eds.), *Progress in behavior modification,* Vol. 1. New York: Academic Press, 1975, pp. 275–305.

VAN HOUTEN, R., MORRISON, E., JARVIS, R., AND MCDONALD, M. The effects of explicit timing and feedback on compositional response rate in elementary school children. *Journal of Applied Behavior Analysis,* 1974, *7,* 547–555.

WALKER, H. M., AND BUCKLEY, N. K. *Token reinforcement techniques.* Eugene, Oreg.: E–B Press, 1974.

WALLACE, I. *The writing of one novel.* Richmond Hill, Ontario: Simon & Schuster, (Pocket Book Ed.), 1971.

WATSON, D. L., AND THARP, R. G. *Self-directed behavior: Self-modification for personal adjustment.* Monterey, Calif.: Brooks/Cole, 1972.

WATSON, J. B. *Behaviorism,* New York: Norton, 1924.

——. Psychology as the behaviorist views it. *Psychological Review,* 1913, *20,* 158–177.

——. The place of the conditioned reflex in psychology. *Psychological Review,* 1916, *23,* 89–117.

WATSON, J. B., AND RAYNER, R. Conditioned emotional reactions. *Journal of Experimental Psychology,* 1920, *3,* 1–14. Reprinted in Ulrich, R., Stachnik, T., and Mabry J. (eds.), *Control of human behavior,* Vol. 1. Scott, Foresman, 1966, pp. 66–69.

WATSON, R. I. The experimental tradition and clinical psychology. In A. J. Bachrach (ed.), *Experimental foundations of clinical psychology.* New York: Basic Books, 1962.

WEIHER, R. G., AND HARMON, R. E. The use of omission training to reduce self-injurious behavior in a retarded child. *Behavior Therapy,* 1975, *6,* 261–268.

WEISBERG, P., AND WALDROP, P. Fixed-interval work habits of Congress. *Journal of Applied Behavior Analysis,* 1972, *5,* 95–97.

WELCH, M. W., AND GIST, J. W. *The open token economy system: A handbook for a behavioral approach to rehabilitation.* Springfield, Ill.: Charles C. Thomas, 1974.

WENRICH, W., GENERAL, D., AND DAWLEY, H. *Self-directed systematic desensitization.* Kalamazoo, Mich.: Behaviordelia, 1976.

WEXLER, D. B. Token and taboo: Behavior modification, token economies, and the law. *California Law Review,* 1973, *61,* 81–109.

WHALEY, D. L., AND MALOTT, R. W. *Elementary principles of behavior.* New York: Appleton-Century-Crofts, 1971.

WHALEY, D. L., AND TOUGH, J. Treatment of a self-injuring mongoloid with shock-induced suppression and avoidance. In R. Ulrich, T. Stachnik, and J. Mabry, (eds.), *Control of human behavior,* Vol. 2. Glenview, Ill.: Scott, Foresman, 1970, pp. 154–155.

WHITE, G. D., NIELSEN, G., AND JOHNSON, S. M. Timeout duration and the suppression of deviant behavior in children. *Journal of Applied Behavior Analysis,* 1972, *5,* 111–120.

WHITEHEAD, W., LURIE, E., AND BLACKWELL, B. Classical conditioning of decreases in human systolic blood pressure. *Journal of Applied Behavior Analysis,* 1976, *9,* 153–157.

WICKES, I. G. Treatment of persistent enuresis with the electric buzzer. *Archives of Disease in Childhood,* 1958, *33,* 160–164. Reprinted in R. Ulrich, T. Stachnik, and J. Mabry (eds.), *Control of human behavior,* Vol. 1 Glenview, Ill.: Scott, Foresman, 1966, pp 151–156.

WILLEMS, E. P. Behavioral technology and behavioral ecology. *Journal of Applied Behavior Analysis,* 1974, *7,* 151–165.

WILLIAMS, C. D. The elimination of tantrum behavior by extinction procedures. *Journal of Abnormal and Social Psychology,* 1959, *59,* 269. Reprinted in L. P. Ullmann and L. Krasner (eds.), *Case studies in behavior modification.* New York: Holt, Rinehart & Winston, 1965, pp. 295–296.

WILLIAMS, R. L., AND LONG, J. D. *Toward a self-managed life style.* Boston: Houghton Mifflin, 1975.

WINKLER, R. C., AND KRASNER, L. The contribution of economics to token economies. Paper presented at the meeting of the Eastern Psychological Association, New York, April 15, 1971.

WOLF, M. M. Comments by a reviewer on methological and assessment considerations in applied settings. *Journal of Applied Behavior Analysis,* 1973, *6,* 532–534.

WOLF, M. M., HANLEY, E. L., KING, L. A., LACHOWICZ, J., AND GILES, D. K. The timer-game: A variable interval contingency for the management of out-of-seat behavior. *Exceptional Children,* 1970, *37,* 113–117.

WOLF, M. M., RISLEY, T., AND MEES, H. Application of operant conditioning procedures to the behaviour problems of an autistic child. *Behaviour Research and Therapy,* 1964, *1,* 305–312. Reprinted in R. Ulrich, T. Stachnik, and J. Mabry (eds.), *Control of human behavior,* Vol. 1. Glenview, Ill.: Scott, Foresman, 1966, pp. 187–193.

WOLFF, R., AND BAUGH, J. Brief communication. *Journal of Applied Behavior Analysis,* 1974, *7,* 446.

WOLPE, J. *Psychotherapy by reciprocal inhibition.* Stanford, Calif.: Stanford University Press, 1958.

WOLPE, J. *The practice of behavior therapy.* New York: Pergamon Press, 1969.

WOLPE, J., AND LANG, P. J. A fear survey schedule for use in behaviour therapy. *Behaviour Research and Therapy,* 1964, *2,* 27–30.

WOLPE, J., AND LAZARUS, A. A. *Behavior therapy techniques: A guide to the treatment of neuroses.* New York: Pergamon Press, 1966.

WOOD, W. S. (ed.), *Issues in evaluating behavior modification.* Champaign, Ill.: Research Press, 1975.

YACORZYNSKI, G. K., AND TUCKER, B. E. What price intelligence? *American Psychologist,* 1960, *15,* 201–203.

YATES, A. J. *Behavior therapy.* New York: John Wiley, 1970.

ZEILER, M. D. Eliminating behavior with reinforcement. *Journal of the Experimental Analysis of Behavior,* 1971, *16,* 401–405.

ZIMMERMAN, E. H., AND ZIMMERMAN, J. The alteration of behavior in a special classroom situation. *Journal of Experimental Analysis of Behavior,* 1962, *5,* 59–60. Reprinted in R. Ulrich, T. Stachnik, and J. Mabry. *Control of human behavior,* Vol. 1. Glenview, Ill.: Scott, Foresman, 1966, pp. 94–96.

ZLUTNICK, S., MAYVILLE, W. J. AND MOFFAT, S. Modification of seizure disorders: The interruption of behavioral chains. *Journal of Applied Behavior Analysis,* 1975, *8,* 1–12.

Author Index

Subject Index